AF529035

CRIME VICTIMS AND JUSTICE

An Introduction to Restorative Principles

CRIME VICTIMS AND JUSTICE

An Introduction to Restorative Principles

Edited by

P. MADHAVA SOMA SUNDARAM

K. JAISHANKAR

S. RAMDOSS

SERIALS PUBLICATIONS

NEW DELHI

First Published - 2008

ISBN: 978-81-8387-163-1

Published by

SERIALS PUBLICATIONS
4800/24, Ist Floor, Ansari Road
Darya Ganj, New Delhi-110002 (India)
Phone : 23245225. Fax : 91-11-23272135
E-mail: serials@satyam.net.in

CONTENTS

PREFACE

Restorative justice, a new philosophical framework for dealing with crime, identifies crime as harm done to both victims and community. It prioritizes restoration as a goal to the justice process. Through efforts to mend and strengthen the social fabric of communities, it is more concerned with "making things right" rather than with fixing blame or dispensing punishment, dramatically different from retributive justice, which is the current prevailing model in many countries. The retributive model concentrates on legal infringement, penalties, and deterrence. The restorative justice is a powerful tool for addressing crime in an effective way. Using informal processes to mediate and reduce conflict through negotiation, restorative justice brings the offender face-to-face with those affected by his or her actions. This approach gives the victim a voice in the justice process; confronts the offender with the human consequences of criminal behavior; requires the offender to make amends through a positive social contribution; reintegrates the individual into the community whenever possible; and builds the community's capacity for resolving and preventing crime.

Considering, the policy pendulum swings between retribution and treatment; and by heavy public expectations, this book which has chapters from criminal justice professionals like Judges, Prosecutors, and Academics and NGO professionals, attempts in developing a new vision for the justice process. As a concrete mission, we feel this book as an attempt to discuss on ways and means for the balanced approach, which allows justice system and agencies to improve their capacity to protect the community and ensure accountability of the offender and the system.

The major focal areas for discussion in this book are

- Transformational dynamics involved in creating and sustaining a restorative system
- Providing a cross-cultural perspective on international experience and expectations
- Contemporary issues in victim typology and classification

- Focusing on special groups of victims like women and children and

- To attempt convergence of services available to victims of crime

Within the context of the restorative justice philosophy, the new balanced approach mission will help justice systems become more responsive to the needs of victims, offenders, and the community and we are aware that this edited volume is an attempt in that direction.

In the following, we will attempt to provide a brief overview of all chapters and highlight what we consider the most important contributions. The overview serves as a tour guide in the "hallway", and points to various "rooms", where readers may explore the rich contents that are of most interests to them.

The first part contains five chapters which deals with the main issue of the book *i.e.* Restorative Justice. In Chapter 2, Sreekumar highlighted the need and importance of Restorative Justice through a comparative evaluation between the theories, practices and consequences of traditional criminal justice systems and also addressed the question of applying principles of restorative justice in serious offences and show the chances of success when certain specific tools are adopted for this purpose. In Chapter 3, Bharat B. Das analyses the position of the victim under criminal justice system and the existing law on the victims' right and compensation in India. In Chapter 4, Marlene Young emphasizes the need for restorative community action both in United States and abroad. In Chapter 5, Jayant Kumar undertook an endeavor to deal with policies and procedures of various countries which strive to achieve the goal of restorative justice. Natti Ronel and Udi lebel's Chapter 6, which is based on qualitative research, describes and interprets the personal experience of 13 bereaved parents in Israel who lost their sons either during military service or in terrorist attacks.

The second part includes four chapters examining several issues related to the Stride towards victim justice system in India. In Chapter 7, Maheshwari and Bhavya Sriram suggest Victim offender Mediation (VOM) as a supplement and not an alternative to sentencing, and advocate its adoption within the present model, as a preliminary step towards a more restorative system. In drawing out the shortfalls of victim compensation and compounding, they showcase the strengths of VOM, and recommend its implementation through making suitable amendments in the Cr. P. C. Chapter 8 of Ramesh and Anirudh Krishnan deals with the need of compensation for them and also proposes the opening of a 'Victim's

Compensation Fund' and provides a detailed analysis of how the fund should function. Highlighting the concept of Restorative Justice, the chapter (9) of Sayantani Guin and Arvind Tiwari aims to study the broad provisions in the Juvenile Justice (Care & Protection of Children) Act, 2000, which conforms with the principles of Restorative Justice and examine the effectiveness of these provisions. Also their chapter attempts to suggest a blueprint for Restorative Justice Approach in the Indian Juvenile Justice System. Maheshwaraswamy in his chapter (10) on Rape Victims suggests a special civil law, with the title of "Compensation for Offences against Women Act" covering all the offences against women including the offence of rape.

The third part is on contemporary victimization issues. An attempt is made by Kailasam in Chapter 11 to identify the important economic factors, which lead to murder victimization in India. An econometric model is developed to identify various economic factors and the results derived from it are quite interesting. In Chapter 12, Karthika and Jaishankar present an empirical micro level analysis on issues related to victimization of labour in brick kiln industry. The aim of the study was to analyze the nature and extent of victimization of labourers in brick kiln industry and the results of this study indicate that abuse and exploitation of labourers are prevalent in this industry. Nanthitha Gopal and Lavanya Paul analyse Street Harassment in Chapter 13. This chapter proposes a draft legislation prohibiting and criminalizing street harassment as a form of gender harassment. Ezhilarasan and Madhavan in their chapter (14) attempt to dwell into the discriminative practices of the male and the female superiors, and to relate whether there is a leadership style that offsets the gender discrimination that is most often prevalent in organizations. Samuel Asir Raj in Chapter 15 examines the situation in the post strike period in a democratic state and emphasizes the right to strike.

The fourth part focuses on Child Victims. Alankaar in Chapter 16 analyses Child abuse from restorative angle and tries to provide solutions to the much debated issue. Indraselvi and Madhava Soma Sundaram in their Chapter 17 focus on the types of punishments adopted by schools in Tenkasi Taluk, Tirunelveli District, Tamil Nadu by an empirical study. In Chapter 18, Mahesh and Jaishankar focus on the child labour issue from victimization perspective. Simhakarna and Ramdoss's Chapter (19) focus on the extent and magnitude of the problem of child trafficking, causes and consequences, legal safeguards and the international agencies involved in the prevention of trafficking. The chapter also suggests measures to prevent trafficking in children and for their rehabilitation. Anantha Ambeth Selvi and Madhava Soma Sundaram in Chapter 20 examine child trafficking is which is a complicated and thorny issue-this study focuses on the rehabilitated victims of child trafficking in a place called moolachi in Ambasamudram Taluk, Tirunelveli district, Tamil Nadu. The study looks into the problems faced by these victims and their requirement for an effective rehabilitation.

The fifth part examines Women Victimization. Chapter 21 by Nandini Rai demonstrates the spatial-temporal variability in the distribution of victimization against women in Delhi by analyzing newspapers over a decade. Stanley Yeldell's Chapter 22 show that Domestic Violence Victims can utilize the "Battered Woman's Syndrome" as a cognizable cause of action in civil litigation in the United States. In Chapter 23, Rashmi Mishra and Sujata Biswal views domestic violence from human rights angle and their empirical study has been designed to study domestic violence against maidservants. Shaha's Chapter 24 is a post mortem study which was conducted over 152 victims of Alleged Dowry Death, for a period of 5 years. The feature of vulnerability with respect to age, socio economic status, occupation, religion, education, place of occurrence, area of occurrence, time of occurrence years since marriage, methods adopted, family type, mode and manner of death were statistically evaluated in this chapter. In Chapter 25, Shohini Basu provides a theoretical analysis of sexual harassment in work place.

The sixth and final part deals with Victim Assistance. Chapter 26 of Stanley Yeldell reports the results of three surveys that investigated three reasons for the need to formulate and develop a victim assistance center at a college or university. Though the chapter focuses on United States, its nature provides universal applicability. Natti Ronel in Chapter 27 presents *Grace Therapy* - an innovative spiritual and restorative therapy for victims of crime, partially based on the well-known 12-step program. Chapter 28 by Rufus and Ramdoss is an empirical study on the beneficiaries of the State Victim Assistance Fund of Tamil Nadu. In Chapter 29, Anna Ryding provides a case study of organized victim support work in Sweden, from an Interactionist and Emotion sociology standpoint. Huddar in chapter 30 presents an analysis of the victim assistance to victims of suicide in Karnataka.

For this edited volume we received over 50 proposals for chapters, which led to 40 draft submissions of full chapters. All submissions were subject to a peer review process, and 30 chapters were finally selected after revisions. The only way for the editors to ensure the success of any edited volume is the high quality and a good quantity of submissions. Peer review process ensures the quality of submissions and most of the contributors served as reviewers for this edited volume. In addition, we also sought the professional insights and detailed comments from the following outside reviewers: Natti Ronel, Bar Illan University, Israel and Stanley Yeldell, Rowan University, USA to whom we are grateful. It was our sole decision whether to include a chapter or not while considering reviewers' comments. In many cases, the rejections were a difficult decision, and some were made merely for balancing the book's coverage of themes. We thank all authors for their support and diligent participation in this project.

We wish to express tremendous thanks to Mr. Vijay Kumar, Business Manager, Serials Publications, New Delhi for his timely help and support. We are appreciative of him and Serials Publications for their continued confidence in our work. Thanks also go to all our contributors who have reviewed the past and have looked to the future of victim justice issues. The compilation of this book was greatly assisted by the enthusiastic support we received from Ms. T. Samyuktha, Intern with Dr. K. Jaishankar in the Department of Criminology and Criminal justice, Manonmaniam Sundaranar University, Tirunelveli, at the time of this publication. Our Sincere thanks go to Ms. Debarati Halder, Advocate, for her painstaking editorial corrections. We also thank Ms. Pariti Bharadwaj, Program Associate. We also thank Ms. Priti Bhardwaj, Program Associate, Chri, New Delhi, for effectively corseating the forewords. Our respective employing establishments, the Manonmaniam Sundaranar University and the University of Madras are due for the debt of recognition for providing a working environment conducive of critical refraction. A special thanks to our families for their patience while we developed this edited volume.

P. Madhava Soma Sundaram, Ph.D.
K. Jaishankar Ph.D.
S. Ramdoss Ph.D.

1. FOREWORD

This book revolves around the notion of "Justice". Every individual strives for justice, be it a man or a woman, a child or an elderly person, an illiterate person or a highly educated person with intellectual capacity, an indigenous person living in a remote locality or a person living in a cosmopolitan city. Despite being a part of the two ends of a spectrum, they all strive for justice. Justice can be viewed as a poetic concept. It combines intellectual and emotional elements. When we hear about a conflict in our neighbourhood, at work, or at home - we attempt to study the facts, examine the details, look at the circumstances - and make a judgment. We tend to judge who is right and what is to be done to solve the dispute.

What is justice? It is a relative term. To understand "justice" one needs to understand what construes "injustice". Injustice is painful as we want to live in a just society. The Oxford English Dictionary (OED) defines justice as *"Conformity (of an action or thing) to moral right, or to reason, truth, or fact; rightfulness; fairness; correctness; propriety"*. But at the same time the OED also defines justice from the perspective of judicial administration of law as, *"Exercise of authority or power in maintenance of right; vindication of right by assignment of reward or punishment; requital of desert."* Justice has many facets which are Distributive, Procedural, Restorative and Retributive. In this book, the editors have tried to look in to Restorative justice facet, which is also known as corrective justice.

Courts of Law at the district, state and national level are conferred with the responsibility to ensure the prevalence of justice in our society. In everyday life people turn to the court of law for justice. We expect the courts and the judiciary to mete out justice. Paradoxically, no court is committed towards this cause. Courts of Law are not necessarily Courts of Justice. As their name indicates, courts deal with legal matters and thus they try by the law. A judge interprets the words and the spirit of law and applies it to each case as he perceives it.

To deliver a verdict, a judge must sit through the trial, hear both parties to provide a fair trial, and then depending on the intensity of the crime, sentence accordingly. By definition, almost half of the people whose case is brought to court lose it. Most of them feel that the verdict, made by the judge or jury is wrong, "*...miscarriage of justice*" they would say. Even people who succeeded in court often feel that the process failed them. True, they won their case but they did not have their 'day in court'. They had their hour, or sometimes only few minutes to articulate their part of the incident. The process was too short, too fast to unfold all aspects of the conflict that took them to court. The court follows strict legal procedures and does not necessarily give the adversarial parties the right to speak or the space to do so.

Some crime victims whose case is tried in court may even feel that they were re-victimized during the judicial process. As the law stands, in criminal cases, crime victims cannot always present their case, especially the pain, suffering and loss incurred by them. The judiciary conveniently shields itself by using "*contempt of court*" as a defense mechanism. The court may not give victims the opportunity to voice their suffering. The court is not tuned nor does it appreciate any personal or anecdotal stories that relate to the case. The bench often orders the parties to stick to the main facts and issues. The legal process leaves no space for discussion pertaining to the impact of the crime and its daily implications borne by the victims. Can we still say that the process is just? In more than a few cases, school children, young women, married women, hard working labourers and older people who were criminally victimized wish to present their case in court, so that justice is meted. Furthermore, the community at large will benefit if it had less crime and violence in its midst. The community, however, is not part of the judicial process, and its pressing mutual interests are not part of the legal discourse. So how and where does justice really show?

Historically, interpersonal conflicts including criminal matters were openly discussed and settled by the people involved usually with the assistance of community elders. However, in the 12th century at the very early stage of nation building, European aristocracy monopolized Criminal Justice System (CJS). Nobility replaced community and interpersonal settlements. Crime was a matter for the monarchs, dukes and barons to deal with. Criminal cases were brought to the local court which was authorized (or not) by the monarch to try people locally. Judgments were passed by the local aristocrats. Among other punishments the court penalized offenders by making them pay fine for their delinquent behaviour. The fine was paid to the judge (or his clerk) who would directly and perhaps even privately benefit from his verdicts. Even today courts order convicts to pay fine and the monies thereof benefit the state treasury. More often this compensation does not reach the victims. .

Criminal victimization is often associated with severe financial, physical and psychological loss. Not only was the victim hurt, and may require expensive medical, dental, plastic treatment or surgery, but most crime victims cannot return, at least for some time to their previous routine. It takes a toll on their life and they need time to recuperate to their initial state depending on the intensity of the criminal act. Surging costs on the one hand and declined income on the other hand leaves crime victims in a difficult, some times long term period with unmet needs. As indicated earlier, the state may fine or sentence the offender depending on the intensity of the crime committed, but the victim is rarely compensated. Not always does the state reimburse crime victims for the expenses they incur, or compensates them for their pain and suffering. In many cases the court suggests the victims to proceed through a civil process, but who has the time, power or means to do so?

If indeed, crime victims have lost their traditional position, what then is their role in the modern criminal process? If the offender plead guilty, the criminal justice process may bypass the crime victim altogether. He/ she might not even know that the offender has been tried already. If the need arises, crime victims are summoned to the court as witnesses. In this role, crime victims are made to answer questions and follow court instructions. Since medieval time a state prosecutor always represented the victim. A judicial process is between the monarch, the state and the offender who, by his illegal acts broke the *Pax Regis* - the King's Peace. Unless called to give evidence, crime victims have no say, whatsoever. True, some crime victims may prefer to be kept aside, and be represented by a prosecutor. However, there are others who strive for justice, and want the court of law to listen to their outcry and listen well.

In his famous article "Conflict as Property", Christie (1977) claims that crime related conflicts are the property of the people involved, the offender and his victim. If the offender admits his wrong doing, he should try and suggest ways to solve the conflict. In a way, Christie gave voice to criticisms stemming from other remote parts of the globe. In New Zealand, some Maori groups insisted on dealing with their internal and external conflicts in their traditional way. They claimed that their traditional method is more just and effective than that applied by the adversarial system. Similarly, the First Nations in Canada preferred using traditional *'healing circle'* and other peace making methods compared to those introduced by the Canadian Criminal Justice System. Arabs on the other hand, prefer having their traditional *'Sulcha'* or *'Attwa'* methods to settle disputes and mete out justice. These people preferred to settle conflicts in what they consider as a well established conventional way to do justice. There is one common underlying principle behind all the above mentioned conventional methods adopted by the various communities across the globe. This principle encourages victims and offenders to meet and discuss their conflict openly among other community members which consequently gives closure to every involved party. Christie (1977) indicated that the affected parties need to meet and resolve their interpersonal conflicts. They can do so themselves, or use others as facilitators or mediators to help them achieve the same. This system of meting out justice is also referred to as *'Restorative Justice'*.

What is the significance of restorative justice? There are at least three reasons to that. Firstly, a conflict can be resolved but a crime cannot be settled. A conflict involves two or more people who may wish to overcome the issue between them. Committing a crime leaves nothing to be said. Conflicts however call for people involved to have a dialogue, justify the reasons for behaving in a certain manner and search for a just solution to resolve the conflict. Secondly, a crime deserves a punishment but a conflict can be settled in different respectful ways. A conflict can be discussed and settled by a joint agreement, whereas court-imposed punishment is often humiliating. Finally, dealing with a crime in court leaves both sides vulnerable. Giving people the option to discuss their own conflict makes the involved parties empowered. They feel that nothing was imposed on them. They reached a fair agreement and justice is done. This often happens if as part of the dialogue, the perpetrator admits his wrong doing and asks for forgiveness and willingness to change. This is also when the offender is ready to cover all costs that the victim has incurred, and even to compensate him for his pain and suffering. This enables victim to meet the perpetrator and listen to his side of the story including some of the explanations and justifications. What may seem as a painful experience has a significant healing effect on both parties involved in the conflict. The victim also experiences closure which is often denied while proceeding in a retributive system. This can only happen when people meet openly to discuss a conflict with an intention to do good and leave behind bitter feelings for their personal welfare and for the benefit of the community and society at large.

What makes restorative justice unique? If it is facilitated locally by community elders, leaders, facilitators or mediators, it may be relatively cheap, much faster and hence more effective than the retributive system. Secondly, when minorities are involved and they often are, they may prefer to settle their disputes outside courts. Doing justice in the traditional way bypasses state administration, symbols and décor that accompany court appearance. Not everyone is happy with the uniforms, flags, coat of arms and ceremonies that are associated with a judicial process. People of minority groups or even of indigenous origin often feel that the state represents a distinct cultural majority, is not necessarily their ally when in real need.

No doubt that crime is the basis of much evil. It is important to study the origins and manifestation of crime. However, the research pendulum seems to shift nowadays from the offender more so towards the crime victim. It is not an accidental shift. Modern theory and evidence suggests that if society wishes to reduce and control crime, it can effectively do so by bringing together the offender and the victim(s). Such a conferencing will make the offender understand the pain, the suffering and damage that he caused to the victim. Conferencing is effective in both preventing further crimes, and helping to heal the criminal conflict between the perpetrator and his crime victim.

In recent years, adopting restorative principles to complement or replace the criminal justice system has been at the centre of theoretical and research literature. Academicians and researchers have studied it and turned it into a multidisciplinary field. Criminology, Victimology, Law, Sociology, Social Work, Psychology, Education and even Economics, among others, have searched selected topics in this domain. What began as a reviving traditional peace making process has turned into an academic discipline. It benefits from much qualitative and quantitative research that is well presented in this book. Furthermore, there are a growing number of national and international organizations that study, shape and market the principles and outcomes of restorative justice programs. The idea of restoring relations, presents a noble universal mission that applies and appeals to many in our incessantly changing world.

India has a long history of peace. Despite its ever growing population, and over crowded cities, for many readers, India has a unique image of a non-violent, peaceful country. Perhaps it was the non-violent approach of Lord Buddha and Mahatma Gandhi that gave India this image. Gandhi's noble saying, *"Non-violence is infinitely superior to violence; forgiveness is more manly than punishment",* encapsulate but only part of his philosophy and the foundation of restorative justice. This book presents a unique contribution to the growing field of Victimology. In addition to discussing, restorative justice, this useful collection also includes various chapters' related to Child victims, Women victims and Victim assistance practices. The editors of this book have taken an outstanding challenge trying to collect and share with the reader a universal, but also an in-depth study of India's experiences in Victimology and restorative principles. Overall, the book offers many insights into Crime Victims and Justice Processes by providing varied information from restorative perspective. This book will well-serve to scholars and students in Criminology, Criminal Justice, Victimology, Psychology, Sociology, Law and Social work.

Uri Vanay, Ph.D.
Prof. Paul Baerwald School of Social Work and Social Welfare,
Bebrew University of Jerusalem, Jerusalem, Israel.

2. FOREWORD

Although restorative justice has victims as its focal point, many problems that victims encounter are still unexplored. Various restorative justice alternatives and supplements to traditional criminal justice practices can be exploited to meet the unfulfilled needs of the victims. Moreover, restorative justice has numerous avenues unexplored. This applies especially to vulnerable victims of serious crimes such as families of murdered victims, victims of sexual crimes, domestic violence, child abuse, terrorism and trafficking of people. On the hind side, restorative justice may not always be the best option for victims - either because the victim is not treated well or because he/she is not ready to meet the perpetrator during the mediation process. This makes the victim prone to re-victimization during the restorative justice procedure as it happens in the adversarial system. There is also a dearth of knowledge and sensitivity about the concerns of victims in restorative justice procedures, as well as on the connection between restorative justice and victim assistance.

The book *Crime Victims and Justice: An Introduction to Restorative Principles* brings forth the highly needed analyses of victims and victimization issues from a restorative justice perspective. It is a successful attempt emphasizing the more efficient and comprehensive approaches to contemporary crime concerns. The publication of this book is important for several reasons. Firstly, it contributes to not so numerous academic literature that deals with the problem of crime victimization in connection to restorative justice. Secondly, it goes into depth by exploring the application of restorative justice in relation to various forms of victimization and different types of vulnerable victims, including those which are rarely mentioned in similar works (e.g. victims of child labor exploitation, child trafficking and street harassment).

The book derives its value as it accentuates the potentials and the limits of restorative justice and based on them it suggests various approaches. The suggested approaches are not in favor of any particular perspective but rather a balance between the two schools of thought i.e. the restorative justice approach and the retributive approach. The contributions published in this book explore innovative ways of dealing with crime and victimization which includes the best practices from both approaches. It also explores some remarkable examples of victim assistance efforts in various parts of the world, including those that use innovative restorative therapy for victims. This approach seems promising in terms of meeting the needs of the victim, but also takes offenders and communities into consideration.

Contributions include valuable theoretical insights and empirical data from distinguished Indian authors as well as leading Victimologists from various parts of the world. The book offers knowledge, ideas and examples of best practices which will be able to instigate the change needed for the benefit of the victims and others prone to being victimized at a global level. It is a highly recommended reading for students, academicians and professionals who are genuinely concerned in various aspects of Justice, Crime and Victimology.

Vesna Nikolic-Ristanovie, Ph.D.
Prof. of Criminology, Department for Prevention and Treatment of Social Disorders, Faculty for Special Education and Rehabilitation, University of Belgrade, Belgrade, Serbia.

CONTRIBUTORS

Mr. Alankaar, Tulir- Center for Prevention and Treatment of Child Sexual Abuse, 183,A, F Block, 9th Street, Anna Nagar (East), Chennai - 600 102. Tamil Nadu.

Ms. A. Anantha Ambeth Selvi, Research Scholar, Department of Criminology and Criminal Justice, Manonmaniam Sundaranar University, Tirunelveli – 12. Tamil Nadu.

Ms. Anna Ryding, Research Scholar, Department of Sociology, Lund University Sweden.

Mr. Anirudh Krishnan, Student, BABL (Hons), NALSAR, Justice City, Shameerpet, Hyderabad, Andhra Pradesh.

Dr. Arvind Tiwari, Associate Professor, Centre for Socio-Legal Studies and Human Rights, Tata Institute of Social Sciences, Deonar, Mumbai 400 088, Maharashtra.

Dr. Bharat B. Das, Reader, P.G. Department of Law, Berhampur University, Berhampur, Orissa.

Ms. Bhavya Sriram, Student, BABL (Hons), NALSAR, Justice City, Shameerpet, Hyderabad, Andhra Pradesh.

Dr. M. Ezhilarasan, Reader, Department of Business Administration, Ayya Nadar Janaki Ammal College, Sivakasi - 628 123. Tamil Nadu.

Dr. M. G. Huddar, Department of Criminology and Forensic Science, Karnatak Science College, Dharwad - 580 001, Karnataka.

Ms. M. Indira Selvi, PG Student, Department of Criminology and Criminal Justice, Manonmaniam Sundaranar University, Tirunelveli – 12 Tamil Nadu.

Dr. K. Jaishankar, Lecturer, Department of Criminology and Criminal Justice, Manonmaniam Sundaranar University, Tirunelveli – 12 Tamil Nadu.

Mr. Jayant Kumar, S/o Shri Surajbhan Singh, Advocate, Dayanand Marg, Radhakishanpura, Sikar, Rajasthan – 332 001.

Dr. L. Kailasam, Shanmugha Bhavanam, Vasantha Apartments, Old No 87/9, New No 137/9, Mundakanni Amman Koil Street, Mylapore, Chennai 600 004. Tamil Nadu.

Ms. R. Karthika, Research Assistant, International Cyber bullying Project, Department of Criminology and Criminal Justice, Manonmaniam Sundaranar University, Tirunelveli – 12 Tamil Nadu.

Dr. Kusa Kumar Saha, Senior Resident, Department of Forensic Medicine & Toxicology, JIPMER, Pondicherry 605 006.

Ms. Lavanya Paul, Student, BABL (Hons), NALSAR, Justice City, Shameerpet, Hyderabad, Andhra Pradesh.

Mr. Lebel Udi, Ben Gurion Research Institute at Sde Boker, Ben Gurion University of the Negev, Israel.

Mr. S. Madhavan, Lecturer, Department of Management Studies, Manonmaniam Sundaranar University, Tirunelveli – 12 Tamil Nadu.

P. Madhava Soma Sundaram, Reader and Head, Department of Criminology and Criminal Justice, Manonmaniam Sundaranar University, Tirunelveli – 12 Tamil Nadu.

Mr. S. M. Mahendra Simha Karna, UGC Junior Research Fellow, Department of Criminology, University of Madras, Chepauk, Chennai 600 005. Tamil Nadu.

Mr. A. Mahesh, PG Student, Department of Criminology and Criminal Justice, Manonmaniam Sundaranar University, Tirunelveli – 12 Tamil Nadu.

Dr. N. Maheshwara Swamy, Asst. Professor of Law, University College of Law, Osmania University, Hyderabad - 500 007.

Ms. S. Maheshwari, Student, BABL (Hons), NALSAR, Justice City, Shameerpet, Hyderabad.

Dr. Marlene Young, Former Executive Director, National Organization for Victim Assistance, NOVA, 510 King Street, Suite 424, Alexandria, VA 22314, United States of America.

Ms. Nanditha Gopal, Student, BABL (Hons), NALSAR, Justice City, Shameerpet, Hyderabad, Andhra Pradesh.

Dr. Nandini Rai, Associate Fellow, Council for Social Development, Sangha Rachna, 53, Lodi Estate, New Delhi – 110 003.

Dr. Natti Ronel, Senior Lecturer, Department of Criminology, Bar Ilan University, Ramatgan-52900 Israel.

Dr. S. Ramdoss, Lecturer, Department of Criminology, University of Madras, Chepauk, Chennai 600 005. Tamil Nadu.

Mr. A. Ramesh, Partner, Ram & Ram, Advocates, Madras High Court, Chennai. Tamil Nadu.

Dr. Rashmi Mishra, Faculty of Sociology, NKC Centre for Development Studies, Bhubaneswar, Orissa - 751 013.

Mr. D. Rufus, UGC Junior Research Fellow, Department of Criminology and Criminal Justice Manonmaniam Sundaranar University, Tirunelveli – 12 Tamil Nadu.

Dr. Stanley B. Yeldell, Associate Professor, Law & Justice Department, Rowan University, Glassboro New Jersey, United States of America.

Dr. S. Samuel Asir Raj, Reader, Department of Management Studies, Manonmaniam Sundaranar University, Tirunelveli – 12 Tamil Nadu.

Ms. Sayantani Guin, UGC Junior Research Fellow, Centre for Socio-Legal Studies and Human Rights, Tata Institute of Social Sciences, Deonar Mumbai 400 088.

Ms. Sohini Basu, Inspiration, GC-1, IInd Floor, Sector III, Salt Lake, Kolkata, 700 106 West Bengal.

Mr. Sreekumar, 380-B, Pocket – 2,Mayur Vihar, Phase-I, Delhi 110 091.

Ms. Sujata Biswal, PG. Student, NKC Centre for Development Studies, Bhubaneswar, Orissa - 751 013.

Part - I

RESTORATIVE JUSTICE: AN INTRODUCTION

P. MADHAVA SOMA SUNDARAM, K. JAISHANKAR AND S. RAMDOSS

1

METAMORPHOSIS OF CRIMINAL JUSTICE SYSTEM TOWARDS VICTIM ORIENTED JUSTICE SYSTEM: THE RESTORATIVE APPROACH

Restorative justice is an approach to crime that recognizes how crime impacts the victim, the community in which the crime was committed and the offender. Its primary focus is

- To repair damage caused by the offence,
- To make reparations
- To the community and
- To the victim, and
- To return the offender to a productive place in the community.

For justice to be truly restorative, the community, the victim and the offender must take active roles. "As a vision for systemic criminal justice reform, restorative justice suggests that the responses to crime must also strike a "balance" between the needs of communities, victims and offenders, involving each to the greatest extent possible in the justice process."

DIFFERENCE BETWEEN THE RETRIBUTIVE JUSTICE SYSTEM AND THE RESTORATIVE JUSTICE SYSTEM

There are certain core differences between the Restorative Justice model and the retributive justice system. In a retributive system, crime is a violation against the state. Restorative justice views crime as an act against an individual victim and the community in which the crime occurs. Since retributive justice emphasizes punishment of the offender, it frequently does not adequately address the issues of community and victim reparation. One of the primary goals of restorative justice is to offer the offender the opportunity to make amends to the victim and to the community.

IMPLEMENTING RESTORATIVE JUSTICE

The manner in which a country implements a restorative system is critical to the success or failure of the new system. Some ways, introduced in developed countries, have proved to be more effective than others. In general, those programs that empower the victims, in the longer run, enjoy greater success than the programmes that offer mere assistance to the victims of crime and abuse of power.

VICTIM IMPACT STATEMENTS AND VICTIM IMPACT PANELS

Involving victims in the justice system is essential to the restorative approach. Many countries have passed victim's rights Acts/Bills, that mandate the victim be informed of court proceedings and have the right to be present at those proceedings. It is often up to the prosecutor to keep victims informed and to encourage their attendance in court.

However, engaging victims in the juvenile justice process requires more than just getting them to the hearings. Prosecutors, in many countries, seek victims' input and encourage active participation in the process. When a victim appears in court, the judge is able to see the real person who was affected by the crime. Victims who are involved in the court process report greater satisfaction with the justice system. Asking the victims if they would like to give a "victim impact statement"' at the time of sentencing, is a good beginning. These statements are an important part of the healing process not only for the victim but also for the offender. The victim has the opportunity to express to the offender the impact the crime has had on his life and the offender is better able to understand how his crime affected a person's life.

Victim Impact Panels are another effective way to create empathy in offenders. They are less individualized than a victim impact statement in which the victim of a particular offender directly addresses his perpetrator. A Victim Impact Panel is a presentation by one or more crime victims to a group of offenders. Through the victims' descriptions of the offence and the long lasting effect of the offence on the victim, the offenders learn to empathize with the victims of their own offences.

COMMUNITY SERVICE RESTITUTION

Community service restitution is designed to repay the community in some way for the offence. It can be court ordered at sentencing or part of an agreement reached in victim offender mediation. For juveniles, community service restitution should in some way address their offence. For instance, if the juvenile is a gang member, the juvenile may be assigned to a locality clean-up crew. If the juvenile has vandalized property, the juvenile may become part of a group of offenders who work together to repair vandalized property in the locality.

PRINCIPLES OF RESTORATIVE JUSTICE AND JUSTICE TO VICTIMS IN INDIAN JURISPRUDENCE

The Principles of Victimology have foundations in Indian Constitutional jurisprudence. The provisions on fundamental rights (Part III) and Directive Principles of State Policy (Part IV) of the Indian Constitution form the bulwark for a new social order in which social and economic justice blossom in the national life of the country. Article 41 mandates, inter alia, that the State shall make effective provisions for "securing the right to public assistance in cases of disablement and in other cases of undeserved want' (Law Commission of India Report, 1996).

The Law Commission in its Report has said further that the principles of compensation to crime victims need to be reviewed and expanded to cover all cases. The compensation should not only be limited to fines, penalties and forfeiture realized. The State should accept the principle of providing assistance to victims out of its own funds, (i) in cases of acquittals, or (ii) where the offender is not traceable, but the victim is identified, or (iii) and also in cases when the offence is proved. In view of the lacunae in the existing provisions for compensation to crime victims under the criminal law, the Law Commission of India has stated that it is necessary to incorporate a new section 357 A in the Code of Criminal Procedure to provide for a comprehensive scheme of payment of compensation for all victims fairly and adequately by the courts (Law Commission of India Report, 1996).

FOCUS ON VICTIM BY JUSTICE MALIMATH COMMITTEE ON REFORMS OF CRIMINAL JUSTICE SYSTEM

Despite the differences of the lawyer community on many of the recommendations of Justice V.S. Malimath Committee, it is to be admitted that this Committee has made recommendations of far reaching significance to improve the position of victims of crime and to provide justice to victims. The committee has noted in its report that an important objective of the criminal justice system is to ensure justice to the victim, yet he has not been given any substantial right, not even to participate in the criminal proceedings. Therefore, the Committee feels that the system must focus on justice to victims and has, thus, made many recommendations, which include the right of the victim to participate in cases involving serious crimes and to adequate compensation.

(i) The victim, and if he is dead, his legal representative shall have the right to be impleaded as a party in every criminal proceeding where the offence is punishable with 7 years imprisonment or more.

(ii) In select cases notified by the appropriate government, with the permission of the court, an approved voluntary organization shall also have the right to implead in court proceedings.

(iii) The victim has a right to be represented by an advocate of his choice, provided that an advocate shall be provided at the cost of the State if the victim is not in a position to afford a lawyer.

(iv) The victim's right to participate in criminal trial shall, inter alia, include:

a. To produce evidence, oral or documentary, with leave of the Court and/or to seek directions for production of such evidence.

b. To ask questions to the witnesses or to suggest to the court questions that may be put to witnesses.

c. To know the status of investigation and to move the court to issue directions for further investigation on certain matters or to a supervisory officer to ensure effective and proper investigation to assist in the search for truth.

d. To be heard in respect of the grant or cancellation of bail.

e. To be heard whenever prosecution seeks to withdraw and to offer to continue the prosecution.

f. To advance arguments after the Prosecutor has submitted arguments.

g. To participate in negotiations leading to settlement of compoundable offences.

(v) The victim shall have a right to prefer an appeal against any adverse order passed by the court acquitting the accused, convicting for a lesser offence, imposing inadequate sentence, or granting inadequate compensation. Such appeal shall lie to the court to which an appeal ordinarily lies against the order of conviction of such court.

(vi) Legal services to victims in select crimes may be extended to include psychiatric and medical help, interim compensation and protection against secondary victimization.

(vii) Victim compensation is a State obligation in all-serious crimes, whether the offender is apprehended or not, convicted or acquitted. This is to be organized in a separate legislation by Parliament. The draft bill on the subject submitted to Government in 1995 by the Indian Society of Victimology provides a tentative framework for consideration.

(viii) The Victim Compensation Law will provide for the creation of a Victim Compensation Fund to be administered possibly by the Legal Services Authority. The law should provide for the scale of compensation in different offences for the guidance of the Court. It may specify offences in which compensation may not be granted and conditions under which it may be awarded or withdrawn.

It is the Considered view of the Committee that Criminal Justice Administration will assume a new direction towards better and quicker justice once the rights of victims are recognized by law and restitution for loss of life, limb and property are provided for in the system. The cost for providing it is not exorbitant as sometimes made out to be. With increase in quantum of fine recovered, diversion of funds generated by the justice system and soliciting public contribution, the proposed victim compensation fund can be mobilized at least to meet the cost of compensating victims of violent crimes. Even if part of the assets confiscated and forfeited in organized crimes and financial frauds is also made part of the Fund and if it is managed efficiently, there will be no paucity of resources for this well-conceived reform. In any case, dispensing justice to victims of crime cannot any longer be ignored on grounds of scarcity of resources.

NATIONAL COMMISSION TO REVIEW THE WORKING OF THE CONSTITUTION AND ITS VIEWS ON VICTIM ORIENTATION AND VICTIMOLOGY

The Commission to review the working of the Constitution (Government of India, 2002) under the chairmanship of the former Chief Justice of India Mr. Justice Venkatachalaiah is of the view that "the assumption that by punishing the offender the victim receives 'Justice' is of doubtful value today because of the decreasing number of successful investigations and convictions. Given the inconvenience, delays, corruption and harassment, many victims tend to keep away from reporting crimes and sometimes there is a tendency to take law into one's own hands."

Among the many reforms canvassed for improving criminal justice is one that advocates a victim-orientation to criminal justice administration. 'Victim orientation' includes greater respect and consideration towards victims and their rights in the investigative and prosecution processes, provision for greater choices to victims in trial and disposition of the accused, and a scheme of reparation/compensation particularly for victims of violent crimes. According to the Commission, the case for a viable, social justice-oriented and effective scheme for compensation to victims is now widely felt. The Government at the Union level and in the states are well advised under the directive principles as well as under International Human Rights obligations to legislate on the subject of an effective scheme of compensation for victims of crime without further delay.

The tremendous support that the criminal justice might derive from the people once the compensation scheme is introduced even in a modest scale, and the possibilities of advancing the crying need for social justice in a very real sense, are attractive enough for the State to find money to float the scheme immediately according to the Commission.

AWARENESS CREATION ON JUSTICE TO VICTIMS

Criminal Justice Systems have a moral and legal responsibility to make all efforts to prevent crime victimization and also to provide relief and satisfaction to the victims. In India, creating awareness at all levels is the basic and immediate need to recognize that the sufferings of victims are unfortunate and the society condemns the acts of people who are responsible for causing such sufferings and to motivate the society and people at large about the importance of preventing victimization and taking care of victims. Even in developed countries where victim support and service systems have been sufficiently established, awareness campaign is an ongoing process.

NEED FOR A NATIONAL LEGISLATION FOR VICTIM JUSTICE

Though in India, there is no legislation or scheme to provide compensation or assistance to victims of crime at the national level, due to the persistent efforts of the Indian Society of Victimology, founded in the year 1992 to spearhead the cause of victims, the Government of Tamil Nadu has constituted a Victim Assistance Fund. This fund created in 1995 by Tamil Nadu, one of the states in South India provides financial assistance to some selected categories of victims of violent crimes such as legal heirs of victims of murder and victims of grievous hurt, rape and dowry victims, particularly to help women and children in distress (Government of Tamil Nadu, 1995). Subsequently some additions and amendments in the scheme were brought in for more effective implementation of the scheme (Government of Tamil Nadu, 1997). As the Victim assistance Fund created by the State of Tamil Nadu is only a scheme applicable to only one state and is only an executive decision without any statutory or legal right for victim compensation or assistance to the victims, the Indian Society of Victimology pursued vigorously by taking several efforts with an ultimate goal of creating a national law on victim assistance which could be applicable to the entire country.

A Model Victim Assistance Bill utilizing the expertise of several experts and Judges and with the support of the National Human Rights Commission was prepared (Indian Society of Victimology, 1996) and sent to the Union Government of India for consideration of adoption by the Indian Parliament. The Committee on Criminal Justice Reforms headed by Justice V.S.Malimath has also in its Report to the Government has recommended for the adoption of the Model Bill on Assistance to Victims. In March 2004, in the 13th Lok Sabha, a Member of Parliament has given notice for the introduction of this Victim Bill prepared by the Indian Society of Victimology for debate and adoption, and now, as the 14th Lok Sabha has been constituted in May 2004, efforts need to be taken to revive the task of introducing the bill again for adoption.

At no period during the evolution of the modern Criminal Justice System, the plight and sufferings of victims of crime and abuse of power and the human rights of victims has been a subject of international attention and debate as of present. Though, the victim, a forgotten element in the criminal justice system was re-born in the later half of the twentieth century, only a few developed countries have brought in some reforms in their domestic laws, providing rights and assistance to victims in the recent decades. The United Nations has made a significant contribution by recognizing the rights of victims through its Declaration on the Basic Principles of Justice for Victims of Crime and Abuse of Power Adopted by the General Assembly in November 1985 and its subsequent efforts to disseminate the principles of victim justice through its two documents, viz., Hand Book on Justice for Victims and Guide for Policy Makers (United Nations 1999 A, 1999 B). India has a long way to go to recognize the rights of victims and to provide assistance/compensation to the victims of crime and abuse of power. Unprecedented in the history, in the recent years, there have been concerted efforts by the higher judiciary of India to recognize the rights of victims and to provide compensation for their sufferings through several precedents.

The Law Commission of India, the Justice Malimath Committee on reforms of the criminal justice system and the Commission to Review the Working of the Constitution have all in one voice unanimously recommended the need to provide justice to victims during the different stages of the criminal proceedings including compensation and assistance as mandatory. It is the most appropriate time for us to enact a national legislation to render justice to victims, in line with the model bill on victims assistance prepared and submitted by the Indian Society of Victimology for consideration of adoption by the Indian Parliament.

One main criticism of restorative justice is that it fails to provide adequate protection for individual rights. Classic models use informal processes of negotiation and mediation, which are designed to resolve conflicts arising out of criminal offences in a way that is constructive for all parties. The values of restorative justice are based on harmony and the good of the community as well as benefits for the parties. It places responsibility for outcomes in the hands of the individuals concerned and it can only operate if the offender accepts the basic facts of the offence. Negotiation takes place in private – not in open court. The presence of lawyers is commonly thought to impair restorative processes because it affects the directness of communication; in Europe, victim/offender mediation tends to involve lawyers as advisers (or experts on levels of damages) rather than as representatives.

As essential participants in restorative justice programs, prosecutors should ensure that these issues are addressed. There are many benefits to implementing restorative justice programs in our country's justice system. Programs such as these divert cases from overburdened court dockets. They empower victims to take an active role in the justice process, and they enable offenders to be reintegrated into the community more effectively. When assessing programs for how they will work in our place, careful consideration of the needs of the community, our victims and our offenders, is a pre requisite. Then, adopting a programs to fit those needs, will lead to success.

Both the United Nations (UN) and Council of Europe have recently set out a number of principles and standards relating to restorative justice, which may provide safeguards for some of these concerns. These deal with:

- The availability of mediation
- Voluntary participation
- The necessity for the parties to be evenly balanced
- The importance of procedural safeguards and
- The question of when legal advice should be available.

They form an important basis for the international movement towards resolution by consensus, and restorative justice measures in particular. The way they are interpreted, and the influence they have had on the emerging European Union commitment to these ideas, in the form of the European Forum on Restorative Justice, is of great significance in terms of both international practice and for the future of domestic criminal justice.

International experience teaches us that the dissemination of information and good practice is crucial for the purposes of monitoring and implementing standards within restorative justice. This book is organized keeping this idea in view. This book should provide a dialogue between theory and practice, as well as play a key role in developing a restorative movement in India and abroad. Realizing that the present form of Justice System is heavily loaded towards retributiveness, the main theme of this book is oriented towards developing a philosophy in which the victims, offenders and communities - all play key roles in achieving justice through reparation of the harm caused by crime.

R. SREEKUMAR

2

NEED AND IMPORTANCE OF RESTORATIVE JUSTICE

INTRODUCTION

We have the following theories of punishments and accordingly, schools of justice, namely–

- Retributive.
- Deterrent.
- Incapacitative.
- Reformative.

RETRIBUTIVE OR DESERT THEORY

Retributive comes from the Latin verb *re* + *tribere*, 'again to give.' As a transitive verb it means 'to give in return', 'to retaliate against person' and 'to repay.'[1] Here punishment is justified, as the natural or appropriate response to crime, a fundamental intuitive claim, and its quantum should be proportionate to the degree of wrongdoing. Proportionality is the key concept in desert theory. Cardinal proportionality requires that overall level of the penalty scale should not be out of proportion to the gravity of the conduct.[2]

DETERRENT THEORY

Deterrence means literally discouraging or restraining somebody through fear or doubt from some course of action. It is derived from the Latin word – *deterrere*, 'frighten from.'[3] This theory regards the prevention of further offences through a deterrent strategy as the rationale for punishing. The premise on which it is justified is that the greatest good of the greatest number represents the supreme value and that the individual counts only for one: it may therefore be justifiable to punish one-person severely in order to deter others effectively.[4]

INCAPACITATIVE THEORY

Incapacitation means a direct prevention of an individual offender from committing a new crime so long as he is actually dangerous to society. As a rule, this procedure is discussed with reference to offenders who are responsible for at least one committed crime. The aim of incapacitation is to restrain·an ex-offender [who may already have been punished justly for the commission of or crimes] from committing a new crime. Its aim is not to punish for a committed crime, nor to rehabilitate. Therefore, an incapacitative measure is not [expressly] intended to be blameful, painful or threatening. The methods of incapacitation include among others – supervision, confinement, banishment, mutilation, surgery and killing. Surgery and mutilation may reduce the capacity to commit a new similar crime to almost zero while killing incapacitates completely.

REFORMATIVE THEORY

The term 'reformation' and nowadays also 'rehabilitation', has literally the meaning of restoring to a former condition. The prefix *re* indicates repetition or return to a state or condition, which has previously prevailed. In penal treatment the term means assisting an offender to improve himself so that he can function in a legally acceptable way in society. Reformation, like incapacitation, is in application primarily confined to the offender himself. Reformation implies a change of character and moral disposition. According to Edward Westermarck's conception of reformation, it aims at the removal of a criminal disposition of mind by improving the offender.[5] Accordingly it has a two-fold aim: negatively to remove the criminal disposition and positively to improve the man socially.[6]

The rationale here is to prevent further offending by the individual through the strategy of rehabilitation, which may involve individual casework, therapy, counselling, intervention in the family, etc. Its behavioural premise is that some or many criminal offences are to a significant extent determined by social pressures, psychological difficulties, or other problems, which impinge on individuals. Offenders are seen as unable to cope and in need of help from experts, and therefore (perhaps) as less than fully responsible individuals. The rehabilitative approach indicates that sentences should be tailored to the needs of the particular offenders. It lays emphasis on the processes of diagnosis and treatment by trained professionals.[7]

A CRITICAL REVIEW OF THE THEORY OF DETERRENCE

The core of deterrence as a specifically moral theory refers to fear of punishment as a motive of law-abidance. In a broader sense, deterrence can be defined as restraint created by doubt or hesitation due to a known rule of behaviour from committing socially undesirable acts. Much legislation and especially criminal legislation is done largely in order to have this effect. Apart from whatever deterrent effect it is expected to have on the concerned offender, the widely held prophesy and objective of deterrence is that it will deter others from committing crimes. However, the big question is – *is it morally right to punish a man for the sake of influencing others to behave in a certain way*?

With regard to criminal conduct, the population is sometimes divided into three groups: firstly, law-abiding people who would not commit a crime even if there was no punishment; secondly, potential criminals who may be deterred by punishment but who without the threat of punishment would commit a crime and, thirdly, actual criminals whose behaviour cannot be influenced by the threat and who commit crimes irrespective of the consequences. In the first instance, punishment is needless; it may even cause anxiety and mental suffering to no good purpose. In the second case, it is the potential criminal, susceptible to the threat of punishment, who is the proper object of deterrence. The third groups, the actual criminals who take the risk or do not mind the risk, are uselessly subjected to deterrence.

Besides those having potential criminal indications but who have not yet committed any serious crime, the first offenders are generally held to be relatively receptive to deterrence, whereas recidivists are harder to influence by punishment irrespective of the increasing amount of injury for every repeated offence.[8] Punishments that are more serious give diminishing returns if the deterrent is addressed chiefly to the class of repeaters or hardened criminals who would commit crimes in any case. Increased seriousness in these cases may primarily result in temporary incapacitation in the form of prolonged detention. We may assume that at both ends of the scale; punishing in order to address either good citizens or the hard core of offenders is unprofitable and vain.

One of the hypotheses of general deterrence is that the less a person has to lose in respect of social integration the less he will be deterred by threats. Social integration relies on his reputation, employment, family relationship, group membership, licenses, and other privileges.[9] Deterrence seems to have most effect on those who have most to lose in terms of social integration, whereas hardened criminals, who have already lost most of this, cannot economically be deterred any more.

It is assumed that the average man in a normal situation can be influenced by the threat of punishment, but a professional criminal and those acting on sudden impulse cannot. Especially serious crimes such as manslaughter and certain moral offences can be little affected.[10] H.L.A. Hart reminds us that no greater punishment may be needed to deter a murderer than a robber, yet legal systems show their allegiance to retributive ideas by punishing the murderer more severely.[11] A research report by Dorothy Miller *inter alia* concludes that it is not clear that the increasing of already existing penalties has an equally increasing deterrent effect. Increased penalties are generally recognized as ineffective in controlling crimes committed against the self, such as drug addiction and prostitution; so also, penalties are regarded as ineffective deterrents of crimes of passion such as murder and assault.[12]

These above inferences seem to shake the assumption that the efficiency of deterrence will vary directly with the amount of punitive injury. Deterrence does not seem to correlate positively with increased punitive injury. Unto Tahtinen goes on to quote from the *Yogasutra* that, "there should be cultivation of the opposite in order to overcome evil.[13] The psychological explanation seems to be that so long as there is emphasis on violence, even though it is on resisting, controlling, limiting and eradicating the use of violence, it is still emphasis on violence in a negative way i.e. our attention is still being directed towards violence. Therefore such opposite moral feelings as social integration should be inculcated in order to overcome criminal violence."[14]

One of the best examples to prove the above mentioned point comes from the story of Jean Val Jean in the classic – *Les Miserables*

['The Poor'] by the French writer Victor Hugo. In this story, Jean val Jean is put in prison for nearly 19 years for having attempted to steal a loaf bread for his sister's starving daughter. The brutality of the insensitive criminal justice system hardens him completely. On being released temporarily on parole, he is invited by a kind Bishop to share his evening dinner. There, on getting enamoured by the silver candlesticks, he steals them and escapes in the darkness of night. On getting caught by the police and being produced before the Bishop, to confirm that the candlesticks were indeed that of the Bishop, the Bishop denies that Jean Val Jean had stolen it from him. The Bishop addresses him as Brother and asks him as to why did he not take the silver spoons too, which the Bishop had gifted to him. This lie of the Bishop based on the Bishop's faith in the inherent goodness of all human beings, broke Jean val Jean down and he decides to reform himself for the last time.

A CRITICAL REVIEW OF THE RETRIBUTIVE NOTION OF JUSTICE

According to Howard Zehr – one of the principal proponents of restorative justice, from the view of retributive justice, "crime is a violation of the state, defined by lawbreaking and guilt" and "justice determines blame and administers pain in a contest between the offender and the state directed by systematic rules."[15] He further points out that, the retributive system is founded on the following assumptions:

1. Crime is essentially *lawbreaking*;
2. When a law is broken, justice involves establishing *guilt*;
3. So that *just deserts* can be meted out;
4. By inflicting *pain*;
5. Through a *conflict* in which *rules* and intentions are placed above outcomes.[16]

The first premise – crime as lawbreaking, results in an emphasis on the act of breaking a defined rule, rather than the harm done or the experiences of those affected. Under this system, the victim is the state and "crime is an offence against the state", not against the individual. The real victims; those who suffered the actual harm; are left out of the equation and called upon only to be witness or other secondary players in the process. The singular focus on legal guilt, not moral, social, or even factual guilt, further isolates the victim.

In addition, much of the society is obsessed with making sure that offenders receive their just deserts or what they "deserve" for what they have done. This approach leads to the view that punishments and the infliction of pain are the appropriate responses to crime. Because of the severity of the punishment if an accused is found guilty, safeguards are put in place to ensure due process. Justice, from this viewpoint, is served when rules and procedures are followed, rather than when a wrong is made right.

The cumulative effect of retributive justice is isolation of the victim and the offender from their personal experiences. This system is not only problematic in that it results in an expanding prison population, but also because it fails to engender empowerment of those directly and indirectly affected. For offenders, there is potentially a greater reward for denying than accepting responsibility. For victims, their limited role in the process makes empowerment difficult. Because the community has little or no say in the outcome, members of the community tend to feel entirely alienated and helpless. The result of retributive justice is a system where few are satisfied with the outcome and many are rendered worse off.

Punishments of a negative nature do not ensure that the offender realizes his mistake and makes the necessary amendments in his life and behaviour and do the needful to redress the harm caused to the victim by him after acknowledging his mistake to the victim. Now, let us examine one of the most outstanding theories ever given on Crime and Justice. Professor John Braithwaite gave this theory in his influential work – *Crime, Shame and Reintegration.*[17]

"The claim of this theory is that the societies that have the lowest crime rates are the societies that shame criminal conduct most effectively. There is an important difference between reintegrative shaming and stigmatization. While reintegrative shaming prevents crime, stigmatization is a kind of shaming that makes crime problems worse. Stigmatization is the kind of shaming that creates outcasts; it is disrespectful, humiliating. Stigmatization means treating criminals as evil people who have done evil acts. Reintegrative shaming means disapproving the evil of the deed while treating the person as essentially good. Reintegrative shaming means strong disapproval of the act but doing so in a way that is respecting of the person. Once we understand this distinction, we can see why putting more police on the street can actually increase crime. More police can increase crime if they are systematically stigmatizing in the way they deal with citizens. More police can reduce crime if they are systematically reintegrative in the way they deal with citizens.

We can also understand why building more prisons could make the crime problem worse. Having more people in prison does deter some and incapacitates others from committing certain crimes, like bank robberies, because there are no banks inside the prison for them to rob, though there certainly are plenty of vulnerable people to rape and pillage. But because prisons stigmatize, they also make things worse for those who have criminal identities affirmed by imprisonment, those whose stigmatization leads them to find solace in the society of the similarly outcast, those who are attracted into criminal subcultures, those who treat the prison as an educational institution for learning new skills for the illegitimate labour market. On this account, whether building more prisons reduces or increases the crime rate depends on whether the stigmatizing nature of a particular prison system does more to increase crime than its deterrent and incapacitative effects reduce it."[18]

This is precisely what Mahatma Gandhi meant so many decades ago when he requested that we 'Hate the Sin and not the Sinner.' The idea was to reclaim the offender as a useful citizen back into the society.[19] The above theory can actualize if the offender is reclaimed back into the social fold. Inter alia, it also requires community participation in the treatment of offenders. This is something that finds approval even in India. The All India Committee on Jail Reforms, popularly known as the Mulla Committee after its Chairman Justice A.N. Mulla, understood the necessity and scope of the issue and devoted one full chapter to it, titled – *Community Involvement in Corrections*.[20]

Now that we have seen the effect of retributive justice from the perspectives of both the victims and the offenders, where do we go to, from here? The answer is quite simple. We go back to the victims and the offenders, together, and help them handle their conflict in a Humane, Harmonious and Positive manner, rather than allow a life-less, fictious third party by the name – 'State' and black-lettered lawyers "to steal"[21] their conflict and leave them unsatisfied. Though this form of dealing with a conflict to arrive at justice is at times known as Deliberative justice since it involves a deliberation between the victim and the offender, it is better known as Restorative Justice since its aim is to restore. However, what restoration are we talking about, here? For an answer to this question, let us understand the concept of Restorative justice.

RESTORATIVE JUSTICE

At the abstract level, "restorative justice is fundamentally concerned with restoring relationships, with establishing or re-establishing social equality in relationships."[22] At a more concrete level, restorative justice "involves the victim, the offender, and the community in a search for solutions which promote repair, reconciliation, and reassurance."[23]

According to Howard Zehr, the assumptions behind restorative justice are –

1. Crime violates people and relationships.
2. Justice aims to identify needs and obligations;
3. So that things can be made right.
4. Justice encourages dialogue and mutual agreement.
5. Gives victims and offenders central roles, and
6. Is judged by the extent to which responsibilities are assumed, needs met, and healing (of individuals and relationships) is encouraged.[24]

Although Zehr speaks in terms of criminal law, restorative justice blurs the line between criminal and civil wrongs by focusing on the harm done and the solutions required for healing, rather than the action itself or the need for punishment.

The Fundamental Principles of Restorative Justice are –

1. Holding the wrongdoer directly accountable for the individual victim and the specific community affected by the wrong act;
2. Requiring the wrongdoer to take direct responsibility for making "things whole again" to the degree that this is possible;
3. Providing the victim(s) purposeful access to the courts and correctional processes, which allows them to assist in shaping the wrongdoers' obligations; and
4. Encouraging the community to become directly involved in supporting victims, holding wrongdoers accountable, and providing opportunities for wrongdoers to reintegrate into the community.[25]

Restoration does not mean returning to the relationship before the conflict.[26] In many cases, this is neither applicable nor desirable. For example, a victim who has never met the offender before the crime may not want further contact with the person. In the case of spousal abuse, the abused spouse is unlikely to wish for a return to the relationship of abuse. Restoration, in the context of restorative justice, refers to "the process of 'righting wrongs' or healing wounds".[27] This means different things for the different parties. Victims may use the process to restore a sense of control over their lives, to obtain answers for questions about the incident, or to express their anger over the wrongdoing and the impact the event has had on them. For Offenders, restoration means "accepting responsibility for their actions by repairing the harm they have caused" and "addressing the issues that contribute to their propensity to engage in harmful behaviour".[28] In the case of the Community, the process of restoration includes "denouncing wrongful behaviour and reaffirming community standards".[29] Restoration also means successful reintegration of the offender into society, particularly in situations where the victims and offenders live in the same community.

Here, it is important to understand the difference between restitution and restoration since, often; restitution is mistakenly used to refer to restoration. Restitution is similar in that it offers "wrongdoers the opportunity to put right the wrong by making good the damage that was caused".[30] However, restitution does not capture the full essence of restorative justice. Restitution assigns a value to the material losses suffered by the victim and requires that the wrongdoer balance the scale by paying that amount to the sufferer. Restoration, on the other hand, looks beyond the material harm to non-material disruptions, such as the loss of a sense of security or the loss of trust. In addition, restitution only considers harm done to the victim; whereas, restorative justice attempts to address the needs of the victim, offender, family members, the community, and others affected by the offence.

May Leung has summarized the comparisons made by Howard Zehr of looking at justice through the Retributive and Restorative lenses in the form of a table.[31] The comparisons are as follows –

Retributive Lens	*Restorative Lens*
Blame-fixing central	Problem-solving central
Focus on past	Focus on future
Needs secondary	Needs primary
Battle model; adversarial	Dialogue normative
Emphasizes differences	Searches for commonalties
Imposition of pain considered normative	Restoration and reparation considered normative
One social injury added to another	Emphasis on repair of social injuries
Harm by offender balanced by harm to offender	Harm by offender balanced by making right
Focus on offender; victim ignored	Victims' needs central
Victims lack information	Victim and offender are key elements
Restitution rare	Restitution normal
Victim's "truth" secondary	Victim's suffering lamented and acknowledged
Action from state to offender; offender passive	Offender given role in solution
State monopoly on response to wrongdoing	Victim, offender, and community roles recognized
Offender has no responsibility for resolution	Offender has responsibility in resolution
Outcomes discourage offender responsibility	Responsible behaviour encouraged
Rituals of personal denunciation and exclusion	Rituals of lament and reordering
Offender denounced	Harmful act denounced
Offender's ties to community weakened	Offender's integration into community increased
Offender seen in fragments, offence being definitional	Offender viewed holistically
Sense of balance through retribution	Sense of balance through restitution
Balance righted by lowering offender	Balance righted by raising both victim and offender
Justice tested by intent and process	Justice tested by its "fruits"
Justice as right rules	Justice as right relationships
Victim-offender relationships ignored	Victim-offender relationships central
Process alienates	Process aims at reconciliation
Response based on offender's past behaviour	Response based on consequences of offender's behaviour
Repentance and forgiveness discouraged	Repentance and forgiveness encouraged
Proxy professions are the key actors	Victim and offender central; professional help available
Competitive, individualistic values encouraged	Mutuality and cooperation encouraged
Ignores social, economic, and moral context of behaviour	Total context relevant
Assumes win-lose outcomes	Makes possible win-win outcomes

Those beings so, let us now look at it from a legal framework. Since our country does not have such a perspective in its substantive and procedural criminal laws, let us see the model prescribed in the provisions and declarations of the United Nations in its different documents prescribing the ideal objectives of a criminal justice system. This can serve as the ideal guideline for us to begin with. What should be the real objectives of a Criminal Justice system? For this purpose, we shall refer to the objectives set out in the *Standard Minimum Rules for Treatment of Prisoners*, 1955 by the United Nations about treating offenders in a different way than the way our present criminal justice system does so. Then we shall examine the salient features of the *United Nations Declaration of Basic Principles of Justice for Victims of Crime and Abuse of Power*, 1985. The first ever-United Nations Congress on the Prevention of Crime and the Treatment of Offenders, held at Geneva in 1955, adopted the *Standard Minimum Rules for Treatment of Prisoners*. This was then approved by the Economic and Social Council of the United Nations by its resolution 663 C (XXIV) of 31st July 1957 and 2076 (LXII) of 13th May 1977.

Part II— Section A deals with Prisoners under sentence who usually known as convict prisoners. Following is what the Standard Minimum Rules provide for –

- The purpose and justification of a sentence of imprisonment or a similar measure deprivative of liberty is ultimately to protect society against crime. This end can only be achieved if the period of imprisonment is used to ensure, so far as possible, that upon his return to society the offender is not only willing but able to lead a law-abiding and self-supporting life.[32]
- To this end, the institution should utilize all the remedial, educational, moral, spiritual, and other forces and forms of assistance, which are appropriate and available, and should seek to apply them according to the individual treatment needs of the prisoners.[33]
- The regime of the institution should seek to minimize any differences between prison life and life at liberty which tend to lessen the responsibility of the prisoners or the respect due to their dignity as human beings.[34]

- Before the completion of the sentence, it is desirable that the necessary steps be taken to ensure for the prisoner a gradual return to life in society. This aim may be achieved, depending on the case, by a pre-release regime organized in the same institution or in another appropriate institution, or by release on trial under some kind of supervision, which must not be entrusted to the police but should be combined with effective social aid.[35]
- The treatment of prisoners should emphasize not their exclusion from the community, but their continuing part in it. Community agencies should, therefore, be enlisted wherever possible to assist the staff of the institution in the task of social rehabilitation of the prisoners. There should be in connection with every institution social workers charged with the duty of maintaining and improving all desirable relations of a prisoner with his family and with valuable social agencies. Steps should be taken to safeguard, to the maximum extent compatible with the law and the sentence, the rights relating to civil interests, social security rights and other social benefits of prisoners.[36]
- The fulfillment of these principles requires individualization of treatment and for this purpose a flexible system of classifying prisoners in groups; it is therefore desirable that such groups should be distributed in separate institutions suitable for the treatment of each group.[37]
- These institutions need not provide the same degree of security for every group. It is desirable to provide varying degrees of security according to the needs of different groups. Open institutions, by the very fact that they provide no physical security against escape but rely on the self-discipline of the inmates; provide the conditions most favourable to rehabilitation for carefully selected prisoners.[38]
- The duty of society does not end with a prisoner's release. There should, therefore, be governmental or private agencies capable of lending the released prisoner efficient after-care directed towards the lessening of prejudice against him and towards his social rehabilitation.[39]

- The treatment of persons sentenced to imprisonment or a similar measure shall have as its purpose, so far as the length of the sentence permits, to establish in them the will to lead law-abiding and self-supporting lives after their release and to fit them to do so. The treatment shall be in a way that will encourage their self-respect and develop their sense of responsibility.[40]
- To these ends, all appropriate means shall be used, including religious care in the countries where this is possible, education, vocational guidance and training, social casework, employment counselling, physical development and strengthening of moral character, in accordance with the individual needs of each prisoner, taking account of his social and criminal history, his physical and mental capacities and aptitudes, his personal temperament, the length of his sentence and his prospects after release.[41]

Then under the section titled – Social relations and after-care, it provides for the following –

- Special attention shall be paid to the maintenance and improvement of such relations between a prisoner and his family as they are desirable in the best interests of both.[42]
- From the beginning of a prisoner's sentence consideration shall be given to his future after release and he shall be encouraged and assisted to maintain or establish such relations with persons or agencies outside the institution as may promote the best interests of his family and his own social rehabilitation.[43]
- Services and agencies, governmental or otherwise, which assist released prisoners to re-establish themselves in society shall ensure, so far as is possible and necessary, that released prisoners be provided with appropriate documents and identification papers, have suitable homes and work to go to, are suitably and adequately clothed having regard to the climate and season, and have sufficient means to reach their destination and maintain themselves in the period immediately following their release.[44]

Now let us examine the provisions from the perspective of the Victims. The *United Nations Declaration of Basic Principles of Justice for Victims of Crime and Abuse of Power*, 1985[45] begins by giving a comprehensive definition of a Victim –

"Victims" means persons who, individually or collectively, have suffered harm, including physical or mental injury, emotional suffering, economic loss or substantial impairment of their fundamental rights, through acts or omissions that are in violation of criminal laws operative within Member States, including those laws proscribing criminal abuse of power.[46]

Under the section titled – Access to Justice and fair treatment, it declares the following principles –

- Victims should be treated with compassion and respect for their dignity. They are entitled to access to the mechanisms of justice and to prompt redress, as provided for by national legislation, for the harm that they have suffered.[47]
- Judicial and administrative mechanisms should be established and strengthened where necessary to enable victims to obtain redress through formal or informal procedures that are expeditious, fair, inexpensive, and accessible. Victims should be informed of their rights in seeking redress through such mechanisms.[48]
- The responsiveness of judicial and administrative processes to the needs of victims should be facilitated by:
  (a) Informing victims of their role and the scope, timing and progress of the proceedings and of the disposition of their cases, especially where serious crimes are involved and where they have requested such information;
  (b) Allowing the views and concerns of victims to be presented and considered at appropriate stages of the proceedings where their personal interests are affected, without prejudice to the accused and consistent with the relevant national criminal justice system;
  (c) Providing proper assistance to victims throughout the legal process;
  (d) Taking measures to minimize inconvenience to victims, protect their privacy, when necessary, and ensure their safety, as well as that of their families and witnesses on their behalf, from intimidation and retaliation;

(e) Avoiding unnecessary delay in the disposition of cases and the execution of orders or decrees granting awards to victims.[49]

It makes a new mark and provides that –

- Informal mechanisms for the resolution of disputes, including mediation, arbitration and customary justice or indigenous practices, should be utilized where appropriate to facilitate conciliation and redress for victims.[50]

Then it makes the most important point when it talks of Restitution to the Victims –

- Offenders or third parties responsible for their behaviour should, where appropriate, make fair restitution to victims, their families, or dependents. Such restitution should include the return of property or payment for the harm or loss suffered, reimbursement of expenses incurred because of the victimization, the provision of services and the restoration of rights.[51]
- Governments should review their practices, regulations and laws to consider restitution as an available sentencing option in criminal cases, in addition to other criminal sanctions.[52]
- Victims should receive the necessary material, medical, psychological, and social assistance through governmental, voluntary, community-based, and indigenous means.[53]
- Police, justice, health, social service, and other personnel concerned should receive training to sensitize them to the needs of victims, and guidelines to ensure proper and prompt aid.[54]

Thus,

1. From the perspective of the offender, the emphasis is quite clearly on his social Re-integration of the offender and not on his stigmatization and ostracization; and
2. From the perspective of the victim, it is Restitution.

However, this cannot happen as easily as it may be wished. When an individual victim or the community at large has been hurt or victimized by the action of the offender that needs to be addressed before we can think of the society showing its willingness to accept the offender back into its fold. Where, relations balance and harmony have been hurt, toppled and destroyed, they need to be Restored and reworked to the best possible extent, before we can talk of the offender's reintegration and re-acceptance.

This cannot happen till the offender understands the damage that he caused in the first place for no fault of the victim or the community and chooses to accept responsibility for his actions. A persistent refusal to accept responsibility only fester the unhealed wounds of the victim and furthers the feelings of anger and hatred.

Denial by the offender hits at the core of a victim's being, at his or her integrity, at the identity and these things are all tied up intimately with a victim's experiences and memory. Denial subverts the victim's personhood.[55]

Once an understanding of the damage caused and acceptance of responsibility is there, the next phase is to redress the damage caused to the best possible extent in the most holistic form possible, within the context of the entire scenario. When a mutually acceptable solution or course of action is reached without any coercion or pressure on either side, particularly on the victim, reconciliation and peace need to be encouraged for which it is necessary that both the victim and the offender get over the past. This is not an easy process. This is particularly so for the victims. This may require them to be able to forgive the offender.

This raises the following important questions –

1. Is there any possibility that the public will accept a changed paradigm like this when we have been rooted in the retributive discourse and practice for so long?
2. How do we make offenders of all varieties, realize the damage they caused and make them own up the responsibility for their acts?
3. Can the victims ever forgive? Is it possible for them? Particularly in serious offences like rape and murder? Should they forgive at all? If so, just why?

Only when there are clear-cut and positive answers to the above mentioned questions that we have any chance of arriving at a new paradigm to the notion and practice of justice. Fortunately and thankfully, the picture is not gloomy and there is a clearly discernible hope since, answers to all the questions are in the affirmative.

Let us now answer the first two questions here.[56]

1. **Is there any possibility that the public will accept a changed paradigm like this when we have been rooted in the retributive discourse and practice for so long?**

Victim-surveys have revealed that the public is not as punitive as had been expected and that many victims would welcome the opportunity to seek some reparation or even reconciliation in place of traditional punishment.[57] This, combined with the growing disillusionment of Academics, Policy makers and criminal justice professionals with the existing paradigm of punishment, has prompted discussion of models of reparative justice oriented towards the aims of mediation and restitution.[58]

Speaking of academics, apart from Howard Zehr and others, Prof. John Braithwaite is one of the leading academics who champion the cause of Restorative Justice.[59] Speaking of policy makers, we can refer to the recommendation of the Committee set up for the Review of the Sentencing Framework for England and Wales. The committee recommended that–

"There is also growing awareness of the contributions that reparation and "restorative justice" can make. The framework could do more to exploit these developing opportunities, within a clearer sense of common purpose. If it could do so in ways that were more transparent, accessible and accountable, it could gain in public confidence".[60]

Though this is of recent development in England, in India, the All India Committee on Jail Reforms had recommended the same, more than twenty years ago. In the chapter titled– *Community Involvement in Corrections*, the committee recommended that "Community groups can be organized as 'Friends of Prisoners' to work for reconciliation between prisoners and their victims or between prisoners and their own families so as to facilitate their smooth return to homes after release."[61]

2. **How do we make offenders of all varieties, realize the damage they caused and make them own up the responsibility for their acts?**

Through different schemes and models of Victim-offender mediation, offenders of the moderate types and the non-hardened and non-habitual types have been sensitized to the damage they caused to the victims and thus make them to take a conscious decision to own up the responsibility of their actions. There are different schemes and models here, spread across different cultures. There are schemes that are run within the context of a prison itself where, the victims are called along with their family and community members to enter into Communication, Deliberation, and Mediation in the presence of a trained mediator. One of the earliest and best-known schemes was the one that was run at the Rochester Youth Custody Centre in England.[62] Another example is Belgium where restorative programmes have been officially introduced.[63] There are some 'Court based' schemes taking referrals from the courts prior to sentencing as is South Yorkshire in England.[64] Others are run outside the prison set up. These are known by different names depending upon the country and the cultural, religious, and spiritual background in which they are organised. In New Zealand, it is known as Family Group Conferencing;[65] Sentencing and Healing Circles in the Yukon valley of Canada;[66] Navajo Peacemaker Court in the Navajo Red Indian territory spread out in the states of Arizona, New Mexico, and Utah in the United States of America, etc.[67]

As things stand today, there are at least 600 such programmes running all over the world.[68] Though most of them are either at an informal level outside the main state legal system, there are some jurisdictions where it has been either integrated into the main criminal justice system itself alongside the dominant approach or has been accepted lock stock and barrel instead of the traditional retributive system. But doubts have often been expressed that 'while such engagement and mediation may have achieved some success in respect of crimes of low seriousness, whether it could really substitute for formal adjudication in the case of serious crimes.'[69]

CAN PRINCIPLES OF RESTORATIVE JUSTICE BE APPLIED IN SERIOUS OFFENCES?

Can we think of substituting the formal adjudication process in the case of serious crimes? We shall seek an answer to the same by seeing whether any attempt has been made in the past which was successful.[70]

India

Here we would be examining only one such success story among the many. In India, it happened outside the formal legal system. Even then, it had the respect, approval, and support of some sections of the formal legal system. We are talking about the Lok Adalat [People's Court] at Rangpur in Baroda district of Gujarat by the veteran Gandhian – Shri Harivallabh Parikh. Prof. Upendra Baxi conducted a preliminary study of the working of this Lok Adalat[71] as part of the project on "Delay in Administration of Criminal Justice in India" undertaken by the Institute of Constitutional and Parliamentary Studies on behalf of the then United Nations Social Defence Research Institute [UNSDRI], Rome. UNSDRI is presently known as the United Nations Interregional Crime and Justice Research Institute [UNICRI] at Turin, Italy.

Prof. Baxi points out that the Lok Adalat continuously tried to promote amicable and mutually acceptable solutions through reconciliation. The final agreements between the conflicting parties were recorded in an agreement sheet which in the local language was known as the 'Kararkhat'. In Part, III of the study report, Prof. Baxi deals with the types of disputes dealt with and sanctions handed out at the Rangpur Lok Adalat. He says that different things are meant by the state and non-state legal systems by the same terminology, and hence use of terms like murder and attempt to murder need not mean the same in the Indian Penal Code and in its usage at the Lok Adalat. Even then, disputes that were taken up at the Lok Adalat could be classified by reference to the nature of the subject matter. From that standpoint, one of the classifications involved – disputes involving the contention that the physical integrity of a person was threatened or injured by use of physical force [ordinarily, in our parlance, "assault", "intimidation", "attack", "rape", "abduction", "grievous hurt", "attempt to murder", "murder", but also beating, child bashing etc.].[72]

Even in such a list, action classified as "rape", "abduction", "grievous hurt", "attempt to murder", "murder" are serious offences. Let us see what Prof. Baxi has to point out further. He goes onto quote from the statistics maintained at the Rangpur Ashram of Shri Harivallabh Parikh and says that out of the 17,254 disputes settled for the period 1949-1971, there were 816 cases of "Attempt to murder" and "Murder" in addition to 2,225 cases of "Violent clashes".[73] This goes onto prove that, even outside the formal state legal system, it is possible to deal with serious offences. Let us now come to a jurisdiction where it was done after a proper legislation was enacted by the Parliament of that country, according sanction to the whole process. We are talking of South Africa.

South Africa

South Africa became a democratic country in 1994 when after the first ever multi party, multi racial, free and fair elections, a government was chosen by the people for the people, of the people. Before this transition to democracy took place, South Africa had witnessed innumerable acts of violence and human rights violations of the gravest nature perpetrated by the ruling minority of whites who followed the racially discriminatory policy of Apartheid. These violent acts included Murder, Abduction, Maiming, Rape, and other forms of grievous offences. After the first ever free and fair elections, when the new Parliament was constituted, it was decided that atrocities committed in the past would not be forgotten. It was decided to deal with the painful past. However, what made the entire difference was the way the South African leadership decided to deal with it.

Since the transition to democracy was the result of a negotiated settlement between the ruling minority and the opposition parties, there were many compelling circumstances under which the agreement to hand over power was arrived at. The army and the police were still dominated by the whites and if they ever felt that they would be hounded out for their past deeds, then they would not have supported the transition and South Africa would have seen more bloodbath. Still the horrific past had to be dealt with. The question was – How?

That is when the newly elected South African Parliament came out with the *Promotion of National Unity and Reconciliation Act*, 1995. Through this Act, a Truth and Reconciliation Commission was created and it provided for the investigation and establishment of as complete a picture as possible of the nature, causes and extent of gross violations of human rights committed during a specified period mentioned therein. In essence, it if where, a former perpetrator of human rights violations made a complete and full disclosure of the atrocities committed by him and met some other criteria laid down in the Act, and then Amnesty "shall" be granted to him. Victims were given the right to oppose applications for amnesty by trying to demonstrate that those conditions had not been met, but they had no right of veto over amnesty.

Why did they seek to do something like that? Why did they seek to encourage amnesty? The answer is to be found in the Preamble to the Constitution.

However, two questions arise here –

1. Why was it that they chose not to prosecute the perpetrators according to the traditional adversarial procedure of criminal trial; what were the compulsions and what were the objectives of taking a different approach, namely that of granting amnesty to the perpetrators? and,
2. Did it succeed in dealing with serious offences in a better and positive manner? If so, in what way and what were the outcomes?

As has been pointed out in one of the earlier paragraphs, the army and the police were still controlled by the whites and if they were to get a dispensation that would have hounded them out by going after them and launching criminal investigations and prosecutions, they would have opposed the peaceful transition to democracy. Hence, a different way had to be found to deal with them. That was why the South African leadership decided to turn the traditional game on its head and came out with a policy that put the onus of getting out on the perpetrators. They came out with the policy of the carrot and the stick. That is why they chose to encourage the perpetrators to come out with the full disclosure of the atrocities in return for amnesty if they fulfilled other requirements too. Those who chose not to do so still faced the prospects of being caught and face the traditional criminal proceedings and its consequences. This was the stick. The carrot was the prospect of being granted Amnesty for their acts, if they made a full disclosure.

One of the most remarkable and unbelievable features of the proceedings of the Commission was that victims or their kin decided to forgive the perpetrators when they made a full disclosure of the unspeakable crimes they had committed. Let us now examine some important questions that would come to the mind of any ordinary person when we see that the Act provided for amnesty in return for a full disclosure –

The first question could be, 'Will it not encourage impunity?' The answer is that, 'it is not true that the granting of amnesty would encourage impunity because amnesty is granted only to those who plead guilty, who accept responsibility, for what they have done. Amnesty is not given to innocent people or to those who claim to be innocent.'[74] There were a number of cases where amnesty was refused to the applicants since they denied in effect that they committed any crime and where they tried to shift the blame onto to other superficial or illogical factors. Thus, the process in fact encourages accountability rather than the opposite. It assists in the cultivation of the new culture of respect for human rights and the acknowledgment of responsibility and accountability by which the new democracy wishes to be characterised.[75]

This is the second question. Is it ever enough that the perpetrators merely apologize and then simply walk away, scot-free? Well, the process was not as simple as that. Taking precisely this factor into account, the Act required that all the applications for amnesty should be dealt within a public hearing unless such a hearing was likely to lead to a miscarriage of justice, as in the case where witnesses were too intimidated to testify in open session. Virtually all the applications have been considered in public in the full glare of television lights. Thus, there was the penalty of this public humiliation and exposure for the perpetrator. Many of those in the security forces who came forward had previously been regarded as respectable members of their communities. It was often the very first time that their communities and even sometimes their families heard of the fact that these persons were actually, for instance, members of death squads or were regular torturers of detainees in their custody. It was so traumatic for some that marriages broke up. That was some price to pay. Thus, it was not entirely the case that the perpetrator was allowed to get off scot-free.[76] Some even wanted to attempt suicide to get out of the trauma and guilt of having tortured and killed innocent black people.[77]

Now the third question. What about justice? It is in answer to this question that we come to realize that it is very much possible to substitute the traditional retributive system with the restorative system. Let us see the form of justice the South African leadership decided to adopt for dealing with its past and as to why did it not do go for retribution when nobody prevented them from doing so? Archbishop Desmond Tutu points out in his book *No Future without Forgiveness*[78] that the Act sought to forgive the perpetrators keeping in mind the traditional African jurisprudence of restorative justice. Here the central concern is not retribution or punishment. In the spirit of *ubuntu*, the central concern is the healing of breaches, the redressing of imbalance, the restoration of broken relationships, a seeking to rehabilitate both the victim and the perpetrator, who should be given the opportunity to be reintegrated into the community he has injured by his offence.

This is a far more personal approach, regarding the offence as something that has happened to persons and whose consequence is a rupture in relationships. Thus, we would claim that justice, restorative justice, is being served when efforts are being made to work for healing, for forgiving, and for reconciliation.[79] This takes us immediately to the fourth question. Since on the grant of amnesty to the offender, all the civil liabilities are expunged, is it fair to deny the victims their right to claim compensation from the perpetrators?

To this, Bishop Tutu says that, 'that is indeed a very high price to ask the victims to pay. That happens to have been the price those who negotiated our relatively peaceful transition from repression to democracy believed the nation had to ask of victims. Our freedom has been bought at a very great price. But to compute the price properly, we should compare the high level of stability that we enjoy with the turmoil and upheaval that have so sadly characterised similar radical change in the former Soviet Union, not to mention the awful carnage and instability in the former Yugoslavia.'[80]

However, the story does not end here. The Commission in its work recommended the payment of a reasonable sum of compensation to the victims of gross human right violations. This reparation was '*nuanced*' and '*individualised*' taking into consideration the needs of each of the families and keeping in mind the best form of balm that would have taken the sting out of their wounds and healed their pain and helped them to move forward. Again, the idea was not to lessen the value of the life that was lost in material terms but to say in effect, to the victims: "We acknowledge that you suffered a gross violation of your rights. Nothing can ever replace your loved one. But as a nation we are saying, we are sorry, we have opened the wounds of your suffering and sought to cleanse them; this reparation is as balm, an ointment, being poured over the wounds to assist in their healing."[81]

Let nobody be cynical that this was not the best deal. It may not have been the most ideal package, given the compelling demands on the resources of the state. However, let us at the same time note something more magnanimous on the part of the victims. Bishop Tutu notes that, 'We at the commission were often deeply humbled that those who came before us were so frequently so modest in their expectations and requests. "Can I have a tombstone erected for my child?" "Could the TRC [acronym for the Truth and Reconciliation Commission] help to find the remains of my loved one, even just a bone so that we could give him a decent burial?" "Could I get assistance to educate my children?"[82]

That brings us to the fifth and the last question: What authority did those who made such a law have, to have acted on behalf of the suffering victims? Was this law made by those sitting in Ivory towers, oblivious to all pain and suffering and concerned only about some highlandishly philosophical and idealistically philanthropically dreaming? The answer to this question is that those who drafted and implemented this law, had all the credentials and claims to have come out with such a law since, almost all of them had suffered immensely under the apartheid regime. They all had either been detained illegally, tortured, tried with bias and thrown into prison for unduly long periods of time which was detrimental to their health and families. They all had suffered immensely and lost a lot in their quest for human dignity and freedom from apartheid. Yet, they decided to forgive and look into the future to build a multi-racial, multi-ethnic, stable and harmonious society.

There are two prominent names among them. One is President Nelson Mandela who had been detained for 27 years at the Ruben Island prison. Even though his family suffered in absence, his health and eyesight were affected and he faced so many other problems, he did not come out as a bitter man harping for revenge but as an advocate for reconciliation, forgiveness, and a better future. The other one was Mr. Mullah Omar the Minister of Justice who introduced the Promotion of National Unity and Reconciliation Act in the newly elected South African Parliament. He was denied a passport at the last minute after obtaining a scholarship to study at the University of London and this devastated him to no end. It was revealed much later that he had been on a death list compiled by a South African Government hit squad. They had tried to swap the tablets he had to take for a heart condition so that he would take the wrong medication. It was this very man who piloted through Parliament the legislation that enabled the men who had tried to kill him to apply for amnesty.[83]

Isn't that proof enough to satisfy the question whether they could legitimately speak for the victims and take tough decisions like the ones that are found in the Act? The fact that the victims accepted their decisions is clearly discernible from the following two incidents. In 1998 when the commission had been working for nearly three years and even when some controversial amnesty decisions were given by the commission, Nelson Mandela and his successor Thabo Mbeki scored nearly eight and seven out a possible ten, in opinion polls while their closest rival was at a distant three. The public opinion would have reflected sharply if they had decided not to reaffirm the mandate in the African National Congress and elect Mr. Thabo Mbeki as the second president after Mandela.[84]

VICTIMS AND FORGIVENESS

In the end, we shall address one of the most important questions raised at an earlier place in this chapter. Can victims ever forgive to complete the process of restorative justice? Is it possible for them? Particularly in serious offences like Rape and Murder? Should they forgive at all? If so, just why?

Two of the most important phrases in this world which can make the biggest difference to our lives and which contain no more than just three words in them, are–

- "I am Sorry", and
- "I Forgive You".

Though these contain just three words each in them, they are the most difficult expressions in the world for humankind not withstanding the fact that, we have conquered the Everest and the Moon. We have already seen that it is possible for offenders and wrongdoers to say that they are genuinely sorry for what they did to others. However, is it possible for victims to say that they have forgiven the offenders? We shall seek an answer to this question through three real life stories where people managed to forgive those who had raped them; had murdered their husbands and brothers; had murdered a person's son.

The July 1995 issue of the Reader's Digest published from India carried an article by the title– *Three Words That Heal* which pointed to the expression 'I Forgive You.' One of the people featured in that article was a woman named Robin Casarjian who had managed to forgive the person who had raped her. The second case is of Babu Bhaya who was convicted in 1983 for murdering three people in five minutes in a gang fight in Ahmedabad, Gujarat. He was sentenced to death which was later on commuted to a sentence of life imprisonment by the Gujarat High Court. In his interview in the film – *Doing Time, Doing Vipassana*,[85] he says that all the feelings of revenge and hatred that he had for the opposite party, got washed away after attending a course of Vipassana meditation. He felt guilty about his past actions and felt a lot of compassion for the family of his victims. He then contacted the family of his victims and sought their forgiveness. They forgave him and the wife and sister of two of the deceased came to the jail and accepted him as their foster brother on the festive day of *Rakshabandhan* in 1992. Today, he is taking care of that family as his own family.

Let us now take one last example to prove the point. To quote from Nobel Laureate Archbishop Desmond Tutu's book– *No Future Without Forgiveness*. Talking about why the South Africans could go ahead with their truth and reconciliation process and not tear the bowels out of each other for what the whites and blacks did to each other in action and retaliation, Bishop Tutu says the following and gives the example of one Mr. Johan Smit, a white Afrikaner. "...we in South Africa have been blessed with some quite remarkable people of all races, not just black South Africans. Mr. Johan Smit of Pretoria lost his young son, who was killed in an ANC [African National Congress] bomb blast. Mr. Johan Smit is an Afrikaner, and conventional wisdom would have led us to expect that he would be bristling with anger and hostility against those the apartheid government propaganda made out to be Communist-inspired terrorists. When Mr. Smit spoke about his son's death, what he said was quite breathtaking. *He said he was not angry*. If he was angry at all, it was against the apartheid government. *He believed that his son's death had contributed to the transition we were experiencing from repression and injustice to democracy and freedom.*"[86]

If all the above-mentioned people who constitute just a miniscule percentage of the largely unreported cases of those who have forgiven, could all forgive, surely, we too can do so. The process may be difficult and time consuming, but it is always better and positive.

Archbishop Tutu sums everything up very succinctly in the following manner – 'Harmony, friendliness, community are great goods. Social harmony is for us the *summum bonum* – the greatest good. Anything that subverts, that undermines this sought-after good, is to be avoided like the plague. Anger, resentment, lust for revenge, even success through aggressive competitiveness, are corrosive of this good. To forgive is not just to be altruistic. It is the best form of self-interest. It gives people resilience, enabling them to survive and emerge still human despite all efforts to dehumanize them.'[87] This is a feature, which is wider, deeper, greater, and more comprehensive than the relative term called – Justice as it is ordinarily understood by all of us.

To conclude this chapter, arrogance on the part of the offender and revenge on the part of the victim is going to take us nowhere. After all, we have got just one place to live in this world – this earth. In addition, we can live peacefully and better by understanding what Mahatma Gandhi tried to teach us through the following message – *"It is man's social nature which distinguishes him from the brute creation. If it is his privilege to be independent, it is equally his duty to be interdependent. Only an arrogant man will claim to be independent of everybody else and be self-contained."*[88]

NOTES

1. Unto Tahtinen, Non-violent Theories of Punishment: Indian and Western [1983] Banarsi Das Motilal, Delhi, at page 74. Hereafter referred to as Unto Tahtinen, Non-violent theories of punishment.
2. Andrew Ashworth, Sentencing in Mike Maguire, et al. edited Oxford Handbook of Criminology [1994], Oxford University Press at page 819. Hereafter referred to as Andrew Ashworth, Sentencing.
3. Unto Tahtinen, Non-violent theories of punishment, at page 88.
4. Andrew Ashworth, Sentencing, at page 821.
5. Edward Westermarck, The Origin and Development of the Moral Ideals, Volume I [1906], Macmillan, London, at page 84. Quoted in Unto Tahtinen, Non-violent theories of punishment, at page 102.
6. Ibid.
7. Andrew Ashworth, Sentencing, at pages 821–822.
8. Johannes Andenaes, Punishment and Deterrence, Ann Arbor: The University of Michigan Press, at page 180. Hereafter referred to as Johannes Andenaes, Punishment and Deterrence.
9. Report of New York Governor's Special Committee on Criminal Offenders (1968), in Gerber, J.I. Rudolph, McAnany, D. Patrick eds., Contemporary Punishments – Views, Explanations and Justifications [1972] University of Notre Dame Press, Notre Dame at page 263.

10. Claus Roxin, Sinn und Grenzen staatlicher Strafe, in Juristische Schulung [1966], page 380. Translated from German and quoted in Unto Tahtinen, Non-Violent Theories of Punishment, at page 93.
11. H.L.A. Hart, Punishment and Responsibility, [1968] Clarendon Press, Oxford at page 237.
12. Dorothy Miller in Stanley E. Grupp, Theories of Punishment, at page 207.
13. Yoga-sutra, II, at page 33.
14. Unto Tahtinen, Non-Violent Theories of Punishment, at page 99.
15. Howard Zehr, Changing Lenses: A New Focus for Crime and Justice [1990] Herald Press, Waterloo, at page 181.
16. Ibid.
17. John Braithwaite, Crime, Shame and Reintegration [1989] Cambridge University Press, Cambridge.
18. John Braithwaite, Restorative Justice and a Better Future, Dorothy J. Killam Memorial lecture delivered at Dalhousie University on 17th October, 1996, at page 3.
19. M.K. Gandhi, Stone Walls Do Not a Prison Make. Compiled and edited by V.B. Kher.
20. Report of the All India Committee on Jail Reforms, Volume II, at pages 255 – 262.
21. Nils Christie, Conflicts as Property, British Journal of Criminology 17:1-15, 1978. Quoted in John Braithwaite, Restorative Justice in Michael Tonry edited Handbook of Crime and Punishment [1998] Oxford University Press at page 329.
22. J.J. Llewellyn and R. Howse, Restorative Justice – A Conceptual Framework (Ottawa: Law Commission of Canada, 1998) Quoted in May Leung, The Origins of Restorative Justice, at page 2, downloaded from the website of the Canadian Forum for Civil Justice, Faculty of Law, University of Alberta, Canada.[http://www.law.ualberta.ca/centers/civilj/fulltext/leung.htm.]. Hereafter referred to as May Leung, The Origins of Restorative Justice.
23. Howard Zehr, Changing Lenses: A New Focus for Crime and Justice Herald Press, Waterloo, Ontario, Canada at page 181. Hereafter referred to as Howard Zehr, Changing Lenses. Quoted in May Leung, The Origins of Restorative Justice, at page 2.
24. Howard Zehr, Changing Lenses, at page 211.
25. May Leung, The Origins of Restorative Justice, at page 2.
26. Law Commission of Canada, From Restorative Justice to Transformative Justice: Discussion Paper [1999] Ottawa at page 33. [Quoted in May Leung, The Origins of Restorative Justice, at page 3].
27. Ibid, at page 27.

28. Id.
29. Id.
30. Ibid, at page 20.
31. May Leung, The Origins of Restorative Justice, at pages 4–6.
32. Rule 58.
33. Rule 59.
34. Rule 60[1].
35. Rule 60[2].
36. Rule 61.
37. Rule 63[1].
38. Rule 63[2].
39. Rule 64.
40. Rule 65.
41. Rule 66[1].
42. Rule 79.
43. Rule 80.
44. Rule 81[1].
45. Adopted by General Assembly resolution 40/ 34 of 29th November, 1985.
46. Principle 1.
47. Principle 4.
48. Principle 5.
49. Principle 6.
50. Principle 7.
51. Principle 8.
52. Principle 9.
53. Principle 14.
54. Principle 16.
55. Adapted with suitable modification from Desmond Tutu, No Future Without Forgiveness [1999] Doubleday, New York at page 30.
56. The third question is addressed at the end of this paper.
57. M. Hough and D. Moxon, Dealing with Offenders: Popular Opinion and the View of Victims in Howard Journal [1985] 24, at pages 160–175. Quoted in Lucia Zedner, Victims in Mike Maguire, *et al.* edited Oxford Handbook of Criminology [1994], Oxford University Press, at page 1234. Hereafter referred to as Lucia Zedner, Victims.
58. R.E. Barnett, Restitution: A New Paradigm of Criminal Justice in Ethics [1977] 87, pages 279 – 301; M. Wright, Making Good [1982], London; M. Wright, Justice for Victims and Offenders [1991] Buckingham. Quoted in Lucia Zedner, Victims, at page 1234.
59. John Braithwaite, Restorative Justice in Michael Tonry edited Handbook of Crime and Punishment [1998] Oxford University Press at page 323.

60. Executive Summary in Making Punishments Work. Report of a Review of the Sentencing Framework For England and Wales [July 2001] Home Office, Britain at page ii.
61. Mulla Committee Report, Volume II, at page 260.
62. G. Launay, Bringing Victims and Offenders Together: A Comparison of Two Models in Howard Journal [1985] 24/3 at pages 200 – 12. Quoted in Lucia Zedner, Victims, at page 1234.
63. Tim Newell, Responding to Crisis – Belgium establishes restorative prisons [2001]. Discussion paper 4 of the International Centre for Prison Studies, King's College, London.
64. D. Smith, H. Blagg and N. Derricourt, Mediation in South Yorkshire in British Journal of Criminology [1988] 28/3 at pages 378 – 395.
65. May Leung, The Origins of Restorative Justice, at page 13.
66. Circles, National Film Board, Canada.
67. May Leung, The Origins of Restorative Justice, at page 11.
68. Ibid, at page 17.
69. Lucia Zedner, Victims, at page 1235.
70. Keeping in mind the limitations of the present purpose, I would also like to just say that Vipassana meditation has been found to be extremely useful, the world over, in transforming hardened offenders irrespective of their ethnic, racial and sectarian backgrounds to realize their mistake, accept responsibility for their wrongdoing and reparate their victims in an individually nuanced manner. That was one of the main areas of research in this author's LL.M. dissertation. General details about the course and its efficacy in prisons across the world are available from http://www.dhamma.org.
71. Upendra Baxi, From Takrar to Karar: The Lok Adalat at Rangpur– A Preliminary Study, in 10, Journal of Constitutional and Parliamentary Studies [1979] Delhi, at pages 52 – 116.
72. Ibid, at page 81.
73. Ibid, at page 78.
74. Ibid, at page 54.
75. Ibid.
76. Ibid, at page 51.
77. Ibid, at page 54.
78. [1999] Doubleday, New York.
79. Ibid, at pages 54 – 55.
80. Ibid, at page 55.
81. Ibid, at page 61.
82. Ibid, at page 64.
83. Ibid, at page 44.
84. Ibid, at page 57.

85. Produced by Karuna Films, Tel Aviv, Israel and directed by Ayelet Menahami and Eilona Ariel in 1997.
86. Desmond Tutu, No Future Without Forgiveness [1999] Doubleday, New York, at pages 35 – 36. Hereafter referred to as Desmond Tutu, No Future Without Forgiveness.
87. Desmond Tutu, No Future Without Forgiveness, at page 31. He further says at pages 271 – 272 that let us understand that, 'Forgiveness is not being sentimental.' The study of forgiveness has become a growth industry. Whereas previously it was something often dismissed pejoratively as spiritual and religious, now because of developments such as the Truth and Reconciliation Commission in South Africa it is gaining attention as an academic discipline studied by psychologists, philosophers, physicians and theologists. In the United States there is an International Forgiveness Institute attached to the University of Wisconsin, and the John Templeton Foundation, with others, has started a multimillion-dollar Campaign for Forgiveness Research.
88. Gandhi Peace Diary [1999] Gandhi Samadhi and Darshan Samiti, New Delhi.

BHARAT B. DAS

3

RESTORATIVE JUSTICE AND VICTIMS: RIGHT TO COMPENSATION

INTRODUCTION

Restorative justice revolves around the ideas that crime is, in essence, a violation of a person by another person (rather than a violation of legal rules); that in responding to a crime our primary concerns should be to make offenders aware of the harm they have caused, to get them to understand and meet their liability to repair such harm, and to ensure that further offences are prevented; that the form and amount of reparation from the offender to the victim and the measures to be taken to prevent remembers of their communities through constructive dialogue in an informal and consensual process; and that efforts should be made to improve the relationship between the offender and victim and to reintegrate the offender into the law-abiding community.

The proponents of the restorative justice argue that punishment society's customary response to crime; neither meets the need of victim nor prevents re-offending. Restorative justice aims at encouraging offenders to take responsibility for the consequences of their actions, express repentance and repair the harm they have done. Restorative justice also emphasizes the reintegration of offenders into communities rather than their control through strategies of punishment and exclusion. Restorative justice is an evolving response to crimes that respect the dignity and equality of each person, builds understanding, and promotes social harmony. This process provides an opportunity for victims to obtain reparation, feel safer and seek closure, allow offenders to gain insight into the cause and effects of their behaviour and to take responsibility in a meaningful way, and enable communities to understand the underlying causes of crime.

The priority of the criminal justice system should be resolving conflict between the offender and the victim therefore the aim should be to meet to (i) Victims needs, (ii) to convince the offender his responsibility of the crime and the loss/injury/harm caused by the crime and (iii) his liability to repair the offender this process more stress is given to reconciling the offender with the victim and the community by voluntarily paying compensation for the harm caused. What required is a paradigm-shift from punitive justice to restorative justice, which will meet to the need for restitution or reparation of harm to the victims and prevail over demand for punishment.

Only recently, society has woken up to the realization of victim's plight and related unfairness of the whole system. The U.N. Congress on Prevention of Crime and Treatment of Offenders took up the cause and contributed substantially in drafting a declaration of victims right (Ottawa, 1984). It was placed on the agenda of the 7th U.N. Congress in Milan, August-September 1985. The U.N. General Assembly adopted the Basic Principles of Justice for Victims of Crime and Abuse of Power; this declaration is specifically concerned with societal response to the needs of the victim. The declaration deals with two focal areas: (a) victims of crime and (b) victims of abuse of power". The first category relates to conventional definition of crime and the declaration lays down norms for providing for (1) standards for access to justice and fair treatment, (2) restitution from the offender, (3) compensation from the State and (4) legal assistance.

The Declaration recognized the following rights of victim of crime:-

(a) Access to justice and fair treatment – This right includes access to the mechanisms of justice and to prompt redress, right to be informed of victim's rights, right to proper assistance throughout the legal process and right to protection of privacy and safety.

(b) Restitution – including return of property of payment for the harm or loss suffered; where public officials or other agents have violated criminal laws, the victims should receive restitution from the State.

(c) Compensation – when compensation is not fully available from the offender or other sources, State should provide financial compensation at least in violent crimes, resulting in bodily injury for which national funds should be established.

(d) Assistance – victims should receive the necessary material, medical, psychological, and social assistance through governmental, voluntary and community – based means. Police, justice, health, and social service personnel should receive training in this regard.

LAWS RELATING TO COMPENSATION IN INDIA

The provision relating to compensation to the victims of crime by the offender are contained in Section 357 of the Criminal Procedure Code, 1973 and Section 5 of the Probation of Offenders Act, 1958 and some other statues.[1] Section 5 of the Probation of Offenders Act empowers a trial court, in its discretion, to order for 'reasonable compensation' to any person for his loss or injury caused to him by the offender who is released under Section 3 or Section 4 of the Act.

The power to compensate the victims of crime under Section 357 of the Criminal Procedure Code is not a new remedy provided under Criminal Procedure Code of 1973. Even Sections 545 and 546 of the Criminal Procedure Code, 1998 provided for compensating victims of crime. Section 543 (1) (a) of the old Code has a social purpose to serve and had to be applied in appropriate cases. But as the Law Commission of India noted in its Forty First Report (1969)[2] our courts did not exercise their statutory powers under this section as freely and liberally as they could be desired. The Commission favored payment of compensation out of fine imposed on the offender. Accordingly, with a view to give a substantive power to the trial court to this effect, it recommended insertion of a substantive provision for payment of compensation to the victim of crime. The Commission observed:

> *"We think, however, that the penal code should give prominence to this aspect of compensating the victims of the offence out of the fine imposed on the offender. At present, the legal provision in this regard is tucked away in the last miscellaneous chapter of the Code of Criminal Procedure. It seems to us that, as a substantive power of the trial Court, it deserves to be mentioned specifically in the Penal Code chapter on punishment along with the provisions relating to fines".*

Under Section 357(1) of the Criminal Procedure Code the court has been empowered to order the payment of compensation to the victim of an offence out of the fine imposed on the accused person while passing an order of sentence of which fine forms a part. Clause (b) of sub-section (1) provides that for compensating the person who has himself suffered injury or loss when compensation is recoverable by a person in a civil court. Clause (c) contains a provision for compensating the heirs and dependents of the person who is victim of a homicide.

Sub-section (3) of Section 357 of the Code, which was introduced for the first time in 1973, provides that when a court imposes a sentence of which fine does not form a part, it may direct the accused to pay compensation. Clauses (a) to (d) sub-section (1) of Section 357 reproduce word for word clauses (a)(b), (bb), and (c) respectively of the old sub-section (1) of Section 545 with the only change that definite article 'The' has been inserted in clause (a) before the word 'expenses'. Section 357(3) runs: 'When a Court imposes a sentence of which fine does not form a part, the Court may, when passing judgment, order the accused person to pay, by way of compensation, such amount as may be specified in the order to the person who has suffered any loss or injury by reason of the act for which the accused person has been so sentenced". It is indeed a step forward in our criminal justice system and reflects the concerns of the legislature for the victims of crime who suffer loss or injury due to the act, neglect or default of the accused. The object of sub-section (3) of Section 357 is to empower the court to award compensation to the heirs and dependents for the loss resulted from the death of the victim of the crime. The compensation should be payable for any loss or injury, whether physical or pecuniary and the court shall give due regard to the nature of the injury, the manner of inflicting the same, the capacity of the accused to pay and other relevant factors. Thus, by the new Section, the jurisdiction of the criminal court has been extended to liberally order for compensating a victim of crime for his loss or injury even in those cases where fine does not form a part of the sentence, which ordinarily lies in the domain of the civil court.

The Supreme Court of India in Harikrishna and State of Haryana V. Sukhibir Singh and others[3] recommended to all criminal courts to award compensation to victims of the Criminal Procedure Code. On the question of compensating the victims of crime, the Supreme Court observed that under Section 357(3), the court can award compensation in cases when no fine can be levied.

The Supreme Court Observed:

> *"It is an important provision but courts have seldom invoked it, perhaps due to ignorance or the object of it. It empowers the court to award compensation to the victims while passing judgment of conviction. In addition to convictions, the court may order the accused to pay some amount by way of compensation to the victim who was suffered by the action of the accused. It may be noted that this power of-the court to award compensation is not ancillary to other sentences but it is in addition thereto. This power was intended to do some thing to reassure the victim that he or she is not forgotten in the criminal justice system. It is a measure of responding appropriately to crime as well of reconciling the victim with the offender. It is to some extent, a constructive approach to crime. It is indeed a step forward in our criminal justice system. We, therefore, recommend to all courts to exercise this power liberally, to meet the end of Justice in a better way. – While awarding compensation the Court must be satisfied that, the victim has suffered loss or injury due to the act, neglect, or default of the accused. This may be physical, mental, or pecuniary loss or injury and the victim is entitled to compensation".*

The restorative and reparative theories that have developed in response to the plight of the victims of crime also underline the necessity to compensate the victims of crime. "Their Argument is that sentence should move away from punishment of offender towards restitution and reparation, aimed at restoring the harm done and calculated accordingly. Restorative theory encompasses the notion of reparation for the effects of the crime. It envisages less resort to custody, with onerous community based sanctions requiring offenders to work in order to compensate victims and also contemplating support and counseling offenders to reintegrate them into community. Such theories therefore tend to act on a behavioral premise similar to rehabilitation, but their political premise is that compensation for victims should be recognized as more important than notice of just punishment on behalf of the state."[4] While explaining the rationale of compensating the victims of crime the Supreme Court of India in State of *Gujarat v. Hon'ble High Court of Gujarat*[5]. observed:

'In our effort to look after and protect the human rights of the convict, we can not forget the victim or his family in case of his death or who is otherwise incapacitated to his livelihood because of criminal act of the convict. The victim is certainly entitled to reparation, restitution, and safeguard of his rights. Criminal justice will look hollow if justice is not done to the victims of crime. A victim of crime cannot be a "forgotten man" in the criminal justice system. It is he who suffered most. His family is ruined particularly in case of death and other bodily injury. This apart from factors like loss of reputation, humiliation, etc. An honour, which is lost or life which is snuffed out cannot be recompensed but then monetary compensation will at least provide some solace'.

The Supreme Court of India observed plight of the rape victims in India and expressed serious concern and suggested that the defects in criminal laws be removed soon. The Court observed as follows in Delhi Domestic Working Women's Forum V. Union of India,[6]

"The defects in the present system are firstly, complainants are handled roughly and are not giving such attention as is warranted. The police, more often than not, humiliate the victims. The victims have invariably found rape trials an experience. The experience of giving evidence in Court has been negative and destructive. The victims often say, they considered the ordeal to be even worse than the rape itself. Undoubtedly the Court proceedings added to and prolonged the psychological stress they had to suffer as a result of the rape itself."

In view of this, the Court laid down the following guidelines for trial of rape cases –

(1) The complainants of sexual assault cases should be provided with legal representation. Such a person must be well acquainted with criminal justice. The victims advocate's role should not be only to explain to her the nature of proceedings, to prepare her for the case and to assist her in the police station and in Court but to provide her with guidance as to how she might obtain help of a different nature from other agencies, for example, mind consulting or medical assistance. It is important to secure continuity of assistance by ensuring that the same person who looked after the complainant's interests in the police station represents her until the end of the case.

(2) Legal assistance will have to be provided at the police station since the victim of sexual assault might very well be in a distressed state at the police station the guidance and support of a lawyer at this stage would be of great help to her.

(3) The police should be under a duty to inform the victim of her right to representation before any questions were asked of her and the police report should state that the victims was so informed.

(4) A list of advocates willing to act in these cases should be kept at the police station for victims who did not have any particular lawyer in mind, or whose own lawyer was unavailable.

(5) The advocate shall be appointed by the Court on application by the police at the earliest convenient moment, but in order to ensure that victims were questioned without undue delay advocates would be authorized to act at the police station before leave of the Court was sought or obtained.

(6) In all rape trials anonymity, (name not to be disclosed), of the victim must be maintained, as far as necessary.

(7) It is necessary, having regard to the directive principles contained under Art.38 (1) of the Constitution, to set Criminal Injuries Compensation Board. Rape victims frequently incur substantial loss. Some, for example, are too terrorized to continue in employment.

(8) Compensation for victims shall be awarded by the court on conviction of the offender and by the Criminal Injuries compensation Board whether or not a conviction has taken place. The Board will take into account pain, suffering and shock as well as the loss of earnings due to pregnancy and childbirth if this occurel as result of rape.

The National Commission for Women should be asked to frame schemes for compensation and rehabilitation to ensure justice to victims of such crimes. The Union of India shall then examine and take necessary steps to implement them at the earliest.

Referring to the state of criminal justice in India today, the Government Notification constituting the Criminal Justice Reforms committee observed:[7]

"………… *People by and large have lost confidence in the Criminal Justice System... Victims feel ignored and are crying for attention and justice ... there is need for developing a cohesive system, in which, all parts work in co-ordination to achieve the common goal".*

The Committee Observed,[8] an important object of the Criminal Justice System is to ensure justice to the victims, yet he has not been given any substantial right, not even to participate in the criminal proceedings. Therefore, the Committee feels that the system must focus on justice to victims and has, thus, made the following recommendations, which include the rights of the victim to participate in cases involving serious crimes and to adequate compensation.

(i) The victim, and if he is dead, his legal representative shall have the right to be impleaded as a party in every criminal proceeding where the offence is punishable with 7 years imprisonment or more.

(ii) In select cases notified by the appropriate government, with the permission of the court an approved voluntary organization shall also have the right to implead in court proceedings.

(iii) The victim has a right to be represented by an advocate of his choice; provided that an advocate shall be provided at the cost of the State if the victim is not in a position to afford a lawyer.

The victim's right to participate in criminal trial shall, inter alia, include:

(a) To produce evidence, oral or documentary, with leave of the Court and/or to seek directions for production of such evidence.

(b) To ask questions to the witnesses or to suggest to the court questions, which may be put to witnesses.

(c) To know the status of investigation and to move the court to issue directions for further investigation on certain matter or to a supervisory officer to ensure effective and proper investigation to assist in the search for truth.

(d) To be heard in respect of the grant or cancellation of bail.

(e) To be heard whenever Prosecution seeks to withdraw and to offer to continue the prosecution.

(f) To advance arguments after the Prosecution has submitted arguments.

(g) To participate in negotiations leading to settlement of compoundable offences.

(v) The victim shall have a right to prefer an appeal against any adverse order passed by the court acquitting the accused, convicting for a lesser offence, imposing inadequate sentence, or granting, inadequate compensation. Such appeal shall lie to the court to which an appeal ordinarily lies against the order of conviction of such court.

(vi) Legal services to victims in select crimes may be extended to include psychiatric and medical help, interim compensation, and protection against secondary victimization.

(vii) Victim compensation is a State obligation in all-serious crimes, whether the offender is apprehended or not, convicted or acquitted. This is to be organized in a separate legislation by Parliament. The draft bill on the subject submitted to Government in 1995 by the Indian Society of Victimology provides a tentative framework for consideration.

(viii) The Victim Compensation Law will provide for the creation of a Victim Compensation Fund to be administered possibly by the Legal Services Authority. The law should provide for the scale of compensation in different offences for the guidance of the Court. It may specify offences in which compensation may not be granted and conditions under which it may be awarded or withdrawn.

It is the considered view of the Committee that Criminal Justice Administration will assume a new direction towards better and quicker justice once the rights of victims are recognized by law and restitution for loss of life, limb and property are provided for in the system. The cost for providing it is not exorbitant as sometimes made out to be. With increase in quantum of fine recovered. Diversion of funds generated by the justice system and soliciting public contribution, the proposed victim compensation fund can be mobilized at least to meet the cost of compensating victims of violent crimes. Even if part of the assets confiscated and forfeited in organized crimes and financial frauds is made part in the Fund and if it is managed efficiently, there will be no paucity of resources for this well conceived reform. In any case, dispensing justice to victims of crime cannot any longer be ignored on grounds of scarcity of resources.

The expanding universe of compassionate criminology must so respond realistically to the new challenge of human rights and social justice as to salvage, solace and resituate victims of crime and abuse of power by resorting to new methodologies of reparative, compensatory, preventive and other judicial remedies. The victims of crime must claim our attention. Injustice to him/her can be fully undone only by recitative justice, beyond punishment of the offender. The most important interest of the victims of crime is restitution, which can be ordered by the courts. The remedy of court ordered restitution makes the victim "whole" and serves as a correctional function. From the victim's point of view, restitution is beneficial because it helps to make whole the victim's crime related loss. As a criminal court's sanction, the victim's right to sue in tort is not impaired. Furthermore, if the restitution is adequate, the victim may be spared the time and expense of bringing civil suits claiming compensation, as well as the emotional strain of enduring a second trial.

The present laws in the absence of legal mandate to pass an order of restitution to the victim of crime in appropriate case only do lip service to them. Making a mandatory provision for compensating the victim of crime by offender may not solve all the problems of the victim of crime, because this provision also will suffer from the same disadvantage that the offender in most of the cases would be discharged or acquitted due to lack of evidence[9] or other technicality in the procedure. As the provision merely emphasizes that the victim of crime be compensated only on conviction, it is not likely to be of real help. There is therefore an urgent need to establish a victim assistance and compensation board to provide assistance and compensation to the victim of crime. Therefore, it is high time that the government of India should come forward with a scheme/program to provide compensation and assistance to the victims of crime for their loss or injury. As we know the victims as well as the accused/offenders in most cases are necessarily poor, restitution alone cannot solve the problems of the victim of crime. Therefore, a consolidated victim welfare fund may be created on a statutory basis, which should be designed to meet both the immediate financial assistance that some victims in distress will need, inclusive of medical and hospitalization expenses, and compensation. The fund will be created from the total amount collected by the State as fine from the offenders/accused and also a suitable and matching grant should be provided by the State. A Board named, as Victim Welfare Board, which will be of non-political composition, will administer the fund. The payment of compensation shall be left to the discretion of the Board and it may refuse payment where there has been undue delay in reporting to police about the occurrence and also where the victim contributed to the commission of the crime.

For too long the victim of crime have been forgotten and forsaken lots of the criminal justice system. If the victims come to regard their treatment as unfair, distorting of reality or little concerned with their own rights, feeling and interest or if the decisions are made which are felt to be unsatisfactory, it is possible that this "Secondary Victimization" by the system may lead to disinterest and future non-cooperation by the victim. When the victim chooses not to cooperate with the system, it will collapse. Therefore, there is a need for renewal of emphasis and enhanced sensitivity to the rights of the victim. Victim's right to assistance is now more acceptable in the developed countries. In India, though there are very limited legal provisions for compensation to the victims of crime by the offender, it received a very cold reception at the hands of judiciary. Hence, there is an urgent need for streamlining the system by legitimately including victim's rights and interests in the system. So also, the victim should be made "whole" with monetary recovery and support service.

In this context, it is pertinent to note that the Supreme Court in *State of Gujarat v. Honourable High Court of Gujarat*[10] directed the state governments to frame law to pay compensation to the victims of crime from the earning during their sentence period. Such compensation should either be paid directly to the victims or through common fund to be created for this purpose or any other feasible mode. Enacting a law on these lines will be in the fulfillment of the constitutional obligation of the State under Articles 39(1) and 41 of the Constitution of India, which vouchsafe justice and equal protection of law. The new enactment will also be in accordance with U.N. Declaration of Basic Principles of Justice for Victims of Crime and U.N. Declaration of Basic Principles and Guidelines on the "Right to Reparation for victims of violation of Human Rights".

NOTES

1. Section 22 of the Cattle Trespass Act, 1872, Section 42 and 76 of the Forest Act, 1972, and Section 1 of the Public Gambling Act, 1967.
2. Law Commission of India, Forty First Report: The Code of Criminal Procedure, Vol..L, (1969), p.356.
3. A.I.R.1988 S.C. 2127.
4. Ashworth A. (1994). 'Sentencing', in M. Maguire, R. Morgan and R. Reiner (eds), Oxford Handbook of Criminology, Oxford: Clarendon.
5. A.I.R. 1998, SC3162.
6. (1995) 1 SCC 14.
7. Committee on Reforms of Criminal Justice System Government of India, Ministry of Home Affairs, March 2003 Volume 1.
8. Ibid.
9. Banerji, P.N. (1976). "Compensation to the Victims of Criminal violence in India", Banaras Law Journal, Vol.12 (1976) P.110.
10. A.I.R. 1998, SC3162.

Marlene A. Young

4

RESTORATIVE COMMUNITY JUSTICE: A CALL TO ACTION

There is an increasing consensus that the current paradigms used by the criminal justice system are proving ineffective. Simply looking for more of the same criminal justice interventions is misleading and depressing because we are asking more of the legal system than it can provide.

—*A. Robert Denton*

All across the United States can be heard expressions of theoretical and practical disillusionment concerning the way society addresses issues of maintaining a just social order, of violence and its prevention, and of the victimization of its citizenry. That disillusionment is the result of twenty years of relatively stable, high crime rates, and of the impotence of government to respond effectively to that antisocial and criminal behavior. Disillusionment sees violence because of a breakdown in community structure and its tenets of reciprocal rights and responsibilities. It is a disillusionment that springs from the fact that most adult citizens will have become a victim of violent crime in their lifetimes, and they see little redress or remorse either from their agencies of government or from their offenders.

The consequences of this disillusionment have been manifested in disparate ways. On the one hand, there have been efforts to get tough on violent and drug-involved offenders in ways one might call punitive, through legislation increasing sentences for certain crimes, re-imposing the death penalty, imposing "three strikes and you're out" sanctions on certain repeat offenders, and paying for a huge increase in prison space.

On the other hand, there have been efforts to try less traditional approaches, ones that address criminal violence, its perpetrators, and its victims in novel, perhaps more holistic, ways:

- The last twenty years have been witness to the revolution that has established bills of rights for crime victims in all fifty states and has led to a movement to amend state constitutions to give victims the right to be informed of, present, and heard at every critical stage of the criminal justice process. The voters in seven states had adopted such amendments by 1991. In 1992, the electorates in five more states ratified such amendments. In 1993, Wisconsin joined those states. In November 1994, six more states became part of the trend. (In addition, it should be noted that California has adopted an amendment that addresses certain victim issues, and Georgia has adopted an amendment in order to establish a victim compensation program.) Arguably, these legislative accomplishments can be seen as part of a broader "human rights" or "consumer" agenda to allow previously disenfranchised and wronged individual's greater participation in institutional decisions that affect their lives.
- For a little over fifteen years, there has been an effort to refocus the criminal justice response to offenders to address not only retribution but also offender accountability. Models of "restorative justice", as this approach is generically called, have focused on victim/offender mediation or reconciliation, dispute-resolution programs, victim restitution, the use of victim impact panels, and so forth. Such models have emphasized that the goal is for victims to feel empowered through a process whereby offenders acknowledge the harm they have done and participate in a process to provide personal redress to their victims.
- Crime- and violence-prevention programs have increased, as illustrated by the establishment of the National Crime Prevention Council, the development of educational curricula on violence prevention and conflict resolution in schools, the development of treatment programs for perpetrators of

violence within the family, the use of crime prevention through environmental design in urban settings, and the move to establish community-wide citizen task forces to address crime and violence as quality-of-life concerns.

While the "law-and-order" and "holistic" camps often argue or talk past each other, it is the position of this monograph that through the use of a new paradigm of justice - Restorative Community Justice - the primary goals of both camps can be reconciled.

For if a local community's known offenders (all of them, for a significant change) are brought to account, and if, in the process, they are both punished and required to settle accounts with the victims and community they have hurt - and if these judicial interventions, punitive and rehabilitative alike, are all executed quickly - and if, finally, all this transpires under the gaze of concerned neighbors, then "swift and certain punishment" may finally get a fair test, using less punitive sanctions than some would prefer yet with increased prospects that victim justice and offender rehabilitation will be achieved.

The purposes of this monograph are, first, to present a theoretical description of Restorative Community Justice (RCJ), contrasting its concepts to those of other models; second, to describe the program elements that would be found in a community that had implemented the model; and third, to suggest areas of legal change that might be desirable to speed the establishment of such programs.

Restorative Community Justice: Constructing A New Paradigm

1. The first principle of RCJ is that criminal justice must be conceived not only as the imposition of justice on the criminal but also as the doing of justice for the victims. This means that a violation of the social order must be seen as an offense against society generally - the traditional "social compact" view - but also as an action that harms individuals. The concern here is on any wrong, even a non-criminal offense that contributes to the weakening of social ties or interferes with community living. The victims of such violations may be defined as the individual whom we traditionally describe as the complaining witness in a criminal prosecution, but they may, in addition, or in the alternative, include community members harmed by the wrongdoing. It should be stressed that, in this expansive concern about violations beyond those

traditionally prosecuted as crimes, the model does not seek to sanction extralegal controls on individual conduct. Rather, it seeks to sanction the greater use of near moribund civil and criminal laws dealing with trespass, nuisance, harassment, and the like.

2. The second principle is that, while governments must establish criminal laws that set the standards of behavior for the general society, the community should often be the locus of implementing those standards in order to be responsive to the cultural nuances that vary by racial, ethnic, geographic, religious, and other backgrounds - all provided that certain equal protection and due process norms are maintained.
3. Third, the "community" from this perspective is more than a cultural filter for sorting out and prioritizing crimes in its midst; the community and its justice partners are to become engaged in defining and attacking community problems, a process that strengthens the important role of community institutions in a democratic society.
4. The fourth principle is that, by responding to crime skillfully, quickly, and locally, those administering community justice improve the chances that offenders and their victims alike will be restored to harmonious relationships with their neighbors.
5. The fifth principle is that all citizens, individually and collectively, have responsibilities for supporting peace and justice within the social order. These can be framed as reasonable expectations (not duties) that are clearly expressed in the RCJ model to three audiences:

OFFENDERS SHOULD BE HELD ACCOUNTABLE FOR THEIR ACTIONS

One element of accountability is retribution or "just desserts". Such sanctions should be just and equitable. Care should be taken to fashion culturally appropriate punishments and to ensure that punishments are proportionate to the criminal action. The perpetrator of a heinous criminal attack has certainly earned the sanction of a lengthy incarceration, and not just to prevent that offender from committing another such attack. But fines, restrictions of privileges, home confinement, temporary exiles or exclusions, work details (not to be confused with community restitution, described below) and the like may be more appropriate for minor infractions.

While accountability should include measured punishment for its own sake, it should go beyond punishment. It should include full restitution to victims. Such restitution should be mandated by law, and should involve a full accounting of damages, past and projected. It should be ordered and, once ordered, remain enforceable until fulfilled. While the courts hold to the legal fiction that restitution is a form of punishment - a designation that has pragmatic benefits to victims in the justice system - one should recognize that payment of restitution is no more a punishment than the repayment of a loan or the expungement of any other debt, however incurred.

Accountability should also involve restitution to the community as a whole. A violation of the social order through crime or other proscribed behavior very often harms a describable community wherein the wrongdoing took place, as when it tears at the social fabric of a neighborhood and drains the larger society's resources to enforce the social order and to ensure that justice prevails. Hence, offenders should be held to perform constructive actions on behalf of the community. While the law and the criminological literature calls this kind of activity "community service," the appropriate name should be "community restitution" in order to stop confusing these activities with services voluntarily given by law-abiding citizens.

Accountability also should involve asking the offender to demonstrate remorse. The act of saying "I'm sorry" may seem trivial in the aftermath of a violent crime, but if the act is accompanied by contrition, it can sometimes help victims begin to reconstruct their own lives. Victims often feel that somehow they have contributed to their own victimization. Demonstrations of remorse help to vitiate the victims' self-blame. Remorse may also be coupled with admissions of shame for violating the social order. Indeed, in a New Zealand model of restorative justice, shame on the offender is considered an integral part of the restorative process.

Plainly, to be ashamed of one's actions is both to acknowledge that they were blameworthy and to be sorry that they caused harm. Many offenders cannot find within themselves the sorrow needed to express genuine remorse, yet can honestly take responsibility for having broken a legitimate societal norm and are prepared to be punished for that upon entering a guilty plea. For some, the lesson learned from that punishment is to go straight; for others, it is, do not be caught again. The RCJ model would continue the long practice of accepting guilty pleas as grounds for imposing lesser sanctions, but would still hold to the principle that remorseful admissions of guilt are better for all concerned than ones delivered with a certain bravado.

VICTIMS ALSO HAVE RESPONSIBILITIES TO THE COMMUNITY

They may not be able to assume those responsibilities due to incapacities brought on by the crime or other circumstances, but ultimately the victims' rights to participate involve parallel responsibilities for participation.

The responsibilities, which we may fairly ask victims to accept, are nothing, more than the responsibilities of citizenship that we should all assume in the justice arena. As citizens (and victims), we should report violations of the social order to the proper authorities, at least when we believe it safe to do so; we should support legal change to improve the administration of justice in the future, if only by exercising our voting rights; we should participate in community crime prevention activities; and we should participate in the administration of justice as witnesses, jurors, and volunteers.

THE AFFECTED COMMUNITIES ALSO BEAR RESPONSIBILITIES

These responsibilities are of two kinds - those of the state, and those of the local community or neighborhood.

The responsibilities of the state should include ensuring that appropriate laws and policies are in place in order to effect Restorative Community Justice and to pay for its implementation. Those legal policies should include the establishment of parallel rights for victims to those available to accused and convicted offenders, notably rights according victims participatory status in the justice system.

The responsibilities of the local community should include establishing and maintaining a practical system of programs and procedures that support Restorative Community Justice. Such a system would include: community policing, community prosecution, community courts, and community corrections, local programs of victim services and violence prevention, and citizen participation in all these efforts. The citizenry here, in most instances, are not just the residents of a neighborhood wherein the community justice system operates but its merchants, office workers, visitors, and friends.

6. The sixth principle of Restorative Community Justice is that justice should aspire to the restoration of both individual dignity and community bonds.

Restoration for offenders involves an act of will on their part as well as support from society. The act of will includes their willingness to acknowledge their participation in the violation of the social order, their acceptance of sanctions, their act of contrition through remorse and shame, and their act of reparations to victims and the community.

- The support from society should involve providing them with opportunity to return to their community with appropriate benefits - such as medical or substance abuse treatment, or social or employment skills - as well as an acknowledgment of their status as a community member. It does not mean that society or victims have to forgive their past behavior or exonerate them, only that they should support opportunities for offenders to construct a new life as law-abiding citizens. Indeed, in some traditional societies where restoration is an integral part of the justice system, community members are not allowed to talk of the crime or the punishment if the offender successfully fulfills the conditions of accountability.

Again, it is not proposed that all offenders deserve an opportunity for restoration. Some may be excluded from restoration permanently through imprisonment, or a form of exile or ostracism, because the offense or pattern of offensiveness was serious enough that their return would only continue the process of community destruction.

- Restoration for the victim should involve the provision of appropriate crisis and supportive counseling, full restitution from the offender and, where that is not forthcoming or immediate, compensation from the state. It should include medical or substance abuse treatment as necessitated by the crime, as well as vocational or other forms of rehabilitation. And victim restoration should include participation rights roughly equal to those of the accused in any criminal justice proceedings (whether in the formal court process or other alternative proceedings).

- Restoration for the community should also involve participation in the decision-making processes of restorative justice and the implementation of its decisions. Groups of community members should be afforded appropriate crisis and supportive counseling, as needed, full restitution from the offender, and the establishment or reestablishment of community structures as the community adjusts to the impact of the social violations.

The purpose of Restorative Community Justice is to take into account that the well being and integrity of communities as well as individuals are harmed by violations of the social order. The new justice paradigm would help restore the community through the restoration of all its injured individuals and groups, a process whereby they can once again contribute to the maintenance of a just social order by helping others.

RESTORATIVE COMMUNITY JUSTICE: PROGRAM ELEMENTS

While no jurisdiction has implemented a full model of Restorative Community Justice, there are examples of one or more of its program elements that have implemented over the last five years. The following review of the elements gives examples of those experimental activities, a great many of them formalized by written community partnerships. A sample partnership agreement from Portland, Oregon, is included in the appendix.

Community Policing

The United States is undergoing the most massive reformation of policing since the anticorruption and "professionalization" reform movements of the first half of this century. In some ways, so-called community policing might be called a "counter-reformation," bringing back the old cop on the beat - a more-or-less permanent beat for a specific officer or deputy, on a more-or-less permanent shift - and often involving the opening of mini-stations not unlike the neighborhood precincts of an earlier time.

But the models involve more than the friendly, peacekeeping officer affectionately portrayed in black-and-white movies of the 1930s. Community policing teaches officers how to round up neighbors to form a block club, or revive a local merchants' association, or encourage students to treat their school and each other with greater respect. In the typical community policing project, there are squad cars still responding to the more urgent calls for service, and investigators still working on felony cases, but the newly assigned officers are more focused on preventing crime than "chasing crooks." The National Institute of Justice has highlighted some of these crime- and violence-prevention efforts. Among the NIJ findings:

- **Boston, Massachusetts:** As part of its neighborhood policing strategy, the Boston Police Department recently announced the deployment of 10 youth service officers, 1 for each of the city's 10 police districts. All 10 officers had volunteered for the position. With 112 hours of training behind them, the officers' job is to reach out to young people by serving as positive role models, speaking against drugs in fifth-grade classes, and referring high-risk youths to public and private social services agencies. The officers are also expected to develop their own after-school and weekend programs for elementary and middle school children. Extra hours, without overtime compensation, are considered part of the job.
- **Columbia, South Carolina:** The Columbia Police Department operates substations at several city housing developments. Over time, the substations have emerged as a nexus for a variety of activities that enhance the life of the community. Officers participate in youth athletic activities, make school visits, and cosponsor social activities such as camping trips, community talent shows, dances, movie matinees, and puppet shows. The officers also serve as mentors, taking special interest in the children and their schoolwork.
- **Houston, Texas:** In Houston, the police department assigned four full-time officers to run a year-round Police Activities League (PAL) program for high-risk youth aged 12-17 from inner-city communities. In addition to sports, the program also features numerous educational field trips and community service projects such as neighborhood cleanups.
- **Jacksonville, Florida:** With its Youth Intervention Program, officers from the Jacksonville sheriff's office meet informally

after school with young men aged 12 to 18 from low-income, gang-plagued neighborhoods. The emphasis is on talking and listening, with the officers working as mentors to strengthen the young men's self-esteem, increase their awareness of the consequences of violence, and provide informal guidance on a range of safety and health topics. The program also provides vocational training, with several community business partners creating work opportunities for the participants.

The scope of this reform movement is enormous. Spurred on by the U.S. Department of Justice, the leaders of the American law enforcement establishment, notably the International Association of Chiefs of Police, the National Sheriffs' Association, the Police Executive Research Forum, and the Police Foundation, have separately pioneered these approaches and collectively pooled their views and experience through the "Community Policing Consortium". The consortium's "Understanding Community Policing: A Framework for Action," spells out the two "core components" of these hundreds, if not thousands, of projects:

- The first component, and perhaps the overarching goal, is problem-solving. Indeed, a few departments embrace a "problem-oriented" style of policing, freeing up a kind of "flying squad" to, say, tackle a rash of local burglaries rather than retool the functions of the regular patrol force. The more typical community police officer is encouraged to be problem-oriented too - often acting as a kind of ombudsman to, say, get city agencies to remove abandoned cars.
- The second component is creating community partnerships - usually in formal documents like the one in the appendix. The roles and assignments meted out between the police, a block club, a group of shops, a school, or other participants, are typically the product of many hours of meetings - ones that often identify problems that the police, on their own, might not have rated in the first tier of community concerns.

The hope of this massive social experiment - fueled by a major Congressional subsidy for new police hires in departments subscribing to community policing precepts (if the Clinton Administration's "Cops on the Beat" program retains Congressional support) - is that bonds of communication and trust will be forged between community leaders and representatives of their frontline criminal justice agencies so that an ethic of law-abiding civility may be restored to community life.

There are interesting by-products of this new style of law enforcement - the antithesis of cool, "just-the-facts-ma'am" professionalism promoted by O.W. Wilson and his admirers two generations ago - that are of interest to those seeking to establish a more ambitious Restorative Community Justice model. First, parallel to the community policing reformation is the advent of victim assistance programs within law enforcement agencies. For two decades, it was America's prosecutors who led the inclusion of such services within criminal justice, but by 1990, over one-third of America's larger law enforcement agencies had established their own victim assistance units. The process of placing these advocates (or advocates in outside, cooperative service programs) into community-policing neighborhoods involves a natural partnership that may well become a commonplace feature of community policing in the future.

Second is the somewhat novel victim assistance program housed in the Delaware State Police, many of whose victim advocates are specially-trained, sworn officers - and some of whose community police officers are graduates of that assignment, and employ the skills and insights of crisis counselors in their community policing assignments.

Third is the interesting partnership of the Redmond, Washington, police department, and the state's corrections department. Volunteer police officers have significantly increased the visits to parolees' homes over what community corrections officers can do - and all of the police officers have become, in effect, eyes and ears of the corrections department so that, for example, the nighttime disturbance that the police quelled without an arrest may nonetheless inform a community corrections officer that a probationer had violated a curfew condition of his release.

As a last example, experimental programs in Native Alaskan villages expect their Public Safety Officers to function not just as law enforcement officers but also as informal judges and as welfare officers. That last role is a reminder that RCJ programs may take on governmental tasks that are seen to be supportive of community cohesion but quite distant from the operations of criminal justice.

Community Prosecution

Proposals and programs on community policing have been in existence for the last twenty years. It was only recently, however, that there has been an initiative to develop community prosecution programs that could work with community police and move prosecutorial functions out of a merely reactive role in prosecuting to a proactive role in preventing crime. Two examples of such programs are exemplary: the Neighborhood District Attorney's Program in Multnomah County (Portland), Oregon, and the Community Prosecution Program in Brooklyn, New York.

Michael Shrunk, Multnomah County District Attorney, chose to name his program the "Neighborhood District Attorney" to emphasize that prosecution is not the primary activity of the attorneys assigned to the program. As one of his deputies said, "We are attorneys for our districts, seeking to solve problems, and using the law only when necessary." Prosecutors elsewhere are more drawn to a title like "Community Prosecutor" to reflect its law enforcement and criminal justice function. Whatever the name of the program, the mission and mandates for the Multnomah County and Brooklyn programs are similar.

The role of the Neighborhood District Attorney is to help develop and implement long-term strategies that address problems in the community in order to enhance its quality of life. To accomplish that purpose, the following sets of activities are encouraged.

Problem-solving

- Community problems must first be identified. The community prosecutors must do this based on citizen and community participation. A serious problem for one community may be objectively just as bad in another community, but not one that will motivate those community members to act. Problem identification can be done through meetings with community members, environmental observations, attendance at civic or community events, or more formal assessment procedures.
- Once problems are identified, the community, with the help of the Neighborhood District Attorney, must prioritize the problems in order to more efficiently analyze the relationship between one problem and another, mobilize resources, and establish a time-line for action.

- The Neighborhood District Attorneys may help the community maximize resources in a number of ways. They may serve as the facilitator of communications. Due to their perceived status and power, they may be able to establish communications between parties where none existed. They can serve as leaders in establishing community partnerships. They can persuade groups to work together that had previously distrusted or were unaware of each other. They can help to coordinate resource development and implementation by exercising a "global vision" in their neighborhoods. By looking at the community as a whole, not just block by block or building by building, they can suggest ways in which different social and economic groups can create synergistic solutions to existing problems.
- After problems are identified and prioritized, and resources are identified or developed, Neighborhood District Attorney can work with the community to design and implement a plan of action to solve the problems. It is imperative that citizens be the primary force behind these plans so that neighborhoods have a long-term commitment to their success. Neighborhood District Attorneys can serve as resources for ideas, advisors with regard to the law, and law enforcers when necessary, but citizen participation is the key to community commitment to the new social order.

Applying the law to Problem-solving

Just as with community policing, the first goal of the community prosecution concept is to solve problems that contribute to the destruction of social order and community life before they become criminal in nature. However, a feature critical to the role of the community prosecutors is their ability to use their knowledge of the law - both civil and criminal - to help the community maintain the social order. There are several ways this legal knowledge and skill has proved useful in Portland:

- The Neighborhood District Attorney can assist community police officers in the enforcement of civil orders and the active prosecution of misdemeanor arrests based on the violation of social order.

- The Neighborhood District Attorney can coordinate with other criminal justice agencies, like the U.S. Attorney's office, the Federal Bureau of Investigation, and the Immigration and Naturalization Service, to ensure that expeditious and aggressive prosecution takes place when crime does occur.
- The Neighborhood District Attorney can assist community involvement in prosecutions through organizing court watches and facilitating victim advocates in informing victims and communities about case status and their rights under the law.
- The Neighborhood District Attorney can ensure that fair and accurate assessments of the impact of crime on individual victims and communities is represented in any case disposition and that full restitution is a part of plea bargains and sentencing requests.

A Sample of Results

Problem-solving with prosecutorial authority as part of the strategy is the essence of community prosecution. Multnomah County's program has been in existence for almost five years. It has expanded from one neighborhood district attorney to five. The program has divided the County into six districts and a final district attorney for the sixth district will be assigned in the coming year. The following is a sampling of the results of the program.

CITIZEN-INITIATED SEARCH WARRANTS

Problem: The community identified lower-level drug houses in the neighborhood as a source of irritation and a degradation of community standards.

Solution: The Neighborhood District Attorney and community police officers put together a program in which neighbors were trained to keep detailed logs of suspected activities. The police department conducted buys at the suspected house. The logs alone were enough to obtain a probable-cause search warrant from the judge. Two people were arrested. They were prosecuted and the neighbors are now willing to be "junior probation officers" to monitor future compliance to probation. The Neighborhood District Attorney is now working with the property owner to resolve the remaining problems at the house.

OPERATION NO DRUGS

Problem: The community identified that the illegal drug activity that occurred on the sidewalks and streets had converted the neighborhood into an open air drug market, seriously affecting the lives of businesses, agencies, and residents.

Solution: The Neighborhood District Attorney and a broad base of partners developed and implemented the following elements of their strategy: increased lighting; increased public awareness of what could be done when illegal activities took place; expanded police patrols; enforcement of "civil exclusions" from the area; and worked with the Immigration and Naturalization Service and the U.S. Attorney's office to aggressively prosecute drug cases and to identify and initiate deportation proceedings where an undocumented alien had been convicted of a drug-related crime. The program was begun in the spring of 1993. By October of that year, there were 200 arrests on drug abuse charges, but in October of 1994, there were only 21 such arrests - evidence of the partnership's success in closing down the open drug market.

TRESPASS AUTHORIZATION PROGRAM

Problem: The downtown business community identified the problem of trespass by vagrants and juveniles during non-business hours. The private premises were accessible because police officers have no right to be there without the owner's permission.

Solution: The Neighborhood District Attorney worked with the owners and police officers to design and implement the following strategy. The owners would designate all precinct officers as the "persons in charge of the property", with authority to exclude people on the premises at unauthorized times or if they were engaged in destructive behaviors. A common exclusion form was developed and police officers were trained in the exclusion policy. Persons found on the premises under the specified conditions were given notice to leave. If they refused to leave, they were arrested. Even if they agreed to leave, those who were regular trespassers were given a "notice of exclusion", as authorized by a city ordinance, and if they were seen on the premises again; they were arrested for violating the exclusion order. In both kinds of arrests, the Neighborhood District Attorney agreed to file complaints on all such arrests, and the misdemeanor staff agreed to prosecute them.

UNLAWFUL CAMPING

Problem: The community identified unlawful camping on public access areas as a source of neighborhood distress due to its unsightliness and the garbage that was distributed around the makeshift campsites.

Solution: The Neighborhood District Attorney worked with the individual residents, the business community, law enforcement, and others to develop a partnership agreement that involved the following. The local Sheriff's Department in conjunction with the Parks Department cleaned up the area. It was then divided up into small territories and certain individuals were identified to monitor those areas for camping activities. Large pink signs saying, "no camping" was erected to help the monitoring activities. Businesses agreed to destroy all large container boxes so that they could not be used for shelter. When someone erected a campsite, citizens confronted them and asked them to leave. If they did not or the monitors wanted assistance in the confrontation, sheriff's deputies would be summoned to effect removal or arrest. The program was one of the first ones established by a Neighborhood District Attorney. In 1989, there were 60 arrests in the area. By 1992, there was only one such arrest - the problem was effectively solved.

MISCELLANEOUS RESULTS

In one area where prostitution was a problem, the Neighborhood District Attorney was able to work with local motels to persuade them to end a "one-hour" rental policy.

Where a burnt-out building was identified as a hangout for unsupervised juveniles, the prosecutor notified the Bureau of Buildings, which cited the owner for a building code violation and ordered him to abate the violation.

Where trees and bushes provided a cover for drug deals and drug usage along a state highway, the Oregon Department of Transportation agreed to replant the area with ground cover that would meet standards for crime prevention through environmental design.

Community Courts

"Community Courts" involve both new ideas and old ones merged in several ways. When judges rode circuit, most judicial proceedings had a high level of citizen participation in that a "jury of one's peers" was sometimes made up of friends or antagonists of the parties, and certainly of acquaintances. Minor disputes or crimes, heard by a local magistrate or a justice of the peace, and were typically resolved around the kitchen table of the judge's house.

The gradual urbanization and centralization of the American justice system left most of the citizen litigants, witnesses, and jurors strangers to one another, which suited those who kept pressing for ever more disinterested methods of decision-making. Ours has become an antiseptic system, and our judges, largely by design, aloof and distant figures.

In many traditional cultures, the judge is expected to be knowledgeable about the parties involved. The judge may be an elder to whom wisdom is attributed and of whom is expected considerable understanding of the parties and of their family and community connections. Or the judicial function may devolve to a kinship or tribal group. Either way, the process is conducted in a manner that seeks to affirm the norms of a familiar community, not a distant society, and, often, to restore both the offender and the offended to the good graces of that community.

The new paradigm would call for integrating such community connections into the court system again. There are several ways that courts might change to accommodate such a system.

(a) The judicial system could become more responsive to community and victim interests. Today's judiciary could be trained to recognize and enforce various bills of rights for victims and their constitutional rights under the nineteen states that have established them. Some would argue that this will eventually entail the recognition of the victim as a third party with standing in the courtroom. That would seem to be the course that the State of Arizona is pursuing as it implements its state constitutional amendment, and where victims have standing and a right to have a lawyer in the criminal justice process.

Even without express legal mandates, judges have the power to ensure victim and community participation through victim impact statements and impact statements from larger communities. The former are now commonplace, while the latter are almost unheard of. Not surprisingly, one of the Multnomah County Neighborhood District

Attorneys was among the first to offer such a community impact statement (in a plea-bargained burglary case.) That the court accepted the statement is a reminder that most courts have inherent authority to receive information that may guide their sentencing decisions and may, in most jurisdictions, effect full restitution to both the victim and any other party manifestly harmed by the criminal act.

(b) Another model for an RCJ approach to judicial decision-making can be derived from New Zealand's "Children, Young Persons, and Their Families Act of 1989". The goals of youth justice in that country are described as follows:

(1) Achieving Justice

"Accountability - emphasizing the importance of young people paying an appropriate penalty for their crime and making good the wrong they have done to others.

"Reducing time frames - making time frames realistic given the age of the child or young person."

"Protecting rights - emphasizing the protection of young people's rights."

"Diversion - keeping young people out of Courts and preventing the use of labels that make it difficult for young people to put early offending behind them.

(2) Responding to Needs

"Enhancing well-being and strengthening families - making available services that will assist the young person and their family."

(3) Providing for Participation

"Family involvement - including families and young people in making the decisions for themselves and taking charge of their lives."

"Victim involvement - involving victims in the decisions about what will happen."

"Consensus decision making - arriving at decisions which are agreed to by the family, the young person, police and victims.

(4) Being Culturally Appropriate

"Culturally appropriate ways of resolving matters - allowing families to choose their own procedures and their time and place of meetings."

(Judge M.J.A. Brown, Principal Youth Court Judge, New Zealand)

It is notable that Judge Brown went on to write, "The philosophies and principles which are being used in the Youth Justice field in New Zealand are, I believe, inextricably based on the communitarian concept. With a greater involvement of families and wider families, we have seen a recognition of the strength of interdependencies - attachments that evoke personal obligation to others within a community of concern. These attachments are not perceived as isolated relationships of convenience but as matters of profound group obligation."

This perspective is unabashedly in harmony with the Maori culture in which Judge Brown was raised. But the statute he drafted and Parliament enacted has been applied to New Zealand's young descendants of Polynesian and European immigrants alike. In the first instance, it has successfully affirmed the legitimacy of the Maori "marae" - a council of one's extended family, which, among other things, seeks through consensus to vindicate its victims and bring its transgressors, repentant, back into the fold.

The system has also worked well with young New Zealanders of European descent, sometimes with the effect of bringing into productive service an extended family that had previously gathered together only to celebrate holidays, not to take collective responsibility for one of their members. In any event, since the law does not impose a definition of the "family group" to whom the sanctioning and reconciliation is delegated, it can be a nuclear family of three or a marae of over a hundred kinfolk.

The procedures for the resolution of justice under these principles involve the following features.

- When a young person is charged with an offence, the case must be referred by the prosecutor to a Youth Justice Coordinator who must investigate the case and arrange for a family group conference before any further action is taken. A family group conference must be convened in cases where a young person has been arrested before any plea, although an exception is made when the young person indicates a non-guilty plea due to legal advice or on certain specific offenses. Similarly, if a child is alleged to have been abused or neglected, the child may be assigned a Care and Protection Coordinator who must convene a family group conference to address the issue.

- There are three stages to the family group conference: the information-giving stage, the family meeting, and the decision stage. At the first stage, the Coordinator provides the background information and may be questioned by the family. At stage two, the family group is entitled to meet in private to decide what must be done, but the victim or representative of the victim is entitled to be present, and there is currently legislation before the New Zealand Parliament proposing an amendment to allow the victim to be accompanied by any reasonable number of persons for the purpose of support. The family arrives at a proposed decision and a plan of action, which then must be discussed with the designated officials. In cases of a youthful offender, the plan should be an alternative to prosecution. In the case of a youthful victim, the plan should be a solution to protecting the child from abuse in the future. If there is not agreement on the plan, the matter will go to court for further adjudication. Even at adjudication, the family has a role in advising the court on its wishes or appropriate sanctions.
- The court must approve and monitor any eventual plan of action or sentence. Community or family members are also responsible for any alternative sentencing or action plan.

While there have been problems in the implementation of youth justice, more remarkable have been its successes. Judge Brown reports, "I would be the first to acknowledge that ours is a very young system. There have been all the teething problems and we will never achieve the level of perfection, which theorists would like to see. Perhaps the most satisfactory response to date, however, has been the complaint expressed by such bodies as the New Zealand Police Association that the system is only working in 90 percent of cases."

While the New Zealanders' culturally-flexible use of "family" might serve some applications of the Restorative Community Justice model, so might an equally-flexible use of "community," which might also borrow from the experience of other kinds of courts, discussed below, operated in, of, or by a community of whatever description.

As will be seen, the primary theme in most of these models is on the sanctioning dimensions of the judiciary, not its fact-finding duties. It is assumed that any case wherein a criminal defendant persists in pleading not guilty will continue to be wrapped up in procedural protections that may demand access to the "efficiencies" of a centralized court system. Yet, the fact that the vast majority of prosecutions in the U.S. are resolved with guilty pleas should be taken into account, as this seems to be the foundation on which localized adjudicative systems are being built.

(c) A third model for community courts can be derived from the experiments in using youth or teen courts as alternatives to judicial processing of juvenile cases. These courts address the goal of using peer community members as participants in the decision-making process. There are over 70 such courts in the United States and, while their procedures differ, some of the guidelines are very similar.

- They are based on a philosophy that young offenders are less likely to recidivate if peers are involved in deciding the appropriate consequences of their acts.
- They are activated after a plea of guilty so that peers in the judicial process do not face as much likelihood of retaliation from the adjudicated offender.
- They attempt to dispense swift and sure sanctions. In order to effect that, they meet often and usually work under predetermined sentencing guidelines. Such guidelines usually include some mandatory community restitution hours, substance abuse testing and treatment, educational or counseling hours, and restitution to the victim.
- If the sentence is successfully completed, the charges are dropped, but if it is not completed, prosecution is resumed in court or through the school administrative process.
- Peers may serve in roles of defense attorney, prosecuting attorney, or the jury. Usually an adult serves in the role of the judge in order to insure neutrality and fairness but there are models in which youth serve in that role as well.

(d) Another model of community oriented restorative justice decision-making is that found in victim/offender mediation programs or dispute-resolution programs. There are three general kinds that can inform the model of Restorative Community Justice more generally and offer alternatives for dealing with violations of the social order and criminal violence.

- One of the more successful programs in this area is the *Resolving Conflict Creatively Program (RCCP)* started in the New York City Public Schools in 1985. RCCP is in place in 250 elementary, junior high, and high schools in the nation, with 4,000 teachers and 120,000 students participating.

The goal of RCCP is to create school change such that there are "Peaceable Schools" which are characterized by community cooperation and communication and shared decision-making. While much of RCCP is devoted to implementing special curricula at all grade levels, teacher training and support, and parent training, it is the student mediation component, which is particularly relevant for Restorative Community Justice. This component attempts to use peers in the mediation process and nonviolent conflict resolution under the supervision of trained faculty coordinators. It also relies upon strong school discipline policies to act as a final deterrent to actual violence. This tends to mirror the community prosecutor approach to enhancing the quality of life in a community through problem-solving but utilizing swift and sure prosecution to enforce the social order when violations of it are criminal.

- The second kind of dispute resolution model is the *Neighborhood Justice Centers and Community Board Programs* begun in the late 1970s and continuing today. The essential goals of these programs have been to encourage community members to resolve disputes themselves through problem-solving techniques and to discourage disputes from escalating from community conflict resolution to formal judicial or law enforcement institutions.
- The Third Kind of Program is *the Victim-Offender Reconciliation Project* - known by its unlovely acronym "VORP" - that embodies what such proponents as Albert Eglash, Dan Van Ness, and Howard Zehr call "restorative justice". The first of the pioneering VORP projects was started in Kitchener, Ontario, in 1974, followed by one in Elkhart, Indiana, in 1978, and many dozens of others were established thereafter. The early programs were inspired by the teachings of the Mennonite Church and other Christian denominations, and are meant to help the victim to understand the offender's

> motivation and the offender to understand the victim's losses. VORP programs, with their stress on restoration, not punishment, have been used as a diversion from the adversarial system, or as part of the court's sentencing process, or even after the outlines of a sentence are set. In their form as a diversion program, they serve to mediate "disputes". In cases where the court retains its sentencing authority, the VORP process has been used to further the understanding of the victim and offender as to the meaning of the violation, and to provide the court additional information as to appropriate sanctions, including restitution.

All of the programs that borrow the techniques of mediation to fashion a sentence have their critics in the victims' movement. It begins with language: to say that two strangers whose only interaction was the criminal violation of one by the other have a "relationship" seems bizarre, and then to say that the relationship suffers from a "conflict" or a "dispute" can sound deeply offensive to victims.

It often does not help matters when the parties do have a previous or even an ongoing relationship with one another. Victim advocates almost universally insist on calling the violence committed by one intimate on another a crime, not a "domestic dispute", or some other palliative.

This is not just a question of semantics. Victim advocates cite many cases in which the mediating agency clearly (if unwittingly) manipulated reluctant victims into cooperating, and then ignored the fact that the victim came in - and left - the mediation process in a position subservient to the offender.

Thus, Ms. Smith, a gentle woman who lives by herself, is asked if she would be willing to have mediated the case against the thirteen-year-old whom she caught leaving her apartment with her television; her religious faith silently compels her to agree to the session, and since her property had already been returned, she raised no objections to the suggestion that the offender's sentence be limited to forty hours of unspecified community service. At no time in the session did she reveal that she is plagued with nightmares of her offender sneaking into her apartment and attacking her, or that her constant fear has caused her to abandon all evening activities at her church, once her favorite pastime.

Though a hypothetical composite, "Ms. Smith" represents actual victims erroneously brought into - or clumsily misused by - well-meaning mediation programs. Likewise, there have been too many schoolyard bullies, abusive spouses, and other chronic predators who have bent a mediation forum to their own ends, defeating the interests of their victims and of justice.

Nonetheless, it has been shown that less formal means of intervention may offer a legitimate method of resolving a public offense when the mediator, judicial officer, or community board is able to balance the process such that all parties are able to make their case with equal force and with an understanding of what their options are (including the option of returning the case to the court). Mediation-type programs which are more selective in the cases they seek to handle and have the knowledge and skill to fortify all the parties to the task ahead have often produced very gratifying results for victims and their advocates as well as for offenders and *their* advocates.

From the Restorative Community Justice perspective, the salient question is not whether mediation models have applicability to the RCJ model but whether they can be used to go beyond the legal facts of a law violation to address issues of social order and its violation.

The Delaware Criminal Justice Council is seeking to do just that in a pilot project it hopes to establish in Kent County. As it is being developed, the plan is that cases would be referred by the prosecutor to the mediation process as a form of "prosecutor's probation". Defendants interested in entering the mediation process must waive their right to a speedy trial. The victim must agree to the process as well, and be screened by trained staff before the mediation. If either the victim or defendant is perceived to be inappropriate for the process, the case will go back to the prosecutor for normal processing.

The mediation process will focus on the harm done to the victim and on the victim's questions of the offender. The mediator will work to design an agreement that restitutes the victim, restores something to the community from the offender, and provides the offender with appropriate treatment if necessary. Project staff will monitor the agreement and its progress. Most referrals will come from the prosecutor, although the plan allows for some cases to come after conviction, from inside a prison, or from self-referrals if mediation is sought to resolve civil disputes before they become a criminal case. A partnership of criminal justice agencies, community groups, and victim representatives has been formed to assist with the program.

(e) A final model for community decision-making is that established in two experiments in New York: the Midtown Community Court in Manhattan, which was opened in October, 1993, and the Red Hook Community Justice Center which is currently being developed. These experiments have been inspired by such phenomena as drug courts, the victims' movement, and community policing, and are demonstrating the efficacy of the judiciary's contribution to Restorative Community Justice. The following precepts guide the New York experiments:

- By arresting, arraigning, and sentencing offenders all in the same neighborhood, justice is swift.
- By paying back the community through community restitution projects, justice is visible.
- By placing drug treatment, health care, education, and court processing under one roof, justice is constructive.
- And by improving communication between the court and the community, the energies of the local police, residents, and businesses are harnessed to improve the delivery of justice.

The goals of the New York courts are to offer community restitution, help steer offenders from further involvement with the criminal justice system, solve community problems, and increase the level of public involvement in court proceedings. John Feinblatt, administrator of the Midtown Community Court, has expanded on the philosophy behind these goals. His views may be summarized as follows:

COMMUNITY RESTITUTION

Community courts recognize that individuals are often victims of crime, but it is equally important that communities be considered victims as well. A priority is placed on having offenders perform needed community-oriented work as part of the sentencing process. Community restitution is ordered to be performed immediately. Such restitution makes a significant contribution to the quality of life in the community. The public performance of the work assures community members that there is a swift response to crime. In its first year, the Midtown Community Court arraigned over 9,000 defendants and nearly 80 percent received sentences of community restitution, social services, or both. Court hearings were held within 17 hours of arrest, and most sentences began within 24 hours of arraignment. Seventy-five percent of the offenders complied with the conditions of their sentences. Community restitution activities included scrubbing graffiti off the walls of 200 businesses and residences, stuffing and sorting over 700,000 pieces of mail for local non-profits, clearing and replacing 6,000 "tree pits" along neighborhood sidewalks, working in soup kitchens, assisting with recycling efforts, and cleaning the court and police precinct.

OFFENDER TREATMENT

Treatment efforts are based on the premise that an arrest creates a crisis in an offender's life, and that such crises make most people vulnerable to change - for better or worse, depending upon other circumstances in the defendant's life. The community court views the arrest as a potential turning point should the defendant want to take advantage of related services. The Midtown Community Court provides opportunities for drug counseling, education, job training, and health care - all on site. More than a dozen city agencies and local non-profit organizations teach English, provide counseling, provide substance abuse treatment, help locate housing, help defendants get jobs, and test for diseases. One mark of success of the court in the first year was that over 1,000 defendants voluntarily returned to the court for further assistance after they had completed their sentences.

PROBLEM SOLVING

Just as the Neighborhood District Attorney focuses on solving noncriminal problems that affect the quality of life in a neighborhood, the community court addresses problems that erode community pride and safety. Court mediators facilitate communication and dispute resolution to restore and build community spirit, as when a bar owner agrees to take steps to keep the noise level down in the late hours.

PUBLIC INVOLVEMENT

Often members of the judiciary and court administrators eschew involvement in community activities because they feel such activities would impair the impartiality and neutrality of the court processes. Community courts are designed to mobilize public interest and to provide leadership in developing new partnerships to enhance community life. The Midtown Community Court encourages residents to visit the court, watch proceedings, and participate in designing community restitution opportunities. Information is disseminated through community advisors, a court newsletter, and even a visible wide-screen video-display of the daily court schedule.

(f) It is suggested that a Restorative Community Justice model of community courts or decision-making processes would be an amalgam of the examples above. It might include the following elements.

- Location in the community.
- Swift justice with community and victim participation in the process. (Representatives of the Midtown Community Court emphasize that the immediacy of sanctions has far more impact on offenders than severity of sanctions.)
- Community and victim participation in the selection of sanctions and in the determination of victim and community restitution.
- Twenty-four hour accessibility.
- Alternative methods of decision-making, including traditional adjudication, community consensus-building, and peer adjudication, plus dispute resolution, mediation, or victim offender reconciliation. The alternatives would be matched to the type of violation of social order or crime that occurred, the age of the victim or offender, and the advice of the community or victim.

The Red Hook Community Justice Center will attempt to take the idea of a community court to its logical conclusion. The community in question is on the Brooklyn side of the New York waterfront, home to some 12,000 people -two-thirds African-American and Hispanic public housing tenants, the rest white and Puerto Rican residents, mostly blue-collar workers. As the Center's, mission statement summarized:

"The vision is ambitious: once completed, the Justice Center will be a multifaceted, multi-service facility, breaking down the walls of distrust, fear and misunderstanding that have traditionally divided courts from low-income communities. By hosting community meetings, mediating quality-of-life problems, offering a variety of social services, and attracting new resources to the community, the Justice Center hopes to transform the nature of a court. In the years ahead, the Justice Center will be an important community resource, a responsible institutional citizen, and a force for positive change in Red Hook."

Community Corrections

The concept of "community corrections" originally embraced the normal work of probation and parole supervision. The term has taken on new meaning when it is used to describe new initiatives in non-incarceration sentencing. The "goals and objectives" of the Model Adult Community Corrections Act show how certain ideas of restorative justice are already found in modern correctional thinking:

(1) To enhance public safety and achieve economies by encouraging the development and implementation of community sanction as a sentencing option;
(2) To enhance the value of criminal sanctions and ensure that the criminal penalties imposed are the most appropriate ones by encouraging the development of a wider array of criminal sanctions;
(3) To increase the community's awareness of, participation in, and responsibility for the administration of the corrections system;
(4) To ensure that the offender is punished in the least restrictive setting consistent with public safety and the gravity of the crime;
(5) To provide offenders with education, training and treatment to enable them to become fully functional members of the community upon release from criminal justice supervision;
(6) To make offenders accountable to the community for their criminal behavior, through community service programs, restitution programs, and a range of locally developed sanctions; and
(7) To foster the development of policies and funding for programs that encourage jurisdictions to minimize the use of incarceration where other sanctions are appropriate.

While most "community corrections" agencies supervise just probationers, at least some also supervise parolees or those who have completed a determinate prison term. Typically, community corrections officers have extensive powers of search and seizure, and can issue their own arrest warrants for violations.

Under the Model Act, a statewide community corrections plan would be developed and monitored by a State Criminal Justice Council made up of criminal justice officials and members of the public. Communities would also establish a local Community Corrections Board with responsibilities for developing and implementing a community corrections plans. That Board would be composed of local criminal justice officials and members of the public. Over a dozen states have instituted community corrections in the manner envisaged by the Model Act.

Its suggested sentencing alternatives include supervised probation, community restitution (or "community service" in the Model Act), home confinement, electronic surveillance, treatment and counseling (either through residential or outpatient facilities), vocational training or mandatory employment, restitution to the victim, fines, and victim-offender education or reconciliation programs.

While the concept of community corrections has been successfully implemented in some jurisdictions, implementation in others has been impeded by structural problems. Community corrections agencies are often understaffed. They do not have formal patrol duties or twenty-four hour on-scene capabilities. While a community corrections officer may supervise offenders who are placed in a community, the officer may not be based there, and in most cases, community members are not actively involved in the supervision or monitoring. Victim participation is also minimal. It is significant that the kind of State Criminal Justice Council or local Community Corrections Board proposed by the Model Act does not designate a role for victim participants. Finally, community service and restitution to individual victims are suggested sanctions rather than debts that the courts must order to be repaid. From the RCJ perspective, this confuses the ideas of restitution, restoration, and retribution.

In the Restorative Community Justice model under review, community corrections can have a much larger role than the Model

Act would suggest. Communities and victims can participate in the corrections process in several meaningful ways:

(a) Community corrections officers can develop partnerships with community members and other criminal justice agencies to develop community-wide monitoring and reporting of suspicious activities. The Volunteer Community Corrections Monitor Program described in the community policing section above could itself be expanded to have not only police officers monitor those under community corrections supervision but also trained citizens. That idea was again suggested in Portland's Neighborhood District Attorney Program in the guise of citizen volunteer "junior probation officers".

(b) Community boards comprised of citizens, including victims, can be used in violation hearings as well as in the establishment of appropriate sentences. Community residents often know far more about the day-to-day activities of people on probation or under community custody status than do community corrections officers.

(c) Community members can also be used to support offenders as they move through the process of providing restitution to the community and the restoration of their own status as a member of that community. A 1991 Public Agenda Foundation study of public attitudes in Delaware revealed strong public support of community restitution because it was a way for offenders to improve job skills, do productive work, and be held accountable by giving something back to the community. It is important to recognize that community restitution in a restorative sense is more than simply doing a designated task. It is critical that the restitution be work that is constructive and restorative in nature for the community, the victim, and the offender. This means that sanctioners need to be creative in their restitution plans.

(d) Finally, community members and victims can be involved in community corrections efforts by participating and supporting victim impact panels and other kinds of victim education programs for offenders. These programs contribute to offenders' understanding the harm done to their victims and to their understanding of the wounds they too have suffered at the hands of others. One of the merits of bringing up an offender's own history of victimization in an educational or treatment setting is that, properly managed, the issue can be addressed without offering the slightest sense of exoneration for their own criminal conduct.

Two examples serve to illustrate creative uses of communities involved in correctional functions.

- In Detroit, Save Our Sons and Daughters (SOSAD) was initially established to help surviving relatives of homicide victims. But soon after its inception, its goals were broadened to address both young victims and offenders involved in inner-city violence. Staff and volunteers work with survivors of violence as they deal with the trauma of victimization. They also work in prisons to encourage offenders to return to the community in good standing after serving their sentences. SOSAD has been successful in promoting the use of Peace Zones in which violence prevention is a priority and reintegrating or restoring young offenders back to their neighborhoods is a major objective.
- In El Paso, Texas, Judge Phillip Martinez handles all juvenile offenses in the court system. When a first-time juvenile offender comes before him, he works with a community organizer to bring together the offender, his family, and representatives of the community and the victim to establish an appropriate sentence. Under this "Conference Committee Program", a probation officer is assigned to each school in his or her district to monitor the implementation of the sentences developed in this way. The community members, school officials, and other students are all involved in holding the juvenile accountable. This has resulted in an 80 percent success rate in handling first-time juvenile offenders (plus a few re-offending property offenders) and has been in operation for almost six years.

Victim Service Programs in the Restorative Community Justice Model.

There are three primary roles for victim service programs in the RCJ model. The first is to help victims and communities address the immediate and long-term trauma of victimization; the second is to help victims and communities access and participate in opportunities to restore justice; and the third is to establish and maintain training and education programs for all agencies and members of the community on victim issues.

(a) When victims and communities are afflicted by crime, emotional trauma is a likely result. It may be greatly exacerbated by financial losses, physical injury, or the death of a loved one, but the impact of sudden, random arbitrary violence, is, in itself, crisis-inducing. Victim advocates play an initial role at the community level in providing immediate practical aid to victims and their families and assisting them with filing for compensation or other forms of financial aid. They also may play a role in connecting them to sources of additional forms of assistance, such as transportation, alternate shelter, document replacement, and the like. But in the course of any other kind of help, the victim advocate's primary goal is to help defuse the psychological crises that face those traumatized by crime.

(b) For victims and communities involved in the restorative justice process, and hence involved in the criminal justice system, perhaps a summary of the victim advocate's role is to "explain, reassure, and support" the victim and community member at every stage of the justice proceedings. This may mean working with law enforcement to defuse victims at the scene of a crime; it may mean working with prosecutors to ensure that there is court accompaniment to individual victims as well as court watchers; it may mean working with victims to translate their thoughts and reactions into a victim impact statement that effectively states their case to a court or decision-making body; it may mean providing accompaniment to victims appearing on victim impact panels or notification of an offender's status upon release.

(c) Finally, victim service programs must be engaged in constant training and education of their allied professionals in current victim needs and rights as well as the training of communities in violence prevention and public awareness of victim assistance. This training and education should be done in collaboration with other agencies but the victim service provider is uniquely placed to continue to ensure that the refocusing of justice from the offender in the courts to the victim and victims in the community takes place.

In fact, it may not too broad a statement to say that the role of the victim advocate can be the glue that makes all the components of the RCJ model hold together. By continuing to express the concerns of the individuals and groups who have been harmed by crime, the advocate can keep the model's principles of responsibility and accountability at the forefront of the day-to-day operations of the cooperative enterprise.

Community Participation in the Restorative Community Justice Model

The sixth program element in the implementation of Restorative Community Justice is the involvement of community citizenry through volunteer work and partnerships. This element has been integrated in the earlier discussions of the five more formalized roles and functions.

However, there are two concerns to which community members should pay special attention.

(a) There is a need to establish as priorities for all community justice agencies a focus on the quality of life, on violence prevention, and on victim assistance issues. Those priorities should be the ultimate goals of every community action plan. If those are priorities and a global vision is maintained, it is easy to see why planting and maintaining a public garden (for example) may improve the aesthetics of the area, prevent the development of an open air drug market, and provide healing opportunities for victims to join with other community members to reconstruct their lives.

(b) In order to maintain those priorities, communities should establish a permanent task force (with rotating memberships) to coordinate specific partnerships in conjunction with their Restorative Community Justice agencies, and also help forge partnership agreements that address specific problems. Such coordination and agreements assist in ensuring accountability of the community as well as individual agencies and people.

Restorative Community Justice: Policy Initiatives

To establish a system of Restorative Community Justice, it is probable that a number of changes in legislation might be required at the state or local level. Two immediate changes are called for.

First, there is a need to change the legislative terminology of "community service" as a sanction to "community restitution". Community restitution should be defined as activities done by offenders that contribute to the quality of life of a community and that "pay back" the community for the harm done. It should not be used or confused with retribution or punishment on the one hand or voluntary service on the other.

And second, in all legislation addressing elements of Restorative Community Justice such as community policing, community prosecution, community courts, or community corrections, an explicit role for victims - as individual and collective consumers of the justice system - should be defined and provided for.

In addition, the following are some policy issues to be considered.

1. Are there violations of social order that should be sanctioned through ordinances or civil processes such that there are legal methods to give notice and establish grounds for arrests that are more serious and prosecution if those violations occur? Portland established "drug-free zones" in 1992 as a part of its ordinances to secure public peace, safety, and morals. In 1994, the ordinance was amended to provide for "civil exclusions" for certain crimes or infractions. If these exclusion orders are violated, wrongdoers are subject to immediate arrest for criminal trespass in the second degree under Oregon law. This provides community police and prosecutors with a potent tool to "hassle" individuals consistently contributing to community disorder. The use of the vernacular here is a reminder that communities should have the ability to respond appropriately to those who crudely despoil community life. But the vernacular is also a reminder that communities and their agents of justice have in the past used such authority to infringe on the rights of individuals whose appearance or conduct may not conform to community norms but whose misconduct does not properly rise to a police matter.

2. What types of crimes or criminals should be processed through alternative courts or decision-making processes with community involvement?

   Some have suggested that alternative courts and the like should primarily be used in cases involving first offenders, juveniles, or misdemeanants. However, Judge F.W.M. McElrea, in reviewing the Youth Justice system in New Zealand, has a more ambitious view:

   "My conclusion therefore is that we indeed do have a new paradigm of justice. It is not simply an old model with modifications ..... It is a spirit, which I would characterize as responsible reconciliation. The term 'reconciliation' connotes a positive, growing process where strength is derived from the interaction of victim, offender, and family in a supportive environment. It is a 'responsible' process in that those most directly affected take responsibility for what has happened and for what is to happen. In the process most of the power previously vested in the court is transferred to the local community, which now carries this new responsibility.

   "Perhaps when the real strengths of the new model have been understood we will be able to take it beyond the Youth Court, find a mechanism for defining a relevant community group for adult offenders, involve victims and the wider process in finding solutions, and in the process remove from the courts and our prisons much of the burden of unrealistic expectation under which they labor." (Emphasis added.)

3. Should judges be mandated to order community restitution whenever communities make a showing of negative impact due to crime? Should personal restitution be mandated to fully compensate all known victims for all losses as a part of any plea? And should "community service" be legislatively redefined to designate voluntary services in the community contributed by citizens in good standing while "community restitution" be used to denote activities that offenders do to satisfy restoration mandates?

4. Should communities be allowed to submit victim impact statements concerning violations of social order and crimes processed in the Restorative Community Justice process?

5. Should communities be given standing to sue drug-related nuisances such that successful plaintiffs can enjoin continuation of the drug nuisance, force a judicial sale of property used in the nuisance, and recover damages from the sale proceeds?

   This is a concept proposed by Congressman Charles E. Schumer in a proposed Community Empowerment Against Crime Act. The cause of action is similar to current civil forfeiture provisions, which target property used to facilitate crime without necessitating a criminal prosecution, and to "private attorneys general" statutes that induce private citizens to bring suits enforcing federal law and keep a share of the recovery.

   Perhaps in the development of Restorative Community Justice, one should look increasingly to these and other civil-law tools of redress and accommodation as ways to assert legitimate community interests while seeking to prevent increases in crime and violence.

JAYANT KUMAR

5

RESTORATIVE JUSTICE: EXISTING POLICIES AND PROCEDURES IN VARIOUS COUNTRIES

In this chapter, an endeavor was taken to deal with policies and procedures of various countries which strive to achieve the goal of restorative justice. A number of resolution processes have been designed worldwide to promote healing of relationships and peacemaking within communities through dialog, negotiation and problem-solving between victims and criminal offenders. These processes emphasize upon victim healing, offender accountability, reparation of losses and, in some cases, forgiveness and the reintegration of the offender into the community. This process occurs instead of, or outside of, any criminal prosecutions of offenders. This approach to crime has gained the name "restorative justice."

NEW ZEALAND

The term "restorative justice" became known in New Zealand by the introduction of *Children, Young Persons and their Families Act, 1989*[1] which introduced the Family Group Conference (FGC). This Act applied to Youth Court proceedings dealing with offenders aged 14-17 and one of the primary objectives of the legislation was to strengthen the ability of families to hold their young people accountable and encourage them to develop in law-abiding and socially productive ways. The major change that was brought by this Act was that it made the involvement of victims as key participants, making possible a healing process for both offender and victim. More or less, this was a piece of legislation, which tried to make the people acquainted with an inbuilt mechanism to follow the norms of the society. The conference followed a very simple process which involved the explanation of their parts by the two parties and discussion by their supporters on the consequences of crime and it ended up with an agreement or any plan resolving the outstanding issue, generally it is as to how to make good the losses to the victims. The basic objectives of FGC can be classified as Empowerment, Restoration, Reintegration, Emotional resolutions and satisfactory outcome. Family group conferences are not just a decision-making process, but much more than that, they are also an experience, an opportunity for human encounter. This is one reason why the victim's presence is so essential. Without a victim present it is almost impossible to get that essential element of encounter and confrontation that challenges a young person's perception of their actions and shows them the human face of crime. In the experience of such an encounter a change of heart is possible.

The Sentencing Act, 2002[2] contains a number of provisions that explicitly endorse restorative justice. Sec. 8 of the same Act states that the courts have to take into account any outcomes of restorative processes that have occurred during the proceedings against the accused. Further, Section 10 is an another step in the same direction, which states that the courts have to take into account any suggestion or contracts between the parties by the accused as to how to make good the losses to the victims.

Restorative justice has also been introduced in New Zealand prisons – on a pilot scheme basis. A full time restorative justice co-ordinator working in the Hawks Bay Regional Prison was put on duty to organize meetings between prisoners and victims. The outcomes have nearly always been very positive. As these meetings occur post-sentence they have no relationship to the sentencing process and are purely for the benefit of the parties themselves. The basic principle lying behind this is to hold the accused accountable[3] from his heart for the act he has committed.

Still, there are cases where the court has refused to accept the offer made by the accused and sentenced him for prison. The classic authority for this is the case of *R v Clotworthy*.[4] The Court held that:

"[T]aking into account the attitude of the victim, one asks the question - what is to be achieved in this particular case by a sentence of imprisonment to commence today? Firstly, there would be the debt to the taxpayer of somewhere between $40-$90,000 per year. Secondly, there would be literally no tangible or realistic benefit to the victim personally - no actual justice. Thirdly, there would be havoc wreaked upon the prisoner's small, ...fragile family...Fourthly, there would be little and probably no prospect of any further reparation beyond the $5,000 payable today.

If there is no serious concern that there should be deterrence personally for the prisoner, then the only purpose served in this particular case by an unsuspended sentence of imprisonment, would be to *satisfy that perceived community need for the court to be punitive.*[5]"

Thus, this is the position of the restorative justice in New Zealand, which shows that though statutory implications have been made for proper practice of restorative justice, still it is easy for the court to compartmentalize restorative justice. Keeping aside all the critiques and exceptions, it is worth noting that New Zealand has given the concept of FGC to the world, which is working fairly well.

AUSTRALIA

Inspired by the success of Family Group Conference in New Zealand, Australia also started FGC. Initially, in Australia the Wagga model of family group conference was occurred on an experimentation basis[6] with a range of innovative local youth initiatives: truancy programs, crime prevention workshops and drug forums for young people. The Wagga Model of FGC is a sort of an offshoot of what was practiced in New Zealand. Instead of FGC, they are called police-run conferences. Wagga-style police conferences involve the perpetrator(s) of an offence and the victim(s) of that offence, together with the families and friends of victims and offenders, and any others significantly affected by that offence. The conference is facilitated by a police officer, whose role is to encourage participants to reach some collective agreement about how best to minimize the ongoing harm resulting from the offending behaviour.

Figure 1
Wagga Conferencing Model[7]

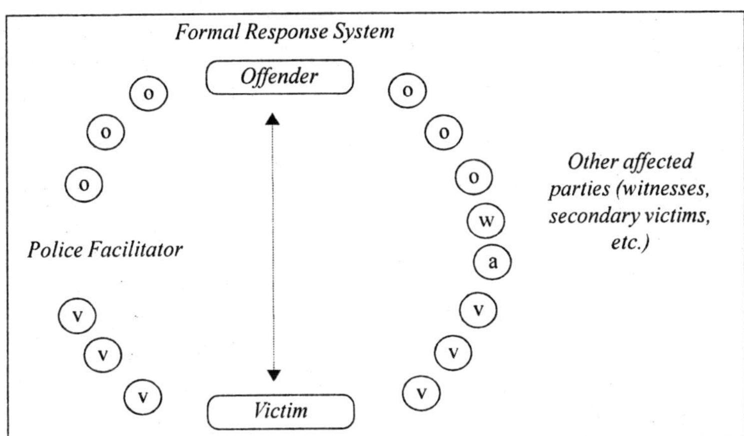

Braithwaite's (1989) Reintegrative Shaming Theory influenced understanding of conferencing, and the police model later developed in Canberra was specifically based upon Braithwaite's theory. The said theory encourages the wrongdoers to experience shame for their offence maintaining their dignity and self respect. This is done by holding the wrongdoers accountable for their act and giving them an opportunity to make the things right.[8] RISE was also funded to test the effects of police conferences as a deterrent to adult drunk-driving offences. The Canberra "drink-driving" conferences are adult diversionary conferences limited to "over-the-limit" driving violations in cases where there is no accident and thus no direct victim. Offenders are required to bring at least six supporters. Volunteer community representatives, ideally from the locale of the offense, serve as stand-in victims as shown in Figure. The central hypothesis of the experiments is that there will be less repeat offending after a conference than after court.

Conferencing in South Australia was also introduced by Young Offenders Act, 1993. According to the Act the conferencing was available to the juveniles of 10-17 years who have committed minor offences and later on also by the Children and Young People Act, 1999.

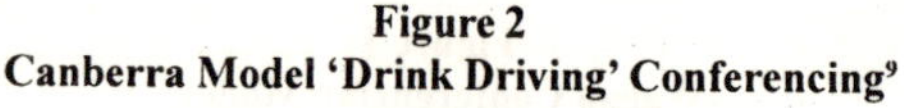

Figure 2
Canberra Model 'Drink Driving' Conferencing[9]

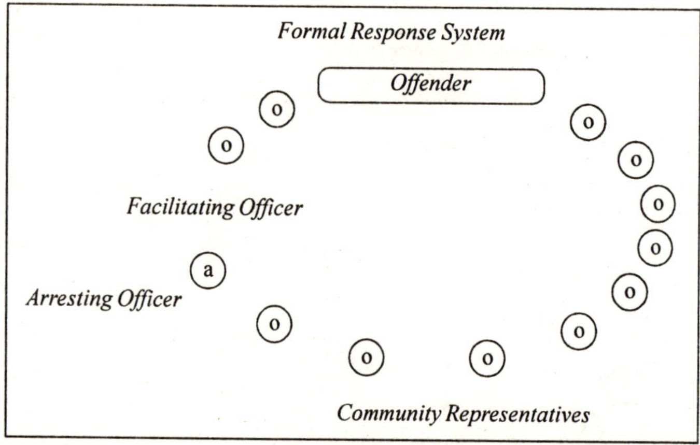

SOUTH AFRICA

In South Africa, the Truth and Reconciliation Commission (TRC) has promoted truth-telling and forgiveness instead of violence and reprisals. Looking at the history of South Africa itself, it can be traced that when South Africa was inhibited by indigenous people only, justice was done by a group of people including the offender and the victim, which was based on the concept of *ubuntu*[10]. Recently, Child Justice Bill was introduced which was again based on the same philosophy. The basic nicety of South African Criminal Administration System is TRC[11], which was also inherent in Promotion of National Unity and Reconciliation Act, 1995 and in the Constitution[12]. *The TRC is simply one mechanism amongst many which is attempting to heal the wounds of the past, in order to create a solid foundation for the future*. Hayner describes the four elements of truth commissions as:

- their focus is on the past
- their aim is to provide a comprehensive picture of human rights abuses and of violations of international law over a period of time, and not simply to focus on one event
- they exist for a limited period of time, usually winding up when their report is complete
- they have authority to access information and demand protection; thus they can examine sensitive issues and maximise the impact of their report

Later on, restorative Justice has become a central part by passing of Crime and Disorder Act, 1998, in which provision for *Referral Order*[13] has been made.

Victim Offender Mediation (VOM) is also a part of South African model of restorative justice. VOM is primarily "dialogue driven," de-emphasizing reconciliation and emphasizing victim healing, offender accountability and restoration of losses. VOM is also distinctive in advocating a "humanistic" model of mediation, a "social work case development approach". In VOM the mediator facilitates dialogue and mutual aid; schedules separate pre-mediation sessions with each party; builds rapport and trust while not taking sides; identifies the strengths of each party; uses a non-directive style of mediation that creates a safe space for dialogue and accessing the strengths of participants; and recognizes and uses the power of silence. Most sessions result in a signed restitution agreement. VOM emphasizes building relationships between parties and establishing trust with the mediator. Generally only the victim and offender may participate because of concern that parents and others may inhibit young offenders from genuinely expressing themselves.

Sec.1 of Child Justice Bill defines restorative justice and the bill gives an alternative to arrest and availability of diversion. Diversion is offered at three levels. Level one includes short duration programmes. The second and third levels, however, are of increased intensity and are of generally longer duration. Family Group Conferences are also made available in the diversion, preferably at, second and third level. The sentencing principles[14] contained in the bill are also based on the principles of restorative justice.

By the above discussion it seems that South Africa by having such strong statutory implications has tried to give a strong mechanism to impart restorative justice. Even after that the most important difficulty in proper implementation of the above is practices of racial discrimination prevalent there. Cases like *Girl Painted White*[15], *Child burn to death*[16] *etc.* are strong revelations of this.

BELGIUM

Belgium is also a leading country in the world with regard to restorative justice practices. From the beginning of twentieth century, by the Children's Act, 1912 Belgium established its policy that children don't need punishment but protection and education. This was later on confirmed by the Youth Protection Act, 1965. One of the basic feature of the Belgian Criminal Justice Administration System is that it distinguishes between adult and child qualitatively. Article 37 of the Youth Protection Act, 1965 provides a legal basis for 'community service and educational projects'. Under this Act, the Judge is empowered to impose a sort of community service and educational projects on the young offenders. Under this, a Compensation Fund has also been created, the purpose of which is that in certain cases the offender is financially helpless to repair the losses to the victim, the offender is asked to go for certain hours of community service or some humanitarian or cultural work. In exchange of that, the offender is paid from the fund by which he can pay the victim. Another policy of Belgian legislation is availability of Victim – Offender Mediation (VOM). There are basically three types of VOM, mediation for juveniles[17], mediation for redress[18] and mediation at police stage[19].

Family Group Conference is also a part of Belgian criminal justice policy. Youth Court judge is empowered to send the cases to FGC. When a person comes before the youth court, the judge assesses the case fitness to send it to FGC. Then, if the judge finds it suitable he narrates the allegation and the case is sent for FGC only if he accepts the facts. If he does not accept, then a normal court proceeding commences. If he accepts the facts, then the judge asks the opinion of youth court's social service representative, which should be relayed within ten days and the latter, in turn, appoints a facilitator to start the conference. The facilitator first approaches the offender and then victim. It is left to the choice of the victim as to whether he wants to remain present personally in the conference or wants to deliberate his views by way of letter or by proxy. A police officer also remains present during the conference. He narrates the facts at the start of the conference and ensures that the offender is in acceptance of the facts because only then the conference can be continued. Then, there comes the phase of storytelling by victim or by his supporter, as to what harm has been caused by the act of the offender. Perhaps, this is the core element of the whole conference because the emotions and sentiments of victim are made evident and then the offender, realizing what he has done apologizes for himself. After the end of the communication, private time is given to offender and victim whereby they discuss what fitting reparation can be made to the victim. Generally, the victims demand is fulfilled. With this, it is also tried to achieve some ancillary objectives like reintegration.

Belgium has also started restorative justice practices in prison also. Since 1998 there has been an action research project in six prisons to test out the possibility of using restorative justice ideas within the most controlled social institutions so that prisoners can be enabled to take responsibility for their actions and that the process can help deal with the conflict between offenders and their victims. The process was evaluated step-by-step to ensure that lessons were regularly learned and good practice identified and spread. Through the results of the initial project the Minister of Justice decided to introduce restorative justice activities in all Belgian prisons. Each of the 30 prisons now has a restorative justice counsellor appointed to work with the governor to introduce concepts and practices in line with those developed within the community[20].

CANADA

Canada was the first nation to use 'Circle Sentencing Policy' to deal with increasing pace of crime in 1980. Circle Sentencing involves offenders, victims, their families and other community members that aim at unfolding the causes of crime and is built on principles of mediation, indigenous peacemaking processes and consensus decision making. The sentencing circle[21] is a method of dealing with members of the community that have broken the law. A sentencing circle is conducted after the individual has been found guilty or if the accused has accepted guilt and is willing to assume his responsibility. This sentencing method encourages the offender and the community to accept responsibility and acknowledges the harm they have done to society and to victims. Sentencing Circle is other way round of FGS and VOM which also aimed at starting the healing process for both the offender and the victim. In this the offender is presented with the impact of their actions in front of respected community members, elders, peers, family, the victim and their family, stimulating an opportunity for real change.

Unlike FGC, it is not that in any case the court can refer the case to Sentencing circle; court has issued guidelines in this regard, particularly in the case of *Joseyounen*[22]*:*

1. The accused must agree to be referred to the sentencing circle.
2. The accused must have deep roots in the community in which the sentencing is held and from which the participants are drawn.
3. There are elders or respected non-political community leaders willing to participate.
4. The victim is willing to participate and has been subjected to no coercion or pressure in so agreeing.
5. The court should try to determine beforehand, as best it can, if the victim is subject to battered women's syndrome. If she is, then she should have counseling and be accompanied by a support team in the circle.
6. Disputed facts have been resolved in advance.
7. The case is one in which a court would be willing to take a calculated risk and depart from the usual process of sentencing.

Figure 3
A Sentencing Circle Model

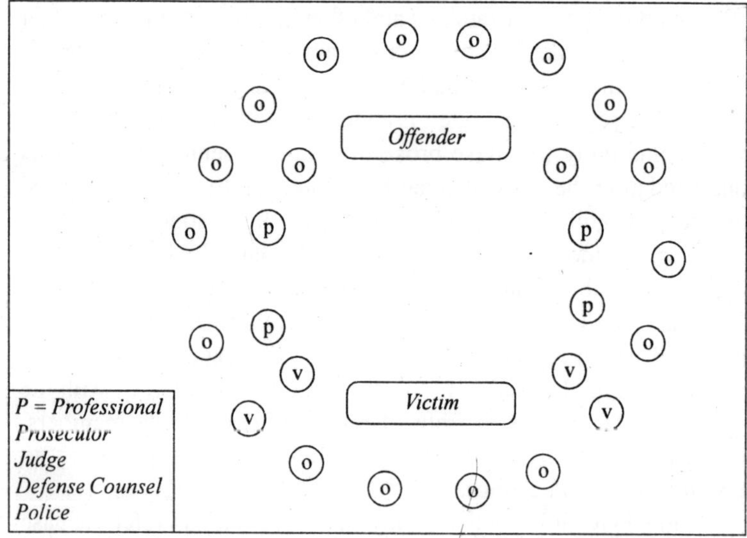

After this a number of sentencing options are available to the community which includes compulsory school attendance/work attendance; referral to specialized programs, i.e. anger management, sexual abuse awareness training; Aboriginal spiritual activities, i.e. sweats, forgiveness/sacrifice ceremonies; curfew rules and regulations respecting residency etc. Apart from this there are certain conditions when Sentencing circle cannot be held like when there is case of repeated offences, when community is not prepared to participate, when community doesn't have any sentencing option etc.

There are two alternative models also present in Canada which achieve the same objective as circle sentences. One is an Elders Panel, consisting of either Elders, or community leaders, or both, or a mixture of citizens and influential individuals. The panel interviews the parties to the circle and also may inquire from other independent/outdoor members. The panel discusses the gravity of the transgression and works out a proposal to the judge about the best way to approach the offender's sentence. The second model is a Sentence Advisory Panel that hears applicants for sentence recommendations. The panel conducts research into the particular case, decides if the candidate is suitable for sentence recommendations, and then formulates a proposal to the judge.

INDIA

The idea of restorative justice is not alien to the Indian Criminal Justice System. Examples of restorative justice can be seen in various Indian legislations and in the Constitution as well. Some important hallmark provisions are mentioned herein:-

- Article 141 of Indian Constitution[23];
- Section 357 of Criminal Procedure Code, 1973[24];
- Section 358 of Criminal Procedure Code, 1973[25];
- Section 359 of the Criminal Procedure Code, 1973[26];
- Section 5 of Probation of Offenders Act, 1958[27].

Though in India no specific policy has been framed such as having TRC o FGC or anything of that sort, initiatives have been taken like the Victim Assistance Fund established in Tamil Nadu in 1995. Few years back, Supreme Court of India while deciding the case of *State of Gujarat V. Hon'ble High Court of Gujarat*[28] held that apart from awarding sentence to the offender, court must also take care to the fact that victims of crime should not be left as 'forgettable man" in the whole process. So, court held that emphasis should also be made to make reparation of the losses to the victim. D. P. Wadhwa J., speaking for the bench held[29]

> *"Reparation is taken to mean the making of amends by an offender to his victim, or to victims of crime generally, and may take the form of compensation, the performance of some service or the return of stolen property (restitution), these being types of reparation which might be described as practical or material. The term can also be used to describe more intangible outcomes, as where an offender makes an apology to a victim and provides some reassurance that the offence will not be repeated thus repairing the psychological harm suffered by the victim as a result of the crime."*

The difference between India and other countries in this regard is that in other countries it is the decision of the offender to do something for the victim meaning thereby that it is offender's inner conscience that makes him do the same but in India it is the court who while delivering the judgment make some provisions for the well being of the victims without any consent of the offenders. The concept of restorative justice must become a real experience in the life of India's society, which is culturally, religiously, linguistically, and ethnically pluralistic. Only with restorative justice can the Kingdom of God can become a reality in India.

Thus, three basic models of community justice or family group conferences have been tried: Wagga Wagga (Australia) where a police officer facilitates the meeting, the New Zealand model where a social worker leads, and the Fresno model where a trained community volunteer guides the process. Apart from these countries there are several other countries in the world that have moved a step towards restorative justice by framing certain methods. In Japan, Victim Compensation Act, 1980 and Victim Protection Act, 2000 and in United Nationsbi and tri partite resolutions have strengthened the process of achieving restorative justice in the respective countries. Same is the case with Sentencing Circles or Peacemaking Circles in the United States and mediation in UK. There is still a long way to go ahead!

NOTES

1. The Act repeals the Children and Young Persons Act of 1974 and has as its objective the promotion of the well-being of children, young persons, and their families and family groups. The membership of children in their families and family groups is to be strengthened, families and family

groups are to receive assistance in caring for their children, and, whenever possible, families or family groups are to be helped to resolve the problems of children who need care or protection or have committed a criminal offence.

2. **Section 7** enlists eight purposes of sentencing, they can be enlisted in the following manner:-

(a) to hold the offender accountable for harm done to the victim and the community by the offending: or
(b) to promote in the offender a sense of responsibility for, and an acknowledgement of, that harm: or
(c) to provide for the interests of the victim of the offence; or
(d) to provide reparation for harm done by the offending; or
(e) to denounce the conduct in which the offender was involved; or
(f) to deter the offender or other persons from committing the same or a similar offence; or
(g) to protect the community from the offender; or
(h) to assist in the offender's rehabilitation and reintegration; or
(i) a combination of 2 or more of the purposes in paragraphs (a) to (h).

3. One facet of accountability is that, accountability lies in the heart of man. When it dies there, no constitution, no law, no court can save it. While it lies there, it needs no constitution, no law, no court to save it.

4. [1998] 15 CRNZ 651. In this case the victim was walking past the offender on an Auckland street in the early hours of the morning. Unprovoked, the intoxicated offender attacked the victim and demanded money. He then proceeded to slash the victim with a knife, cutting his face and stabbing him in the chest and stomach. The victim received six stab wounds and underwent surgery. This left permanent scarring. Judge Thorburn in the District Court described the offender's behavior as utterly bizarre, defying explanation, understanding or any intelligent appreciation. The offender pleaded guilty. Sentencing was delayed while a restorative justice conference was held. The conference resulted in the victim accepting the offender's sincere apology. The victim wanted cosmetic surgery for the severe scarring. The offender offered to assist with the cost. Consequently the offender agreed to pay $25,000 to the victim for surgery by way of reparation. The victim was adamant the offender should not go to jail.

   In the District Court, Judge Thorburn ordered $15,000 as reparation for the victim. He further imposed a suspended sentence of 2 years together with 200 hours community service. The principles applied by the Judge in sentencing display an awareness of the principles of restorative justice and the means of giving effect to them.

5. [1998] 15 CRNZ 651.

6. The first "conferencing" in Wagga Wagga involved four young offenders who had stolen a $10,000 motorcycle and had caused $1,000 damage and the victim, offenders and their families were very satisfied with the conference result.
7. http://iirp.org/library/vt/vt_mccold.html last visited on 3rd November, 2004.
8. The Wagga model of conferencing was designed to facilitate this process of reintegrative shaming.
9. Supra Note 7.
10. Archbishop Desmond Tutu explains about ubuntu that it is very difficult to render into a western language. It speaks of the very sense of human. When we want to give high praise to someone we say 'yu, u nobuntu'; 'hey, he or she has ubuntu'. This means they are generous, hospitable, friendly, caring and compassionate. They share what they have. It also means my humanity is caught up, is inextricably bound up, in theirs. We belong to a bundle of life. We say, 'a person is a person through other people.'
11. There is no commonly accepted definition of what a truth commission is or what it should do. A truth commission is typically a body set up at a time of political transition to investigate past violations of human rights in a particular country over a defined period. TRC began its first hearings in April 1996 in East London in South Africa's Eastern Cape chosen because it was the site of intense repression in the 1970s and 1980s. It was also the home of Steve Biko who died in police detention in 1977. The TRC has attracted extensive national and international attention.
12. Schedule 6, paragraph 22 of the Constitution of 1995 says: "Notwithstanding the other provisions of the new Constitution and despite the repeal of the previous Constitution, all the provisions relating to amnesty contained in the previous Constitution under the heading "National Unity and Reconciliation" are deemed to be part of the new Constitution for the purposes of the Promotion of National Unity and Reconciliation Act, 1995 (Act 34 of 1995), as amended, including for the purposes of its validity."
13. Referral Order in Youth Justice System means that youth offenders are referred to Youth Offenders Panel. The panel then allows the victim to play a par in the whole process as to suggest how to make reparation.
14. The bill set out sentencing options as follows:-
    1. community based sentence;
    2. restorative justice sentences;
    3. sentences involving correctional supervision; and
    4. sentences with a compulsory residential requirement.

15. Lorraine, a 15-year old girl went to a departmental store. While she was there the store manager accused her of shoplifting. The store manger asked a male security guard to strip off her T-shirt and paint her white from head to waist. She suffered humiliation. Later on, the security person was found guilty and store manger was left free.
16. Kagiso, a 14-year child with his four friends broke into and entered in a shop. The owner of the shop locked them in store room, poured petrol on the children and lit a cloth. As a result of this, Kagiso died.
17. This is made available to deal with juvenile offenders exclusively. Juvenile offenders are given option to have VOM with their parents and victim.
18. This is designed for some serious cases. Generally, the court accepts the agreement of VOM, but this mediation is between adult offenders and victim in serious cases wherein the prosecutor has decided to prosecute the offender irrespective of any result of VOM.
19. Herein, the police deliver the case for mediation. This is done in cases of minor offences.
20. http://www.restorativejustice.org.uk/about-rj/prisons2.htm last visited on 4th November, 2004.
21. Victim, offender, their supporters and community members sit in a circle without tables or other furniture. An object, called a talking piece, circulates in order among participants who speak only when they are holding the talking piece. The use of the talking piece reduces the role of the facilitator and eliminates cross-talk or interruptions because the talking piece designates who may speak while all others listen. The process may involve separate circles for the victim and offender before all parties are brought together to determine an action plan to address the issues raised in the process. The talking piece moves in clockwise direction so that everyone gets an opportunity to speak and no one can interrupt other in between. By consensus the circle may develop the sentence for the offender and may also stipulate responsibilities of community members and justice officials as part of the agreement.
22. [1995] W.W.R. 438 at 442-46
23. The State shall, within the limits of its economic capacity and development, make suitable provision for securing the right towards, education and to public assistance in case of unemployment, old age, sickness and disablement, and in other cases of undeserved want.
24. Sec. 357 states that when a Court imposes a sentence of fine or a sentence (including a sentence of death) of which fine forms a part, the Court may, when passing judgment, order the whole or any part of the fine recovered to be applied to pay compensation to the victim or any other related function.

25. Section 358 deals with Compensation to persons groundlessly arrested.
26. Section 359 deals with Order to pay costs in non-cognizable cases.
27. Section 5 gives the power to court to require released offenders to pay compensation and costs.
28. AIR 1998 SC 3164.
29. Ibid.

NATTI RONEL AND UDI LEBEL

6

BEYOND RESTORATION: THE ROLE OF NON-FORGIVENESS FOR BEREAVED PARENTS

INTRODUCTION

Usually, forgiveness by victims to the "bad guys" who harmed them is a restorative option that may serve both as a goal and path for recovery (Ronel, this issue). However, it is a goal set by therapists or victimologists, based on our professional experience and knowledge about the process of victimization, restoration and recovery. How much this knowledge corresponds to the subjective experience of offended victims themselves? Can victims have a different experience, when and why?

The emerging field of Victim's Victimology identifies the subjective experience of victims as a meaningful source in the accumulation of an experiential knowledge of victimization (Ben David, 2000). In view of that, the current paper, based on qualitative research, brings forward the personal experience of suffering victims, of bereaved parents in Israel, in relation to the continuum from anger to forgiveness and its impact on their personal struggle with the loss and subsequent social activities. The parents who participate in this research lost their sons during their military service or by terrorism. Most of them serve as opinion leaders in Israel, therefore they exemplify victims' advocacy endeavours.

THE NATURE OF FORGIVENESS

Although forgiveness is central to the teachings of the Judeo-Christian tradition, its introduction into modern research and practice is relatively new (McCullough & Worthington, 1999). Enright and The Human Development Study Group, who pioneered the research on forgiveness, suggest a highly moral definition (1991): "Forgiveness is the overcoming negative affect and judgment toward the offender, not by denying ourselves the right to such affect and judgment, but by endeavouring to view the offender with compassion, benevolence, and love while recognizing that he or she has abandoned the right to them" (p. 126). In this view, forgiveness is directed beyond the harm itself, at the offender as a human being (Haber, 1991), and displays a marked readiness to respond ahead of the principle of justice (Enright & The Human Development Study Group, 1994).

Another, slightly more flexible definition, perceives forgiveness as a pro-social change in the individual toward the harm causing person, which includes relief from the past injury and related bitterness (Berecz, 2001). The pro-social change takes place in the interpersonal motivation of people following their personal injury (McCullough, 2000). It is an active decision of the offended to give-up one's former state of non-forgiveness (Worthington & Wade, 1999), taken after the offended reached a state of strength (Flanigan, 1992). This decision is experienced as related to one's relationship with oneself and with the world (Rowe & Halling, 1998). It can guide one to search reconciliation with the offender (Worthington & Wade, 1999), besides other means of doing justice. However, it is emphasized that forgiveness is distinct from reconciliation (Fow, 1996).

Another distinction is between amnesty and forgiveness (Kaminer, Stein, Mbanga & Zungu-Dirwayi, 2000). Amnesty is a law-related category, that can be provided only by state authorities and therefore it is irrelevant to interpersonal relationship where forgiveness may take place.

Four major models introduce forgiveness in research, theoretical or clinical literature (Scobie & Scobie, 1998): (a) the Christian model - human forgiveness should reflect the unconditional divine forgiveness (Scobie & Scobie, 1998); (b) the pro-social model – the role of forgiveness in relationships (Scobie & Scobie, 1998). This model may relate to individuals as well as to communities that are kept up by the means of forgiveness. The act of forgiveness is perceived to be able to liberate the community of continuing negative situations (Andrews, 1999); (c) philosophical models – analyzing forgiving as a moral virtue

(Haber, 1991); (d) health-related models - the benefits of forgiveness to the mental health of the forgiver (Freedman & Enright, 1996; Maltby, Macaskill, & Day, 2001; Sells & Hargrave, 1998). For example, research conducted in South Africa with 134 black survivors of abuse, found a significant negative correlation between psychiatric symptoms and scores on the forgiveness test (Kaminer, Stein, Mbanga, & Zungu-Dirwayi, 2001).

THE AFTER-BEREAVEMENT PROCESS

Bereavement is considered a two-track phenomena (Rubin, 1981, 1992, 1993). The first track indicates the immediate changes in the behavior and personality of bereaved individuals just after the trauma. The second track refers to the further adaptation of bereaved individuals including dealing with the deceased in their inner world, renewing emotional ties with the loved one, reminiscing, and shaping feelings towards them (Parkes & Weiss, 1983). The restoration of the overall functioning, as well as of satisfaction in life, is enabled after the conclusion of the first track, while the second track processes still accompany the person. More often than not, this process of adjustment ends with the recovery of normal functioning. Bereaved individuals who deviate from this process may develop a "complex grief response" (Ginzburg, Giron, & Solomon, 2002; Middelton, Raphael, Martinek, & Nisso, 1993). When bereaved individuals do not progress to the second track of grief, their condition is referred to as "pathological grief" or "prolonged grief" (Faschingbauer, Zisook, & Devaul, 1987). Some researchers claim that such behavior is influenced by social-cultural variables. In the Israeli context, for instance, there are those who argue that society encourages prolonged mourning (Malkinson & Bar Tur, 2000).

A familiar phenomenon after loss is the tendency of bereaved people to idealize the fallen, accompanied by the parents' sense of guilt for contributing to their child's death (Kubler-Ross, 1979; Lifton, 1979). Another tendency of individuals after loss is the effort to find meaning and significance in the painful events (Wheeler, 2001). This effort sometimes leads to intensive activity and public or political initiatives, which provide those in crisis with an understanding and a sense of meaning.

THE POLITIC OF BEREAVEMENT

The current research targets bereaved parents in Israel that lost their sons as part of the unique military situation in Israel. As the Israeli society is fighting for its existence since its independence, military bereavement is inseparable from the Israeli experience. Therefore, bereavement is considered to be owned by the public or by the state and it constitutes a continuing topic in the public arena. Consequently, the victims, the bereaved families, have gained a treatment different than that of families who struggle with other kinds of loss. During the years bereaved families went out publicly and played a moral role in the communal arena. Their individual bereavement became a resource to be used by the state as well as by other power groups, including them. From its start, military bereavement was a political issue which served political figures (Doron & Lebel, 2006). Bereaved persons – particularly parents – turned out to be opinion formers (Lebel, 2006).

Although the politization of bereavement is a known phenomena, its meaning for the recovery of the bereaved individuals was less investigated. The experiential knowledge about recovery of bereaved parents who gained a public influence has not yet explored. Consequently, our research targets the role of the anger - forgiveness continuum in the recovery process of bereaved parents who are opinion leaders. However, this current paper describes a segment of the broader research (see also: Lebel & Ronel, 2005; Ronel & Lebel, 2006). Our current research question is to describe the meaning of the anger for the parents and to understand their reaction to the possibility of forgiveness.

METHOD

The present research is a phenomenological-hermeneutic study that focuses on the personal experience of the participants (Bryman, 1988; Spinelli, 1989; Van Manen, 1997).

Participants

The participants were 13 bereaved parents, who can be divided into three groups:

1. Four parents of sons who fell in battle (in Lebanon, by Syrian or Palestinian fire).

2. Four parents of sons who were killed in acts of terror by Palestinians (during the Intifada [the Palestinian uprising]).
3. Five parents of sons who were killed in accidents during military service.

Major characteristics of the parents are presented in table 1. Most of the parents (eleven of the thirteen) were socially or politically active. Sometimes this activity began before their bereavement, but became more prominent after the tragic event.

Table 1
Main Characteristics of the Parents

Group	*Pseudonym*	*Gender*	*Age range*	*Years after loss*	*Socio-political activism Anger*	*Anger*	*Willingness to forgive*
Battle	Yael	Mother	50-60	5	strong	mild	No need
	Eve	mother	60+	20	strong	strong	definitely not
	Rose*	mother	60+	19	medium	was stronger in the past	no
	Yitzchak*	father	60+	19	medium	was stronger in the past	no
Terror	Abraham	father	50-60	7	strong	medium	definitely not
	Moses	father	50-60	1	strong	strong	definitely not
	Reuben	father	50-60	7	strong	strong	definitely not
	Sharon	mother	40-50	4	strong	strong	definitely not
Acci-dent	Yuval*	father	50-60	5	strong	strong	definitely not
	Betty*	mother	50-60	5	mild	strong	definitely not
	Simon	father	50-60	5	strong	strong	definitely not
	Lea	mother	50-60	5	none	medium	definitely not
	Sarah	mother	60+	3	very mild	mild	no need

* A married couple (parents of the same dead child)

Procedure

Various methods were employed to locate participants for this study. Our initial acquaintance with several of them was the result of their being relatively well known figures who received press coverage. They, in turn, referred us to others (the snowball effect). The parents participated in one or more intensive interviews conducted according to our own guidelines.

The data analysis followed the phenomenological method (Giorgi, 1975; Polkinghorne, 1989; Shkedi, 2003). To improve the authenticity, we first performed each step of analysis separately, and then repeated them as a group (with our research assistant), ultimately reaching consensus. The results represent the integration of this entire process. Furthermore, the findings were presented to a group of professionals and researchers in the bereavement field (at least one was also a bereaved parent), and their reactions are incorporated in the following discussion.

FINDINGS

The 'Parents' anger was a major component of the interviews, spoken as well as lying behind the words. It was accompanied with their pain to constitute a distinct experience of bereavement. Sometimes the parents were unable to make a clear distinction between the anger and the pain; it seemed that the expressions of anger were the parents' way of crying out their pain. Following, we will describe three categories of the experience of participants related to their anger: their "enemy", their views about anger and their no-forgiveness.

The "Enemy"

The anger of the participant was mostly explicit and directed towards an object. Parents sought the figure that they perceived as guilty for their son's death. This defined blameworthy became an object for the parents' rage and their public efforts. Eventually this figure was impersonalised and constituted "an enemy", against whom one must fight for justice.

For example, Eve, whose son fell in Lebanon, has dedicated her life to ongoing reproof of the Defense Minister at that time. Her anger towards him has increased since the tragedy: "He had a wicked and morally unsound plan." She is convinced that "He lied to everyone ... a dangerous man." When she sees him on television, she claimed, she feels exposed to "evil and arrogance" that evoke "not only anger and perhaps hatred but also revulsion."

Typically to our participants, the main guilty figure was not the one who actually killed their sons, but those who carry the responsibility for the creation of the tragic event. Thus Rose expressed no anger against the terrorist who killed her son: "I have no feelings...

[Our son] was a kind of a representative of the IDF [Israel Defense Force]. We see nothing as personal…" Similarly, the parents of soldiers killed during training accidents did not blame the soldier or officer who accidentally caused the death of their sons. Simon said, "I'm not angry at those who were involved in the accident. I am angry because we were deceived."

A more complex situation emerged among the families of terror victims. Perhaps the fact of their sons were murdered by individual, identifiable terrorist aroused anger towards this individual, as well, but nevertheless he or she was not the object of their activity and they, too, sought the responsible party among the Israeli political ranks. It seems that among these parents, the two themes coexist. Sharon, a public activist, said: "my son's murderer is wandering freely … I would be happy to see that terrorist dead. … Any other form of justice misses the mark … punishment is punishment. *The problem is with the Oslo accords, the problem is with us...*" (emphasis added).

During the interviews a great part was devoted to different aspects of the definition of "the enemy," the person truly responsible for the loss. The parents' definitions of the enemy can be divided according to two different motives.

First, an "institutional enemy", revealed in the army's response to the loss: This motive characterized most of the parents of victims of accidents. These parents experienced a secondary blow in their experience of the army's response, which took the form of a whitewash and an attempt to protect those truly responsible, thereby failing to learn lessons, both organizational and personal. Their anger was directed strongly towards the organization that failed to take responsibility and allowed this to happen. The parents found the senior officer that they considered responsible for the error, the concealment, and the cover-up, and were angry with him or her. For instance, Yuval accused the head of the committee that investigated the accident after his son's death: "He is a traitor. Cooperation with the enemy is betrayal. Since most of the deaths in the IDF are in accidents, he cooperated with the enemy!"

Second, a "political enemy" based on an ideological perspective: The parent's definition of a political enemy reflects their views prior to the bereavement. In their opinion, their personal bereavement was caused by the implementation of a flawed policy, which made their son's death possible. Among these parents, the meaning ascribed to the grief-related anger reinforces their political views, whatever they may be. Thus, for instance, for Moses, the blame for his bereavement served to reinforce his opinion: "We are surrounded by enemies, terrorists. Jews need to protect themselves. That night, they didn't protect my son and me. "Period".

The parents who were angry sought justice that should begin with a confession of guilt. The parents sought justice and confession of guilt from those people whom they considered the true enemy, and not those who actually killed their sons. Parents whose anger was political wanted the person responsible for the political failure to take responsibility, admit his or her mistake, and, of course, resign. Similarly, parents who defined an institutional enemy wanted the person truly responsible for the failure to admit the error and bear responsibility. For parents from both these "anger groups," the punishment was removal from their positions, or at least, a criminal justice process. For example, Yuval said: "I don't think that in a normative society you can cause someone's death and go on with no trial. You may get 'no guilty', but justice must be." As long as those responsible for the failure fulfill public, political, or military positions, the parents will feel that justice has not been done and will seek it. There were parents who expressed the justice they sought extremely harshly, almost disregarding the humanity of those responsible.

The Anger

Parents who remained ardent activists for years after their children's death indicated that their anger and inability to forgive do not necessarily reflect their personal opinions but rather the perceived wishes of their departed loved ones. For their son's sake, there can be no option for forgiveness. It would constitute a denial of responsibility towards him, as Yuval noted: "When you have children, some kind of parent-child compact is forged... I owe him this protection because someone ended his life unnecessarily..."

Some parents apparently channel their energies into anger and initiative instead of pain. According to Eve, "anger gives us a lot of strength. Anger is not a destructive element. It boosts adrenalin, like fuel. It provides motivation. You know what to do with it, while you don't know what to do with pain." It seemed that the participants minimized the introspection necessary for processing loss and directed their feelings towards public activity and expressions of anger towards personalities and institutions – thus ignoring a necessary step for completing the first track of mourning.

In some cases, the parents' anger seemed to increase every time they were exposed to deaths in similar circumstances to those of their sons. Our impression was that out of their pain and anger they identified with any new loss that happened in similar circumstances. The "accumulation" of losses naturally increased their sense of injustice and therefore their furious reaction. "Every time soldiers were killed in Lebanon, there was wild anger," Yael recalled. It can be said that among the parents there was a steady re-victimization experience, sometimes being interpreted as the responsibility of the same 'enemy' who had led to their own sons' death. The parents continued to demand public proof of the responsibility of this "guilty party" for a chain of failures and disasters. A generalization of this activity may turn parents into social initiators. The willingness to fulfill this unofficial role was explained by Moses, whose son was murdered in a terror attack: "I made a decision after the incident: I would not limit my work to benefiting my own home. I would act on behalf of the public, in any field."

No-forgiveness

The most prominent and unequivocal finding of the present research is that the forgiveness option does not exist for most parents interviewed, although their anger can be moderated somewhat. Most parents refused any attempt to raise the forgiveness option, as they were threatened even by discussing it. Rose, for example, after 20 years of bereavement, said: "Forgiveness? No way. No, definitely not!" Abraham admitted, "Forget forgiveness… I, as left wing as you can find, perhaps at the furthest left-wing extreme within Zionism … I tell you there is no forgiveness… If I have the opportunity to see the two who succeeded in killing my son, I imagine I will want to kill them." Interestingly, Abraham didn't describe his son's killer as his true enemy, but even for them there was no forgiveness.

There were cases when parents presented pretentious willingness for forgiveness, but immediately outlined impossible conditions for it, for example, that the Prime Minister will resign and will voluntary go to court (Eve).

For other parents, it was possible to discern the beginnings of a tendency toward forgiveness, out of weariness. It was de facto forgiveness, evolving in the course of time, after years of intensive activity. The anger that accompanied the activity fanned the fire of the pain, and sometimes, time worked to soften the anger by coping with the pain. Although the research participants did not testify to this directly, Yael told us indirectly: "The softening is a forgiveness we don't admit, but it is, undoubtedly, forgiveness."

However, Eve showed an opening for forgiveness from an unexpected direction. She told us that after her son's death in battle, she wrote a letter to the military and political leadership of the time. One of the army commanders immediately met her and spoke about her son, whom he knew personally. The personal, intimate meeting with a man who had totally different political views to hers, and who had been defined as belonging to the "enemy" camp, broke the ice. After that, she could no longer see him as the enemy, and she defined their relationship as friendly, even though he continued to adhere to his views, which differed from hers. The exceptional nature of this story lies in the intimacy that was created; this is what served as the basis for forgiveness and even reconciliation.

CONCLUSION

Why our participants refused even to discuss the forgiveness option? What can we learn from this special population that can contribute to our understanding of victimological processes?

First, there was a perception of the parents that their anger serves their public activity, and therefore forgiveness, even potential, can endanger this activity. These parents, when channelled their private victimization into public activity, became missionaries. Their public activity is their main mission in life, perceived to be greater than their private needs. The more the parents perceive their personal bereavement through public eyes, the more aware they are of the circumstances surrounding their tragedy in its broader contexts, the more familiar they become with the organizational and political culture in which they experienced their tragedy, the more their personal pain is translated into public rage. Since their mission hadn't fulfilled its goals – their enemy is not yet punished and the system is not yet transformed to prevent further victimization – they could not risk it by forgiveness.

Second, the parents created an impersonal enemy with whom it is impossible to reconcile or even to forgive. This impersonal enemy, usually located far away from the parents' everyday lives, is mostly unaware to the projection of guilt by the parents, or denies any responsibility to the event. Moreover, in the parents' public mission, the enemy plays the role of the impersonalized bad person. Forgiveness, which is personal, would then cut off this figure from the "good – bad" impersonal illustration. Therefore there are no conditions for forgiveness.

Third, the parents' activity is a Sisyphean mission that demands an investment of significant personal resources. Forgiveness, on the other hand, is perceived as demanding also an investment of personal resources, but in an opposite direction. It becomes an 'either-or' choice, and the parents choose their more urgent mission.

Obviously, the parents suffered from their victimization. Their individual recovery was sacrificed, consciously or unconsciously, for their public mission. In a way, the parent's mission was directed at a national recovery from the evil that causes their own victimization, and personal recovery wasn't a requirement for them. Although the literature review suggests the benefits of forgiveness (e.g., Kaminer, Stein, Mbanga, & Zungu-Dirwayi, 2001), yet the parents refused to participate in this process, but found a whole meaning in their struggle against their enemy as part of their quest for national recovery.

In a broader consideration, we can anticipate that when victims find meaning in their activity, a meaning connected to their victimization in the form of a mission for life, they will continue with this activity regardless of its personal cost. In addition, when the initial track of the victimization process (Rubin, 1992) provides a meaningful experience for recovering victims, and simultaneously the further tracks may risk this meaning, the victims may prevent any transformation of themselves. One may hypnotise that other forms of politically loaded victimization, *e.g.* women's abuse, attract victims who may become opinion leaders to sacrifice their individual effort for recovery for the sake of societal recovery. While from the outward one may question these victims' recovery, their own experience may question the need for further individual recovery efforts. In other words, experiential knowledge of victims may discover soothing meaning in conditions and activities which usually are considered as disturbing. Our victimized parents, for example, perceived no acute need for further personal recovery, but found a soothing meaning in their effort for a "national recovery". However, these generalized assumptions call for further explorations.

Still in a broader consideration, the experience of our participants indicates the importance of personalization in any restorative process. According to the literature, forgiveness is related to a person and not an act (Haber, 1991). In order for it to occur, the figure defined as the "enemy" should become a human figure – a person – and not remain in the one-dimensional representation of an enemy. For this purpose, there must be a human encounter, like that experienced by just one of the research participants. In a political or institutionalized offending and victimization, such as the current study, remote figures who play an indirect role could assist the restorative process by becoming closer to the event and personalized to the people directly involved, especially the victims. At least in Israel, considering the military bereavement topic, this implication is applicable and can be implanted in the local policy. We can assume that it can be achieved in other victimizing circumstances as well.

REFERENCES

Andrews, M. (1999), Truth Telling, Justice, & Forgiveness: A study of East Germany's "Truth Commission." *International Journal of Politics, Culture and Society, 13* (1), 107-124.

Ben-David, S. (2000), Needed: Victim's Victimology. In P. C. Friday and G. F. Kirchhoff (eds), *Victimology at the transition from the 20th to the 21th century (pp. 55-72)*. Monchengladbach: Shaker Verlag & WSVP.

Berecz, J. M. (2001), All that Glitters is not Gold: Bad Forgiveness in Counselling and Preaching. *Pastoral Psychology, 49* (4), 253-275.

Bryman, A. (1988), *Quantity and Quality in Social Research (Chap. 2)*. London: Unwin Hyman.

Doron, G., and Lebel, U. (2006), Postmortem Politics: Competitive Models of Bereavement and Civil-military Bargaining over Military Secrecy. *Journal of Modern Jewish Studies, 5* (2), 163-181.

Enright, R.D., and The Human Development Study Group (1991), The Moral Development of Forgiveness. In W. M. Kurtines and J. L. Gewirtz (Eds.),

Handbook of Moral Behavior and Development (Vol. 1, pp. 123-152). Hillsdale, NJ: Lawrence Erlbaum Associates.

Enright, R.D., and The Human Development Study Group (1994), Piaget on the Moral Development of Forgiveness: Identity or Reciprocity? *Human Development, 37* (2), 63-80.

Faschingbauer, T.R., Zisook, S., and Devaul, R. (1987). The Texas Revised Inventory of Grief. In S. Zisook (Ed.), *Biopsychological aspects of Bereavement (pp. 11-124).* Washington DC: American Psychiatric Press.

Flanigan, B. (1992), *Forgiving the Unforgivable.* NY: Macmillan.

Fow, N.R. (1996), The Phenomenology of Forgiveness and Reconciliation. *Journal of Phenomenological Psychology, 27*(2), 219-233.

Freedman, S.R., and Enright, R.D. (1996). Forgiveness as an intervention goal with incest survivors. *Journal of Consulting and Clinical Psychology, 64* (5), 983-992.

Ginzburg, K., Giron, Y., and Solomon, Z. (2002), Grief Response Patterns Among Bereaved Parents. *Megamot, 41* (4), 566-583 (in Hebrew).

Giorgi, A. (1975), Convergence and Divergence of Qualitative and Quantitative Methods in Psychology. In A. Giorgi, C. Fischer and E. Murray (Eds.), *Phenomenological Psychology (Vol. II, pp. 72--79).* Pittsburgh: Duqesne University Press.

Haber, J. G. (1991), *Forgiveness.* Savage, MD: Rowman & Littlefield.

Kaminer, D., Stein, D. J., Mbanga, I., and Zungu-Dirwayi, N. (2000). Forgiveness: Towards an Integration of Theoretical Models. *Psychiatry, 63* (4), 344-357.

Kaminer, D., Stein, D.J., Mbanga, I., and Zungu-Dirwayi, N. (2001), The Truth and Reconciliation Commission in South-Africa: Relation to Psychiatric Status and Forgiveness Among Survivors of Human Rights Abuse. *British Journal of Psychiatry, 178,* 373-377.

Kubler-Ross, E. (1979), *On Death and Dying.* NY: Macmillan.

Lebel, U. (2006), *Politics of Memory.* London: Routledge.

Lebel, U. & Ronel, N, (2005), Parental Discourse and Activism as a Response to Bereavement of fallen sons and Civilian Terrorist Victims. *Journal of Loss and Trauma, 10* (4), 383 – 405.

Lifton, R.J. (1979), *The Broken Connection: On death and continuity life.* New York: Simon & Schuster.

Malkinson, R., and Bar-Tur, L. (2000), The aging of Grief: Parental grief of Israeli soldiers. *Journal of Personal and Interpersonal Loss, 2-3,* 247-261.

Maltby, J., Macaskill, A., and Day, L. (2001), Failure to forgive self and others: A replication and extension of the relationship between forgiveness, personality, social desirability and general health. *Personality and Individual Differences, 30,* 881-885.

McCullough, M.E. (2000), Forgiveness as Human Strength: Theory, measurement, and links to well being. *Journal of Social and Clinical Psychology, 19* (1), 43-55.

McCullough, M.E., and Worthington, E.L. (1999), Religion and the Forgiving Personality. *Journal of Personality, 67* (6), 1141-1164.

Middelton, W., Raphael, B.; Martinek, N., and Nisso, V. (1993), Pathological Grief Relations. In M.S. Stroebe, W. Stroebe and R.O. Hanson (Eds.), *Handbook of Bereavement: Theory, Research, and Intervention (pp. 44-61)*. New York: Cambridge University Press.

Parkes, C.M., and Weiss, R. (1983), *Recovery from Bereavement*. NY: Basic Books.

Polkinghorne, D.E. (1989), Phenomenological Research Methods. In R.S. Valle and S. Halling (Eds.), *Existential-phenomenological Perspectives in Psychology (pp. 41–60)*. New York: Plenum Press.

Ronel, N. (2007), Grace Therapy for recovering victims: A restorative 12-step based therapy. In M. S. Sundaram, P. K. Jaishankar and S. Ramdoss (Eds.), *Crime Victims and Justice: An Introduction to Restorative Principles*. New Delhi: Serial Publications.

Ronel, N, and Lebel, U. (2006), When Parents lay their Children to rest. *Journal of Social and Personal Relationships, 23*(3), 445-460.

Rowe, J.O., and Halling, S. (1998). Psychology of Forgiveness. In R. Valle (ed.), *Phenomenological Inquiry in Psychology (pp. 227-246)*. New York: Plenum.

Rubin, S. (1981), A two-track Model of Bereavement: Theory and application in research. *American Journal of Orthopsychiatry, 51* (1), 101-109.

Rubin, S. (1992), Adult child loss and the two-track Model of Bereavement: Outcome to loss among Israeli Parents. *Omega, 24* (3), 183-203.

Rubin, S. (1993), Loss and Bereavement: Landmarks in Theory, Research, and Therapy. In R. Malkinson, S. Rubin, and A. Witstom (Eds.), *Loss and bereavement in Israeli society (pp. 21-38)*. Jerusalem: Kaneh - Ministry of Defense (in Hebrew).

Scobie, E.D., and Scobie, G.E.W. (1998). Damaging Events: The Perceived need for Forgiveness. *Journal for the Theory of Social Behavior, 28* (4), 373-401.

Sells, J., Dan Hargrave, T. (1998), Forgiveness: A review of the Theoretical and Empirical Literature. *Journal of Family Therapy, 20* (1), 21-36.

Shkedi, A. (2003), *Words of Meaning*. Tel Aviv: Ramot (in Hebrew)

Spiegelberg, H. (1976). *The Phenomenological Movement (Vol. II, chap. XIV)*. The Hague: Martinus Nijhoff.

Spinelli, E. (1989), *An Introduction to Phenomenological Psychology*. London: Sage.

Van Manen, M. (1997), From Meaning to Method. *Qualitative Health Research, 7* (3), 345-369.

Wheeler, I. (2001), Parental Bereavement: The Crisis of Meaning. *Death Studies, 25* (1), 51-66.

Worthington, E.L., Jr. and Wade, M.G. (1999). The Psychology of Unforgiveness and Forgiveness and Implications for Clinical Practice. *Journal of Social and Clinical Psychology, 18* (4), 385-418.

Part - II

STRIDE TOWARDS VICTIM JUSTICE SYSTEM

S. MAHESHWARI AND BHAVYA SRIRAM

7

VICTIM-OFFENDER MEDIATION AND CRIMINAL JUSTICE

INTRODUCTION

India's criminal justice system may be said to be a combination of several models of justice, like the preventive, deterrent, and reformative models. However, it still focused on punishing the offender for his/her wrongdoing, and in that sense, our system is largely retributive in nature.[1] *Retributive Justice* is a theory of *Criminal Justice* wherein *Punishments* are justified because the criminal has created an imbalance in the social order that must be addressed by action against the criminal.[2] As per this model, once an offender has paid his debt to society, justice is considered to have been done. However, the question we need to ask here is, justice for whom? The victim or the State? Because of the single-minded, focus of the State on the offender, disregarding the need for victim participation, the criminal justice system, as a means of formal social control represents the take over of the State to the exclusion of the victim. In fact, victims of crime feel increasingly frustrated and alienated by our current system of justice.

Even though the justice system exists precisely because individual citizens' rights have been violated by criminal behavior, crime victims have virtually no legal standing in the process of doing justice in the courts. The crime is against "the state" and state interests drive the process of doing justice. Individual crime victims are left on the sidelines of justice, with little or no input.[3] Since our society defines justice in this manner, the victims of crimes sometimes seek the most severe possible punishment for their offenders. They believe this will bring justice, but it often leaves them feeling empty and unsatisfied after getting what they sought. This is because other important needs of victims are not addressed by punishing the offender. That is, it cannot restore their losses, answer their questions, relieve their fears, or heal their wounds.[4] The only way such things may be achieved is if there is a shift from the prevalent retributive model to a restorative model.

Restorative justice emphasizes the importance of elevating the role of crime victims and community members, holding offenders directly accountable to the people they violate, restoring the emotional and material losses of victims, and providing a range of opportunities for dialogue, negotiation, and problem solving, whenever possible, which can lead to a greater sense of community safety, conflict resolution, and closure for all involved. In essence, restorative justice represents a very different way of responding to crime through more active involvement of crime victims and the community.[5]

VICTIM-OFFENDER MEDIATION

Victim-offender mediation[6] (VOM), with its focus on *Restorative Justice*, is one way in which this paradigm shift may be incorporated into our present system. A proper introduction to VOM is necessary for a better understanding of how to move towards restorative justice for the victims.

VOM involves a face-to-face meeting, in the presence of a trained mediator, between the victim of a crime and the person who committed that crime. The practice is also called victim-offender dialogue, victim-offender conferencing, victim-offender reconciliation, or restorative justice dialogue. In some practices, the victim and the offender are joined by family and community members or others. In the meeting, the offender and the victim can talk to each other about what happened, the effects of the crime on their lives, and their feelings about it. They may choose to create a mutually agreeable plan to repair any damages that occurred because of the crime.[7]

Through VOM, victims might finally receive answers to any questions, which had been bothering them, and have a chance to find peace of mind from the justice they may get out of the process. They take an active role in getting their material and emotional needs met.

Research indicates that victims who participate in VOM receive more restitution than those who do not and feel safer and less fearful afterwards than those who do not.[8]

On the other hand, VOM also requires the offenders to take responsibility for their actions by mediating a restitution agreement with the victim, to restore the victims' losses, in whatever ways that may be possible, depending on that particular situation. They learn the impact of their actions on others, and take an active role in righting their wrongs. The agreement may result in monetary or symbolic compensation, i.e., it may consist of work for the victim, community service, or anything else that creates a sense of justice between the victim and the offender. This mediation process personalizes the crime making the offender completely aware of not only the consequences of his action but also what needs to be done to compensate the victim as may be necessary.

The goal of VOM is to hold offenders directly accountable and to impress on them the full impact of what they did while providing important support and assistance to victims. The idea of bringing together a victim of a crime and the person who committed that crime is based on age-old values of justice, accountability, and restoration.[9] VOM is primarily *"dialogue-driven"*, with emphasis upon victim empowerment, offender accountability, and restoration of losses. This dialogue addresses emotional and informational needs of victims that are central to both the empowerment of the victims and the development of victim empathy in the offenders.[10]

The reasons for adopting VOM can be found in the deficiencies of the retributive model. To elaborate, the retributive model rests on high rates of conviction, which only serves to burden the State with rising prison population[11] and high costs of incarceration. Further, the model's belief in punishment has not resulted in any significant deterrence. On the other hand, VOM has led to reduce fear among victims and reduced criminal behaviour.[12]

Mediation is being used in an increasing number of conflict situations, such as divorce and child custody cases, community disputes, commercial disputes, and other civil court-related conflicts. These forms of mediation may be differentiated from VOM on several points. Firstly, in the aforementioned settings, the parties are called "disputants", and the assumption is that both are contributing to the conflict and, therefore, need to compromise to reach a settlement. Often, mediation in these cases focuses heavily upon reaching a settlement, with less emphasis upon discussing the full impact of the conflict on the disputants' lives. In victim-offender mediation, the involved parties are not "disputants". Generally, one party has clearly committed a criminal offense and has admitted doing so, whereas the other has clearly been victimized.[13] Therefore, there is no need to mediate on the issue of guilt or innocence. This leads us to the second difference, which is that, there is no expectation that crime victims compromise or request less than what they need to manage their losses. Thirdly, VOM, unlike other forms of mediation, is not *settlement driven* and emphasises on *dialogue*. Lastly, the mediator's role is distinct from arbitration; the responsibility falls on the victim and offender to arrive at a solution acceptable to both. The process and the solution are thus both crucial.[14]

An essential issue to be addressed in the implementation of VOM is whether it can be used for all crimes and if not which crimes can it be used for? In response, victim-offender mediation is clearly not appropriate for all crime victims, and consequently, a majority of cases handled by VOM are property offences and minor assaults. VOM may be useful at any stage of the criminal justice process. For young offenders and first or second time offenders, mediation may provide diversion from prosecution. In these cases, charges may be dismissed if the offender mediates an agreement with the victim and complies with its terms. But as a general rule, VOM is used prior to sentencing, where a successful outcome can subsequently be used to justify leniency in sentencing. Cases are also referred to VOM after a formal admission of guilt has been accepted by the court, or after conviction, with the mediation being a part of the sentence or a term of probation, if the victim is interested.[15] VOM is thus commonly not an *alternative* to more conventional sentences, but a *supplement* that allows greater participation, and potentiai for reduced sentences.

More violent cases are also sometimes referred to VOM, although this is not commonplace. In a growing number of victim-offender programs, victims and survivors of severely violent crimes, including murder and sexual assault, find that confronting their offender in a safe and controlled setting, with the assistance of a mediator, returns their stolen sense of safety and control in their lives.[16]

Restorative justice is almost non-existent in Indian criminal jurisprudence, not to mention VOM. The progress made in the sphere of victimology is yet to pervade criminal justice practices in India. The main reason is perhaps that the procedural law here does not provide much scope for these practices. The victim is still restricted to the role of witness. The criminal justice system, as a means of formal social control, is still steeped in the retributive model, and centres on the State. This is the *"vertical dimension model"* of the criminal justice system,[17] which persists in India, based on an outdated colonial model. The restorative justice paradigm however, advocates replacement of the vertical criminal justice system with a *"horizontal line of justice"* where the punishment system is sought to be substituted by a mediation system, which gives a central role to the victim.[18]

A progressive step has been taken in the *Malimath Committee Report* (2003), which strongly advocates the rights of the victim. It mentions the need to formulate a witness protection programme, re-classify offences, and involve the victim in all stages of the trial. Another notable issue addressed by the Report is compensation to victims. However, the Report does not empower the victim outside of the retributive system.

The Report remains silent on issues such as restorative justice and VOM. The Committee has also recommended that the offence of cruelty under Section 498A of the Indian Penal Code, 1860 be made compoundable and bailable in order to facilitate mediation between the spouses. However, the Committee's insistence on reconciliation raises concern in those who are keen on restorative justice. A large percentage of women who approach the state or even non-governmental organizations for help are sent back into continuing violent situations following a process of *"mediation"* between husband and wife in which the woman is at a severe disadvantage because of the patriarchal nature of the process. These women who approach the judiciary may in these instances feel that the system has failed them. The Committee's recommendation would not only condone but also encourage such solutions. Thus, the one prescription for mediation made by the Report seems a completely imprudent choice.

There is undoubtedly a need to have new laws and institutions for the incorporation of restorative justice. However, a beginning has been made under the existing provisions of the Code of Criminal Procedure, 1973. For instance, the compounding of offences under Section 320 of the Code has been allowed for in an effort to incorporate restorative justice in the prevailing system.[19] Under this provision, the victim may opt to compound the case, thus providing an opportunity for the victim to affect a compromise or to mediate with the accused. This ostensibly brings the victim to the forefront. Though it is required that the Court be satisfied with the terms of the proposed compromise or mediation, there is no guarantee that this will in fact be effectuated. That is to say, the compounding of offences need not necessarily result in mediation at all, and the victim may be left bereft of a remedy, particularly because the victim and the offender are often not placed on an equal footing, coercion, and corruption being rampant. This renders the entire exercise a mere means to dispose off cases in the name of restorative justice, the result of composition being acquittal.

There is only one basic difference between the compounding of offences and VOM, compounding results in an acquittal, while VOM, being a supplement to the sentence, does not absolve the offender of his liability to the State. In the event of the compromise remaining unfulfilled, subsequent criminal proceedings are precluded by virtue of Article 20(2) of the Constitution of India,[20] thereby defeating the entire objective of restorative justice. In VOM, on the other hand, even non-observance of the restitution agreement by the offender will not leave the crime unaddressed, as the offender will still be liable to the State, and punishment will still be exacted.

With regard to victim compensation, Section 357 of the Code of Criminal Procedure provides for compensation that may be awarded irrespective of whether the offence is punishable with fine and whether the fine is actually imposed.[21] This payment by the offender to the victim as a consequence of the court's order may be viewed as a form of restitution. However, S. 357 is invoked sparingly and inconsistently by the courts,[22] due to a variety of reasons such as lack of awareness and indifference on the part of the judiciary.[23] Further, the implementation of this provision is dependent entirely about the court to that effect.[24] As a solution to this, guidelines may be given to the judges to give primacy to victim compensation at the time of sentencing.

This provision merely seeks to appease the victim by providing monetary relief, while continuing to exclude the victim from playing any significant role. Therefore, the redressal of individuated grievances does not feature to the same extent as in VOM. However, as far as some sort of restitution is provided to the victims, this provision pays attention, although in a very pecuniary manner, to the victim, and is still a step towards a restorative paradigm.

VOM is not a viable panacea for all offences. Before adopting VOM into the present system, a classification of offences to which it will be applicable is imperative. As it has already been established that the only flaw in the current provision for compounding under the Code of Criminal Procedure lies not in its substantive, but its procedural aspect, VOM may be applied to the same set of offences set out in section 320. However, it is recommended that while referring cases for VOM, the Court should exercise its discretion in determining whether the existence of power relations between the victim and the offender would adversely influence effective meditation.

Keeping in mind the shortfalls of the existing provisions in furtherance of restorative justice, a new provision may be introduced into the Cr. P.C. to fill in the lacunae. It is proposed that the provision may be as follows:

> *"Upon the request of the victim, and the consent of the offender, the Court shall refer the case for VOM in offences to which Section 320 applies, provided that the Court is satisfied that the power relations in such case do not preclude the possibility of an effective mediation. Such reference shall be made only after the guilt of the accused has been either proven or admitted. Further, such mediation shall be taken into consideration by the Court as a mitigating factor while imposing sentence."*

Such a provision would serve to incorporate VOM as a specific method of restorative justice within the framework of the current system, as a paradigm shift to a completely restorative system is neither possible nor desirable. Techniques like restorative justice and VOM carry great promise for India. Indian heritage testifies to the fact that the socio-cultural fabric contains intrinsic mechanisms to bring conflicting parties together and help them settle their disputes in an informal manner. In fact, the caste panchayats and other social groups in the rural areas have been effective in dispensing justice.[25] The interests of the victims have been paramount, and the offenders have often been directed to compensate or restore the harm done to the victims. The effect and impact of social expectations and social sanctions on the behaviour of the people have always been decisive. It is highly desirable that this mechanism adopted by the panchayats should be extended to the criminal justice system.

In light of the existing system and its inherent deficiencies with regard to victim participation, the situation calls for a shift from the *"vertical criminal justice system"* towards a *"horizontal line of justice"*,[26] where the punishment system is to be supplemented by a mediation system, empowering the victim within the retributive paradigm. The goal envisaged by the restorative paradigm may be achieved by inducting VOM into the existent model, thus furthering the interests of society without prejudicing the needs of the victim.

CONCLUSION

In conclusion, restorative justice attempts to draw upon the strengths of both, the offenders and the victims, rather than focusing upon their weaknesses. While denouncing criminal behaviour, restorative justice emphasizes the need to treat offenders with respect and to reintegrate them into the larger community in ways that can lead to lawful behaviour. Thus, it is the empowerment of affected stakeholders on both sides that is the crucial feature of restorative justice, the absence of which causes both conventional and retributive justice systems to fail. Restorative justice also facilitates faster re-integration into society of the former offender taking us in the direction of a kinder and gentler Nation.

NOTES

1. As per Mark Umbreit's characterisation of retributive and restorative justice, retributive justice focuses on punishment, whereas the restorative paradigm emphasizes accountability, Infra (n) 4. It is in this sense that the term "retributive system" has been used in this paper.
2. The theory is often associated with harsh punishment, and the phrase an eye for an eye, a tooth for a tooth' is often used as a justification for this theory. However, proponents of the theory point out that the retribution should be proportional to the crime, and that minor crimes should have mild punishments while major crimes should have harsh punishment. The theory is sometimes justified by the belief that

punishment is expected to act as a deterrent. http://en.wikipedia.org/wiki/Retributive_justice.

3. Umbreit, Mark S. 1998. "Restorative Justice Through Victim-Offender Mediation: A Multi-Site Assessment. Western Criminology Review 1(1). [Online] Available: http://wcr.sonoma.edu/v1n1/umbreit.html, last visited on 1-11-2004.
4. Marty Price, J.D, Crime and Punishment: Can Mediation Produce Restorative Justice for Victims and Offenders?, http://www.vorp.com/articles/crime.html, last visited on 1-11-2004.
5. Supra (n) 3.
6. Also known as Victim-Offender Reconciliation Programs (VORP).
7. http://www.voma.org/abtvom.shtml, last visited on 1-11-2004.
8. Ibid.
9. The principles of restorative justice are consistent with those of many indigenous traditions, including Indian, Native American, Hawaiian, Canadian First Nation people, Aborigines in Australia, and the Maori in New Zealand. These principles are also consistent with values emphasized by nearly all of the world religions, Umbreit, Mark S., Restorative Justice Through Victim-Offender Mediation: A Multi-Site Assessment; http://wcr.sonoma.edu/v1n1/umbreit.html, last visited on 1-11-2004.
10. Dr. Mark S. Umbreit, a leading authority in this field, refers to this "dialogue-driven" mediation as Humanistic Mediation. It is a nondirective style of mediation in which the parties primarily speak to each other with minimal intervention by the mediator. The mediator maintains an attitude of unconditional positive regard and concern for all parties while remaining neutral; Umbreit, Mark S., Creating a Safe, if not Sacred, Place for Dialogue; http://www.ojp.usdoj.gov/ovc/publications/infores/restorative_justice/bulletin1/rjmc_2.html#when.
11. In its Inaugural Annual Report (1993-94), the National Human Rights Commission has expressed its alarm at the appalling condition of prisons across the country, including overcrowding, lack of sanitation and poor medical facilities.
12. Before mediation, victims feared re-victimization in 25% of the cases; afterward only 10%; http://www.ojp.usdoj.gov/ovc/publications/infores/restorative_justice/bulletin1/rjmc_2.html#when, last visited on 1-11-2004.
13. http://www.ojp.usdoj.gov/ovc/publications/infores/restorative_justice/bulletin1/rjmc_2.html#when, last visited on 1-11-2004.
14. Mawby, R.I. (et al), Crime Victims, (1987), Tavistock Publications, London, p.54.
15. Where a defendant maintains a not guilty plea in contemplation of a genuine defense - self-defense, diminished capacity, etc. - there is no

place for mediation until such issues are resolved. Where a defendant maintains a pro forma not guilty plea only to preserve the possibility for plea negotiations, a restorative justice process may be appropriate. Price, Marty, J.D., Personalizing Crime: Mediation Produces Restorative Justice for Victims and Offenders, http://www.vorp.com/articles/justice.html, last visited on 1-11-2004.

16. Ibid.
17. Muralidhar, S., Rights of Victims in the Indian Criminal Justice System, Forthcoming in National Human Rights Commission Journal, 2004, p.88.
18. Ibid.
19. Under Section 320, the offences under the IPC that may be compounded have been listed along with the persons by whom they may be so compounded. The Section makes a distinction between offences for the composition of which the permission of the Court is to be sought [Section 320(2)] and those for which such permission is not necessary [Section 320(1)].
20. Article 20(2) of the Constitution of India provides as follows: "No person shall be punished for the same offence more than once."
21. Under Section 357(1) when the Court imposes a sentence of fine or one of which fine forms a part, the Court may order that the whole or any part of it may be paid as compensation to the victims in certain circumstances. In addition, sub-section (3) of Section 357 provides that the Court may order the payment of such compensation even in the imposition of a sentence of which fine does not form a part.
22. In 1960-61, out of 182 cases of violence tried in Pune, compensation was awarded to the aggrieved party only in 13 cases. A study conducted in 1980 found that no compensation was given to victims of dacoit gangs, but limited ex gratia assistance was provided in about 15 percent of the cases; Singh, D.R., Victimological Studies in India, Paper Submitted for the 11th International Symposium on Victimology, 2003, South Africa.
23. Chockalingam, Kumaravelu, Evaluation of the Implementation of the Victims Assistance Fund in Tamil Nadu, http://www.aqpv.ca/diffusion/abstracts/abc_a/chockalingam_nk.html, last visited on 1-11-2004. The Government of Tamil Nadu created a Victims Assistance Fund in 1995 under which for the first time in India, State Government has allocated ten million rupees to provide relief to three categories of victims of violent crimes viz., dependents of murder victims, victims of rape and grievous injury.

24. In Hari Singh V. Sukhvir Singh (1998) 4 SCC 551, the SC had to exhort the criminal courts to use this provision since "this power was intended to do something to reassure the victim that he or she is not forgotten in the criminal justice system." p. 558, para 10.
25. Bajpai, G S, Conflict Management Through Restorative Justice, Indian Police Journal, 2001. http://forensic.to/webhome/drgsbajpai/Restorative%20art.doc , last visited on 21st October 2004.
26. Although the terminology used by S. Muralidhar has been borrowed, our suggestion is in contrast to his views in so far as he suggests the replacement of the vertical system by the horizontal system; Muralidhar, S., Rights of Victims in the Indian Criminal Justice System, National Human Rights Commission Journal, 2004, p. 88.

A. Ramesh and Anirudh Krishnan

8

COMPENSATION FOR VICTIMS- THE NEED OF THE HOUR

INTRODUCTION

Black's law dictionary defines 'criminal law' as follows "The substantive criminal law is that law which for the purpose of preventing harm to society, a) declares what conduct is criminal, and b) prescribes the punishment to be imposed for such conduct."[1] The criminal justice system refers to 'the network of courts and tribunals which deal with criminal law and its enforcement'[2].

A successful criminal justice system is one, which enforces the criminal laws of a country effectively. It is harsh reality that the criminal justice system in India may not have achieved its ends. Delay in prosecution, witnesses' repeatedly turning hostile, unimaginably low percentage of convictions etc is eloquent testimony to the above fact. The major criminal law in India, *i.e.* the Indian Penal Code has been hailed to be well drafted Statutes. The Criminal Procedure Code and the Evidence Act are also equally well drafted. Why, then has the enforcement of criminal law proved to be ineffective? Has the shift in criminal jurisprudence from the theory of retaliation, i.e. "A tooth for a tooth" and an "eye for an eye", to the deterrence theory, which revolves around using punishment as a means of deterring offenders, proved ineffective due to the fact that the reparative and restorative theories, which dwell on the well-being of the victims, have been pushed to the background?

Further, a successful criminal justice system, from a common person's point of view refers to an expeditious disposal of criminal cases coupled with an adequate punishment for offenders. On the contrary, in this part of the globe the conviction rate is very low and the delay is prevalent to such an extent, that the phrase "justice delayed is justice denied" has become very common. The question is whether the system is being implemented properly. Is the defect due to the inept working of the executive or does the fault lies with the judiciary? Alternatively, is it the legislature, which has faulted?

This article discusses a suitable answer for the above question, placing the onus on the issue of compensation to be given to victims of crime, being treated with scant disregard by the Indian Legislature and Courts. All these years, the victim of a crime has been a neglected man. Giving the victim of crime his due would make the system work fruitfully. The first part of this article looks into the need for compensation for victims.

IMPORTANCE OF COMPENSATION FOR VICTIMS

What has to be kept in mind is that for the criminal justice system to achieve its objectives, i.e. safeguarding society, not only must the cases in Court be decided justly, but also every victim must bring the case before the Court. By considering a crime to be a crime against society, the interests of the victim must not be forgotten and subordinated to that of the State, else victims may develop a tendency to take law into their own hands to seek revenge and it may be a case of 'popular justice' taking over from 'formal justice'[3].

The above would lead to a state of anarchy and a rule of law would be impossible. Further, the current criminal justice system offers no incentive to the victim to file a complaint. Conviction of the accused, which itself seldom happens, is rarely accompanied by an award of compensation to the victim. This means that when the offender is punished, the victim receives no benefit whatsoever except for the fact that he/she gets the satisfaction of having got the wrongdoer punished.

Conversely, in the case of an acquittal, there is mortification for the victim and witnesses. The humiliating questions asked during the cross examination, prevent victims from knocking on the portals of justice. This is more so in cases of rape. The Supreme

Court has recognized this fact. As observed in *State of Punjab v. Gurmit Singh*[4]

> *"There has been lately, a lot of criticism of the treatment of the victims of sexual assault in the court during their cross-examination. The provisions of Evidence Act regarding relevancy of facts notwithstanding, some defence counsels adopt the strategy of continual questioning of the prosecutrix as to the details of the rape. The victim is required to repeat again and again the details of the rape incident not so much as to bring out the facts on record or to test her credibility but to test her story for inconsistencies with a view to attempt to twist the interpretation of events given by her so as to make them appear inconsistent with her allegations. "*

The infamous *Tukaram case*[5], widely criticized by many legal stalwarts like Dr. Upendra Bakshi, involved an acquittal of a police officer accused of raping a young married girl. In this case, the Court also impugned a sexually promiscuous nature to her.

Because of such instances, access to justice has been impeded. Providing compensation to victims will prove as an incentive for them to approach courts. This should be done even if the accused is acquitted. This can be done by a statutory board outside the purview of courts as well, as is done in many foreign countries (this has been dealt with later on).

Another effect of the victims not being compensated for their loss is that compensation does flow from the accused to the victim, but unofficially, in exchange of the victims and other witnesses turning hostile. This has resulted in a disproportionate number of acquittals leading to the suppression of justice. When this happens one wonders whether the criminal justice system is indeed meeting its ends.

It can always be argued that the victim can claim damages in civil courts and under remedies for torts, but this argument *prima facie* fails due to the inaccessibility of the courts to the common person, which is a result of the expenses and delay in courts.

In the light of the above-mentioned reasons, a conclusion can be reached that compensating victims for their losses is of paramount importance to the successful functioning of the criminal justice system. It is also a fact that the same has not been implemented satisfactorily in India. What has to be considered at this stage is whether the fault lies with the Legislature or the Judiciary. The statutory provisions have been explained below.

PROVISIONS FOR COMPENSATION UNDER THE CRIMINAL PROCEDURE CODE

Sec. 357 of the Criminal Procedure Code, 1973 deals with compensation for victims. This provision is *in pari materia* with sec. 545 of the Criminal Procedure Code, 1860. While Sec. 357(1) and Sec. 357 (2) deal with cases where the court imposes a sentence, which includes a fine, sec. 357(3) extends to cases where fine does mot form a part of the sentence.

Sec. 357 (1) (a) and (b) deal with the award of compensation in defraying the expenses of prosecution and in indemnifying any person who may have suffered any loss as a result of the offence, if that person could have recovered the same in a civil case, respectively. Sec. 357(1)(C) states that if a person is capable of claiming damages under the Fatal Accidents Act, 1855 from the accused for the death of the victim, that person can claim the same amount of damages as compensation under the criminal case itself. One important phrase used in this sub-section is "caused the death". This would include cases of culpable homicide not amounting to murder also.

Sec. 357(1)(d) states that if a person is convicted for theft, criminal misappropriation, criminal breach of trust, cheating, or of having dishonestly received or retained, or of having voluntarily assisted in disposing of stolen property or property which he had reason to believe to be stolen, the Court may order such a person to compensate the *bona fide* purchaser for the loss suffered by him as a result of the property being returned to the rightful owner.

The next sub-section of Sec. 357, which is relevant to this article, is Sec. 357(3), which stipulates that where the sentence does not include a fine, the court may order the accused to compensate the victim for loss suffered by him.

Thus, there is a statutory provision related to compensation for victims. The question, though, is whether these provisions are adequate. Though there is a provision that deals with compensation for victims, it remains silent on what action should be taken if the offender fails to pay, on how a just and reasonable compensation should be determined etc. One would get a better idea on how the Statute should have been by comparing India with foreign countries in this respect.

COMPENSATION PROVISIONS IN FOREIGN COUNTRIES

Compensation for victims of crime is one of the earliest forms of victim assistance. The first compensation programs in modern society were established in New Zealand and Great Britain in 1964 based on the concept suggested by British Magistrate Margery Fry in the late 1950s. In the United States, the first compensation program was established in California in 1965. New York, Hawaii, Massachusetts, Maryland, and the Virgin Islands soon followed suit. Today, all 50 states, the District of Columbia, and the Virgin Islands operate victim compensation programs. Compensation programs provide financial assistance to victims of nearly every type of violent crime including rape, robbery, assault, sexual abuse, drunk driving, and domestic violence. The programs pay for expenses such as medical care, mental health counselling, and, in cases of homicide, funerals and loss of support[6].

The amount of money spent by the Federal States of USA as compensation for victims of crime is substantial. In 1996, state compensation programs paid approximately $240 million to more than 110,000 victims nationwide[7]. The range of total payments among states is considerable, varying generally by the size of the state. Ten states pay less than $500,000 annually and about 15 pay more than $3 million. The states with the two largest programs, California and Texas, pay out nearly one-half of all compensation benefits. California operates the nation's largest program, paying nearly one-third of all compensation benefits nationwide (approximately $75 to $80 million annually). The second largest program, Texas, pays out approximately $20 to $30 million to victims each year. Where then, does the funding for these states in this respect come from? 40 % of the funding flows from a Fund established under the Victims of Crime Act, 1984, which is the federal funding source for the State programs. The remaining money comes from two sources-the money collected from offenders and funding from general revenue appropriations from Legislatures. According to the National Association of Crime Victim Compensation Boards (NACVB), more than four-fifths of the states are in the first category, gaining most of their income from offenders.

State compensation programs are represented by these Boards (*i.e.* NACVCB), an organization founded in 1977 to provide advocacy, training, and technical assistance, and to foster communication among state programs. NACVCB provides a strong national voice on all matters affecting state compensation programs before Congress and the Office for Victims of Crime (OVC). In addition, it provides extensive training to its members on a wide range of issues facing programs today, from administration and funding matters to coverage of emerging areas of victimization.

The compensation programmes in USA not only provide an incentive for victims to bring the case before court but also make it mandatory for them to do so, by making filing a complaint a pre requisite for claiming compensation. The eligibility criteria have been carefully monitored to ensure that the victims co-operate with the prosecuting body to facilitate delivery of justice.

Each state, in USA has eligibility requirements that victims must meet to qualify for compensation benefits. While eligibility requirements vary from state to state, virtually all programs require victims to:

1. Report the crime to law enforcement bodies, normally within 72 hours although a few programs have shorter or longer periods. Nearly all states have a 'good cause' exception applied liberally to children, incapacitated victims, and others with special circumstances.
2. Cooperate with police and prosecutors in the investigation and prosecution of the case.
3. Submit a timely application to the compensation program, generally within one year from the date of the crime. A few states have shorter or longer deadlines, and most have the ability to waive these deadlines for exceptional circumstances.
4. Victims , generally, are not eligible for compensation if their victimization is a result of their own criminal activity or misconduct[8].

Compensation programmes in the USA have reached such high proportions that every year, one week is celebrated as the "National Crime Victims' Rights Week" . In 2005, April 10-16 will be the National Crime Victims' Rights Week.

The importance of compensation of victims has been recognized in many other countries as well. Canada-Manitoba enacted the Justice for Victims of Crime Act, 1986 that is on the same lines as the Victims of Crime Act,1984 of the USA . In the United Kingdom, Criminal Justice Act, 1988 serves the same purpose. New Zealand has also enacted Victim of Offences Act, 1987.

An additional provision introduced in New Zealand is the system of "Victim Impact Statements"(VIS) . According to the Victim of Offences Act, 1987 , before an offender can be sentenced, a VIS should be prepared for the judicial officer sentencing the offender so that he or she understands how the offence has affected the victim. A police officer or Victim Support worker should seek information from the victim for drafting a VIS. A victim is encouraged, but not required, to provide this information.

The VIS should include information on physical or emotional harm, loss of or damage to property, and any other effects the victim has experienced because of the offence. It should not include what the victim thinks the sentence should be.

People who are not victims, but who have been disadvantaged by the offence, may be asked by the prosecutor to provide a VIS. In these cases, the judicial officer decides whether the VIS is to be submitted to the court at sentencing.

Before seeking the information, the official must ensure that the victim is advised of the purpose for which the information is sought, that it will be recorded and verified, and that it must be true.

This additional provision introduced in New Zealand has proved to be very successful and ensures a system where the victim is treated with sympathy and is given his/her due and at the same time, he/she provides all such details as may be required for the prosecution.

In other respects, the Statutes mentioned in all the countries are *in pari materia* with each other. They are all based on the U.N. Declaration of 1985. In most nations, the compensation for victim's movement has been very effective. It has been deemed to be the "growth industry of the decade" in Canada at the 1st National Conference of Victims of Crime held at Toronto in 1985.In UK it has been termed as the "fastest growing voluntary movement". However, in India, this movement has not really taken off and seems to be suffering from teething trouble.

POSITION IN INDIA

The Statutory provisions under Indian law have already been explained. These provisions suffer from inherent limitations as the extent of the fine and the capacity of the criminal to pay the fine has not been considered by the Legislature. The discretion of awarding a just and reasonable compensation has been left with the Courts. The Courts, in turn, have not made use of S.357 adequately.

This was recognized by the Supreme Court in Hari Singh v. Sukhbir Singh[9], where the Court observed as follows:

> *"Section 357(2) is an important provision but court have seldom invoked it. Perhaps due to ignorance of the object of it. It empowers the court to award compensation to victims while passing judgment of conviction. In addition to conviction, the court may order the accused to pay some amount by way of compensation to the victim who has suffered by the action of the accused. It may be noted that this power of courts to award compensation is not ancillary to other sentences but it is in addition thereto. This power was intended to do something to reassure the victim that he or she is not forgotten in the criminal justice system. It is a measure of responding appropriately to crime as well as reconciling the victim with the offender. It is, to some extent, a constructive approach to the crimes. It is indeed a step forward in our criminal justice system."*

Even when the courts have used S. 357, more often than not they seem to have used it rather conservatively, very often giving the financial position of the accused as an excuse. The Courts while awarding compensation ought, also, to take the financial position of the accused into account. This is true not only for compensation but also for fines. The Supreme Court keeping this in mind reduced the fine from Rs.42, 300/- to Rs 4000/- in *Adamji Umar Dalal v. The State of Bombay*[10].

This award seems relatively just when one compares it to the case *Palaniappa Gounder V. State of T.N*[11], where the accused was convicted for murder and ordered to serve a sentence of life imprisonment and pay a fine. The High Court keeping the heirs of the victims in mind awarded a compensation of Rs 20,000. The Supreme Court, stressing on the poor economic condition of the accused, reduced the sum to a mere Rs 3000, completely ignoring the plight of the victim. Then, should the victim suffer due to the lack of ability of the offender to pay? In addition, what if the offender defaults in paying the fine?

The Supreme Court in *Sarwan Singh V. State of Punjab*[12] held that such a default would result in an additional 6 months simple imprisonment for the offender. In that particular case, the punishment already included 5 years rigorous imprisonment. One fails to understand how an extra 6 months simple imprisonment would affect a person who has already undergone 5 years rigorous imprisonment. From the point of view of the offender defaulting, would indeed be a better option!

An alternative would be awarding rigorous imprisonment for a fixed period and using the wages earned by the prisoner as compensation money for the victim. The Supreme Court in *State of Gujarat v. Hon'ble High Court of Gujarat*[13] suggested the above and suggested that the payment can be made either directly or through a fund.

The Supreme Court, though, in a few cases has given due regard to S. 357 and taken into consideration the interests of the victims. One such case was *Hari Singh V. Sukhbir Singh*[14], where the Supreme Court clearly laid down the guidelines to be followed while awarding compensation. The Court observed as follows:

> *"The payment by way of compensation must, however, be reasonable. What is reasonable may depend on the facts and circumstances of each case. The quantum of compensation may be determined by taking into account the nature of the crime, the justness of claim by the victim and the ability of the accused to pay. If there are more than one accused they may be asked to pay in equal terms unless their capacity to pay varies considerably. The payment may also depend on the acts of each accused. "*

In this case, the Court increased the compensation amount from Rs 2,500 to Rs 50,000 taking into account the fact that victim's power of speech had been permanently impaired.

Similarly, in *Dr Jacob George v. State of Kerala*[15], where a woman died because miscarriage was caused without her consent, by the doctor, the compensation to her heirs was increased from Rs 4,000 to Rs 1 lakh. Cases like the above two, though, are exceptions in India's criminal jurisprudence where the victims have been given their due.

We can go further to say that compensating victims is a duty of the State. Right to compensation can be considered as a fundamental right by bringing it within the ambit of Article 21, *i.e.* right to life and personal liberty. The State should be responsible for the breach of this right.

In order to prevent the breach of this right, a Statute that deals with the compensation for victims, is the need of the hour. The Statute should provide for a fund, which should be used to compensate victims of crime, whether the offender is convicted, or not. Under the current law, compensation for victims is available only when the accused is convicted. This has to change.

Further, the fund must consist of money recovered from offenders. The amount collected from convicts should be based on their ability to pay as well as the nature of the crime. Well to do offenders must be made to pay hefty sums so that it would also have a deterrent effect.

Further, as regards the amount of compensation that has to be awarded, a fixed method of calculation should be specified. This should depend on the loss suffered by the victim or in the case of murders, the loss suffered by the victims, near and dear ones as well as their future expenses. The method that is followed to determine damages under torts may be suitable. This method as laid down in *General Manager Road Transport Corporation v. Mrs Susamma Thomas*[16], is as follows:

> *"The assessment of damages to compensate the dependants is beset with difficulties because from the nature of things, it has to take into account many imponderables, e.g., the life expectancy of the deceased and the dependants, the amount that the deceased would have earned during the remainder of his life, the amount that he would have contributed to the dependants during that period, the chances that the deceased may not have lived or the dependants may not live up to the estimated reasonable period of their life expectancy , the chances that the deceased might have got better employment or income or might have lost his employment or income altogether."*

Legislations to this effect are already being followed in foreign countries. It is only India, which has not implemented the same. India needs to come up with legislations, which are based on the foreign legislations.

Compensating victims for their losses is of paramount importance for the working of a Welfare State like India. India has to prove that it has come out of the laissez-faire era, by coming up with well-drafted legislations that deal with rights of victims.

NOTES

1. Henry Campbell Black, M.A," Blacks law Dictionary", 6th ed., 1990, p.374.
2. Ibid.
3. While Formal Justice Refers to the Justice Meted out by Courts, Popular Justice Refers to other means resorted to by the citizens in furtherance of Justice.
4. (1996) 2 SCC 384.
5.
6. National Association of Crime Victim Compensation Boards, Crime Victim Compensation Program Directory, 1.
7. Nation Wide Analysis, Victims of Crime Act, 1996 Victims of Crime Act Performance Report, State Compensation Program,Washington, D.C.: U.S. Department of Justice, Office of Justice Programs, Office for Victims of Crime,April, 14 1997.
8. The US Department of Justice-OVC Bulletin, "New Directions Advocating for the Fair Treatment of Crime Victims".
9. (1988) 4 SCC 551.
10. (1952) SCR 172.
11. (1977) 2 SCC 634.
12. (1978) 4 SCC 111.
13. (1998) 7 SCC 392.
14. Supra n.9.
15. (1994) 3 SCC 430.
16. AIR 1994 Sc 1631.

SAYANTANI GUIN AND ARVIND TIWARI

9

JUVENILE JUSTICE SYSTEM IN INDIA: A RESTORATIVE JUSTICE APPROACH

INTRODUCTION

The Juvenile Justice System involves the organization and process of juvenile justice. This is a unique system of justice for the children devised and developed for the purpose of socializing and controlling children. The Juvenile Justice approach accords high priority to reduce the need for legal interventions in children's cases to avoid the devastating ill effects of criminalization, penalization and stigmatization. In India, the Juvenile Justice System is broadly administered under the Juvenile Justice (Care & Protection of Children) Act, 2000. The Act is friendlier to children and provides for the proper care and protection as the ultimate rehabilitation of children. Although, the Act has provision of community service for the juvenile offender as a sentencing process, it neglects the involvement of the juvenile victim, the child offender and the community in the juvenile justice process. This calls for a balanced approach of Restorative Justice. This chapter aims to study the broad provisions in the Juvenile Justice (Care & Protection of Children) Act, 2000, which conforms with the principles of Restorative Justice and aims to examine the effectiveness of these provisions. Finally, the chapter attempts to suggest a blueprint of Restorative Justice approach in the Indian Juvenile Justice System.

THE CONCEPT OF JUVENILE JUSTICE

The concept of justice in the case of juveniles has two dimensions:

1. **Justice before the onset of Delinquency**: This involves the devolution and even imposition of social responsibilities on the child while at the same time demonstrating societal concern for him.
2. **Justice after the onset of Delinquency**: It involves the elements of protective intervention both in the sense of the child and in the sense of the society.

The Juvenile Justice System not only provides for the special needs of children who commit crime, but also extends a protective umbrella to those vulnerable or endangered to do so under situational compulsions. It aims to serve the best interests of the child while providing correctional treatment to juvenile offenders. The foregoing discussion highlights the application of the concept of Restorative Justice in the Juvenile Justice (Care & Protection of Children) Act, 2000 with the objective of delivering justice to juveniles after the onset of delinquency and prevents juveniles in indulging in the same act before the onset of delinquency.

JUVENILE JUSTICE SYSTEM IN INDIA

In India, Juvenile Justice System is Broadly Administered under the Juvenile Justice (Care & Protection of Children) Act, 2000. The Act aims to provide for *proper care, protection and treatment of juveniles in conflict with law and child in need of care and protection by catering to their development needs and by adopting a child friendly approach in the adjudication and disposition of matters in the best interest of children.* The Act also aims to provide for *their ultimate rehabilitation through various institutions* established under this Act.

The Act takes into consideration the provisions of the *Indian Constitution, United Nations Standard Minimum Rules for the Administration of Juvenile Justice, 1985 (the Beijing Rules), United Nations Convention on the Rights of the Child, 1989, and United Nations Rules for the Protection of Juveniles Deprived of their Liberty, 1990.*

It is pertinent to mention here that the Juvenile Justice (Care & Protection of Children) Act, 2000 is a major step forward in terms of being a progressive and proactive legislation for the care, protection, treatment and rehabilitation of 'children in need of care and protection' and 'juveniles in conflict with law'. It is a comprehensive legislation for justice to the children in the situation of abuse, exploitation and social maladjustment. This law is not only the basic legislation for the children in the country but also it provides a 'blueprint' for the welfare of the children. The Act provides for the safety and security from abandonment and for the development of character and personality of the juveniles and to become useful citizens of the country. It enjoins the *State* to make provision for the proper care, treatment, development and rehabilitation of the children/juveniles. It also calls upon the State to develop a network with the *voluntary organizations* to come forward and to shoulder the responsibility with the State, of the Children in distress situations.

The legal framework under the Act provides for 'Juvenile Justice Boards' and 'Child Welfare Committees', the legal bodies for trial of 'Juvenile in Conflict with Law' and 'Child in need of Care and Protection' respectively. Thus, the Act enables increased accessibility to a juvenile or the child by establishing Juvenile Justice Boards and Child Welfare Committees and Homes in each district or group of districts.

The Act provides for role of *social worker and voluntary organizations* at various levels. Besides, the Act also has highly innovative provisions for the *social reintegration of these children through non-institutional care system of adoption, foster care and sponsorship programmes.*

Although the Act is much more child friendly and aim towards their ultimate rehabilitation, a major gap in the Act is overlooked. *The Act has little or no scope for the juvenile offender, the victim and the community to be directly involved in the juvenile justice process.* The following few sections of the Act provides for the role of juvenile offender and the community:

1. ***Section 15 (1)*** of the Act provides that the Juvenile Justice board may order the juvenile to perform *Community Service* when it is satisfied on inquiry that a juvenile has committed an offence. However, the Act does not specify the various activities that could be given as community service to the offenders. Thus Community Service often becomes punitive rather than constructive.

2. ***Section 32 (1)*** states that any child in need of care and protection can *Voluntarily Produce him/herself* before the committee, among others.

PRESENT SCENARIO

In order to ensure speedy implementation of the new law on Juvenile Justice, the *Ministry of Social Justice & Empowerment, Government of India*, framed *Model Rules under the Act* for the guidelines of State Governments/UT administrations. These Rules were published in the Gazette of India (Extra Ordinary) dated 22nd June, 2001 and were also circulated to all the State Governments/UT Administrations with the request to either adopt these Model Rules or frame their own Rules on the basis of these Model Rules.

However, while looking into a complaint of alleged murder of 2 children by a female juvenile, it came to the attention of the *National Human Rights Commission* that only some States appear to have implemented the various provisions of Juvenile Justice (Care & Protection of Children) Act, 2000. It immediately directed that a notice be issued to the Chief Secretaries of all the States and Union Territories to furnish the information to the Commission with regard to the implementation of the provisions of Juvenile Justice (Care & Protection of Children) Act, 2000 and especially on whether:

(1) The Juvenile Justice (Care & Protection of Children) Act, 2000 been implemented in the State,

(2) Juvenile Justice Board and Protective Homes have been set up in the State, if so, details thereof,

(3) There are certified Homes or Special Homes in which the child will be kept if not released on bail,

(4) There are Child Welfare Committees and Children's Homes. Based on the feedback received from all the State/UTs, it was found that only 11 States have implemented the provision of the Juvenile Justice (Care & Protection of Children) Act, 2000, which include Chandigarh, Chattisgarh, Delhi, Goa, Gujarat, Haryana, Manipur, Orissa, Rajasthan, West Bengal and Uttar Pradesh. The State Government of Jammu & Kashmir has stated that the Juvenile Justice (Care & Protection of Children) Act, 2000 is not applicable to the State of J.K. Other States have not implemented the provision or implemented them

partially. The Commission has sought further information from the States where the implementation of the provision of the Juvenile Justice (Care & Protection of Children) Act, 2000 has not been made (NHRC, 2004).

It is reported that the Act is seeing very poor implementation everywhere and especially in Mumbai, where large number of street children need special attention. The child often remains isolated and alienated through his/her stay in the juvenile institutions. The skills that they are taught like carpentry or electrical work are outdated and taught in en masse. For girls, rehabilitation often becomes equal to marrying the girl off (Times News Network, 2004).

MAGNITUDE OF THE PROBLEM OF JUVENILE DELINQUENCY IN INDIA

Crime in India 2004 Reported that the share of Crimes Committed by Juveniles to total IPC (Indian Penal Code) crimes reported in the country during the 1997 to 2000 was static at 0.5%. However, in 2001, this share rose to 0.9% and further marginally increased to 1.0% in 2002 and remained static in 2003 and 2004. During 1999 and 2000 juvenile crime rate was 0.9 whereas in 2001 to 2004, it has shown a mixed trend of crime rate 1.6, 1.8, 1.7 and 1.8 respectively. The juvenile IPC crimes in 2004 have increased by 7.9% over 2003 as 17,819 IPC crimes registered against juveniles in 2003 gone up to 19,229 cases during 2004. The increase in the incidence of juvenile crimes for some heads like Cases of Cheating, Arson and Theft has been observed (NCRB, 2004).

Thus, it can be stated that the frequency of offence committed by the juvenile have increased over the years. Also, often the national dailies reports changing variation in the nature of crimes committed by the juvenile. In this situation of increasing changing pattern in the nature of offence committed by children, it becomes essential that an alternative juvenile justice method be adopted so as to imbibe in the children the values and morals of life through collective efforts.

NEED FOR A RESTORATIVE JUSTICE APPROACH

From the above, it is clear that the Act has been partially implemented in the country and the implementation of the Act is very poor in the few States where it has been implemented. Apart from this, there is very little or no scope in the Act to involve the juvenile offenders, the victim of the crime and the community in responding to the crime committed. Thus, an integrated approach to juvenile justice is required wherein the juvenile offender, the child victim and the community can play an effective role in realization of the true spirit of the Act. This calls for a balanced approach wherein the victim, the juvenile offender and the community could play a role in the juvenile justice process in the best interest of the child. The concept of Restorative Justice could provide a viable solution. Before discussing how Indian Juvenile Justice System can become restorative in nature, it is important to understand some of the overall principles and goals of restorative justice.

THE CONCEPT OF RESTORATIVE JUSTICE

Restorative Justice is a Theory of Justice that Emphasizes Repairing the harm caused or revealed by criminal behaviour. It is best accomplished through cooperative processes that include all stakeholders. It is a new movement in the fields of Victimology and criminology. It outlines an alternative philosophy for addressing crime. When viewed from a restorative lens, crime is a violation of people and relationships- the relationship between an offender and his or her family, friends, victims and the community- as opposed to merely an act against the State. Acknowledging that crime causes injury to people and communities, it insists that justice repairs those injuries and that the parties be permitted to participate in that process. Restorative Justice programs, therefore, enable the victim, the offender and affected members of the community to be directly involved in responding to the crime. They become central to the Criminal Justice process, with State and legal professionals becoming facilitators of a system that aims at *offender accountability, reparation to the victim and full participation by the victim, offender and the community.* Thus Restorative Justice provides an opportunity for victims, offenders and sometimes representatives of the community to communicate about an offence and how to repair the harm caused (retrieved from *http://www.restorativejustice.org/intro/* on May 18, 2006)

DEFINITION OF RESTORATIVE JUSTICE

Restorative Justice is a process whereby parties with a stake in a specific offence resolve collectively how to deal with the aftermath of the offence and its implications for the future.

STAKEHOLDERS AND GOALS OF RESTORATIVE JUSTICE

There are three *Primary Stakeholders* in Restorative Justice-*victims, offenders and the community. Goals* of Restorative Justice include *accountability, community development and community protection.* The emphasis on *Victims* role in Restorative Justice is about choice. Restorative Justice cannot exist without giving the victims the opportunity to participate in the justice process and making every effort to respond to their needs and desire for participation. The emphasis for *offenders* in restorative justice is on change. The goal is to hold offenders accountable by providing opportunities for them to understand the effect their actions have on others and to assist the offenders in enhancing and developing skills that will make them more productive and competent citizens by identifying and building on their strengths. For the *community*, the emphasis in restorative justice is on bonding and building relationships. Communities are also victims of crime. Certainly, the Juvenile Justice System has a responsibility to protect the public from juvenile offenders in the system.

KEY VALUES

Restorative programmes are characterized by four key values:

1. **Encounter:** Create opportunities for victims, offenders and community members who want to do so to meet to discuss the crime and aftermath,
2. **Amends:** Expect offenders to take steps to repair the harm they have caused,
3. **Reintegration:** Seek to restore victims and offenders as whole, contributing members of society,
4. **Inclusion:** Provide opportunities for parties with a stake in a specific crime to participate in its resolution.

AIMS OF RESTORATIVE JUSTICE

The key aims or outcomes of Restorative Justice are as follows:

1. **Victim Satisfaction**: reducing the fear of the victims and ensuring they feel "paid back" for the harm that has been done to them;
2. **Engagement with the Young Person**: to ensure that they are aware of the consequences of their actions have the opportunity to make reparation and agree to plans for their restoration in the community.

3. **Creation of Community Capital**: Increasing public confidence in the criminal justice system.

PRINCIPLES OF RESTORATIVE JUSTICE

The following are some of the principles on which restorative justice is based on:

1. **Repair:** Crime results in harm to individual victims, communities and juvenile offenders and creates an obligation to make things right. Essentially, justice requires healing or repairing harm and rebuilding broken relationships.
2. **Involvement:** All parties, including the victim (if he/she wishes), the community, and the juvenile offender should be provided with opportunities for input and participation in the justice process.
3. **Justice System Facilitation:** Repairing harm requires that the respective roles of the government and the community be rethought in terms of how to repair the crime. In other words, restorative justice based practices change the role of the justice system from being an expert in a case driven response to crime towards the justice system acting in a facilitative role that focuses more on problem solving and community capacity building.

THE RESTORATIVE JUVENILE JUSTICE VISION

From a *Practical Perspective,* the concept of Restorative Justice requires the juvenile justice system to respond to crime by devoting attention to the following:

1. Enabling offenders to understand the harm caused by their behavior and to make amends to their victims and communities,
2. Building on offender's strengths and increasing offenders competencies,
3. Giving victims an opportunity to participate in the justice process,
4. Protecting the public through a process in which the individual victims, the community, and offenders are all active stakeholders.

In India, incorporating the Restorative Justice approach in the Juvenile Justice (Care & Protection of Children) Act, 2000 may help in delivering justice to children before and after the onset of delinquency in the following ways:

1. **Support from the Community:** The community involved defining the harm experienced, and participating in the decision-making about steps for repair may result in increased victim recovery from the trauma of crime. Thus not only the victim gets a support from the community to deal with the harm and pain, the juvenile offender also gets an opportunity of acceptability from the community.
2. **Community Protection:** The community involved in preventing and controlling juvenile crime, improving neighbourhoods, and strengthening the bonds among community members may result in community protection.
3. **Rehabilitation of the Juvenile Offenders:** The juvenile offenders, while interacting with the victim and the community, get an understanding of the human impact of their behavior. They tend to accept responsibility for their action, start expressing remorse, and prepare themselves to take action to repair the damage through developing their own capacities. Thus the juvenile offenders may become fully integrated, respected members of the community, which may accelerate their rehabilitation in the community.
4. **Constructive Resolutions to Delinquency:** Juvenile justice professionals, as community justice facilitators may organize and support processes in which individual crime victims, other community members, and juvenile offenders are involved in finding constructive resolutions to delinquency.

PROGRAMMES

The following are some of the programmes and outcomes typically identified with restorative justice, which may be applicable in the Indian Juvenile Justice System:

1. **Victim-Offender Mediation**: This is a process that provides an interested victim the opportunity to meet his offender in a safe and structured setting, engaging in a discussion of the crime with the assistance of a trained mediator. The goals of victim offender mediation include: permitting victims to meet their offenders on a voluntary basis, encouraging the offender

to learn about the crime's impact and to take responsibility for the resulting harm, and providing victim and offender the opportunity to develop a plan that addresses the harm. With the assistance of the mediator, the victim and the offender begin to resolve the conflict. Both are given the opportunity to express their feelings and perceptions of the offence.

2. **Conferencing**: The aim of conferencing is to divert offenders from the justice system by offering them the opportunity to attend a conference to discuss and resolve the offence instead of being charged and appeared in court. Conferencing is not offered where offenders wish to contest their guilt. The conference, which normally lasts 1 to 2 hours, is attended by the victims and their supporters, the offenders and their supporters and other relevant parties. The conference coordinator focuses the discussion on condemning the act, without condemning the character of the actor. Offenders are asked to explain what happened, how they have felt about the crime, and what they think should be done. The victims and others are asked to describe the physical, financial and emotional consequences of the crime. This discussion may lead the offenders, their families and friends to experience the shame of the act, prompting an apology to the victim. A plan of action is developed and signed by key participants. The plan may include the offender paying compensation to the victim, doing work for the victim or the community, or any other undertaking the participants may agree upon. It is the responsibility of the conference participants to determine the outcomes that are most appropriate for these particular victims and these particular offenders.
3. **Circles**: This is a process designed to develop consensus among community members, victims, victim supporters, offenders, offender supporters, judges, prosecutors, defence counsel, police and court workers on an appropriate sentencing plan that addresses the concerns of all interested parties. The goals of circles include: promoting healing of all affected parties, giving the offender the opportunity to make amend, giving victims, offenders, family members and communities a voice and shared responsibility in finding constructive

resolutions, addressing underlying causes of criminal behaviour, and building a sense of community around shared community values.

4. **Restitution:** It is the payment by an offender of a sum of money to compensate the victim for the financial losses caused by the crime. It is justified in a restorative perspective as a method of holding offenders accountable for their wrongdoing, and as a method of repairing the victim's injury. Restitution can be determined in the course of mediation, conferencing or circles, it can also be ordered by a judge. In other words, it is a potentially restorative outcome that may result from either a restorative or a conventional process.
5. **Community Service:** This involves work performed by an offender for the benefit of the community. It is justified in a restorative perspective as a method of addressing the harm experienced by communities when a crime occurs and the effort to ensure that the offender's community service repairs that particular harm.

As mentioned earlier, the provision of Community Service is already present in the Indian Juvenile Justice System. However, the Act does not specify the various activities that could be given as community service to the offenders. Thus Community Service often becomes punitive rather than constructive. Among the other four processes of Restorative Justice viz. Victim-Offender Mediation, Conferencing, Circles and Restitution, the processes of Victim-Offender Mediation and Conferencing could be more applicable in the Indian situation with the help of the Voluntary and Non-Governmental Organizations and social workers.

SUGGESTIONS

Based on the above discussion of the various concepts of Restorative Justice and its possible implication in the current Juvenile Justice (Care & Protection of Children) Act, 2000, the following suggestions could be offered:

1. **Amendment in the Act:** Section 15 of the Juvenile Justice (Care & Protection of Children) Act, 2000 has to be amended in the light of the various programmes in Restorative Justice.

2. **Community Service:** Community service work should be oriented to community needs and linked with broader community issues. Community service should be constructive and educational-not punitive. Juveniles should not feel isolated while doing community service; rather they should feel connected to the community. To facilitate the development of a more meaningful community service, specific community service orders (e.g. cleaning a specific community space, conduct discussions or educational workshops, work with a neighbourhood group on neighbourhood repair, assist elderly or disabled persons with household projects, conduct community surveys about the needs of the community, maintain a community garden, etc should be mentioned in the Juvenile Justice (Care & Protection of Children) Act, 2000.
3. **Educational Workshops:** To meet competency development goals espoused in restorative justice, educational workshops and projects need to be designed to assist youth in developing skills and in gaining some social capital. This allows the youth to build relationship with others and have an ongoing role in their community based on something of value that they have to offer.
4. **Apologies:** Oral and written apologies to victims could be recommended. However, the apology must be sincere. If the respondent feels and is able to articulate his/her remorse in a sincere and respectful manner, then an apology can be therapeutic option for offenders and victims. However, it depends on the victim's wish to receive an apology.

CONCLUSION

Although the Juvenile Justice (Care & Protection of Children) Act 2000 is a progressive legislation, it has not been implemented properly in the country. Only eleven states in the country have practically implemented the Act. Also, the Act lacks important provisions like the involvement of the community, juvenile offender and the victim in the justice delivery process. Looking into the wide anomalies, the need of the hour is to incorporate the Restorative Justice approach in the Act and the proper implementation of the Act throughout the country. Broadly, it can be said that the Restorative Justice model can be included into the present Juvenile Justice System in India by providing needed services available for victims of crime and giving the victims opportunities for involvement and input. Also, community members, including individual crime victims and offenders could be widely involved in making decisions and carrying out plans for resolving issues and restoring the community. The Non-Governmental Organizations and the Community Based Organizations can also play an effective role in this process. This would necessarily enhance the juvenile justice process in the best interest of the child.

REFERENCES

Bare Act (2001), Juvenile Justice (Care & Protection of Children) Act, 2000, Allahabad, Law Publishers (India) Private Limited *http://www.restorativejustice.org/intro/:* website visited on May 18, 2006.

http://www.restorativejustice.org/rj3/intro_default.htm retrieved from internet on October 20, 2004.

http://www.youthcourt.net/publications/article1.pdf retrieved from internet on October 20, 2004.

NCRB, (2004), Crime in India, 2004, *National Crime Records Bureau, Ministry of Home Affairs*, Government of India

NHRC, (2004), "National Human Rights Commission: Juvenile Justice Act 2000 not implemented in 23 States/ UTs", retrieved from http://www.nhrc.nic.in/dispArchive.asp?fno=811 on October 20, 2004.

Srivastava, S.P. (1989), *Juvenile Justice in India*, Delhi, Ajanta Publications.

Times News Network (2004), "Troubled Children's Dilemma: After 18, What?" *Reported in the Times of India dated Monday,* October 11, 2004.

N. Maheshwara Swamy

10

RESTORATIVE JUSTICE TO THE VICTIMS OF RAPE– THE INDIAN LEGAL SCENARIO

INTRODUCTION

One of the heinous crimes against female folk is "Rape". This phenomenon could be witnessed at all times and in all regions of the world and its occurrence is more common where the victims of the crime are helpless females or minor girls. It is a peculiar offence where the victim has to suffer mentally, physically, psychologically, socially, culturally, and economically, for the rest of her life. While sexual instinct is too natural, availing sexual satisfaction by applying force on the person of a female is obviously unnatural, unethical, immoral, and illegal. It is also against the public policy and social justice.

In India, rape is a cognizable offence punishable under the provisions of the Indian Penal Code, 1860 (hereinafter referred to as IPC), in accordance with the provisions of the Code of Criminal Procedure, 1973 (hereinafter referred to as Cr.P.C.). The punishment to be imposed is to the person who commits the rape but no measure of appropriate relief is provided to the victims of the rape. In the eyes of the society with regard to rape, "once a victim always a victim". This is the dictum of the majority.

Today, the sympathy is in favour of the offenders whether of rape or otherwise, based on the foundation of "Human Rights", and the "Theory of Reformation", throughout the world. Various reformative and rehabilitative measures are under sway for the protection and welfare of the criminals. However, no such attempt is wisely made to compensate the loss caused to the victims of the offence of rape. The existing law is not as effective as it ought to be and whatever the legal measures available are practically engrafted with ambiguous language, permitting payment of meagre compensation to the traumatic victims of the ghastly offence of rape. This is a glaring discrimination towards the "fair sex" - victims of rape.

Rape is a Psychophysical Phenomenon Instigated by environment and the culture in which the people are brought up. While ancient Indian culture and heritage inherited the quality of respecting women and in extending them all possible welfare and protective measures beginning from birth to bereavement. In modern times, although such an ideology is continued in theory, but in practice there is every threat to the safe existence of women for a variety of reasons. Conditions are such that a woman is always exposed to the risks of sexual violence in the form of rape, molestation, and harassment for dowry, eve teasing, and so on. Reports are not scant to establish that women in India are ill-treated, under-estimated, harassed, raped and even killed or made to commit suicide at some place or the other on some ground or the other. The growing number of rape cases shocks the conscious of any civilized society. Today, reported incidents indicate situations where a father committing rape on his own daughter, a teacher on his student, a police man on a civilian or a woman under custody, a superintendent/ manager of a protective home on the inmates, an officer on his subordinate, and so on.

According to the information provided in "Crime in India 2001" (p.48), published by the National Crime Records Bureau (NCRB), Ministry of Home Affairs, Government of India, the total number of rape cases in India has been estimated at 16075 during the year 2001. Similarly, commission of rape on the Scheduled Caste/Scheduled tribe women, custodial rapes, rapes even on disabled girls in the Observation Homes are not unknown (see page 197 of the National Human Rights Commission's Annual Report 2001-2002.). The still worst situation is commission of rape on the pregnant women, age-old women, or months-old children.

On the face when the incidence of rape in and around the country is as indicated above, there is every compelling need to look into this social menace and to provide them sufficient protection and to safeguard the welfare of the victims of rape by means of an appropriate legislation so that they can feel assured of all their hopes and aspirations for a happy and congenial living on par the rest of the female world. The present paper examines these aspects of the factual position vis-à-vis the existing legal provisions governing rape and its victims, and makes suitable suggestions to meet and mitigate the injustice being caused to the victims of rape in the present day Indian scenario.

VICTIMS OF RAPE – INDIAN LEGAL SCENARIO

The available statistical reports indicate that the incidence of rape in India is growing day by day. Even minor girls are not spared in certain instances. The problems of rape victims are innumerable in the present day system of criminal justice and social set up. A victim of rape is victimized repeatedly, initially in the hands of the police when a complaint is lodged or an investigation is ordered, secondly, when the trial of the case starts, and lastly, which may never be the least, is when the society behaves like a beast against the victims of rape. The net result is defamation and degradation of the victim of the rape in particular and the womanhood in general, which contingencies have to be faced by the victim through out her remaining life, thus making her life meaningless. At any rate, it becomes impossible for the victim to forget the trauma and tragedy of rape, in as much as every existing protective procedures and legal provisions react as factors in the renewal of the incidence of rape continuously.

As early as in 1995, the Supreme Court of India in the case reported as Delhi Domestic Working Women's Forum v. Union of India, (1995) 1 SCC 14, observed that "It is rather unfortunate that in recent times, there has been an increase in violence against women causing serious concern. Rape does indeed pose a series of problems for the criminal justice system. There are cries for harshest penalties, but often times such crimes eclipse the real plight of the victim. Rape is an experience, which shakes the foundations of the lives of the victims. For many, its effect is a long-term one, impairing their capacity for personal relationships, altering their behavior, values and generating fears. In addition to the trauma of the rape itself, victims have had to suffer further agony during legal proceedings".

As already stated above, there is no specific law governing the rights and protections of the victims of rape, except certain limited relief under Cr.P.C. "With the passage of time and due to increasing interactions with the western civilization, the focus of the penologists, jurists, criminologists and the Government was shifted to the rights of the under-trials and reformation of the convicts and the victims became the forgotten men of our criminal justice system" (see "Perspectives on Victimology in the context of Criminal Justice System", R.K. Bag, Reference Material, Refresher Course on Criminology and Forensic Science for University College Teachers, NICFS, MHA, GOI, 2004, p. 80).

VICTIMS OF RAPE – LEGAL RELIEF

Under the Criminal law, there are two relief available to the victims of rape, namely:

(I) The relief of Compensation

(II) The relief of Conducting Trial in Camera, and

(III) The relief under the Constitution of India

Each of the above first two relief are discussed below briefly in combination with the relief provided for under the Constitution of India as also the selected case-law emanated thereon:

(I) Relief of Compensation

There are two relevant enactments which govern the subject of rape under the Indian Law, namely, IPC and Cr.P.C. While, IPC, vide its various Sections from 375 and 377 provides for the description, nature and scope of the offence of rape, the Cr.P.C. vide its Section 327 and 357, etc., provides for the procedure to be followed during the trial of the offence of rape and imposing punishment in the nature of imprisonment for life or for a term of 10 years and fine. The word "and" used after the figure and word "10 years" under sub-Section (1) of Section 357 of the Cr.P.C., makes it clear that the Court trying for an offence under that Section has to impose invariably fine. Section 357 empowers the Court to order to the payment of compensation out of the fine imposed on the accused. This Section when analyzed brings out the following information:

1. Sub-section (1) of Section 357 contemplates that when a Court imposes a sentence of fine or a sentence (including a sentence of death) of which fine forms a part, the Court may, when passing the judgment, order the whole or any part of the fine recovered to be applied:

(a) in defraying the expenses properly incurred in the prosecution; and
(b) in the payment to any person of compensation for any loss or injury caused by the offence, when compensation is, in the opinion of the Court, recoverable by such person in a Civil Court;
(c) *not relevant
(d) *not relevant

2. Sub-Section (1) of Section 357 which is a general provision applicable in all cases of punishment including death sentence, can obviously be invoked in case of the offence of the rape, subject, of course, to the following conditions:
   (a) In case of clause (a) of Sub-Section (1) of Section 357 in its application to the offence of rape, the expenses to be defrayed must have been properly incurred in the prosecution, and
   (b) In case of clause (b) of Sub-Section (1) of Section 357 in its application to the offence of rape, the victim of rape must have incurred any loss or injury for which compensation is, in the opinion of the Court, recoverable by such person in a Civil Court.

It is yet to be an established ascertainable principle of law as to whether the right of a woman injured in the offence of rape includes the right to recover compensation by filing a suit in a Civil Court. However, now it is well settled principle of judicial precedent that rape is a crime against basic human rights, and is also violative of the victim's most cherished of the Fundamental Rights i.e., the Right to Life contained in Art. 21 of the Constitution of India. (See State of Punjab V. Ramdev Singh, AIR 2004 SC 1290; see also Shri Bodhisattwa Gautam V. Miss Subhra Chakraborty, AIR 1996 SC 922).

An Acquitted Accused is not liable to pay Compensation

The person who commits an offence must be sentenced, and in case of acquittal, the accused is not under any liability to pay the compensation. As was held by the Supreme Court in Giridhari Lal v. State of Punjab, (1982) 1 SCC 608, the sentence to be imposed under clause (a) of Section 357(1) must be a substantive sentence of fine.

Power of the Court to award compensation under Section 357(3)

Sub-Section (3) of Section 357 of the Cr.P.C., which is yet another legal provision empowering the court to award compensation. It reads as follows:

"When a Court imposes a sentence, of which fine does not form a part, the Court may, when passing judgment, order the accused person to pay, by way of compensation, such amount as may be specified in the order to the person who has suffered any loss or injury by reason of the act for which the accused person has been so sentenced"

The above provision of Section 357 though looks like attracting the cases of rape victims, but it cannot possibly be made applicable to such cases covered by Section 376 insofar as the punishment provided for the offence of rape is not only imprisonment but also fine. Further, sub-Section (3) is not as clear as it ought to be as to whether a Court can impose the sentence of imprisonment without imposing fine, so that it could award compensation to the victims of the offence of rape. However, it was held by the Supreme Court of India that "The object of S. 357(3) is to provide compensation payable to the persons who are entitled to recover damages from the person sentenced even though fine does not form part of the sentence." (See Sarwan Singh v. State of Punjab, (1978) 4 SCC 111).

It would be pertinent to quote here the interpretation of sub-Section (3) of Section 357 of Cr.P.C., made by the Supreme Court in yet another case, i.e., State of Punjab v. Gurmej Singh, AIR 2002 SC 2811, wherein it was held that "A reading of sub-section (3) of S. 357 would show that question of award of compensation would arise where the Court imposes a sentence of which fine does not form a part of it.

Power of Revisional Court to Award Compensation

As provided for under sub-Section (4) of Section 357, an order under Section 357 may also be made by an Appellate Court or by the High Court or the Court of Sessions while exercising its powers of revision.

Compensation awarded by the Criminal Court has to be taken into account while awarding compensation by a Civil Court

At the time of awarding compensation in any subsequent civil suit relating to the same matter, the Court shall take into account any sum paid or recovered a compensation under Section 357, as contemplated in Sub-Section (5) of Section 357.

Factors to be considered while awarding compensation

As was held by the Supreme Court in Hari Singh V. Sukhbir Singh, (1988) 4 SCC 551, "The Compensation should be payable for any loss or injury whether physical or pecuniary, and the court shall have due regard to the nature of the injury, the manner of inflicting the same, the capacity of the accused to pay and other relevant factors."

Need to set up Criminal Injuries Compensation Board

Recommendations No. 7 and No. 8 of the Apex Court in the Bodhisattwa Gautam's case cited above, envisages as follows:

"7. It is necessary having regard to the Directive Principles contained under Article 38(1) of the Constitution of India to set up a Criminal Injuries Compensation Board. Rape victims frequently incur substantial financial loss. Some, for example, are too traumatized to continue in employment".

"8. Compensation for victims shall be awarded by the Court on conviction of the offender and by the Criminal Injuries Compensation Board whether or not a conviction has taken place. The Board will take into account pain, suffering and shocks as well as loss of earnings due to pregnancy and the expenses of the child but if this occurred because of the rape.

Payment of Interim Compensation

In the above case of Bodhisattwa, it was further held that if the court trying an offence of rape has jurisdiction to award compensation at the final stage, there is no reason to deny to the Court the right to award interim compensation which should also be provided in the Scheme stipulated in the Delhi Domestic Working Women's Forum's case cited above.

Compensation in Case of Gang Rape

In Tangirala Venkateshwarlu and another v. State of A.P., 2003 Cri.L.J. 4034 AP, the Andhra Pradesh High Court speaking through Hon'ble Justice L.N. Reddy, awarded compensation of Rs.3,000/- each to the prosecutrix in view of the fact that "Keeping the earning members of the family (the offenders in this case) in jail for 10 years would virtually slattern the entire family."

II. Relief of conducting trial in camera:

Section 327 of the Cr.P.C., provides the relief of conducting trial in camera while dealing with a rape case. Accordingly, Sub-Section (2) of Section 327 specifically contemplates that "Notwithstanding anything contained in sub-section (1) the inquiry into and trial of rape or an offence under Section 376, Section 376-A, Section 376-B, Section 376-C and Section 376-D of the Indian Penal Code (45 of 1860) shall be conducted in camera:

Provided that the presiding judge may, if he thinks fit, or on an application made by either of the parties, allow any particular person to have access to, or be or remain in, the room or building used by the court".

Sub-Section (3) of Section 327 of the Cr.P.C., reads as follows:

"Where any proceedings are held under sub-section (2), it shall not be lawful for any person to print or publish any matter in relation to any such proceedings, except with the previous permission of the court."

Sub-Section (3) of Section 327 has to be read in conjunction with sub-Section (2) thereof.

In State of Maharashtra V. Chandraprakash Mewalchand Jain, AIR 1990 SC 658, the Supreme Court expressed the view that "The court must not be obvious of the emotional turmoil and the psychological injury that a prosecutrix suffers on being molested or raped. She suffered a tremendous sense of shame and the fear of being shunned by society and her near relatives, including her husband. Instead of treating her with compassion and understanding as one who is an injured victim of a crime, she is, more often than not, treated a sinner, and shunned. It must therefore, be realized that a woman who is subjected to sex-violence would always be slow and hesitant about disclosing her plight. The court must, therefore, evaluate her evidence in the above background."

In Shri Bodhisattwa Gautam v. Miss Subhra Chakroborthy, AIR 1996 SC 922, the Supreme Court held, inter alia, that a large number of women still fail to report rapes to the police because they fear embarrassing and insensitive treatment by the doctors, the law enforcement personnel or the cross-examining defiance attorneys. The fear has to be allayed from the minds of women so that if and when this crime is committed, the victim may promptly report the matter to the police and on a charge-sheet being submitted, the trial may proceed speedily without causing any embarrassment to the prosecutrix who may come in the witness box without fear psychosis.

NAME OF THE VICTIM OF RAPE SHOULD NOT BE PRINTED IN THE JUDGMENTS OF THE COURTS

In State of Punjab V. Ramdev Singh, AIR 2004 SC 1290, the Apex Court opined that the name of the victim should not be printed or published in the judgments. In this case, the Hon'ble Supreme Court further held that the courts are expected to deal with cases of sexual crime against women with sensitivity. Such cases need to be dealt with sternly and severely.

LEGAL ASSISTANCE TO THE VICTIMS OF RAPE

In Delhi Domestic Working Women's Forum v. Union of India, (1995) 1 SCC 14, the Supreme Court laid down, inter alia, and the following parameters in assisting the victims of rape:

> *"The complainants of sexual assault cases should be provided with legal representation. It is important to have some one who is well-acquainted with the criminal justice system. The role of the victim's advocate would not only be to explain to the victim the nature of the proceedings, to prepare her for the case and to assist her in the police station and in Court but to provide her with guidance to how she might obtain help of a different nature from other agencies, for example, mind counseling or medical assistance. It is important to secure continuity of assistance by ensuring that the same person who looked after the complainant's interests in the police station represents her till the end of the case."*

CONCLUSIONS AND SUGGESTIONS

The foregoing discussion makes it obvious that the compensatory relief to be provided to a victim of the offence of rape under the existing law in India is under an embryonic stage. Although, the highest courts have opened new vistas in awarding compensation to the victims of rape, the consequential effects thereof in the post-decision events compel the need for taking further effective steps to execute the laudable principles laid down by the highest judiciary of the country. Establishment of a Criminal Injury Compensatory Board suggested by the Supreme Court is a welcome step, but it requires further procedural steps to make the enforcement of the same. In view of these conclusions it is suggested that a special civil law, more so with the title of "Compensation for Offences against Women Act" shall be enacted, contemplating, inter alia, appropriate relief measures covering all the offences against the women including the offence of rape, apart from bringing necessary modifications in the provisions of IPC, Cr.P.C., and the Evidence Act, in parity with the presently proposed new Act, by taking into consideration the following aspects:

1. The person responsible for rape shall be subjected to marry the victim, provided both of them are in the age group of marriage and are not already married. In case of gang rape, the leader of the gang shall be made to marry the victim.
2. Marriage between the offender and the victim of rape shall not be a ground for the court in not sentencing the offender, but in such a case, the sentence of imprisonment could be for a term not exceeding one year, as a measure of deterrence.
3. In case of rape other than the cases covered by the above entries, the court should award compensation invariably in all cases and such compensation must be pooled into a fund, for which Government should also add its own contribution. Each of the victims of the rape shall be paid on monthly basis a sum not less than Rs.3,000/- with provision for gradual increase depending upon the degree of violence, out of the said funds, regularly until the death of the victim, irrespective of her economic standard or social status or cultural heritage.
4. In case of rape of a minor, the compensation to be awarded shall be exemplary which could be sufficient to make future livelihood of the minor, and where the offender is not in such a position to pay the compensation, the State should compensate the victim accordingly.
5. Employment opportunities shall be extended to the victims of rape as also to their off-springs, wherever it is felt expedient.
6. Incentive schemes should be introduced to encourage women to report about the commission of rape, well in time.
7. Awareness programs through mass media and newsreels in cinema theatres, etc., covering the need to protect the interests of the women in general and the victims of rape in particular and promote their welfare, along with the consequences of committing the sexual violence against women.

Part - III

VICTIMIZATION: CONTEMPORARY ISSUES

L. KAILASAM

11

VICTIMS OF VIOLENT CRIMES

INTRODUCTION

While analyzing the official statistics of crime levels in India, it is found that the crime incidences grow rapidly during the last five decades. The incidence of Indian Penal Code (IPC) offences was increased to 17.71 lakhs in 1999 from 6.25 lakhs in 1971. The incidence of violent crimes was increased from 0.49 lakhs in 1961 to 2.38 lakhs in 2000. The percentage of property crimes and economic crimes were decreased by 36.2 % and 1 % respectively compare to the year 1961 and 2000. On the other hand, the percentage of violent crimes to the total incidences of crimes is increased by 4.6 % compared to year 1961 and 2000. The graphical representation of the share of the above crimes with the total IPC crimes is given below.

Perecentage of Increase of Violent, Property and Economic Crimes

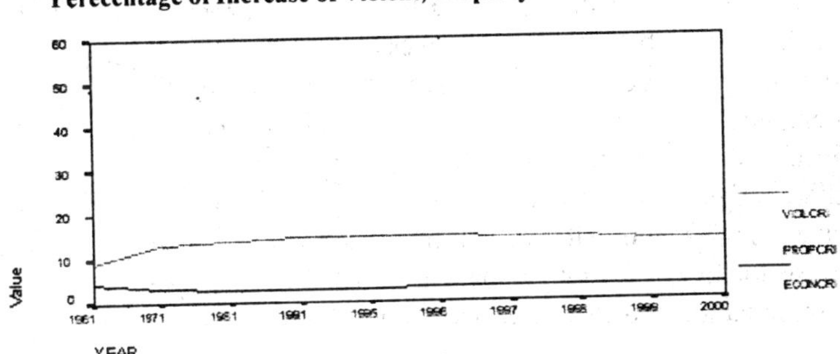

While analyzing the percentage of increase over the years, it is seen that the violent crime are increasing more quickly compared to other types of offences. As a consequence of the increase in the violent crimes, the victims of the violent crimes might have multiplied evenly. Therefore it becomes necessary to analyze the consequences of the increase of the violent crimes in specific the victims of the violent crimes. In this chapter a preliminary attempt is made to concentrate the victimization of murder. The purpose of the study is to analyze the factors of murder victimization from an econometric perspective with objective to suggest useful strategies to reduce the net social loss due to murder victimization.

OBJECTIVE OF THE STUDY

The preliminary objective of the study is to

- Study the existing literature and economic factors leading to victimization.
- Develop an Econometric Model to analyze various factors in order to identify the crucial factors of victimization of violent crimes in specific victimization of murder in India with the objective to reduce the number of victims.
- Suggest useful strategies to reduce murder victimization in India.

REVIEW OF LITERATURE

The Declaration of Basic Principles of Justice for Victims of Crime and Abuse of Power was adopted by the General Assembly of the United Nations on 29 November 1985. In the said declaration it was declared that victims should be treated with compassion and respect for their dignity and that they are entitled to prompt redress for the harm that they have suffered, through access to the criminal justice system, reparation and services to assist their recovery. The Declaration recommended that measures to be taken on behalf of victims of crime to improve access to justice and fair treatment, restitution, compensation and assistance at the international, regional and national levels. The main steps to be taken to prevent victimization linked to abuse of power and to provide remedies for the victims was outlined in the declaration. After declaration, various studies on victimization were taken up. Some of the important studies relating to violent victimization and its causes are given below.

Fajnzylber et al (2000) discussed the recent upward trend in crime rates of developing countries and the risk factors of *victimization*. They found that economic growth and income inequality are robust determinants of violent crime rates and its victimization. They stated that there was clear evidence that the above factors are responsible for *violent crimes* and its consequent victimization.

Andrienko (2003) found the link between crime and wealth. Using the simple probabilistic model of heterogeneous criminals and a victim, they showed that individual risk of crime victimization is the positive function of additional utility received from a victim and negative of its protection. It is negative function of the variance of the initial utility distribution of potential offenders for victim attractive to the average offender and positive otherwise. They found that the risk of crime *victimization* is closely connected with individual wealth, protection and income distribution. They further found that individual wealth have U-shape form influence on *victimization risk* from *violence* and property crimes.

Tella et al (2003) identified that the relationship between crime *victimization* and income distribution. They identified which social group is the main victims of the crimes. They found that poor have suffered mainly due to crime rises in Argentina.

Bar-Gill and another (2000) in their article "Crime Rates and Expected Sanctions: The Economics of Deterrence Revisited" stated that a higher expected sanction lowers the crime rate. They studied the effects of the crime rate on the expected sanction. They studied the effects of the crime rate on deterrence and on optimal law. The optimal deterrence policy may reduce the crime rate and *victimization* accordingly.

Greenfield et al (1998) analyzed the Crimes committed by Current or Former Spouses, Boyfriends, and Girlfriends. The report prepared by the Bureau of Justice Statistics, based on their findings presents a summary of the statistical information about violence committed against intimates. Their finding is based on information gathered from *victims*, law enforcement agencies, hospital emergency departments, and those convicted of crimes against intimates. They also found that Intimate violence predominantly affects women as *victims*.

Krejny (1999) studied the *recidivist victims* and found that despite efforts to control and prevent it, crime is still a serious problem, suggesting that policies aimed at criminals may not be having the desired effect. In order to best allocate scarce resources, policymakers must begin to turn their attention to victims. By understanding what makes a person more likely to be victimized, policymakers can identify high-risk groups and formulate policies that directly, and more efficiently, reach these potential *victims* and prevent crime. This study attempts to identify common characteristics of one particular subset of victims: so-called "recidivist victims," or individuals who have been victimized more than once. Whereas a person who was victimized only once may simply have been in "the wrong place at the wrong time," a person who has been victimized several times may possess some characteristics that make him or her a more attractive target to criminals. The "lifestyle" or "routine activities" framework formulated by sociologists and other researchers to explain personal criminal victimization is discussed and tested using an econometric approach. Some unexpected results indicate that the routine activities theory may not adequately explain an individual's repeat victimization risk.

Rodrigo (2002) discussed the heterogeneity in crime rates across countries. He focuses on two aspects as possible of those differences; reporting rates and economic development. The behavior of the reporting rate was explicitly analyzed by comparing data from a *victimization* survey with official crime records. The results indicated that reporting rates tend to be strongly correlated with development so that richer countries report a higher fraction of committed crimes. The positive relation between development and crime systematically found in previous studies in criminology was shown to be a result of the correlation between development and reporting rates. Once the presence of the reporting error was accounted for income per capita does not have any significant effect on crime. Inequality has positive effect on crime. Growth rates and education have negative effects on crime.

Robert (2001) in his article "Modeling Crime *Victimization* and the propensity to report crime to police" applied regression and small area estimation model. He used a Logit model to report and to test the significance of socio-economic factors that affect individuals reporting decision. The results of model will give better understanding of which groups have a higher or lower propensity to report crime.

Andromachi (2002) and two others in the article "Modeling property crime using the British crime survey" applied simulations to illustrate the roles of household and area characteristics in respect of the following; how household types differ in predicted property crime *victimization* both in aggregate and differentially by crime type; how area characteristics are associated with rates of victimization how household victimization histories affect predictions of subsequent crime events.

Felson et al (2001) examined suspect's relationship to an assault *victim* affects when the police make an arrest. The results indicate that in cases of minor assaults the police less likely to make an arrest when the suspect was an intimate partner of the crime than when the suspect was an identifiable stranger. In addition victims who know the suspect in any way are reluctant to sign complaints and this reluctance inhibits arrest. Men are less likely than women to sign complaints, particularly when the suspect was a partner.

Sheila and two others (2000) discussed the Impacts of childhood abuse of Juvenile violence. They estimated the relationship between childhood abuse and subsequent involvement in juvenile violence either as victim or perpetrator.

Graham and another (1993) in their article "Once bitten, Twice bitten: Repeat *Victimization* and its implications for crime Prevention" discussed the problems of victimization of various types of offences including violent crimes.

Matt (2002) in his article "Crimes Against Business the way forward for future research" considered the reasons such as nature and extent of *victimization* against business.

DATA

From the survey of literature mentioned in the previous para, it is found that economic factors may play prodominat role in determination of victimization in India too. An econometric analysis of the various factors may help to identify the causes of murder victimization.

Therefore it is proposed to analyse the data econometrically to suggest useful strategies for reducing murder victims.

As the objective of the study is to analyze the various factors of murder victimization in India from a cross-country perspective, the official data published by National Crime Records Bureau, Government of India was extensively used. The data relating to economic factors were collected from Economic survey, published by Economic Division, Ministry of Finance, Government of India. The above secondary data was used to develop an econometric model for deriving useful strategies.

The important factors of murder victimization were classified into two categories.

- Individual Characteristics Variables
- Community Variables.

The characteristics of the variables are discussed below

Individual Characteristics Variables

The following individual characteristics variables were analyzed in order to estimate how much they interrelated to murder victimization.

- *Gender*
- *Age*

Gender

Gender plays a vital role in murder victimization. The following table indicates the percentage of male and female victims for the last two years 1999 and 2000.

Table 1
Percentage of Male and Female to total Victims

Year	*Male*	*Percentage of Male to Total Victims*	*Female*	*Percentage of Female to Total Victims*	*Total*
1999	30460	79.59 %	7812	20.41 %	38272
2000	31755	78.65 %	8618	21.35 %	40373

The graphical representation of the above are given below for easy visualization

Graph 1

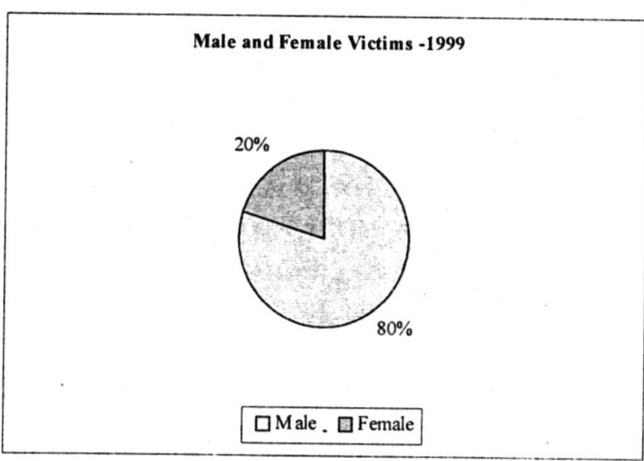

Graph 2

It is seen that Male are more vulnerable victims compare to Females. More than 80 % of murder victims are males and only 20% are females.

Age

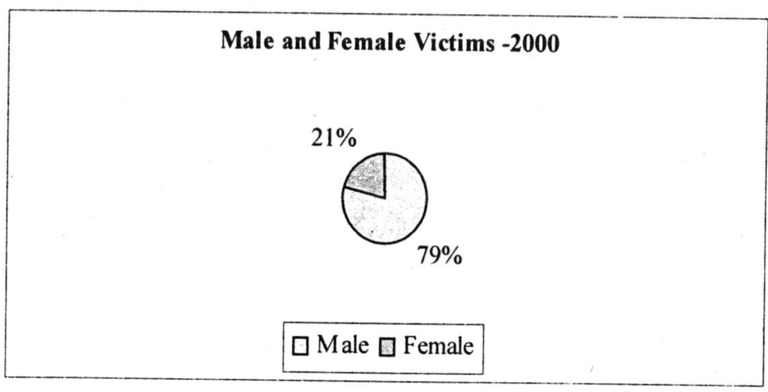

For the purpose of the analysis, the following categories of age were considered

- Up to 10 years
- 11-15 years
- 16-18 years
- 19-30 years

- 31-50 years
- Above 50 years

The following table represents the percentage of murder victims sex wise and age wise for the year 1999 and 2000.

Table 2
Murder Victims –Age Wise Sex Wise Percentage

Sl. No.	*Age*	*1999* Male	Female	Total	*2000* Male	Female	Total
1.	Upto 10 years	1.50	1.18	2.68	1.45	1.35	2.81
2.	11-15 years	1.36	0.60	1.96	1.24	0.62	1.85
3.	16-18 years	4.68	1.61	6.30	5.10	1.74	6.84
4.	19-30 years	32.79	9.27	42.06	33.04	9.86	42.90
5.	31-50 years	32.40	6.25	38.66	30.98	6.40	37.38
6.	Above 50 years	6.85	1.49	8.34	6.84	1.38	8.22
	Total	79.59	20.41	100.00	78.65	21.35	100.00

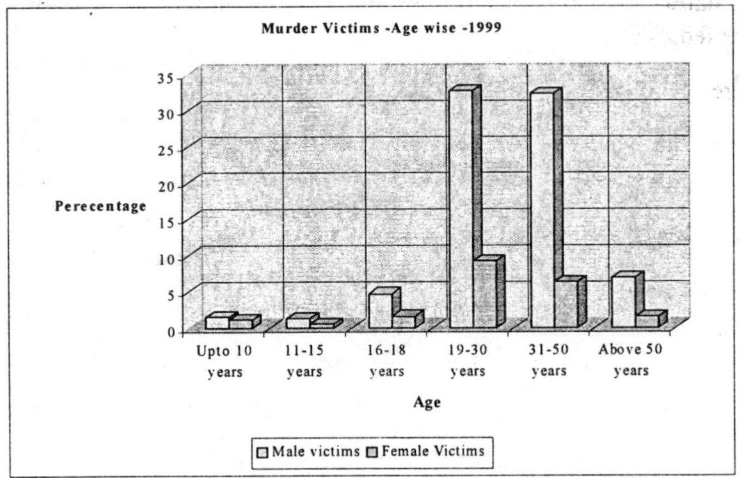

On analyzing the above table and graph it is found that Male age group falling 19-30 years are the most vulnerable group of murder victims in India.

Community Variables

The second type of variables represents community indicators. The following indicators are considered important and affect the murder victims for the purpose of analysis.

- Firearms
- Worker's Participation
- Literacy rate
- GDP
- Police strength

Fire Arms

The majority of the victims of murder were due to use of firearms by the criminals. Eight thousand three hundred and seventy persons were killed by using licensed and unlicensed firearms during 2000. It represents 20.73% (24.28 % for the year 1999) of victims are died due to the firearms only. Compare to the year 1999, the number of persons died due to firearms was decreased by 3.55%. As the firearms plays a vital role in victimization of murder cases, the above variables were considered.

Worker's Participation

The unemployment plays vital role in commission of any crime. The unutilised and under utilized mind is always seed ground for any criminal activities. Many of violent crime are due to unemployment. The workers participation rate is good indicator for measuring the unemployment.

Literacy Rate

Education is one of the important factors of criminality and victimization. It is commonly seen that the offender of murder victims is less educated and on the other hand the victim is educated slightly higher or at least more compare to offender. The inequality in the education leads to commission of offences. Therefore this factor was taken into consideration for confirming whether it plays a vital role in commission of murder offences.

Per Capita

This important economic indicator and plays a vital role in deciding the crime incidences and victimization accordingly. In this chapter an attempt has been made to confirm whether per capita net domestic Product at current prices has an impact in the criminality in India.

Police Expenses

The number of police officials plays a vital role in preventing the occurrence of crimes in the society. If the number of policemen is employed more, the criminals might not be possible to continue their activities. Therefore expenses incurred on the police authorities are taken for confirming whether they have impact on the victimization in India.

Table 3
Correlation Between the Various Factors of Victimization with the Number of Victims

Name of the Factor Leading Victims of Murder	*Correlation Coefficient*
Arms	0.8087
Worker's participation	-0.1068
Literacy	- 0.4965
Per Capita	0.6821
Police expenses	0.8729

The correlation coefficients of the various variables considered with the victims of murder are evaluated and given below.

The empirical approach for analyzing the cross county evidence requires to develop a model for deriving useful conclusions. The model developed is explained in the next section.

MODEL

For the purpose of analyzing the impact of the variables discussed above, K-Linear Model can be developed as follows. This model helps to quantify the impact of the various variables discussed above. The number of victims, which is dependent variable, could be quantified when a particular situation exists. By making slight adjustment in the dependent variable by taking appropriate decision by the policy makers, it may be possible to reduce the number of victims and hence net social loss. The basic model developed is of the following form.

Number of Victims = F
(Arms, Worker's Participation, Literacy, Per Capita and Police Expenses) (5.1)

Where Number of Victims is the Dependent Variable and Arms, Worker's Participation, Literacy, Per Capita and Police Expenses are independent variables

Econometrically it can be written as

$$Y = b_1 * X_1 + b_2 * X_2 + b_3 * X_3 + b_4 * X_4 + b_5 * X_5 + u \qquad (5.2)$$

Where,

Y represents number of victims
X_1 represents *Arms*
X_2 represents *Worker's participation*
X_3 represents *Literacy*
X_4 represents *Per capita*
X_5 represents *Police Expenses and*
b_1, b_2, b_3, b_4, b_5 are constants and u is the disturbance term

The dependent variable in the model is *'Victim'* a count data, showing number of persons was victim of murder during a previous year.

By running the K-Linear regression the following results were obtained.

$$Y = 923.9398 + 1.2814 * X_1 + 17.7136 * X_2 - 24.62 * X_3 + 0.011008 * X_4 + 0.748158 * X_5 + u \qquad (5.3)$$

Where,

Y represents number of victims
$\mathbf{X_1}$ represents *Arms*
$\mathbf{X_2}$ represents *Worker's participation*
$\mathbf{X_3}$ represents *Literacy*
$\mathbf{X_4}$ represents *Per capita*
$\mathbf{X_5}$ represents *Police Expenses*

CONCLUSIONS

On analyzing the above equation, the following conclusions can be derived

- If all the dependent variables *i.e.* Arms, Worker's Participation, Literacy, Per Capita and Police Expenses kept at zero level, the average number of victims would be 923

The partial coefficients with negative value have the impact of reducing the incidences of victims. There is only one negative coefficient i.e. literacy rate

- The partial coefficient 24.62 means that the incidences of victims will have an average decrease by 25 incidences for every unit of increase in Literacy

The impact of positive partial coefficients is discussed below.

- The partial regression coefficient 17.7136 means that the incidences of victims will have an average increase by 18 for every unit increase in number of Worker's Participation.
- The partial regression coefficient 1.2814 means that the incidences of victims will have an average increase by one for every unit increase in the percentage of Arms.
- The partial regression coefficient 0.7481 means that the incidences of victims will have an average increase by 0.7481 for every unit increase in Police Strength.
- The partial regression coefficient 0.011008 means that the incidences of victims will have an average increase by 0.011 for every unit increase in Per capita.

Based on the above analysis it can be concluded that

- As regard murder victims are concerned, more than 80 % of victims are male. The male members of the age group 19-30 are the most vulnerable group of murder victims. By educating this vulnerable group about the consequences of murder and other violent crimes it is possible to reduce the victims of murder to a major extent
- Since the literacy plays a very vital role, appropriate measures are to be taken to increase the literacy to a maximum possible extent in specific in the areas where the illiteracy is more
- The worker participation should be made evenly, which may reduce the murder victims.
- The presence of licensed and unlicensed arms in the society is one of the main reasons for murder victimization and it has positive impact on the increase of victimization and hence adequate measures to be taken to remove the unlicensed arms and provide more restrictions for issue of license arms.
- The expenditure on police leads to more number of victims. However the coefficients are meagre. Therefore, appropriate allocations to victim's assistance are to be made, which may lead to reduction of murder victimization.
- The coefficient of per capital in the analysis is meagre and hence it is not much relevant in determination of murder victimization.

- At present, there is no specific provision in Indian Penal Code for paying cost and damages to the victims by the killer. Necessary amendment to be made in Section 301 of Indian Penal Code itself so that the offender, apart from punishment and fine should pay appropriate cost and damages to the victims, as ordered by the competent court. This suggestion give relief to victims without any burden to the exchequer

REFERENCES

Andrienko Yuri, (2003), *Crime and wealth: Evidence from international crime victim surveys*, Center for Economic and Financial Research, Moscow, June 2003.

Ards, D Sheila, L Samuel Myers, Jr and Wan Fang, (2000), *"The Impacts of childhood abuse of Juvenile violence,* A paper presented for presentation at the International conference "Violence in the Family", Novermber 28, 2000.

Baller, D Robert, Anselin Luc, Messner F. Steven & Hawkins F Darnell, (2001), "Structural Co-variates of US country homicide rates: Incorporating spatial effects" *Criminology* Volume 39 Number 3, 2001.

Bar-Gill Oren and Harel Alon (2000), *"Crime Rates and Expected Sanctions: The Economics of Deterrence Revisited* The Eitan Berglas School of Economics, Tel-Aviv University, Tel-Aviv, Israel 69978. June 2000.

Economic Division, Ministry of Finance, Government of India, "Economic Survey 2000-2001.

Fajnzylber Pablo, Lederman Daniel and Loayzal Norman, (2000), *Crime and Victimization: An Economic Perspective*, This paper has been prepared for presentation at the 1st Meeting of the Latin America Economic Policy Review, New York, 2000.

Felson, B Richard, & Ackerman Jeff, (2001), "Arrest for Domestic and other assaults, *Criminology* . Volume 39 Number 3, 2001.

Graham, Ousey C, Lee R Matthew, (2002), "Examining the conditional nature of the illicit drug market – homicide relationship: A partial test of the theory of contingent causation", *Criminology.* Volume 40 Number 1, 2002.

Greenfeld Lawrence and others, (1998), *"Violence by Intimates: Analysis of Data on Crimes by Current or Former Spouses, Boyfriends, and Girlfriends"* U.S. Department of Justice, Office of Justice Programs, March 1998.

Hopkins, Matt, (2002), "Crimes Against Business the way forward for future research", *British Journal of Criminology* (2002) 42, 782-797, 2002.

Krejny L Meredith, (1999), "*Answering the Question: Who gets victimized?* Regional Research Institute, West Virginia University, March 1999.

National Crime Record Bureau, Ministry of Home Affairs, Government of India, *"Crime in India 2000"*.

Soares, R Rodrigo, (2002), *Development, Crime and Punishment: Accounting for the International Differences in Crime Rates*, 5-Sep, 2002.

Tella Di Rafael, Galiani Sebastian, Schargrodsky Ernesto (2002). *"Crime Inequality when Victims Adapt"*. Inter-American Development Bank Regional Policy Dialogue Poverty Reduction and Social Protection Network Studies on Poverty and Social Protection May 2002.

Tella Di Rafael, Galiani Sebastian, Schargrodsky Ernesto, (2002). *"Crime Victimization and Income Distribution"* . Inter-American Development Bank, Regional Policy Dialogue Poverty Reduction and Social Protection Network, Studies on Poverty and Social Protection. May 2002.

Tseloni, Andromachi, (2000), "*Comparing multilevel and single level negative binomial regression models of personal crimes: Evidence from the National Crime victimization survey,* Department of Criminology and Criminal Justice, University of Maryland.

United Nations (1999), *Handbook on Justice for Victims: On the use and application of the United Nations Declaration of the basic principles of Justice for Victims of Crime and Abuse of power*. Office for Drug Control and Crime prevention, Center for International Crime prevention. Retrieved on August 25, 2005 at www.ojp.usdoj.gov/ovc.

R. KARTHIKA AND K. JAISHANKAR

12

VICTIMIZATION OF LABOURERS IN BRICK KILN INDUSTRY

INTRODUCTION

"They work, work since dawn to sunset, work in the midst of creation or destruction of empires, work in the middle of birth and death" said Nobel Laureate Rabindra Nath Tagore, about the labourers (Haldar, 2003). They are the engines of the financial stability of a country. But they are the unfortunate victims of ignorance when it comes to the question of their human rights, freedom of speech of action or regarding personal security. In a developing democratic country like ours, though the exploitation of labourers are lesser than capitalist countries due to various Trade unions and Labour laws, but the daily wage workers are still in the dark (Haldar, 2003). Daily wage labourers are the victims of poverty, the ever-changing employment situation and the fascism of the capitalist society. As they are illiterate and poor, these daily wageworkers are ignorant of their rights. The employer, taking advantage of the poor condition of the workers dictated by their own terms and conditions with regard to wages, hours of work, leave etc., The workers were left with no choice, but to accept such terms because service was the sole means of earning their livelihood (Haldar, 2003).

The effects of victimization hit, particularly hard on the poor labourers who are the disable, the powerless, and the socially isolated. For the victimized labour, longer-term employments are adversely affected. It may be possible for the victim to return to work after a long time but their work performance will be adversely affected, resulting in demotion, loss of pay and possible dismissal. This is particularly likely where the victimization occurred at work, as it may be difficult for the victim to avoid people or situations, which led to their initial victimizations. Researches show that shock waves from victimization touch, not only the victim but also the victim's immediate family and the next of kin, neighbours and acquaintances. This holds true for the emotional as well as the financial consequences, and the effects can endure for years or even for a lifetime. The victims of abuse of power have particularly difficulty in gaining recognition of the fact that they have been victimized. The essence of abuse of power is that, those who should be expected to protect the population commit it. The shock and loneliness incurred by the victimization can be much greater by these victims (Haldar, 2003).

BRICK KILN INDUSTRY AND PROBLEMS

The Brick kiln industry focuses its work on preparing bricks for building new structures, as well as additions, alterations, and repairs. Most Brick kiln workers work full time, with many working overtime. They often are required to work evenings, weekends, and holidays to finish a job. Brick kiln workers need to be physically fit. Work often requires prolonged standing, bending, stooping, and heavy lifting. Exposure to extreme weather conditions is common because much of this work is done outside or in partially completed structures. Workers may be required to work with potentially dangerous tools and equipment, often on temporary scaffolding or in bad weather. Therefore, Brick kiln workers are more prone to injury than in other occupations

People may enter the industry without any formal classroom training after high school. However, skilled workers such as carpenters either need many years of on-the-job training, or apprenticeship training where they pick up their skills by working alongside experienced workers. As they acquire these skills they move progressively to more challenging work. After several years of moving up the ladder, they reach journey level. Apprenticeship programs are often administered by local unions. Training usually lasts between 3 and 5 years and consists of both classroom and real work experience.

Brick Kilns are a complementary industry to the Construction Sector. The process of production is largely manual and consequently, the Brick Kiln industry is a major employer of workers. According to the All-India Brick Kilns & Tiles Manufacturer's Federation (at New Delhi), there are 50, 000 Brick kilns all over India employing, on an average, 100 workers (as per muster rolls)per unit. The Brick kilns are of three sizes: large kilns producing 45,000 - 60,000 bricks per day, medium kilns producing around 25,000 bricks per day and small kilns producing 12,000 - 15,000 bricks per day

Workers at Brick kilns belong to the lowest economic strata of the labour force. Out of the 51 brick kiln workers interviewed, about six out of ten (60.8%) were landless labourers who spent about 6 to 7 months at Brick kilns and the remaining period as agricultural workers. The remaining Brick kiln workers did own marginal fragments of land and combined income from self-cultivation with wages from Brick kilns. Brick kiln workers are recruited through labour agents of the kilns owners. The recruitment process generally involves payment of advance to workers at their native places for a specific period of employment. Consequent to the payment of advance, the entire family comprising of husband, wife and children moves to a given Brick kiln and works there during the Brick making season. It is worth noting that only adult males are registered as workers on the muster rolls of the employers and the rest of the family members remain 'invisible' to the social production and accounting system. Women accompanying the male worker can be wife, sister or widowed mother. Children accompanying a worker include younger brothers apart from his own children.

Ercelawn and Nauman (2003) explored the situation in brick kilns with a view to emphasizing the feasibility of socially effective, prompt relief and remedy. It is based on rapid assessments through short visits of over 100 brick kilns in and around the urban and semi-urban areas of the districts of Hyderabad, Multan, Lahore, Rawalpindi, Peshawar and Haripur; A study on brick kilns conducted in New Delhi by ILO (2003) has found out that the work at Brick kilns is a seasonal activity occurring largely between October and June. The Brick kilns shut-down during the monsoon period. The study showed that 13.7% of the workers were less than 14 years old at the time of first migration to Brick kilns. This is indicative of the significant presence of child labour in the Brick kiln industry. Churchill and Guerin (2003) in their study on the brick kiln workers analyzed the situation of the brick kiln workers in Tiruvallur and considered as a milder form of bondage. Brick kiln work is seasonal, for six or seven months, until the rains come. Workers are usually brought in from poorer communities by a middleman who provides a salary advance (which was advanced to him by the kiln owner). Although the working conditions are unattractive, wages are around the poverty level. Since they often come from dry areas, during the low season, workers typically have few other income opportunities. Consequently, their primary means for acquiring cash is to pledge their labour for the following season, launching a perpetual cycle of commitments. Figures are preliminary results of an empirical study conducted by the French Institute of Pondicherry for the ILO and are based on a sample of 250 brick kiln workers.

Bhukuth (2005) in his study highlights some of the findings from a study carried out in the brick kiln industry in Tamil Nadu. This was both a qualitative and a quantitative survey. As child labour is a common factor in the brick kiln industry, he showed that in the interlinked credit-labour market employers do not directly employ children, but they have implemented a system that constrains parents to use their children to improve their productivity. In such an environment parents use child labour to improve their bargaining power.

It is found that there are few studies on workers in brick kiln industry. However, most of the studies deal with general problems of workers and not on victimization due to specific abuse or exploitation. The purpose of this study is to fill the gap in the literature on labour victims of brick kiln industry in the Indian context.

NEED AND SIGNIFICANCE OF THE STUDY

The Present Study aims at Studying the Victimization of labourers. This Study is an attempt to explore the various forms of Victimization in brick kiln industry. This Study aims to find the nature and extent of Victimization in brick kiln industry, and the problems faced by labourers. The main purpose of this research is to analyze the victimization of labourers in Brick Kiln Industry. It is situated in Panagudi, Tirunelveli District, Tamil Nadu, India. The area of this industry is 4 acres. Nearly 150 workers are working. The workers were treated cruelly by owners. The womens of this industry were physically, psychologically, and sexually abused. Women and children were abused by male co-workers, and employers. Daily wage workers face many problems inside this industry. The present study tries to analyze the problems faced by the labourers inside the Brick kiln industry and tries to provide suggestions.

METHOD

The universe of the study comprised of the labourers of Panagudi in Tirunelveli district, Tamil Nadu, India. Purposive sampling method was adopted to choose the sample for the present study. A total of 110 respondents were selected for the present study from Panagudi area. An interview schedule was constructed to collect data from the respondents. This study comprises 110 samples, of which 41 were male, 60 respondents were female and 9 respondents were Transgender. For the Pilot study 10 victims of abuse were taken from the universe of the study. The Purpose of the pilot study was to test the comprehension of the tool by the respondents and the face validity of the interview schedule was fixed after consulting experts in the field of Criminology. After the pilot study in the interview schedule, certain items were incorporated or modified. The main study was conducted with the help of final draft or interview schedule. The data collected in main study were processed by using the statistical package for social sciences (SPSS – version 11) Programme and percentage analysis was done to elicit the results.

RESULTS AND DISCUSSION

I. Socio-economic Characteristics

Table 1
Socio-economic Characteristics

Age	*N*	*%*
10-20	15	13.6
21-30	34	30.9
31-40	27	24.5
41-50	34	30.9

Contd....

Age	*N*	*%*
Sex		
Male	41	37.3
Female	60	54.5
Transgender	9	8.2
Education		
Uneducated	48	43.6
Below 8th std	33	30.0
Below 10th std	20	18.2
Below 12th std	7	6.4
Under graduates	2	1.8
Community		
OC	14	12.7
BC	32	29.1
MBC/DNC	17	15.5
SC/ST	47	42.7
Mode of Work		
Daily coolie	82	74.5
Monthly coolie	28	25.5

The Table 1 shows that 30.9% of the respondents were in the age group between 21-30 and 41-50, 24.5% of the respondents were in the age group between 31 - 40, 13.6% of the respondents were in the age group between 10-20. So here these age group respondents are mostly child labourers. 54.5% of the respondents were female workers, then 37.3% of the respondents were male workers, then 8.2% of the respondents were transgender workers. 43.6% of the respondents were uneducated, 30% of the respondents had their education below 8th, 18.2% of the respondents were below 10th std, 6.4% of the respondents were below 12th std, 1.8% of the respondents were under graduates. 42.7% of the respondents were SC/ST, 29.1% of the respondents were BC, then 15.5% of the respondents were MBC/DNC, and 12.7% of the respondents were OC. Majority of the respondents belong to SC/ST group. 74% of the respondents work for daily wages and 25.5% of the respondents said that they were monthly workers.

II. Victimization by Harassment

Table 2
Type of Harassment

	Type of Harassment			
	Yes		*No*	
Type of Abuse	*N*	*%*	*N*	*%*
Physical	56	50.9	54	49.1
Sexual	84	76.4	26	23.6
Mental and Verbal	66	60.0	44	40.0
All the above	79	71.8	31	28.2

Table 2 shows that 76.4% of the respondents were sexually harassed. 60% of the respondents were mentally and verbally harassed by owner, and co-workers. 50% of the respondents were harassed physically of the respondents were harassed physically, sexually, mentally and verbally.

Table 3
Forms of Physical Abuse

	Forms of Physical Abuse			
Physical abuse	*Yes*		*No*	
	N	*%*	*N*	*%*
Slapping	0	0.00	110	100.0
Hitting with sticks	4	3.6	106	96.4
Beating and using vulgar words	51	46.4	59	53.6
Making to work more than required	102	92.7	8	7.3

Table 3 shows the various forms of physical abuse. 92.7% of the respondents said that the most used form of physical abuse is making to work more than required and 46.4% of the respondents experienced beating and using vulgar words.

Sexual Abuse

Table 4 shows that more than 93.6% of the respondents were sexually abused and the forms of sexual abuse is physical contact and advances, demand or request for sexual favour, sexually collared remarks, unwelcome physical conduct of sexual nature, unwelcome verbal or non-verbal behaviour of sexual nature. 49.1% of the respondents felt unwelcome physical contact of sexual nature, and 40% felt physical contact and advances.

Table 4
Forms of Sexual Abuse

Sexual Abuse	*Forms of Sexual Abuse* *Yes* *N*	*%*	*No* *N*	*%*
Physical contact and advances	44	40.0	66	60.0
Demand or request for sexual favour	34	30.9	76	69.1
Sexually collared remarks	42	38.2	68	61.8
Unwelcome physical conduct of sexual nature	54	49.1	56	50.9
Unwelcome verbal or non-verbal behaviour of sexual nature	40	36.4	70	63.6
All the above	7	6.4	103	93.6

Table 5
Forms of mental abuse

Mental Abuse	*Forms of Mental Abuse* *Yes* *N*	*%*	*No* *N*	*%*
Using vulgar words	63	57.3	47	42.7
lack of leisure	26	23.6	84	76.4
Not providing leave	15	13.6	95	86.4
Reducing wages	32	29.1	78	70.9
All the above	43	39.1	67	60.9

This Table 5 shows the various forms of mental abuse. 57.3% of the respondents felt abuse by using vulgar words, 39.1% of the respondents experienced abuse by vulgar words, lack of leisure, not providing leave, reducing wages, and 29.1% of the respondents felt wage reduction as the reason of mental abuse.

Nature of the Resistance

Table 6 shows that the nature of resistance in various abuse. 53.6% of the respondents disobeyed abusers orders, 36.4% of the respondents became silent, totally neglected the abuser, told that they will resign and 39.1% of the respondents got angry.

Table 6
Nature of Resistance

Nature of Resistance	*Nature of the Resistance*			
	Yes		*No*	
	N	*%*	*N*	*%*
Got angry	43	39.1	67	60.9
Become silent	40	36.4	70	63.6
Totally neglected him	40	36.4	70	63.6
disobeyed his orders	59	53.6	51	46.4
Told that you will resign	40	36.4	70	63.6
All the above	27	24.5	83	75.5

First Reaction

Table 7
First Reaction Towards Harassment

First Reaction	*First Reaction*			
	Yes		*No*	
	N	*%*	*N*	*%*
Shock	38	34.5	72	65.5
Anger	31	28.2	79	71.8
Trauma	39	35.5	71	64.5
Nervousness	33	30.0	77	70.0
Helplessness	32	29.1	78	70.9
Resistance	41	37.3	69	62.7
All the above	53	48.2	57	51.8

Table 7 shows that the first reaction of the abuse. 48.2% of the respondent's reaction was shock, anger, trauma, nervousness, helplessness, resistance. 35.5% of the respondents experienced trauma, 37.3% of the respondents resisted and 34.5% of the respondents felt shock.

Reasons for not Complaining Against the Abuser

Table (8) shows the reasons that they did not complained to the higher authorities. 48.2% of the respondents were of the feeling of humiliation, fear of mocking by other workers, it may create problem in their work, it may create in family life, and afraid of higher authority, and 15.5% of the respondents were afraid of the higher authorities.

Table 8
Reasons

Reasons for not Complaining Against the Abuser				
Reasons	*Yes*		*No*	
	N	*%*	*N*	*%*
Feeling of humiliation	10	9.1	100	90.9
Fear of mocking by other workers	8	7.3	102	92.7
It may create problem in my work	10	9.1	100	90.9
It may create problem in my family life	14	12.7	96	87.3
I am afraid of my higher authorities	17	15.5	93	84.5
All the above	53	48.2	57	51.8

III. Impact of Harassment

Table 9
Impact of Harassment

Impact of Harassment	*N*	*%*
Scaring		
Always	5	4.5
Often	38	34.5
Seldom	46	41.8
Never	21	19.1
Feel their life is Useless		
Always	16	14.5
Often	31	28.2
Seldom	42	38.2
Never	21	19.1
Depression		
Always	12	10.9
Often	41	37.3
Seldom	38	34.5
Never	19	17.3
Feeling of Revenge		
Always	21	19.1
Often	36	32.7
Seldom	29	26.4
Never	24	21.8

Impact of Harassment	*N*	%
Feel to Resign the Job		
Always	18	16.4
Often	39	35.5
Seldom	29	26.4
Never	24	21.8
Full Concentration of duties in past		
Yes	1	0.9
No	74	67.3
Not applicable	35	31.8

Table 9 shows the impact of harassment. 34.5% often felt scarred. 67.3% felt that they were not able to concentrate in their duties as they did in the past.

FINDINGS

- Majority of the female respondents were abused.
- 10 respondent's wives were sexually harassed.
- Most of the respondents felt harassment in workplace.
- Majority of the respondents were abused physically by making to work more than required.
- Majority of the respondents were sexually, mentally and verbally abused.
- Majority of the respondent's first reaction of abuse were shock, anger, trauma, nervousness, helplessness, resistance.
- Most of the respondents did not complain about their abuse to higher authority, the reason was it may create problem in their family life, and many were afraid of higher authorities.
- Majority of the respondents felt that they were not satisfied with the action taken by the higher authority and police.
- Majority of the respondents were scared by the employer / abuser.
- Majority of the respondents felt that their life is useless.
- Majority of the respondents were in depression
- Majority of the respondents have the feeling of taking revenge.
- Majority of the respondents felt that they should resign their job.
- Majority of the respondents are not able to perform their duties, with full concentration as in past.

CONCLUSION

It is found in this study that most of the workers are SC/ST people. In other studies done on brick kiln labourers also the same trend is found. Some victims were daily coolies, because they are very poor. Most of the respondents said that they were physically, sexually, mentally and verbally abused by owners or co-workers. Some women labourers tried to resist the abuse. Most of the victims were found suffering of depression. Mostly women respondents were sexually abused by owners or co- workers. The labourers of this industry are widely abused. Awareness should be created among the labourers, public, owners, regarding the plight of victimization. Most of the respondents did not complain the abuse to the higher authority or police. The reasons were

- The fear of humiliation.
- Fear of Mocking by other workers.
- They may create problem in their daily work.
- They may create problem in their family life.
- Fear of higher authority or police.

Special training must be given to the owners, and Co-Workers, so that they would not abuse the labourers in the work place. This study would help providing the empirical information about the labourers' abuse by the owners. The Society, NGOs, other government organization should take appropriate measures to stop the abuse of labourers. The development of every nation solely depends on labourers. Therefore efforts must be taken to address the issue of labourers abuse by owners, Co – workers, higher officers in work place.

REFERENCES

Ercelawn A and M Nauman (2003), "Forced Labour in Pakistan Debt Bondage in Brick Kilns", *Asia Pacific Research Network Journals:* Volume 9 December 2003 http://www.aprnet.org.

Churchill C. and Guerin I. (2003), "Micro led finance to eliminate bonded labour" A study of ILO. Available at http://www.ilo.org/public/english/employment/finance/download/churchguer.pdf.

Bhukuth Augendra (2005), "Child Labour and Debt Bondage" *A Case Study of Brick Kiln Workers in Southeast India Journal of Asian and African Studies*, Vol. 40, No. 4, 287-302 (2005).

Haldar Debarati (2003), Victimization of Labour in India: A shrouded Episode. Unpublished Article. (by Personal Communication).

NANDITHA GOPAL AND LAVANYA PAUL

13

CRIMINALISING STREET HARASSMENT: RECLAIMING PUBLIC SPACE

INTRODUCTION

Congested Traffic. Crowded markets. Long queues. While in public spaces, one encounters a range of minor accustomed annoyances. Most of these are irritations that we have grown to become accustomed to as inevitable and normal. However, there is a subcategory of situations that impact only a part of the population. A woman walks on a street. A man whom she does not know approaches her and makes an obscene remark or gesture. The woman counters it with a retort, or more typically, ignores him and walks on. Does this seem like a common sequence of events? The reason that every woman would answer that in the affirmative is because that is the harsh reality. It happen everyday of the year. On the surface, the above described situation would seem like a most simple and ordinary encounter. A deeper look however, would reveal a complexity of feeling, thought and intention that, despite decades of feminist theorizing, we have just begun the process of decoding. Hidden in this complexity are the personal and political contradictions of women's lives, making the experience of street harassment the quintessential moment of feminity in our culture.

On a horrifyingly frequent basis, women are approached by unfamiliar male perpetrators and are subjected to acts of tort and crime that have been trivialised over the years. These women find themselves targets of lewd remarks, gestures, solicitations etc. One common thread that runs through these offences is that they are premised on sexual undercurrents. Another popularly observed cause of street harassment is that it stems from the urge of male perpetrators to assert their perceived position of power in the most proximate forum that they can do so – the street.

A substantial portion of feminist jurisprudence over the years has highlighted the tendency of the law to not take seriously, events that affect the lives of women. The eye of the law, they opine, either fails to 'see', or trivialises factors which have a profound effect upon women's consciousness, physical well-being and freedom. A direct consequence of street harassment is the ghettoisation of women into private spheres. It is the near universalisation of the offence that has ironically and unfortunately resulted in the universalisation of its acceptance. There are, however, a section of women that refuse to accept this victimisation as inevitable. The existing criminalisation of the undefined act of 'outraging modesty' imposes its own costs on the victims in determining the crime. This chapter seeks to speak out for all those women who do not regard the frequent violations of their body and space as normal.

This chapter seeks to primarily take the first step in identifying and naming the offence of street harassment. The chapter, in doing so, draws from common practical experiences of women on the street. The researchers have then examined the current legal redress available with regard to the issue, its judicial discourse, and its consequent ineffectiveness. The analysis seeks to deconstruct existing myths that have only facilitated the perpetuation of patriarchal morality. The chapter then proposes a draft legislation seeking to criminalise this very 'normal', 'everyday' event.

DEFINING STREET HARASSMENT: *NAMING THE CRIME*

A wide variety of behaviour would come within the purview of the conduct that is generally considered by targets, survey respondents, and commentators to constitute street harassment. These would include both verbal and non-verbal conduct such as lewd remarks, lewd gestures, unwelcome body conduct, stalking, "catcalls", "wolf whistles" etc. The remarks are frequently sexual in nature, and comment exhaustively on a woman's physical appearance and her presence in public. They range from "hello baby" to vulgar suggestions and outright threats.

At the outset we would like to submit the following reasons for using the term "street harassment" as opposed to "sexual harassment in public places":

- To tie the phenomenon to conduct that is currently punishable in the workplace;
- To emphasise the conduct component over the speech in apprehension of any counter assertions about Freedom of Speech and Expression and;
- To emphasise that this conduct is not essentially sexual in nature so much as it motivated by and instrumental to male power and hierarchy. [1]

Further, although the 'street' is a common venue of harassment of this kind, the term 'street' is to signify a range of public places; such harassment takes place quite commonly in venues such as buses, bus stations, cinema halls etc.

We have however, identified the following common characteristics that run through all of these acts:

- The typical targets of street harassment are female;
- The harassers are male;
- The aforementioned are commonly unacquainted;
- The encounter is usually face to face;
- The forum is a public one; a place to which the substantial portion of the public has access;
- The contents of the speech, if any, are not intended as public discourse.

While all individuals may define street harassment in varying terms, it is imperative that the law requires taking a more static vision. In attempting to define street harassment, it is likely that some women may differ in their opinions on what kind of comments may be legally sanctioned and what may not.

What we have primarily identified as important is to define the term in terms of the action and not the intention. This would to a certain extent, help in establishing objective standards for judgement. Further, it would help recognise that street harassment must be examined as a tool of male oppression with all its complexities and its context based nature. In addition, as a legal problem, it must be shaped into a more specific description that can withstand debate.

During the course of the study however, we found that not always were the harassers entirely unacquainted with their targets. They have typically also included colleagues, college mates, jilted boyfriends and the like that find the public place a safe haven for such expression that they would otherwise find themselves restricted from doing because of social pressure. The street on the other hand, is popularly perceived where men may stake their claim as male space. The legislation therefore, seeks to include even acquainted perpetrators within its purview. The researchers acknowledge that this may be problematic with regard to the man's judgement of when his acts have turned unwelcome. The chapter and the legislation seeks in no way, to criminalise the mere approach to a woman[2]. Instead, the chapter is premised on what most feminist groups have sought to teach the sexes:

"NO MEANS NO MEANS NO". Therefore, even if the harasser and the victim are people that have moved intimately for a period of time, the researchers seek to incorporate the right of the woman to nevertheless, say NO at any point, even if it was previously welcomed. Any act subsequent to this would therefore then constitute harassment. Thereby, the starting point of the criminalisation is with regard to acts that are unwelcome. The paper has sought to however, deconstruct existing unacceptable myths of what is welcome and what is not and counters that the 'reasonable man' would be the best judge of it. Secondly, in addition to "...unwelcome to the woman...", the researchers have chosen to append the word "disrespectful". This is in furtherance of a contention to incorporate the respectfulness standard as opposed to the reasonableness standard, in the light of the evident inadequacy of the later. Further, in pursuance of our earlier mentioned argument to broaden the concept to include acts that are not necessarily overtly sexual in nature, the words "...includes but not limited to..." are proposed to be introduced.

The final definition we submit would be more tenable is thus: *"Street harassment occurs when one or more persons accost one or more women in a public place on one or more occasions, and intrude or attempt or intrude upon the woman's privacy in a manner that is disrespectful and unwelcome to the woman, with language and/or actions that include but are not limited to those that are explicitly or implicitly sexual."*

STUDYING STREET HARASSMENT: *THE GHETTOISATION OF WOMEN*

Public places can engender a characteristic set of incivilities that can injure an individual's self esteem either fleetingly or, since the occurrence of these incivilities is repetitive and recursive, more momentously and even permanently. Women often see the dilemma and dissatisfaction of public harassment as evocative of larger issues in their relations with men as men often see them as evoking their own perceived gender dilemmas. We as a society have neglected public harassment, especially the heterosexually romanticized public harassment that women experience from men: the vulgar slur that pretends to be flattery, the act of caressing a breast or posterior that a man might explain was compelled because the woman was so alluring, the screams and blows from playful men who harass women because men believe them lovely or because they believe them to be no better than mere sexual objects. Instead of examining the breached rules of public places per se, society prefers to examine tangential issues architecture, city life, etiquette, and civility that reflect some, although customarily few, of these public harassment abuses. This neglect is regrettable. In women's lives, public harassment abuses are frequent reminders of the ever-present relevance of their gender. In the history-less present of public places, gender norms need to be constantly established and are being constantly accomplished. Public harassment reinforces the basic division between the sexes and prescribes the conduct or mere presence of some while punishing others.

Street harassment, much contrary to popular male perception, cuts across women of all shapes, sizes and colour. The targets of street harassment are literally any women between the age when her body begins to develop sexually to an undefined point when she is no longer believed to be a sexual being because she is dismissed as being "too old". It is important to not however, that the experience of street harassment varies between women. For a very young girl, it is one of the earliest and defining sources of a girl's disempowerment. Street harassment teaches women that their sexuality is their vulnerability. In addition, street harassment impacts vulnerable groups within women as a sect. Lesbians, prostitutes etc., find themselves continually subjected to acts of harassment not only by virtue of their feminity, but also doubly for being socially labelled as moral deviants. Street harassment clearly has an impact upon the psychological well being of women, as well as upon their conduct. In the cold light of the law, however, the question posed is whether this impact rises above the ordinary annoyances that people must endure as the price of living in society.

The Impact of Street Harassment upon Women.

Street harassment evokes emotional responses from its targets ranging from moderate annoyance to intense fear. Two themes occur repeatedly in women's responses to inquiries about the effects of harassment: the intrusion upon privacy and the fear of rape. Each time a woman is addressed by a strange man on the street, she must entertain the possibility that he might rape her. Although most encounters may turn out to be innocuous after the fact, this fear is not an unrealistic one given the statistics about rape in our society, which indicate that as many as one in three women have been victims of rape or attempted rape at some time in their lives. Women who are harassed on the street typically do not respond to the harassment but instead try to ignore it, or, more accurately, *pretend* to ignore it; this common reaction may result from unwillingness to admit their powerlessness in the situation, from fear of physical attack,[3] or merely from reluctance to draw attention to themselves or to displease. They freeze; they put on a blank face; they attempt to pretend that nothing is happening. The combination of these evasive actions with the feelings of invasion, anger, and fear described above takes a considerable psychological toll, described by one author as a form of schizophrenia. Even more insidious may be the erosion of self-esteem and disempowerment, which result from no response to these "little rapes".

After reducing a woman to a sexual object by their comments and conduct, harassers proceed to force this perception upon the woman herself. While schizophrenia or madness may seem extreme descriptions of this distress, studies of sexual harassment in the workplace show that its victims do indeed experience a variety of psychological and emotional problems, including depression, anxiety, stress, loss of motivation and guilt, as well as simple disgust, hurt and anger. Similarly, according to psychologists, a woman subjected to public insults on the street suffers a psychological toll from feeling degraded, embarrassed, angry, and helpless. Harassment may also teach women to be ashamed of their bodies and to associate them with fear and humiliation, thus contributing not only to problems with self-esteem but also to potential difficulties developing as sexual beings.[4]

Finally, it is clear that street harassment has consequences for the physical and geographical mobility of women. It not only diminishes their feelings of safety and comfort in public places but also restricts their freedom in major respects, significantly depriving them of their life in the public sphere. Women in the survey have mentioned as a solution; avoiding certain places, sites or activities. Thus, street harassment forms part of a whole spectrum of means by which men objectify women and assert coercive power over them, one which is in many ways the more invidious for being so pervasive and appearing, deceptively, to be trivial.

The Consequences of Street Harassment for Women, Gender and Society

The fear, psychological trauma, and restrictions on personal liberty described above have obvious consequences for women as individuals. Not so obvious, perhaps, are the consequences for society as a whole. In fact, the harms of street harassment extend its impact upon the relationship between the sexes, upon the construction of gender in our society, and upon social and political relationships in general.

First, street harassment increases the dependence of women upon men at the same time as it adds to the pervasive distrust and hostility between the sexes. One obvious result of street harassment and the related danger of sexual assault is that they encourage women to seek male escorts in public - men to protect them from harassment by other men. Second, contrary to the folk wisdom that "sticks and stones may break my bones but words will never hurt me," language is manifestly instrumental in the construction of reality, locating individuals within that reality and thus constructing their gender identities. Street harassment teaches women to associate their bodies with shame, fear, and humiliation, thus making it difficult to feel comfortable as sexual beings. Women also learn their place from language, and they learn that place is not a public one. The remarks women hear from harassers on the street carry the implicit message that women belong not in public, where they draw attention by their mere appearance, but in the private sphere, in the home. The continuation and near-general tolerance of street harassment has serious consequences both for women and for society at large. It inflicts the most direct costs upon women, in the form of fear, emotional distress, feelings of disempowerment, and significant limitations upon their liberty and mobility. But it also increases distrust between men and women and contributes to the reinforcement of rigid gender roles, hierarchy, and the confinement of women to the private sphere. Street harassment thus performs a function as a social institution, which is antithetical to the acceptance of women into public life on terms equal to men.

THE DEFENCE: *THAT THERE IS NONE*

" Women must learn to behave; and in consequence to that, men will automatically behave."

" Women should know their limits; this is India, not the US"

" Know your limits and help create an eve teasing free atmosphere"

" Women wear revealing clothes"

"... Men who are of course frustrated would never mind a prize as good as the woman who bares it all..."

" She doesn't look like she might mind the attention"

Why do men harass? 36% of men that took the survey said it was a harmless means of passing time. 16% felt that it would never happen unless the woman asked for it. A number of other men cited male camaraderie as a popular reason driven by general peer pressure. Still others said the comments were meant as compliments; as harmless expressions of appreciation. This result supplements the effort of the researchers to define the offence in terms of action and not the intention. The idea was to break through such common excuses, which are quite the contrary perspective to how women are impacted by harassment; as, explained before.

One common response that was received on any questioning was that the woman that wears anything that revealed skin was "asking for it". The instant part of the chapter forms a significant portion of the crux of the argument. The instant chapter seeks to assert that there is no such thing as 'provocation'. To accept provocation as a defence would be to perpetuate an unfortunately existing myth that men have no control. The researchers sincerely hoped that the survey conducted on the women would reveal that the way they dress and the frequency of harassment has no relation whatsoever. Unfortunately, the result was contrary. Now it would be common for most people to then use this number to conclude and justify provocation as a valid defence to harassment. On the other hand, the researchers instead seek to use this number as proof of the heightened burden on women to prevent and guard themselves from the offence and not on the male perpetrators to refrain from the same. All existing literature that seeks to find solutions to the problem of street harassment quite strangely, all address the women. All debate on the issue begins on a much-accepted premise that men are going to engage in the activity and that this is a fact and that this is an undisputable reality. The construction of the instant penal legislation seeks to deconstruct this foundational notion.

Therefore, we submit that the defence of provocation is mythical and per se unacceptable. A complaint of harassment does not legitimise the scrutiny of the sexual conduct and character of the woman in any way, as is currently done. In order to avoid the rampant secondary victimisation therefore, the statute makes a provision stipulating that the woman's dress and prior sexual conduct is irrelevant to the issue of whether the conduct was welcome or unwelcome to her.

THE ARM OF THE LAW: *AND IT'S GROPING OF VICTIMS*

It is possible to identify a number of existing legal redress for the behaviour described as harassment. One common remedy that women have sought over the years is the offence of 'outraging of modesty'. This remedy will be dealt with towards the end of this chapter to credit it with its due thorough analysis. The chapter will briefly run through alternative remedies before that. The judicial process of determining this undefined act has imposed its own costs on the victims consequently resulting in a secondary victimisation. Other areas of redress are the tort of assault; the tort of defamation. The Indian Penal Code further, permits every individual a right to self-defence and therefore condones acts of violence that are done in the cause of the same. This would constitute not a direct legal redress, but perhaps a source of the condonation of retaliation on the part of the woman.

The Right to Freedom of Movement

The Indian Constitution guarantees to every citizen, the right to move freely throughout the territory of India.[5] "Liberty" as John Locke envisaged "is to be free from restraint and violence from others, which cannot be where there is no law." The liberty of women, in this most fundamental sense of freedom from restraint, is substantially limited by street harassment, which reduces their physical and geographical mobility and makes them reluctant to appear alone in public in many areas. In this sense, street harassment accomplishes an informal ghettoization of women - a ghettoization to the private sphere. Yet the most fundamental definitions of liberty include the right of an individual to go where she chooses in spaces, which are public. Thus when the law fails to protect women from street harassment, it deprives them of one of the basic goods for which government was ordained, leaving them in a Hobbesian wilderness, which men do not share. In order to participate as equal citizens in the polity, women must reclaim the public space. This is one of the goals of what is called "reconstructive feminist jurisprudence": to reconstruct the reforms necessary to the safety and improvement of women's lives and to do so in language that is true to their own experience and their own subjective lives. Central to the freedom to be at ease in public spaces is the capacity to pass through them retaining a certain zone of privacy and autonomy about the person - a zone of interpersonal distance that is crossed only by mutual consent. If, by contrast, women are forced to submit to violation of that zone of personal privacy when they enter public areas, that very invasion of privacy has the effect of driving them back into the private sphere, where such violations may be avoided. By turning women into objects of public attention when they are in public therefore, harassers drive home the message that they do not belong there.

Assault

The tort of assault, on the surface, is seemingly an effective remedy. The offence of assault has been commonly defined as

"A person commits an assault when, without lawful authority, he engages in conduct which places another in reasonable apprehension of receiving a battery."

On its face, assault appears to have a lot of promise, particularly in light of the accounts women give of the fear harassment arouses in them. Moreover, assault not only captures the fear of rape, which underlies women's response to harassment but also embodies the liberal values of freedom and mobility that are restricted by harassment. The judicial discourse on the remedy has however, proved to present a range of obstacles. As in rape prosecutions, a woman appears likely to succeed on an assault claim for harassment only if she is married, "chaste," or "of good character." the standard elements of the law of assault may also pose problems in the context of street harassment. One obstacle is posed by the fact that both the crime and tort of assault require a finding of intent on the part of the harasser. If the survey and research is any indication, most men who harass women on the street deny that they proceed from any hostile or alarming intent and instead plead that they were just having fun or intended a compliment, demonstrating the problems associated with describing the offense in terms of the perpetrator's intent or perception. So unless a plaintiff is able to demonstrate intent to cause fear of an offensive contact from either the content of the communication itself or from the context, she will have difficulty proceeding on a cause of action for assault.

In addition, there is a high likelihood of reluctance to impose liability for "mere words" or "mere solicitation. This is especially clear in the supposed analogy between solicitation to prostitution and the harassment of women on the street. The typical street harasser is not in fact making a good faith solicitation to sexual intercourse, even though his words may state that he is. For related reasons, an assault case may founder upon a requirement that the victim's fear be perceived by the court or jury as "objectively" reasonable. To male judges or observers, street harassment may not seem intimidating. It would not be surprising if this were so, because the study revealed significant sex differences in the perception and interpretation of street harassment, with female respondents believing that targets of harassment feel significantly less safe in the situation than male respondents think they do. A common reaction that the researchers witnessed in the course of the survey was a typically alarmed and appalled reaction of the men with regard to the frequency of harassment that women are subjected to. It is unfortunate indeed already that women, the world over have grown to become accustomed to acts of harassment. This in turn has caused the men, perhaps understandably, to be completely oblivious to them. Therefore, a cause of action based on assault would address street harassment effectively only if it is combined with a respectfulness standard.

In sum, the following are the obstacles to locating redress within the tort of assault:

- a history of selective enforcement, both to protect only women deemed by the court to be "of good character" and to punish primarily harassers who are poor;
- an intent requirement;
- possible judicial reluctance to impose liability for "mere words";
- a requirement that the plaintiff's fear have been objectively reasonable, measured by the reactions of the reasonable man; and
- a tendency to require that the harasser's behaviour has been repetitive.

Defamation

The tort of slander provides yet another ancillary redressal. Slander is defined by Section 499 of the Indian Penal Code is the publication of a defamatory statement in a transient form. The Bombay and Madras High Courts have held that when there is imputation of unchastity to a woman by spoken words, the wrong was actionable without proof of special damage.[6]

The Tamil Nadu Prohibition of Harassment of Women Act, 1998

A couple of years ago, in what would be popularly perceived as a 'casual' encounter of eve teasing, Sarika Shah of Chennai met her brutal death. A few men returning from a Youth Congress meeting accosted the girl while on their motor vehicles and in the tussle Sarika Shah died. In the wake of the furore of public reaction, the Tamil Nadu Government promulgated a stopgap measure in the form of the *Tamil Nadu Prohibition of Eve Teasing Ordinance, 1998*. This was then repealed by the instant Act in the year 2002. The instant legislation has been a huge source of contribution to the statute drafted by the researchers. A general issue of concern as observed in the analysis has always been the identification of authorities to tackle harassment. In this regard, the Tamil Nadu legislation identifies existing management authorities of public places and crew of public service vehicles as authorities of enforcement and imposes stringent obligations on them to do so. The Act further, defines and criminalizes harassment death and harassment suicide. The researchers however did not agree with the definition of 'harassment' in the Act, which stipulates thus:

> *" Harassment means any indecent conduct or act by a man which causes or is likely to cause intimidation, fear, shame or embarrassment, including abusing or causing hurt or nuisance or assault or use of force."*

It is quite evident that the wording of the definition would in all probability, cause the same problems that existing legal redress does incorporating measures and standards of 'indecency', 'shame' and 'embarrassment'. The researchers submit that the use of such definition bears a grave apprehension of secondary victimisation.

Outraging "Modesty"

The groping arm of the law is perhaps at its worst as is evident from the judicial discourse on the instant undefined act. The Indian Penal Code, in Section 354, criminalizes the assault or criminal force inflicted upon a woman with intent to outrage her modesty. The intention of the provision is apparently to punish sexual offences that are of lesser gravity than rape. The courts have over the years, placed large focus on the issue of the woman's 'modesty'. It is an imperative to all cases that allege the instant offence to prove that the assault in the minds of right-minded people would be perceived as 'indecent' and that the offender intending on behaving in such an indecent manner. As held in the case of *S P Mallik*[7] therefore, "unless culpable intention is proved, the mere touching of the belly of a female in a public bus cannot be called a deliberate act of outraging modesty…the act is under the circumstances, purely accidental and unintentional."

We submit that the primary objection to the instant provision is the dilution of the offence of rape. Section 354 has provided an escape route to offenders that have in actuality committed the offence of rape or attempt to rape. In a case where the accused caught hold of a married woman and tried to open the string of her *salwar* with intention to rape her, the woman managed to prevent the crime by an act of violence in self-defence. The court appallingly, held that the man's action displays no show of determination to have sexual intercourse, despite the resistance. The victim therefore, could only find remedy under the offence of outraging of modesty.[8] In another case, where a married woman accused two persons of having dragged her home and having raped her, and medical examination further showed evidence of semen on her clothes, the court opined that the case of rape was not made out. The court stated as its primary reason, that the presence of semen on a married woman's clothes is nothing unusual.[9]

It is submitted as our second objection of the provision, the discourse on 'modesty'. In the long line of cases that have attempted to define the term, the case of *Rupan Deol Bajaj v Kanwar Pal Singh Gill,*[10] to put it mildly, is not surprising. The Supreme Court, defines for us, the term modesty as the quality of being modest and in relation to woman means "womanly propriety of behaviour; scrupulous chastity of thought, speech and conduct". The word `modest' in relation to woman is defined in the above dictionary as "decorous in manner and conduct; not forward or lewd; shame fast." The meaning of the word `modesty' is further explained as "womanly propriety of behaviour; scrupulous chastity of thought, speech and conduct (in man or woman); reserve or sense of shame proceeding from instinctive aversion to impure or coarse suggestions". The researchers object to such definition of modesty as the criterion for determination of the offence. In doing so, the judiciary imposes serious social costs on the woman by shifting an unacceptable burden on her to provide justification for why she should not be subjected to such acts.

The third objection to the instant provision is its essential ingredients. A number of cases have held the following to be essential for a conviction under Section 354:

- That the person assaulted must be a woman.
- Accused must have used criminal force on her intending thereby to outrage her modesty.
- The essence of a woman's modesty is her sex.
- Act of pulling a woman, removing her dress coupled with a request for sexual intercourse, is such as would be an outrage to the modesty of a woman.
- Knowledge, that modesty is likely to be outraged, is sufficient to constitute the offence without any deliberate intention having such outrage alone for its object.[11]

We have already elaborated on the problems with the criteria of overt use of force and that of the proof of intention. Despite the existence of the aforementioned legal redress, the survey displayed also a general ignorance of the law and any remedies therein. Moreover, even the knowledge of the law has not proved to be an empowering factor. The case of *Bharadwaja Bhoginbhai Hiranbhai v State of Gujarat*[12], enlists exhaustively the factors that invariably stop a woman from speaking out against a case of harassment:

- A girl or a woman in the tradition bound non- permissive Society of India would be extremely reluctant even to admit that any incident which is likely to reflect on her chastity had ever occurred.
- She would be conscious of the danger of being ostracised by the Society or being looked down by the Society including by her own family members, relatives, friends and neighbours.
- She would have to brave the whole world.
- She would face the risk of losing the love and respect of her own husband and near relatives, and of her matrimonial home and happiness being shattered.
- If she is unmarried, she would apprehend that it would be difficult to secure an alliance with a suitable match from a respectable or an acceptable family.
- It would almost inevitably and almost invariably result in mental torture and suffering to herself.
- The fear of being taunted by others will always haunt her.
- She would feel extremely embarrassed in relating the incident to others being over powered by a feeling of shame on account of the upbringing in a tradition bound society where by and large sex is taboo.
- The natural inclination would be to avoid giving publicity to the incident lest the family name and family honour is brought into controversy.
- The parents of an unmarried girl as also the husband and members of the husband's family of a married woman would also more often than not, want to avoid publicity on account of the fear of social stigma on the family name and family honour.
- The fear of the victim herself being considered to be promiscuous or in some way responsible for the incident regardless of her innocence.

- The reluctance to face interrogation by the investigating agency, to face the court, to face the cross examination by Counsel for the culprit, and the risk of being disbelieved, acts as a deterrent.

To summarize, none of the efforts we have examined has yet provided an effective remedy for street harassment. No legal category quite "fits" the harassment experience, though many are near-remedies.

THE SOLUTION: *TOWARDS AN EFFECTIVE REMEDY*

NO MEANS NO MEANS NO

Why turn to the law yet again

The sub chapter on freedom of movement explained John Locke's definition of liberty that stated in clear words, that such freedom is the right against restraint, which cannot be where there is no law... "Which cannot be where there is no law". As much as the faith of the women in the judiciary, and understandably so, has dwindled, the law, if effectively tailored can prove to be the long pending answer to the issue. The instant chapter proposes a central penal law – *The Prohibition of Street Harassment of Women Bill, 2004,* seeking to take the first step in naming the crime.

Before proceeding to design any new remedies or to reform the ones, which exist, it is important to review precisely what we want to accomplish through such measures. The most general goal, of course, is to change the behaviour of harassers. Thus the aim of any legal action should be the general deterrence of harassing behaviour. To accomplish this, remedies must be defined in manner that they are both realistic and effective. Based upon the review of previous efforts to fit harassment into other legal categories, it is concluded that the remedy must:

- not define the offence or liability in terms of the intent of the harasser;
- incorporate a respectfulness standard both as to the offensiveness of the conduct and the woman's reaction to it;[13]
- apply to both verbal and non-verbal conduct;
- not require repetition or a course of conduct,
- apply to behaviour in public places but be limited to speech which is not public discourse;

- specify, if possible, that it applies to street harassment, so that the judiciary may not opt out of applying it to this situation;
- be "worth it" to pursue, either because it is "cheap" for victims to employ, involving a simple procedure; and
- "hurt" enough to provide general deterrence.

The source of authority of the proposed bill

While drafting the instant legislation we have drawn authority from entry 1 of List III – the Concurrent list enshrined in Schedule 7 of the Indian Constitution. The said entry 1 vests power in both the Union and the State Governments to legislate on criminal law.

Definitions

The first chapter has sufficiently explained the defining of the term 'street harassment' and the reasons for the same. The researchers sought to include a comprehensive definition for the term 'public places' as to not leave any loopholes for offenders to bypass the law on the jurisdiction of the offence. For the purpose, the researchers have relied on the definition provided by the New York Penal Law.[14] With minor modifications, the researchers submit that an effective definition of the term is:

"Public Place" means a place to which the public or a substantial group of persons has access, and includes, but is not limited to, roads, public service vehicles, places of amusement, places of worship, parks, playgrounds, educational institutions and hallways, lobbies and other portions of apartment houses and hotels not constituting rooms or apartments designed for actual residence.

Drawing from the Tamil Nadu legislation, we have also made stipulations that penalises more seriously, 'harassment death' and 'harassment suicide'.

Authorities

We have firstly, imposed a proactive obligation on the part of the management of any public place to take preventive steps against street harassment within their premises. The researchers envisage here, measure such as adequate lighting, separate queues, security guards etc. A similar duty has been imposed on the crew of a public service vehicle. Beyond this, the bill imposes a duty on the aforementioned authorities to duly inform the police on the receipt of a complaint by an aggrieved person of harassment within their premises, and penalises for the failure to do so. In the case of public roads, the researchers have chosen to identify traffic police as an authority. The construction of this clause is also keeping in mind the costs of enforcement. It is for this reason we have chosen to use existing authorities, saving the costs of the creation of new ones.

The Prohibition

The statute makes a blanket ban on any acts of street harassment of women. The legislation also herein has sought to do away with any burden of proof of modesty. Essentially, the provision has consciously distanced the determination of the crime from any moral criteria that has so far, only perpetuated patriarchy. Since the statute is one of strict liability, the researchers have decided to concede and maintain the burden of proof of the offence on the woman. Thereby, as long as the action is proved, no further proof of *mens rea* of any kind is requisite. The earlier draft of the bill had reversed the burden on the man in the light of rampant secondary victimisation. However, in choosing to dilute one of the stringent standards, the researchers have afforded priority to retain strict liability.

Punishment and Penalties

The statute has made stipulations for the imposition of imprisonment and/or fine. With regard to both, the bill provides for a *maximum* limit and not a minimum one. The reason for this is the apprehension that otherwise, the courts would find it convenient to impose minimum penalties in the light of the existing normalisation of the offence. Therefore, by imposing a maximum limit it is hoped that it would then impose a process of application of mind on the part of the court. Judicial discretion would then perhaps be more effective, in deliberating on the gravity of the offence.

A growing concern has been expressed about the misuse of such legislation by a woman. It is for this reason that the bill does not make a definite awarding of damages. The bill does not exclude it entirely in appreciation of the need for damages to compensate for medical expenses and emotional and physical trauma. However, the bill has chosen to leave that at judicial discretion with regard to the facts and circumstances and on clear determination of the guilt. The bill has also made recognition of a range of street harassment that occurs whilst the offender is operating a motor vehicle. In light of the need to provide a more realistic deterrence that involves the deprivation of a benefit, the bill provides for the revocation of license of the offender to operate the motor vehicle in such circumstances. The bill does not bar any alternative remedies in the form of damages for defamation etc. The instant proposed law seeks not to act in derogation of other laws and therefore, the offences of attempt to rape and rape continue to be remedies available outside of this law.

Rule making power

Although the chapter proposes a central legislation, the researchers have chosen to give states the rule making power under the Act and not the Central Government. This is in acknowledgement of the fact that the gravity and the frequency of the offence vary drastically between states and thereby; it would be more effective for states to tailor the legislation to their particular circumstances.

CONCLUSION

During the course of the study, we discovered that often, women suppress feelings about street harassment and may even repress the experience itself. Repression of this sort does not seem surprising, for the experience of street harassment is so common that it has simply seemed an inevitable part of life. Yet the subject is broached, asking female students and friends about their experiences and their opinions, they have invariably been responsive, have talked eagerly, and have reacted with a sense of solidarity and anger. They have seemed hopeful with regard to suggestions that there might be legal remedies, which could address their pain; but this hope was often accompanied by expressions of incredulity, reflecting disbelief that the legal system would pay any attention to the problem.

This dialogue and this anger are healthy; and they are creative. As Cynthia Bowman points out, "we must give voice to the hurting self, . . . even when that hurting self voices "trivial" complaints; even when the hurting self is ambivalent toward the harm and even when (especially when) the hurting self is talking a language not heard in public discourse. Only by so doing will we *ourselves* become aware of the meaning of the suffering in our lives, and its contingency in our history. Only when we understand the contingency of that pain, will we be free to address it and change the conditions, which cause it through legal tools.

This chapter has been an attempt to continue and to broaden that dialogue.

NOTES

1. Bowman, Cynthia, Street Harassment and the Informal Ghettoisation of Women, (1991) Harvard Law Review, 334.
2. During the course of the survey, a number of responses indicated that in criminalizing street harassment, a consequent situation that would render young people that willingly want to get acquainted in public places an impossibility, would be undesirable. This is in response to that concern.
3. USA Today, July 19, 1991: "I was walking down the street the other day, wearing nothing revealing. This man was flicking his tongue at me and asked me if I tasted as good as I looked. There is nothing you can do about it. What if you get someone mad? You don't know who they are, and you might end up raped or killed."
4. Jennifer Nedelsky points to the connection between the shame women are taught to feel about their bodies and a more general sense of inadequacy. Jennifer Nedelsky, Inadequacy and Disentitlement: Internal Barriers to Women's Equality, unpublished paper presented at the Annual Meeting of the American Political Science Association, August 1991. Iris Young also speculates that the general lack of confidence that women frequently have about their cognitive and leadership abilities is traceable in part to doubt about their bodies, which is exacerbated by repeated invasions of their personal space. Iris Marion Young, Throwing Like A Girl and Other Essays in Feminist Philosophy and Social Theory 155-56 (1990).
5. The instant freedom is enshrined in Article 19(1) (d) of Part III of the Constitution. The only restrictions that are permitted on such freedom are general public interest and the protection of a scheduled tribe. The act of street harassment clearly fails to fall within the ambit of either. The infringement of such a right therefore, finds no justification whatsoever.
6. Hirabhai Jehangir v Dinshaw Edulji (1927); A D Narayana Sali v Kannamma Bai (1932).
7. 1982 Cr LJ 19 (Pat).

8. Rameshwar, 1984 Cr LJ 786 (P&H).
9. State v Musa 1991 Cr LJ 2168 (Orissa).
10. 1995 Supreme Court.
11. Aman Kumar v State of Harayana (2004) Supreme Court.
12. 1983 Supreme Court.
13. The respectfulness standard essentially promotes the notion that there is a certain amount of respect that a woman is entitled to as a matter of right, simply by virtue of the fact that she is human. It is not the same as respect in appraisal. It is the basic respect due to a human by virtue of their being so. Such a standard helps counter the problems of differing notions of reasonableness.
14. The researchers found the same also having been incorporated in the Pennyslvania Statute Criminalizing Harassment.

REFERENCES

Baxi, Pratiksha (2001), *Sexual Harassment,* www.seminar.org.

Bowman, Cynthia (1991), *Street Harassment and the Informal Ghettoisation of Women,* Harvard Law Review, 334.

Dierde, Davis (1994), *The Harm that has no name: Street Harassment, Embodiment and Afrcian American Women,* 4 UCLA Women's L.J. 133.

Gardner, Carol Brooks (1980), *Passing By: Gender and Public Harassment,* 50 Sociological Inquiry 328.

Heben, Tiffanie (1994), *A radical reshaping of the law: Interpreting and remedying street harassment,* 4 S. Cal. Rev. L. & Women's Stud. 183.

Kapur, Ratna, *Sexcapades and the Law,* www.seminar.org.

Thompson M. Deborah (1994), *The Woman on the Street: Reclaiming the Public Space from Sexual Harassment,* 6 Yale J.L. & Feminism 313.

ANNEXURE
THE PROHIBITION OF STREET HARASSMENT OF WOMEN BILL, 2004

An Act to prohibit and criminalize harassment of women in public places within the territory of India

CHAPTER I
PRELIMINARY

1. Short Title, Extent and Commencement

(1) This Act may be called the Prohibition of Street Harassment of Women Act, 2004

(2) This Act shall extend in Operation to the Whole Territory of India.

(3) It shall be deemed to have come into force on the __________.

2. Definitions

(1) "Street harassment" occurs when one or more persons accost one or more women in a public place on one or more occasions, and intrude or attempt or intrude upon the woman's privacy in a manner that is disrespectful and unwelcome to the woman, with language and/or actions that include but are not limited to those that are explicitly or implicitly sexual.

(2) "Language" includes but is not limited to reference to male or female genitalia; or female body parts; or to sexual activities; or solicitation of sex; or reference by word/action to target of harassment as object of sexual desire; or similar words that by their very utterance inflict injury or naturally tend to provoke violent resentment even if the woman did not herself react with violence.

(3) "Public place" means a place to which the public or a substantial group of persons has access, and includes, but is not limited to, roads, public service vehicles, places of amusement, places of worship, parks, playgrounds, educational institutions and hallways, lobbies and other portions of apartment houses and hotels not constituting rooms or apartments designed for actual residence.

(4) "Public service vehicle" shall have the same meaning as defined in clause (35) of Section 2 of The Motor Vehicles Act, 1988 (Central Act 59 of 1988);

(5) "Harassment Death" means where the death of a woman is caused by bodily injury or occurs otherwise than under normal circumstances and if it is shown that soon before her death, she was subjected to street harassment that caused the injury and/or circumstances.

(6) "Harassment suicide" occurs when any woman commits suicide and it is shown that soon before her death, she was subjected to street harassment by any person.

(7) Words and expressions used but not defined in this Act shall have the same meanings assigned to them in the Indian Penal Code, 1860 (Central Act XLV of 1860);

CHAPTER II
AUTHORITIES

3. Responsibility of Management of any Public Place

(1) Any person who is in charge of any public place shall;

(a) take such steps as he may deem fit to prevent street harassment within the public place;

(b) on a complaint made by an aggrieved person, give information to the police about the street harassment.

(2) Any person who fails to take action under sub-section (1) shall be liable to fine which may extend to two thousand rupees.

4. Duty of Crew in Public Service Vehicle

(1) The crew of a public service vehicle shall take such steps as they may deem fit to prevent street harassment of women in the vehicle.

(2) Where such street harassment is committed in a public service vehicle, the crew of such vehicle shall, on a complaint made by the aggrieved person take such vehicle to the nearest police station and give information to the police.

(3) Any crew that fails to take steps under sub-section (2) shall be liable to fine which may extend to one thousand rupees.

5. Duty of Traffic Police

The traffic police on duty in an area shall, on the complaint made by an aggrieved person, give information to the police about the street harassment.

CHAPTER III
PROHIBITION OF STREET HARASSMENT

6. Prohibition of Street Harassment

Street Harassment of women at any public place is prohibited

7. Burden of Proof

When a person is accused of any offence under this Act, the burden of proving the commission of the offence is upon the woman, and the Court shall presume the absence of the same until proved.

8. Presumption as to Harassment Death and Abetment of Harassment Suicide

When the question is whether any person had caused harassment death or abetted harassment suicide of a woman, the court shall, unless the contrary is proved, presume that such person had caused the harassment death or abetted the harassment suicide, as the case may be, when it is shown that before her death, such woman had been subjected to harassment and bodily injury was caused in furtherance of such street harassment or commission of the said offence by or at the instance of that person and it resulted in death or suicide, as the case may be, of that woman.

9. Extent of relevance of harasser's intent

The harasser's intent, except his intent to say the words and/or engage in the conduct is not an element of this offence.

10. Woman's Sexual History Irrelevant

The woman's dress and prior sexual history are irrelevant to the issue whether the street harassment was welcome or unwelcome to her.

CHAPTER IV
PENALTIES

1. Short Title, Extent and Commencement

11. Penalty for Street Harassment of Women

Whoever commits or participates in or abets street harassment of woman in or within the premises of any public place or any public service vehicle or any other place shall be punished with imprisonment which may extend to three years and/or fine which may extend to twenty thousand rupees or both.

12. Harassment Death

Notwithstanding anything contained in Section 11, whoever commits harassment death and if the act by which the death is caused,

(1) is done with the intention of causing death or of causing such bodily injury as is likely to cause death, shall be punished with imprisonment of either description for a term which may extend to imprisonment for life and with fine which shall not be less than fifty thousand rupees;

(2) is done with knowledge that it is likely to cause death but without any intention to cause death or such bodily injury as is likely to cause death, shall be punished with imprisonment of either description for a term which may extend to ten years and with a fine which shall not be less than fifty thousand rupees;

(3) is rash or negligent, shall be punished with imprisonment of either description for a term which may extend to ten years and with fine which shall not be less than twenty five thousand rupees.

13. Harassment Suicide

Notwithstanding anything contained in Section 11, whoever abets harassment suicide shall be punished with imprisonment of either description for a term which may extend to ten years and with fine which shall not be less than fifty thousand rupees.

14. Order to pay compensation

The court may, when imposing a penalty under this Act, order the accused to pay, by way of compensation, such amount as may be specified in the order, to the person who has suffered any loss or injury or disability or mental agony by reason of the act which the accused person has been so sentenced to or to her legal heir.

15. Revocation of motor vehicle license

Any person who commits or participates in or abets street harassment while operating a motor vehicle shall be subject to revocation or suspension of his license to operate a motor vehicle or driver's license.

16. No bar to alternative remedies

The penalties under this Act do not in any manner, preclude the victim from claiming any other remedies under existing civil and/or criminal law.

CHAPTER V
MISCELLANEOUS

1. Short Title, Extent and Commencement

17. Operation of other Laws

The provisions of this Act shall be in addition to and not in derogation of, any other law for the time being in force.

18. Power to Make Rules

(1) The Government of a State may make rules for carrying out the purposes of this Act

(2) All rules made under this Act shall be published in the Gazette of the respective State Government and unless they are expressed to come into force on a particular date, shall come into force on the date on which they are so published.

Every rule made under this Act shall, as soon as possible after it is made, be placed before the Legislative Assembly, and if, before the expiry of the session it is so placed or the next session, the Assembly makes any modification in any such rule, or the Assembly decides that the rule should not be made, the rule shall thereafter have effect only on such modified form or be of no effect, as the case may be, so, however, that any such modification or annulment shall be without prejudice to the validity of anything previously done under that rule.

M. EZHILARASAN AND S. MADHAVAN

14

LEADERSHIP AND GENDER DISCRIMINATION: A VICTIMIZATION PERSPECTIVE

INTRODUCTION

The 1995 Commonwealth Plan of Action on Gender and Development presents a vision of: *"a world in which women and men have equal rights and opportunities at all stages of their lives to express their creativity in all fields of human endeavor, and in which women are respected and valued as equal and able partners in establishing values of social justice, equity, democracy and respect for human rights. Within such a framework of values, women and men will work in collaboration and partnership to ensure people-centered sustainable development for all nations."*

The 1995 Fourth World Conference on Women in Beijing provided a renewed global commitment to achieving gender equality and equity. The final clause of the Beijing Declaration states as follows, "We hereby adopt and commit ourselves as Governments to implement the Platform for Action, ensuring that a gender perspective is reflected in all our policies and programmes."

Despite considerable progress in some areas of women's lives since the UN named 1975-1985 as the Decade for Women, gender inequality/inequity persists in all areas of life and all countries of the world. The 1995 UN Human Development Report, which had a particular focus on gender, indicated that no country treats its women as well as its men, and in almost all countries of the world women are over-represented among the unemployed and those living in absolute poverty. The gaps between women and men have closed over the last 20 years in terms of educational enrolment, literacy and life expectancy. But women still lag behind in terms of political and economic participation.

And gender inequality under the law and violence against women are stark indicators of "the low status accorded women in societies everywhere" (UNDP, 1995).

The proportion of women in decision-making positions in governments worldwide, although it has increased in some countries, still falls far short of the 53 per cent that would represent the female proportion of the world's population, and indeed the target of 30 per cent endorsed by Commonwealth Heads of Government and by the UN Economic and Social Council. In general women are disadvantaged when it comes to opportunity and learning (Laura, 2002).

"Gender" refers to the socially and culturally determined roles, rights, duties, resources, and interests of men and women (European Commission, 2001). Although many believe that women's low representation among top executives and lower average income is primarily a result of socialization and discrimination, findings of psychology, biology, and anthropology suggest that evolutionarily derived temperamental sex differences exist that may explain much of these disparities. Stereotypes of men as more competitive and more inclined to take risks than women, and stereotypes of women as more attached to their children and more risk averse than men are true as generalizations. Traits, for which average sex differences exist, such as aggressiveness, desire for status, and risk preference, are highly correlated with workplace outcomes (Kingsley, 1999).

Workplace romances and sexual harassment are pervasive in today's organizations. However, despite the fact that these two phenomena share a social-sexual component, they have primarily been treated as unrelated organizational issues (Charles &Herman, 1998). Survey says: Sexual harassment complaints went up about 10% each year between 1995 and 1998! And even worse, 2 out of 3 complaints had some merit! Clearly, organizations need to learn how to manage this issue, not just be compliant with the law (Timothy & Sue, 2001). When women think about victims of harassment they are concerned with a woman's assertiveness and work effectiveness, while men are more concerned with the psychological state of the woman and how provocative she is when they think about victims of sexual harassment (Linda et al., 2000).

Results indicated that the team leader was more frequently attributed blame, yet attribution of blame was affected by the marital status of both the team leader and the coworker. Both the team leader and the coworker were most frequently attributed an ego motive for the involvement (Gwen, 2000). In this pretext, the role played by leader-member dyadic situations seems to be of much relevance in gender discrimination. A leader's emotional display is proposed to affect his or her audience (Kristi, 2000).

Different leadership styles initiate different behavioral patterns among the subordinates. The major thrust of the leader is two fold – one is the type of influence on the subordinates and the other is the attainment of common goals. Gone are the days wherein the male were the earners and the female were the housekeepers. With the massive industrialization and modernization of the economy, the co-existence of both the genders in the key roles of the organization has become inevitable. There is an equal chance for the female as well as the male employee to serve under the opposite gender.

This chapter is an attempt to dwell into the discriminative practices of the male and the female superiors, and to relate whether there is a leadership style that offsets the gender discrimination that is most often prevalent in organizations. The deliberations in the chapter are the outcomes of research carried out by the authors among an equal number of male and female occupying superior roles across an array of organizations.

METHOD

Objectives

The present study was taken up in a multi industry context among a varied set of respondents with the following as its objectives.

1. To identify the leadership styles prevalent among the respondents,
2. To identify the general leadership practice of the respondents,
3. To study the prevalence of gender discrimination and its extent of prevalence among the respondents, and
4. To identify a leadership style or leadership styles that were gender neuter.

Research Design

The present research may be fit into the exploratory research design as it tried to explore into the possibilities of relationship between the leadership style and the gender orientation of the respondents and come out with propositions.

Sample

A total of 150 respondents in superior positions were taken into consideration for the present study. The composition of the respondents is as in tables 1(a) to 1(c). The male female composition was maintained at 1:1 in order to facilitate the study. Thus, 75 male and 75 female respondents were considered in the study.

Data Collection

The primary data collection tool was questionnaire. Two questionnaires were administered to each respondent. One was administered to identify the leadership style and the other for determining the gender orientation level. The leadership style inventory was an indigenous version of the leadership ability evaluation inventory of the IPAT, Illinois, which was pre-tested. However, for the gender discrimination purpose, a questionnaire was designed and pre-tested. For both the questionnaires review of literature was carried out and the items were finalized on that basis.

Tools of Analysis

Various tools of analysis were adopted in the study that suited the purpose of research. Simple statistical tools such as mathematical average and standard deviation were used for the leadership style analysis and the level of gender discrimination. Pearson's correlation analysis was used to enumerate the nature and level of relationships among the variables under study.

Both t-test and chi-square tests were used to analyze the significance of the relationships under study. The t-test was adopted to study the significance of the relationship among the variables directly under study and the chi-square test was used to determine the presence of impact of the demographic variables on the gender discrimination.

Limitations of the Study

The basic limitation of the study was the difficulty in determining the sampling method as the researchers intended to take into consideration a wide array of respondents into consideration. Further, there was also an extent of withdrawal of respondents due to their basic personal inhibitions on the gender discrimination subject.

The Results

Table 1 (a)
Age Classification of the Respondents

Age	*Male*	*Percentage*	*Female*	*Percentage*
< 30	18	24	26	34.67
30 - 40	27	36	31	41.33
40 - 50	14	18.67	9	12
>50	16	21.33	9	12
	75	100	75	100

Table 1 (b)
Experience Classification of the Respondents

Experience	*Male*	*Percentage*	*Female*	*Percentage*
< 5	19	25.33	23	30.67
5 to 10	11	14.67	12	16
10 to 15	18	24	16	21.33
15 to 20	16	21.33	13	17.33
> 20	11	14.67	11	14.67
	75	100	75	100

Table 1 (c)
Work Nature Classification of the Respondents

Nature	*Male*	*Percentage*	*Female*	*Percentage*
Shop-floor	19	25.33	11	14.67
Office	13	17.33	22	29.33
Service	15	20	13	17.33
Banking	11	14.68	14	18.67
Government	10	13.33	13	17.33
Others	7	9.33	2	2.67
	75	100	75	100

General Gender Orientations

Table 2
Orientation Scores

	Overall		*Male*		*Female*	
	Aver.	*S.Dev*	*Aver.*	*S.Dev*	*Aver.*	*S.Dev*
Task Orientation(Max: 20)	12.42	3.04	12.10	2.33	12.73	3.66
Human Orientation (Max: 15)	8.00	2.30	7.30	2.36	8.64	2.16
Female Orientation (Max: 25)	11.04	4.39	10.30	3.95	11.73	4.84
Male Orientation(Max: 25)	12.24	4.32	12.10	2.13	12.36	5.77

Table 3 (a)
Age-wise Gender Orientation

	Male			*Female*		
Age	*F.O*	*M.O*	*Total*	*F.O*	*M.O*	*Total*
< 30	12	6	18	16	10	26
30 - 40	8	19	27	9	22	31
40 - 50	10	4	14	6	3	9
>50	8	8	16	3	6	9
	38	37	75	34	41	75

Male orientation was found to be higher at the overall level. However, the respondents seem to be more balanced than the female respondents in the sense that out of 75 respondents 38 were female oriented and 37 were male oriented. But the female respondents were more male oriented (41 out of 75).

In the age-wise analysis it could be mentioned that the middle age was a period of reverse inclination. That is, the males were female oriented and the female were male oriented to a larger extent. The male respondents in the age group of less than 30 years and 40 to 50 years were highly female oriented. The female respondents had an alternating swing in the inclination. Those in the age group of less than 30 years were female oriented, in the age group of 30 to 40 years were highly male oriented, in 40 to 50 years they were male oriented and in the above 50 years they were again female oriented. This could lead to an inference that the female respondents were more swaying in their orientations than the male respondents. The age-gender relationship was found to be significant at $p>0.05$ level for both the male and the female respondents in the chi-square test.

Table 3 (b)
Experience-wise Gender Orientation

	Male			Female		
Experience	*F.O*	*M.O*	*Total*	*F.O*	*M.O*	*Total*
< 5	14	5	19	11	12	23
5 to 10	8	3	11	10	2	2
10 to 15	7	11	18	6	10	16
15 to 20	5	11	16	4	9	13
> 20	4	7	11	3	8	11
	38	37	75	34	41	75

In the case of experience, there was found to be a tilt from the female orientation to the male orientation as far as the male respondents as well as the female respondents were concerned.

Thus it could be inferred that with experience, the orientation shift from female inclination to male inclination is a common phenomenon, that is, while respondents were new to the job they were female oriented and as they become experienced they become more male inclined. The experience-gender relationship was also found to be significant at p>0.05 level for both the male and the female respondents in the chi-square test.

Table 3 (c)
Work Nature-wise Gender Orientation

	Male			Female		
Nature	*F.O*	*M.O*	*Total*	*F.O*	*M.O*	*Total*
Shop-floor	5	13	18	4	7	11
Office	10	2	12	12	10	22
Service	9	4	13	6	7	13
Banking	7	4	11	6	8	14
Government	3	7	10	4	9	13
Others	4	7	11	2	0	2
	38	37	75	34	41	75

The work nature, that is, the type of job the respondents were engaged in, was found to play a role in the gender orientation. The male respondents in the shop floor area, and government offices were more prone to be male oriented, and those in the office, service and banking jobs were more female oriented. As far as the female respondents were concerned except in the shop floor area and government office jobs, in which they were male oriented, there was only a marginal female inclination. The work nature-gender relationship was found to be significant at p>0.05 level for the male in the chi-square test. However, in the case of female respondents there was no significant relationship between work nature and gender orientations in the chi-square test.

Leadership and Gender Orientations

Table 4 (a)
Leadership – Gender Orientation (Male respondents)

Female Orientation		*Human Orientation*	
		low	high
Task Orientation	low	low	high
	high	low	high
Male Orientation		*Human Orientation*	
		low	high
Task Orientation	low	low	high
	high	high	low

Table 4 (b)
Leadership – Gender Orientation (Female Respondents)

Female Orientation		*Human Orientation*	
		low	high
Task Orientation	low	low	high
	high	low	high
Male Orientation		*Human Orientation*	
		low	high
Task Orientation	low	low	low
	high	high	low

In general task orientation was found to be less consistent than the human orientation as the standard deviation of task orientation was higher than the human orientation. Between the two genders the male respondents were more consistent than the female respondents. While the average scores of both the genders were close to the overall levels, the male respondents had slightly lower scores than the female respondents.

Table 5
Pearson's Correlation Coefficient Values

Orientations	*Overall*	*Male*	*Female*
Task – Human	0.40	0.06	0.46
Task – Female	-0.16	-0.29	-0.16
Task – Male	0.69	0.76	0.71
Human – Female	0.46	0.73	0.37
Human – Male	0.23	0.33	0.21
Female – Male	-0.15	-0.19	-0.15

The correlation analysis between the two leadership orientations and the two gender orientations reveal the following.

Table 6
Significance of Relationship (t-test)

Orientations	*Overall*	*Male*	*Female*
Task – Human	4.068*	2.877*	4.189*
Task – Female	4.846*	4.894*	3.769*
Task – Male	5.924*	3.368*	5.293*
Human – Female	3.480*	2.972*	3.535*
Human – Male	3.456*	4.467*	6.092*
Female – Male	3.604*	6.607*	7.052*

* All values are greater than t-table value of 2.576 at p>.005 level

Task orientation was found to have a positive correlation with human orientation, and male orientation. It had a negative correlation with female orientation, which meant that higher the task orientation lower would be the female orientation. This pattern was consistent in both the genders.

On the other hand, human orientation seemed to possess a positive correlation with both the male and female orientations. However, the human orientation to female orientation was found to be stronger. This pattern was also consistent in both the genders, but in the male respondents the human orientation to female orientation was found to be very strong.

Thus, it could be inferred that the human oriented leadership style was more female inclined and the task oriented leadership style was more male oriented.

The female-male orientation correlation was found to be negative which means that in a high female orientation environment the male orientation may be expected only at a lower level.

Table 7
Significance of Relationship (Chi-square)

	Respondents	*Chi-square Value*	*Significance Level*
Age – Gender Orientation	male	9.042	0.029
	female	8.255	0.041
Experience– Gender Orientation	male	10.481	0.033
	female	10.06	0.041
Work Nature– Gender Orientation	male	10.264	0.036
	female	0.964	0.857

The four possible leadership style environments – low task–low human, low task–high human, high task–low human, high task–low human – and the four gender orientation environments – low male–low female, low male–high female, high male–low female, low male–high female – were also studied.

It was found that female orientation was found to be low in the low human orientation environments and high in the high human orientation environments in both the male and the female respondents. On the other hand, male orientation had an oscillating prevalence in the various leadership environments.

On the whole it could be inferred that the high task-high human leadership environment was having a high concern for both the male and the female and also the gender discrimination in this style was lower than in any other style.

CONCLUSION

The above few pages of discussion lead to the conclusion that there exists gender discrimination among the superiors in all work environments. The amount of orientation towards the male seems to be higher than towards the female. Among the various leadership styles the one with a high task orientation is inclined towards the male and the one with a high human orientation is inclined towards the female workers. Hence, a leadership style with a high level of both the task and human orientations would be better off in a more positive disposition.

REFERENCES

Charles A. Pierce, Herman Aguinis, (1998), Bridging the gap between romantic relationships and sexual harassment in organizations, *Journal of Organizational Behavior*, Volume 18, Issue 3, Pages 197 – 200, Published Online: 4 Dec 1998.

European Commission (2001), *Equal Opportunities for Women and Men in the European Union - Annual Report 2000*. Luxembourg: Office for Official Publications of the European Communities. 2001. ISBN 92-894-1213-5.

Gwen E. Jones, (2000), Hierarchical workplace romance: an experimental examination of team member perceptions, *Journal of Organizational Behavior*, Volume 20, Issue 7, Pages 1057 – 1072, Published Online: 4 Jan 2000.

Kingsley R. Browne (1999), An evolutionary account of women's workplace status, *Managerial and Decision Economics*, Volume 19, Issue 7-8, Pages 427 – 440, *Published Online:* 22 Feb 1999.

Kristi M. Lewis (2000), When leaders display emotion: how followers respond to negative emotional expression of male and female lead, *Journal of Organizational Behavior*, Volume 21, Issue 2, Pages 221 – 234, *Published Online:* 16 Feb 2000.

Laura L. Bierema (2002), Women, Work, and Learning, *New Directions for Adult and Continuing Education*, Volume 2001, Issue 92, Pages 53 – 62, *Published Online:* 20 Mar 2002.

Linda E. Hurt, Richard L. Wiener, Brenda L. Russell, R. Kelley Mannen, (2000), Gender differences in evaluating social-sexual conduct in the workplace, *Behavioral Sciences & the Law*, Volume 17, Issue 4, Pages 413 – 433, Published Online: 1 Feb 2000.

Timothy S. Bland, Sue S. Stalcup, (2001), Managing Harassment, *Human Resource Management*, Volume 40, Issue 1, Pages 51 – 61, Published Online: 4 Apr 2001.

UNDP (1995), *Human Development Reports. New York: United Nations Development* Programme.

S. Samuel Asir Raj

15

DEMOCRATIC STATE AND RIGHT TO STRIKE: RETRIBUTIVE JUSTICE IN THE ERA OF RESTORATIVE JUSTICE?

INTRODUCTION

In modern democracies the adoption of social security as a basic human right to which all individuals are entitled is one of the great social achievements. Fundamental international treaties such as the Universal Declaration of Human Rights and the International Covenant on Economic, Social and Cultural Rights include the right of everyone to social security. Formal social security programmes have been created by governments of both industrialised and developing countries as an instrument for the realization of this principle.

The progress of democracy in many nations witnessed significant broadening of social security and welfare programmes, which in many cases was due to the result of protracted struggles by workers and others. Recent pressures from global capital and World Bank for reduction in taxes and labour costs has impelled many governments to roll back social welfare programmes and entitlements drastically. This 'retreat of the state' from the realm of social welfare points to a transition from one paradigm of state intervention to another. This transition reveals a clear shift in the discourse on democracy where the traditional values such as human dignity, freedom, equity and justice are ignored and is progressively leading to weakening of working class.

Modern democracies have endeavoured to expand the scope of substantive freedoms that people possess so that broad ranges of the choice are available to them. Constraints on substantive freedoms such as right to strike can be called deprivation and people can be deprived even if they are not necessarily poor. One purpose of a democratic and representative government is to guarantee rights to its citizens. This is usually done by a 'Bill of Rights' detailing the rights of citizens that is enshrined in the country's constitution. And how does the government enforce rights? The rights are enforced by the local civic authorities, the police, and an independent judiciary. What happens if the constitution enshrines human rights but the government fails to enforce them? According to Amartya Sen (2005) "Democratic institutions give people the opportunity to participate in deliberations and dialectics, to press for justice and equity, and to reject socially unacceptable policies. These are matters of public action. Institutions make room for such action and allow its free use. But institutions alone cannot yield public action in any mechanical way. Democratic institutions cannot substitute for public action and participatory politics".

Traditionally the state guarantees human rights as it codifies and implements it for its citizens. Any change in the nature of the state or its authority directly affects its capacity for implementation of human rights. The shift in the discourse on democracy has direct consequences for human rights where there is a real danger of rights losing their right to be rights and citizens have to face a loss of entitlements. India witnessed such a deformation of democracy in July 2003, when the state of Tamil Nadu launched a vindictive onslaught against its own striking employees which forebode ominous portents not only for the trade union and labour rights but also for the democratic rights and institutions as well. The indefinite strike on July 2, 2003 by over 13 lakh employees of the state government and teachers was a product of resistance to the government's retrograde move of downsizing; the restoration of rights taken away and the drastic curtailment of pension and other benefits.

In March 2003, the Joint Action Council of Teachers Organisations and Government Employees Organisations (JACTO-GEO) was compelled to call a token strike against the state government's cuts to superannuation benefits. The Confederation of Teachers Associations and Government Employees Associations (COTA-GEO) called for a mass hunger strike on the same day. Confronted with widespread anger among their members, the unions called for an indefinite strike on July 2 to fight for a series of 15 demands—the main ones relating to the restoration of pensions and other benefits. After ignoring the demands of the workers for over two months, on June 26, the Chief Minister called the unions into talks, only to inform them that the full force of the draconian Essential Services Maintenance Act (ESMA) would be used if they went on strike. Then in a pre-emptive move to break the strike, the union members and leaders were arrested from midnight on June 30, 2003. These actions angered workers and instead of the next day as scheduled, the indefinite strike began from the afternoon of July 1 as office workers and teachers walked out of their offices and schools. Consequent to the failure of two strikes during 2002 to win any concessions from the government, the response to the strike call was overwhelming. An estimated 90 percent of the public sector workforce stopped work on July 2, 2003.

The massive participation in the strike shook the Chief Minister of Tamil Nadu, India and an emergency amendment to the ESMA was rushed through on July 4, providing retrospective powers to dismiss strikers and to impose substantial fines and jail terms on anyone found guilty of striking or instigating a strike. The newly-incorporated Section 7 (1) of the ESMA states: "... if any notification under Section 3 of the Act has been published by the government in the official gazette expressing its intention to prohibit strikes in respect of the service defined under Section 2 of the Act, any government servant to whom the Act applies shall at once report to duty where he\she was reporting prior to the strike prohibited by the notification. In case of failing to do so, the said government servant is deemed to have admitted having committed the misconduct knowingly and voluntarily warranting the punishment." And, the penalty for the "misconduct" could be "dismissal from service, or in the alternative, a break in service, as the case may be, without conducting any enquiry."

The ordinance added an explanation, which said: "It will not be obligatory on the part of the appointing authority or the government as the case may be to individually serve the order of dismissal or the order of break in service or any other punishment on the employees by issuance of separate order and it will be sufficient if the said order is published in the notice board of the office where he\she was working, or if a newspaper publication is made either en masse or individually stating the decision made in terms of sub-section (2) in respect of the said employee". The right of the government servant against whom an order of dismissal or any other punishment has been passed, was restricted to just approach the Appointing Authority and "prove that his\her non-reporting to duty was not due to his\her participation in the strike but due to bona-fide reasons other than participation in the strike".

Over the next few days, almost 200,000 workers were summarily sacked in the largest mass dismissal in Indian history. Workers not only lost their jobs but, in many cases were made to vacant their housing as well, while at the same time, police continued to make arrests. The government was intent upon crushing the strike by any means asked heads of departments and Collectors to "freeze the attendance registers" as on July 3 and not to allow those who turned up for duty after that day to sign attendance. This unprecedented wholesale offensive against the democratic rights and social position of the working class was upheld by the Tamil Nadu High Court and the Indian Supreme Court.

Despite the enormity of the attack on basic democratic rights, the trade unions and opposition parties, made no move to seek broader support from the working class and directed the sacked employees into a series of futile legal actions. The unions challenged the action by a writ petition in the Madras High Court. A single Judge made an interim order directing the government that the "suspension and dismissal of employees without conducting any inquiry be kept in abeyance until further orders and such employees be directed to resume duty". The State appealed against this interim order. The employees also challenged the validity of the Tamil Nadu Essential Services Maintenance Act, 2002 and the Tamil Nadu Ordinance 3 of 2003. On appeal, a Division Bench of the Madras High Court ordered release of employees who were arrested and put in prison. The High Court dismissed legal petitions to overturn the sackings on the grounds that the workers had not sought reinstatement through the State Administrative Tribunal—a body consisting of one judge already inundated with cases. Out of jail, the union leaders promptly convened a meeting of the strike committee and on July 12 unconditionally called off any further industrial action.

Appeals and writ petitions were filed in the Supreme Court challenging the dismissal order. The Division Bench of the Supreme

Court held that the discretionary rule of alternative remedies cannot apply in a case like this. "In a case like this, if thousands of employees are directed to approach the Administrative Tribunal, the Tribunal would not be in a position to render justice to the cause. Hence, as stated earlier because of very exceptional circumstance that arose in the present case, there was no justifiable reason for the High Court not to entertain the petitions on the ground of alternative remedy provided under the statute." Further the bench held that: "Now, coming to the question of right to strike - whether Fundamental, Statutory or Equitable Moral Right - in our view, no such right exists with the government employees. Law on this subject is well settled and it has been repeatedly held by this court that the employees have no fundamental right to resort to strike."

As A.G. Noorini notes, "Since no one claims a "statutory" right to strike, the observation was uncalled for. Nor was it for the court to embark on the "moral" right to strike since it had not considered the mass of literature on the subject; literature which, sadly, is a closed book to very many. On the narrow issue of the "fundamental" right to strike, Justice Shah was content to cite three precedents since 1962 which held that no such fundamental right existed". In a 21-page ruling thoroughly permeated with hostility to the working class, the judges declared: "No political party or organisation can claim a right to paralyse the economic and industrial activities of a state or nation or inconvenience citizens." After stating that strike action was "mostly misused," they suggested that, for redressing grievances, employees should do "more work honestly, diligently and efficiently" to impress their employer. Following the reinstatement of some 165,000 workers, the Supreme Court brought down its final judgment on August 6 which dismissed the challenge to the ESMA law and declared that employees had "no fundamental, legal, moral or equitable right" to strike.

THE RIGHT TO STRIKE

India is a party to the International Covenant on Economic, Social and Cultural Rights adopted by the United Nations General Assembly on December 16, 1966. Article 8 (1) (d) of the Covenant reads thus: "The States Parties to the present Covenant undertake to ensure... (d) The right to strike provided that it is exercised in conformity with the laws of the particular country." "This article shall not prevent the imposition of lawful restrictions on the exercise of these rights by members of the armed forces or of the police or of the administration of the State". "Nothing in this article shall authorise State Parties to the International Labour Organisation [ILO] Convention of 1948 concerning Freedom of Association and Protection of the Right to Organise to take legislative measures which would prejudice, or apply the law in such a manner as would prejudice, the guarantees provided for in that Convention." Thus only "lawful restrictions" are permissible; not total denial. Therefore, the right to strike becomes a crucial instrument for warranty of basic socio-economic rights of workers and all citizens,

Right to Strike has not been gifted to the working class by any Government or by any provision of the Constitution, Conventionally over decades, it has become an integral part of trade union movement, even considered to be inseparable from the process of the collective bargaining, workers and employees who are subjected to terror and exploitation take recourse to strike action as being the last resort only when all the provided avenues fail to bring the remedy. Nowhere the right to strike has been allowed to be abrogated by the International Working Class movement. To work in a reasonably equitable manner, the process requires that all the liberal principles of organising and pressing one's interests be respected and protected by law. The impairment of basic democratic rights and entitlements of any organised force would skew the social contract and tilt the balance of economic welfare.

The Tamil Nadu administration's pre-emptive decision to crush a strike by teachers and government employees, using the provisions of a draconian law made harsher by post facto amendment through ordinance, was a blow aimed at the foundations of the liberal order. The subsequent Supreme Court decision upholding the dubious sequence of decisions and extinguishing the right to strike is a still more lethal setback. Asked to adjudicate on the merits of one particular strike and the Tamil Nadu government's ruthless response of mass arrests and summary dismissals, the Supreme Court sought to fashion a system of relief that would provide the State government a face-saving exit. In the bargain, the two-member Bench of the court issued an extraordinary ex cathedra denunciation of the right to strike. Effectively, the ruling handed down by Justices M.B. Shah and A.R.

Lakshmanan turns the clock back on the enlightened jurisprudence evolved since the 1960s, upholding the right to collective bargaining and industrial action as a basic democratic entitlement.

Right to strike is fundamental trade union right and the Indian Trade Union Act of 1926 and the Industrial Dispute Act of 1947 deal with right to form trade unions and collective bargaining by the workers. The working class of India, for that matter throughout the world, have established their rights through struggle and sacrifice. Whether industrial working class or government employees, they cannot forego their right to collective bargaining including the right for strike in furtherance of their legitimate interests whatever may be the circumstances. Besides, the right to strike is organically linked with the right to collective bargaining and will continue to remain an inalienable part of various modes of response/expression by the working people, wherever the employer-employee relationship exists, whether recognized or not.

The International Labour Organization- a tripartite body of the UN system in its Conventions 87, 98 and 154 have accepted those rights and Convention 151 which is meant for the Public Service has specifically mandated that 'Public Employees shall have, as other workers, the Civil and Political rights which are essential for the normal exercise of freedom of association, subject only to the obligations arising from their status and the nature of the functions'. ILO's Convention is a tripartite decision – Government, employer and the Labour and Govt. of India as a founder member of ILO cannot morally ignore it. Whether the Govt. of India has ratified this Convention or not is a different matter. The trade union movement has all through demanded ratification of this Convention by the Govt. and go ahead to assert their rights.

WHAT IS THE 'RIGHT TO STRIKE'?

The 'Right to Strike' refers to the cluster of rights, immunities and protections that allow a group of workers to cease work without terminating their employment relationship with their employer without exposing themselves to civil liability for their actions. Most countries distinguish between legal and illegal strikes. The right to strike thus refers to taking protected industrial action within the legal framework of a particular country. The right to strike is internationally accepted as a legitimate means for the redressal of grievances of workers. While it is not clearly articulated as a fundamental right, it is recognised as an implied right that can be inferred from other rights such as the right to collective bargaining, to form trade unions and to fair and decent working conditions.

The right to strike has been recognised as crucial in the process of collective bargaining, as it is the only means by which workers can withdraw labour services for obtaining some form of benefit. Additionally, the right to strike is intrinsically linked to the freedoms of association and of expression and the right to peaceful assembly, thereby making it an unassailable and fundamental part of any democratic machinery. It is essential, therefore, that strike action must not be prohibited, nor so heavily regulated that its role is illusory.

DOES THE RIGHT TO STRIKE EXIST IN INDIA?

While the right to strike is not explicitly included in the list of fundamental rights specified in the Constitution of India, Article 19 enumerates the right to freedom of speech and expression, to assemble peaceably without arms, and to form associations or unions (Art 19(1)(a)-(c)). The right to strike is thus a corollary of these expressly stated rights. The Industrial Disputes Act 1947 (IDA) and the Trade Unions Act 1926 (TUA) are the primary pieces of Central legislation regulating this right in India. The IDA establishes the conditions regarding notice and arbitration that must be complied with before industrial action is undertaken (Sections 22, 23), and the circumstances in which such actions may be deemed illegal (Section 24). The IDA by virtue of its regulation of the legality of a strike, thus explicitly recognises that strikes exist as a legitimate means of negotiation, including for government employees (Section 22). The TUA protects the activities of registered trade unions by providing that a trade union, office bearer or member of a registered trade union, shall not be subject to a suit or claim in a civil court alleging conspiracy or interference in trade or business (Section 18).

While these provisions effectively grant workers and unions the right to legal strike, the recognition of this right in India, has been inconsistent. For example, in TK Rangarajan v Government of Tamil Nadu and Others (2003), Justices M.B. Shah and A.R. Lakshmanan stated that government employees had no moral or legal right to strike, unequivocally disregarding established industrial jurisprudence. Instead of referring to the Central legislation described above, the bench relied solely on the provisions of the Tamil Nadu Essential Services Maintenance Act 2002 (ESMA) and the Tamil Nadu Ordinance No 3 of 2003. Both these Acts reiterate Rule 7 of the Central Civil Services (Conduct) Rules, 1964, which prohibits the right of government employees to strike.

Significantly, in B.R. Singh v. Union of India (v), ex-Chief Justice of India, A. M. Ahmadi, heading a three-member bench, had stated that "the bargaining strength [of trade unions] would be considerably reduced if it is not permitted to demonstrate by adopting agitation methods such as… 'strike'…The right to strike is an important weapon in the armoury of workers, recognized by almost all democratic countries as a mode of redress." This judgment justified a strike by certain employees on the grounds that the Trade Authority of India had dismissed them without referring them to a tribunal. This judgment, which should at least have been referred to in TK Rangarajan, was completely ignored, resulting in a decision per incuriam.

The Court not only denied the right to strike on statutory grounds, but also rejected the 'moral' and 'equitable' right of government employees to strike. It further stated that government employees did not have a right to strike even if their cause was just. The legal argument advanced in the judgment appeared to be a mere cover for the actual concern – that "business is adversely affected" by a strike. The fact that 169,000 employees of the government of Tamil Nadu had a legitimate grievance – that their pension and other benefits were being withdrawn without negotiation – was not found to have a mitigating effect on the 'illegality' of the strike under ESMA, which allows for employees to be dismissed for participating in agitations and penalises the instigation of strikes with sentences of up to three years imprisonment, possibly with fine. Further, the court had no words of censure for the preventive arrests of 2,200 employees the previous night as a pre-emptive measure. The right of workers to strike in India is thus far from secure. It has yet to be recognised by authorities and has inexplicably been left undisputed by workers' unions.

The substance of the ruling in this landmark case amounted to denial of justice. It was "an extraordinary case of deployment of State power against its own employees" and "summary dismissal and the overnight arrest of hundreds of thousands of employees ... are in profound conflict with fundamental rights, the basic norms of democracy, and enlightened self-interest".

The first verdicts, involving 2,937 employees attached to the State Secretariat and other government offices in Madras, were handed down on November 15. Of these, 587 were sacked with the remainder receiving various forms of punishment, including pay cuts, compulsory transfers and demotions. Dismissed workers have yet to be told what charges they are being punished for. Only 132 personnel were exonerated.

LABOUR AND RETRIBUTIVE JUSTICE

Examining the actions of the state in accordance with the paradigms of retributive justice, it is evident that the government and Indian state handled the striking employees in a retributive manner as opposed to the tenets of restorative justice. Restorative justice policies and practices have had an enormous impact on public policy, individual and community attitudes, and the quality of justice experienced by the individuals most directly affected.

The state by defining the strike by its employees for restoration of superannuation and other benefits as collective violation of their responsibilities towards society, moreover by imposing the Essential Services Maintenance Act it was fanatical to establishing blame and guilt on its employees. Instead of promoting dialogue and negotiation, the state promoted an adversarial relationship and imposed pain, punishment and deterrence to prevent/ control the strike. Describing the strike in purely legal terms, the judiciary and state government represented its employees abstractly to the public and devoid the strike of moral social, economic and political dimensions. Characterizing strikers as offenders and compounding their loss of rights, the drastic curtailment of pension and other benefits, further punishment was handed by way of orders for dismissal which amounted to being twice victimized. In order to legitimise these actions, the state sought to focus on society's disaffection on employee past behaviour and the rights of the strikers were projected as unreasonable.

In recent Indian experience, the working class as whole has been relatively responsible and only used strikes in extreme cases when negotiations have failed completely or when employers have appeared to be completely insensitive to genuine demands of labour. Denial of this right would lead to a massive deterioration of the bargaining power of workers, which has already been weakened by various macroeconomic processes such a global integration and the withdrawal of the state from important areas of regulation and provision.

In any society, the socio-economic rights of all citizens, including workers, have never really been freely gifted by the state or employers; their recognition and implementation have always been the result of prolonged struggle on the part of workers and other groups. Changing the conditions of such struggle amounts to changing the possibility of ensuring these basic rights, which are even recognised in the Constitution of India. Therefore, the right to strike for workers remains an important instrument for ensuring the basic economic rights of all citizens. This is most unfortunate and obviously a open support for the most vindictive action against the employees and teachers by the political leadership of the Government and the bureaucracy to suppress a justified collective action by the employees and teachers for redressal of their grievances when all other means of negotiated settlement failed.

The point, however, is not that the right to strike needs to be established in India – a fact that is clearly internationally accepted, protected and well-documented – but what particular steps need to be taken to ensure that it is categorically respected in every sphere. This is crucial at a time when the Central Government is proposing to undertake economic reforms and policies that could have serious ramifications on workers' welfare.

For a start, the Central government must link its economic policies to the international standards established by the International Labour Organisation (ILO) and the international community, by ratifying the relevant ILO conventions (87, the Freedom of Association and the Right to Organize Convention; and 98, the Right to Organize and the Collective Bargaining Convention). As a founding member of the ILO, India is bound to respect the 1998 Declaration on Fundamental Principles and Rights at Work, as an "expression of commitment" that governments and employers alike are dedicated to equitable working conditions. The Declaration states that member-states are obligated to "to respect, to promote and to realize, in good faith and in accordance with the Constitution", the freedom of association and the effective recognition of the right to collective bargaining, among others, specifically adding that even if member states – such as India – have not ratified the relevant conventions, they are obligated to respect and abide by the norms by virtue of their voluntary membership in the organization. Similarly, the Government of India should reconsider Article 8(d) of the International Covenant on Economic, Social and Cultural Rights, which recognizes the right to strike.

According to Amartya Sen democratic politics requires the protection of political freedom (such as free speech, uncensored media, freedom from political prosecution or persecution), as well as public participation and social deliberation. The government should clearly pronounce the right to strike in India by amending the IDA and other existing legislation to explicitly uphold the exercise of lawful strikes. In addition, it is necessary to repeal the Essential Services Maintenance Act and the corresponding state acts, where they exist. Finally, unlike the unilateral approach adopted by the Second National Commission on Labour, a broader survey of worker's opinions would ensure that labour reforms are supported by democratic participation.

P.S.

The AIADMK government was voted out of power in May 2006. The DMK which came into power, in their first budget restored all benefits including superannuation benefits and other benefits. Moreover, the new government declared that priority will be given to the legal heirs of Government employees and Teachers who died during the strike period and those of Road Gang Mazdoors who died during the period of termination of their services for appointment on compassionate grounds.

REFERENCES

Chandrasekhar C. P. and Ghosh, Jayati (2004), The right to strike and labour repression in India, Business Line, February, 03,. Retrieved on September 14, 2006 from http://www.thehindubusinessline.com/2004/02/03/stories/2004020300100900.htm 05/02/2004.

Dev, Ganesh and Ratnayake K., (2003), Tamil Nadu sackings signal new offensive against Indian workers. *World Socialist Website,* 3 September. Retrieved on October 19, 2006 from http://www.wsws.org/articles/2003/sep2003/ind-s03.shtml.

Human Rights Features (2005), *Right to Strike Indispensable for worker's rights*, HRF/121/05, June 24.

Noorani, A.G., (2003), A. Legitimate Right, *Frontline*. Retrieved on September 9, 2006, from http://www.frontlineonnet.com/fl2020/stories/20031010002509000.htm.

Rajan Varada, W. R., (2003), State Terrorism against Striking Employees *People's Democracy*. Vol. XXVII, No. 29, July 20.

Rastogi, Anirudh & Srivastava, Siddharth (2004), *Combat Law*, Volume 2, Issue 6.

Sen, Amartya (2005), Indian democracy and Public Reasoning. *Frontline*. Retrieved on October 6, 2005 from http://www.frontlineonnet.com/fl2204/stories/20050225005401300.htm.

Sridhar, V., (2003), To legalise exploitation *Frontline*, Volume 20 - Issue 18, August 30 - September 12. Retrieved on September, 19, 2006 http://www.frontlineonnet.com/fl2018/stories/20030912007500600.htm.

Umbreit Mark S. (2000), *The Handbook of Victim Offender Mediation: An Essential Guide to Research And Practice.*

Part - IV

CHILD VICTIMS: A NEED BASED INTERVENTION ANALYSIS

16

RESTORING JUSTICE TO CHILD VICTIMS OF ABUSE: DRAWING INTERLINKAGES BETWEEN THE MACRO AND THE MICRO

INTRODUCTION

Child abuse is one of the most appalling crimes our society is suffering from today, and it is a cause of serious concern for many professional arenas. A significant level of attention is being paid to the victims of child abuse at the global level, even though we in India as a state and a society have not given it the consideration the enormity of its magnitude demands and deserves. Justice for the child victims of abuse has always been one of the primary areas of focus in the international debate on child abuse and the issues falling within its gamut. Also, the justice-delivery system shares a mutually influencing relationship with the socio-cultural realities. This chapter discusses some of the issues about such relationships, in the wake of certain emerging trends and debates on the nature of justice.

Child Abuse and Neglect can be defined as "the intentional, non-accidental injury, maltreatment of children by parents, caretakers, employers or others including those individuals representing government/non-government bodies which may lead to temporary or permanent impairment of their physical, mental, psycho-social development, disability or death." (The definition evolved at the National Seminar on Child Abuse in India, 1988, as quoted in Bajpai, 2003). Child abuse can further be divided into three broad categories – physical abuse, emotional abuse, and sexual abuse.

Child Physical Abuse can be defined as "a situation in which a child suffers, or is likely to suffer, significant harm from an injury inflicted by the child's parent or care-giver. The injury may be inflicted intentionally or may be the result of physical punishment or physically aggressive treatment of a child". (Victorian Government Department of Health and Community Services, 1994).

Child Emotional Abuse can be referred as a" pattern of behavior that impairs a child's emotional development or sense of self-worth". This may include constant criticism, threats, or rejection, as well as withholding love, support, or guidance." (National Clearinghouse on Child Abuse and Neglect Information, 2004).

Child Sexual Abuse is defined as "contacts or interactions between a child and an older or more knowledgeable child or adult, when the child is being used as an object of gratification for the older child's or adult's sexual needs. These contacts or interactions are carried out against the child, using force, trickery, bribes, threats, or pressure." (United Nations definition, as quoted in Bajpai, 2003).

CHILD ABUSE: EXISTING LEGAL RESPONSES

Appropriate responses by the legal system in India to child abuse are virtually non-existent. There are forms of abuse towards which the legal justice system has not responded at even the most rudimentary level. Where there have been responses, they have tended to be inappropriate, inefficient and inadequate.

India does not have a comprehensive law on child abuse. The existing laws pressed into action when a case of child abuse is reported to the police are either the various sections of the Indian Penal Code, or the Juvenile Justice (Care and Protection of Children) Act of 2000. In spite of these provisions, there are various forms of abuse, of which the existing laws fail to take cognizance. Also, the sections within the Indian Penal Code are not gender-neutral, and presume that certain types of sexual abuse cannot target boys as victims. It is now a well-argued and well-discussed opinion that the Indian Criminal Justice System essentially has the offender at its center, the focus being his/her apprehension and sentencing. The victim gets sidelined, in this process that begins usually by reporting the crime at the Police Station level and concludes with the judgment pronounced by the court of law, followed by further punitive action against the accused, if convicted. No steps are usually taken to help the victim to deal with the emotional loss suffered through the offence. The way in which this process is executed by the agencies like police and courts can be insensitive and damaging to the victim, especially in the subject under discussion where the victim is a child within the context of a very delicate issue of child abuse. The Supreme Court of India itself has made such observations in case of rape victims in its judgment on Delhi Domestic Working Women's Forum v UOI [1995(1) SCC 14, 18 to 21], stating that complaints are being handled roughly and are not being given due attention, that the victims are more often than not humiliated by the police, and that the experience of furnishing evidence in court has been negative and destructive (Bajpai, 2003). When the system is so intimidating for an adult victim, how petrifying can it possibly be for a child victim of abuse can well be imagined.

SOCIAL FORCES AND JUSTICE–DELIVERY

The law and the associated justice-delivery processes of any country or society are in many ways a reflection of the norms, values, and practices followed by its population. The law and its processes cannot be viewed as antiseptically isolated from the social fabric of the society they arise out of, for the simple fundamental reason that these are formulated, interpreted and enforced by the people from the same socio-cultural milieu. Hence, legal justice vis-à-vis a particular social concern is largely influenced by the prevailing socio-cultural attitudes and beliefs related to that issue. In this way, the macro-level forces of social patterns that include norms, values, and practices determine the micro-level responses to the problem in terms of the process of justice-delivery to the victim. These macro-level issues are political in character and decide the distribution and/or concentration of power among various stakeholders as far as that issue is concerned.

No culture and society explicitly permits the abuse of its children. But the unfortunate fact remains that child abuse happens, and there are certain social factors that directly or indirectly allow it to happen. And later on, these factors come in the way of child victims and the justice they deserve. Therefore, to combat abuse of children within the society, it is important to explore the politics of child abuse, that is, what are the norms that impact and abet the abuse of society's children.

It is worth mentioning here that the area of developing a political analysis of child abuse, especially in India, is under-explored and many socio-political factors that contribute to child abuse are still to be deliberated and debated upon. In the following text, an attempt is being made to present and discuss some of the social factors that not only lead to, but also fuel the perpetration of abuse against children. The first four norms in the list, that is, 'children as property of parents', 'learned helplessness', 'sexual entitlement', and 'shroud of secrecy' have been taken from an article discussing the politics of sexual abuse by Jim Struve (1990). An effort is also being made to discuss how these norms affect the justice-delivery process in the Indian context:

Children as Property of Parents

Our society holds this norm strongly that parents have the ownership of their children. As Struve (1990) puts it, "perceiving a ... child as a property provides a justification for controlling him or her. Women and children in our society are encouraged to be passive, thereby conditioning them to accept a position of being controlled. In fact, strong negative and social sanctions are focused on women and children who choose not to be passive: strong women are perceived and labeled as "aggressive" and "hostile" while *strong children are perceived and labeled as "defiant" and "rebellious"* [emphasis provided]."

Thus, within this socio-cultural context, a so-called "defiant" child demonstrates parental inefficacy while a "compliant" one displays otherwise. This leads to the practice of using virtually any means possible by the parents to ensure compliance on the child's part in the name of disciplining the child. Such "disciplining" can taken the form of harsh corporal punishment, but still gets justified by the society. Hence physical and emotional abuse not only goes unnoticed, they find social legitimacy as well. Examples of such legitimacy can be found ingrained in folk-culture. A popular idiom in Punjabi means - "Tongue-lashings by your parents are joyful and healthy". Also, incest (sexual abuse of a child by a member of the immediate or the extended family) is not a rare form of abuse. A large number of news-reports in the recent times on incest bear testimony to this fact. Going by the norm under discussion, the society denies the sexual abuse of a child at the hands of his/her own parents, grandparents etc. Social attitude like this does not allow the children to voice such a concern in case they are suffering from this type of abuse. Children who disclose are often disbelieved, at times even by the law enforcement machinery (Virani, 2000).

Learned Helplessness

Struve (1990) defines this as "the ability to accept one's position of passivity in relationship to those who are defined as being more dominant, to such a degree that a person experiences psychological paralysis". The cultural environment of our country is such that children are economically, socially, and legally completely dependent on their parents/guardians. The power hierarchies between the children and the adults are made clear to the children through verbal and non-verbal communication (Bharat, 1997). Highly inadequate steps are being taken to empower the children by making them aware of their social, cultural, and legal rights, and in terms of creating an environment where such rights can be articulated and actualized by the children themselves. Against such a backdrop, a child facing abuse may find it to be a situation of "no escape". For instance, children are often taught not to trust and speak to strangers. But in situations of a threat or occurrence of abuse, at times a stranger might actually be the one who could help if the child asked for it. But the child's learned helplessness would come in the way of seeking help from such a person, thus blocking the possibility of a rescue from abuse.

Sexual Entitlement

It is a common and prevalent social belief that sex is a privilege and entitlement for the dominant person in an inter-personal relationship. It is a popular belief that men are sexually aggressive and dominant, and must have their sexual urges satisfied by their partners in relationship. Very often women and children are presented and promoted as commercialized commodities for the sexual fulfillment of men. In a sexually abusive situation either or both the offender and the child might think that it is the right of the former to seek sexual gratification from the latter.

Shroud of Secrecy

Sex is a taboo subject in our society. Sex is also perceived as a dangerous and/or corrupting issue. This develops an exaggerated anxiety in the mainstream society with regard to sexuality. The rigid norms arising out of such an anxiety do not accept information-seeking behavior on this aspect of life, especially by women and children. This also develops in the society a general and widespread shame regarding matters concerning sexuality. For this reason, a large number of victims of sexual abuse suffer from shame and feel embarrassed to seek help. When they do seek help, these very social norms curb the child's initiative of seeking assistance as the people whom the children tell might themselves be too embarrassed to handle the subject. Therefore, it becomes difficult for the child in such a repressive environment to access justice in any form.

Also, this norm keeps sexuality (and thus sexual abuse as well) from entering the mainstream social dialogue, resulting in the ill-informed and ill-equipped laws that we have today, the case in point because we lack a law, which could comprehensively tackle the issue of child abuse. The Indian Penal Code sections regarding sexual abuse and harassment fail to take note of many forms of child sexual abuse, thereby allowing the perpetrators an easy escape.

Patriarchy and Rigid Gender-Role Stereotypes

In a male-dominated patriarchal society like ours, adherence to gender-role stereotypes is an expectation the society has of every individual. Compliance with the norm is not only appreciated, but celebrated too, whilst deviance is looked down upon. These stereotypes clearly define the power and role relationships between boys and girls, men and women – a man ought to be aggressive, physically and mentally strong and should play the role of the provider and the protector, while a woman ought to be soft, compliant and should play the role of the care provider and the nurturer. Also, a man must exercise restraint on emotion whereas it is expected of women to be emotional (Ross, 1961; Dube, 1988; Bharat, 1997). These stereotypes refuse to acknowledge that males too can be in victim-roles. Therefore, in the case of abuse of boys, it becomes particularly difficult for them to deal with their own victimization without facing a conflict with the "invincibly aggressive" popularly defined masculine traits the gender-role stereotypes expect them to possess. At the same time, the society too is not ready to view males as possible victims, hence leading to further victimization in terms of the societal denial of their trauma (Hunter,

1990; Mathews, 1996; Lisak, 1997). Such a conflict adds to the pain of the victims and the denial of this pain on the part of the society takes away many of their support systems as well. But the fact remains that boys are abused – physically, sexually, and emotionally.

Several studies that were done abroad peg the prevalence of sexual abuse in males at between 2.5% and 16% (Hunter, 1990). The prevalence of physical abuse among boys has been found to be around 17% (Lisak et. at., 1996). Research has also shown that victimization of boys in terms of physical abuse is higher than that of the girls, especially under the age of 12 years (Rosenthal, 1988 as quoted in Mathews, 1996). Corporal punishment, a common form of physical abuse, is also high among boys. In Canada, 70% of the victims of non-sexual assault under the age of 12 are boys (Statistics Canada, 1991 as quoted in Mathews, 1996). There are various studies, which state that boys are hit more than the girls, but they are also less likely to report such abuse (Mathews, 1996).

Even though such abuse exists in the case of boys, the legal justice system in India offers little support and solace. The extent of this indifference against the boys is so much that the Indian Penal Code does not even acknowledge that boys too can be sexually molested and raped. The sections that pertain to these offences (IPC Section 354 about "Outraging the modesty of a woman" and IPC Section 375 about rape) are solely applicable to females. The sexual abuse of males has to be in this case tried under IPC Section 377 which is not primarily meant for abuse or violence, but against the so-called "unnatural sexual offenses" and intends to punish "whoever voluntarily has carnal intercourse against the order of the nature with any man, woman or animal". Such a state of affairs mirrors the social stereotypes that males cannot be victimized. Also, there is no acknowledgement in the IPC Section 375 that defines rape, that a woman too could perpetrate this crime. In reality, women can, and do, commit sexual crimes against children (Finkelhor & Russell, 1984; Miletski, 1995; Valios, 2002). But it is most tragic that the society and the law are unmindful of such violations of childhood.

Adults Always Know What is Best for the Child

This is a very popular notion held by our adult society, and happens to be yet another manifestation of the famous adage – "children are meant to be seen and not heard". With regard to the justice-delivery process, this norm surfaces in the shape of a child victim who is reduced to a mute spectator in a battery of events, with the strong likelihood of his/her role having already been defined by the system as that of a mere informant.

Sanctity of the Family

In our society, family sanctity in considered paramount and families are seen as bricks, which build the foundation of the whole society, and that these are to be saved from "breaking up" at any cost. In an environment of patriarchy, this gets even more accentuated and the family honor becomes a primary concern for the individual, the families and the society as a whole, at times even over-riding the interests of the individuals constituting them. It is now a proven fact that most cases of child abuse are perpetrated by someone known to the child, and many times the offender is member of the immediate or extended family (Mathews, 1996; Panchal & Shaikh, 1997; Sakshi, 1997 as quoted in Virani, 2000; RAHI, 1997 as quoted in Virani, 2000). But when the child seeks support from inside or outside the family, this social norm is likely to prompt the significant adults in the family to silence the matter within the four walls and behind the closed doors in order to protect the so-called "family honor". For this reason, chances are that the child may never be able to access any social, legal, or psychological support from the support systems available outside the family.

The social norms discussed above have substantial repercussions on the issue of child abuse, and on the journeys of the victims of such abuse from hurt towards healing. Some of the areas in which social norms have influenced the justice-delivery process have also been discussed. This discussion is at best only suggestive, and by no means exhaustive. The issues brought up through the discussion need change by way of law reforms. However, more than that, these social norms themselves need to be questioned and deconstructed. Such norms, values, and practices affect a whole range of factors in society, of which legal justice is only a part. To bring about a more widespread and structural change in the larger landscape, it is pertinent that change be brought in these norms. In addition, the relevance of social justice cannot be underestimated. All of these norms influence the social-justice process as well by influencing the ways in which society will perceive these victims and react or respond to the abuse suffered by them. For the justice to be holistic in nature, it is necessary that social change be brought about in the attitudes, beliefs, and norms prevalent in the society affecting the victims of abuse. Law reforms alone shall hold no meaning if the culture of silence, oppression and inaction continues to surround the issue of child abuse in the society.

The legal justice system also needs to undergo a structural change in terms of its role as a component and catalyst of providing holistic justice to the child victims, and to free itself from the shackles of negative and unhealthy social norms and practices. The law reforms are certainly needed, but more than just law reforms it is the entire approach of legal justice system towards working with the child victims that requires nothing short of a metamorphosis.

The premise on which the Criminal Justice System has operated so far needs to undergo a paradigm shift. This shift should be in the direction of a switch from offender-centrality to a victim-centered system of justice. One of the major purposes of any justice system has to be apprehending the offender, but the primary motive, which should hold the center stage, must be to help the victim. Justice to a victim not only and not always means punishment for the offender. Justice means to support and assist the victim in overcoming the aftermath of the violence – physically, financially, emotionally and/or spiritually. Justice also means to deal with the victim sensitively, empathetically, and compassionately. Justice also means not to further victimize the victim. And most importantly, justice means to empower the victim to live a life as optimally and normally as s/he would have lived had the abuse not taken place. And this holds special significance in the context of the child victims of abuse, as they are still in the formative years of their life – they are as vulnerable as they are impressionable. Thus, the justice-delivery process should prepare itself as per the needs of such victims and dedicate itself to developing multifaceted strategies and interventions to address the trauma caused by the abuse. This becomes even more relevant in the wake of the fact that research suggests a significant link between victimization in childhood and later involvement in violent crimes (Widom, 1992). But as a U.S. Department of Justice report on improving the criminal justice response to child victims and witnesses says, "The criminal justice response can be a critical turning point in defining how experiencing violence will impact a child's life".

Therefore, it is crucial for this system to be very process-oriented and participatory. It must be process-oriented because the process is as important as the outcome itself. Even regardless of the outcome, the process in itself can go a long way in healing the hurt caused by the abuse, if it is sensitive to the emotional and developmental needs of the child. Participation is of essence in this process. So far, the child in such cases has often been a passive viewer. The need now is to allow the child his/her right of participation in the process in the capacity of an active stakeholder. Article 12 of the United Nations Convention on the Rights of the Child, of which India is a signatory, defines, and declares this right to participation. This does not indicate that adult stakeholders shall hold no decision-making power. It simply means that a child be allowed to participate actively in mattes concerning her/him, in view of the child's evolving capacities with age and experience. At the same time, an enhanced participation also results in a greater likelihood of securing a successful final outcome (Reno et al. 1999).

As can be observed, this shift from children being silent beneficiaries of the criminal justice system to being active stakeholders in the victim justice system is fundamentally a shift from welfare-based approach to a rights-based one.

INTEGRATING AND DEBATING RESTORATIVE JUSTICE PRINCIPLES AND APPROACHES

The aforementioned transformation in the structure and approach of the current Criminal Justice System of India would also suggests incorporation of several of the principles of Restorative Justice, such as the process of justice- delivery being highly important in its own right irrespective of the final outcome, participation of the victim throughout the process, emphasis on empathy and emotional restoration of the victim, and an increased and more active involvement on the part of the victim. The advocates of Restorative Justice have done a commendable job in bringing many of the shortcomings of the current Criminal Justice System to the fore, and accommodation of several of these Restorative Justice principles can indeed enrich the process of providing justice to the victim. Having said this, it is emphasized that, not all Restorative Justice Principles and approaches can be made universally applicable to all situations of offending and victimization. The case in the point here is one of the basic proposition of Restorative Justice, which is that "Crime is primarily conflict between individuals resulting in injuries to victims, communities and the offenders themselves; only secondarily is it lawbreaking" (Van Ness, 1993, as quoted in Strang, 1999).

One of the main modern approaches of Restorative Justice is the Restorative Justice offender-victim conference aimed at reconciling the parties in order to repair the injuries caused by the crime (Strang, 1999; Morrison, 2002). Also, the Restorative Justice conference also requires participation of both the offender and the victim. When viewed in the context of an issue as sensitive as child abuse, it might not be a very effective, sensitive and hence an advisable proposition, keeping in mind the dynamics involved in this issue. This is an issue where not only the child's body has been violated, but in most cases the trust has also been breached because as stated earlier, it is someone known to the child who perpetrates the abuse. In cases of child sexual abuse, very often the abuser approaches the child in a very insidious way and cleverly manipulates the child's vulnerabilities through a process known as "grooming". During this process of grooming, the offender in most cases befriends a child after identifying him/her as his target, gradually starts touching the child and through this desensitizes the child to touch, isolates the child from support systems, and makes the child feel responsible for these happenings while he begins to abuse him/her (Dam, 2001).

This brief overview of process of sexual abuse can help us comprehend the child's feelings of ambivalence towards the abuse, and the delicacy of the issue in terms of disclosure, reporting, and the victim's struggle to deal with it. Keeping all this in mind, a face-to-face conference with the abuser may actually do more harm than good. Many times the child might be so traumatized by the abuse that facing the offender might further victimize the child. For this reason only, in camera trials have been initiated in court proceedings. Also, it is important that the victim resolves his/her internal conflicts arising out of the abuse first before entering into an exercise targeted at his/her conflict-resolution with the offender. Considering the confusing, insidious, and manipulative nature of such a crime, and the age and power differentials between the two parties, it can be suggested that such an idea does not hold good under the given circumstances. So, it has to be realized that child abuse is a very special type of crime containing a range of distinctive dimensions and dynamics that might render such a conference unadvisable.

However, there could be certain strategies and interventions based upon Restorative Justice Principles that could be weaved into the current Criminal Justice System in order to make it more victim-friendly. A few of these are suggested below:

(i) Multi-disciplinary Support Teams: Various professionals who could help a child victim of abuse, for instance social worker, pediatrician, psychologist, psychiatrist, lawyer etc., would form this team which would then work with all the cases of child abuse that are reported to the Criminal Justice System. This team would help the child testify in a way that all the information required is obtained early on in the case and the child would not need to testify again and again before the court. Also, this team could help the child in coping with abuse and/or the anxieties and pressures pertaining to the case.

(ii) Court Awareness Programme: This programme would aim at providing easy-to-understand age-appropriate information regarding the ongoing case proceedings to the child victim at different stages of the criminal justice process, and preparing the child for each of these stages so the child knows what to expect and what is expected of him/her. This would encourage participation and provide information on court proceedings and the outcome.

(iii) Victim Impact Statement: Victim Impact Statement is a statement that the child victim could make to the court stating in his/her own words how she/he feels about the abuse; about the way it has affected her/him. Apart from being an evidentiary tool, it helps the court feel the impact of the victimization as felt by the child. Also, in the routine proceedings the child might not have had the opportunity to articulate some of his/her thoughts and/or feelings. This could provide that opportunity and verbalizing the impact might be a cathartic process for the child. The significant adults in a child's life, such as the parents, siblings etc., may also be allowed to make such statements. The victim impact statement must be optional and should be left to the choice of the child.

Our socio-legal justice system has for long stayed insensitive and blind to the needs and pain of victims of child abuse. As long as we continue to stay this way, we will keep punishing them for the crimes committed by the perpetrators. Now is not the time for inaction, the children are waiting ...

REFERENCES

Bajpai, A. (2003), *Child Rights in India: Law, Policy, and Practice*. New Delhi: Oxford University Press.

Bharat, S. (1997), Family Socialization of the Indian Child. *Trends in Social Science Research*. Vol. 4, No. 1, 201-216.

Dam, C. V. (2001), *Identifying Child Molesters: Preventing Child Sexual Abuse by Recognizing the Patterns of the Offenders*. New York, USA: The Haworth Maltreatment and Trauma Press.

Dube, L. (1988), On the Construction of Gender: Hindu Girls in Patrilineal India. *Economic and Political Weekly*. 23, 11-19.

Finkelhor, D., & Russell, D. (1984), Women as Perpetrators. In Finkelhor, D., *Child Sexual Abuse: New Theory and Research*. 171-187. New York, USA: The Free Press.

Hunter, M. (1990), *Abused Boys: The Neglected Victims of Sexual Abuse*. New York, USA: Fawcett Columbine.

Lisak, D. (1997), Male Gender Socialization and the Perpetration of Sexual Abuse. In Levant, R. F. & Brooks, G. R. (Eds.), *Men and Sex: New Psychological Perspectives*. 156-177. USA: John Wiley and Sons.

Lisak, D., Hopper, J., & Song, P. (1996). Factors in the Cycle of Violence: Gender Rigidity and Emotional Constriction. *Journal of Traumatic Stress*. 9, 721-743.

Mathews, F. (1996), *The Invisible Boy: Revisioning the Victimization of Male Children and Teens*. Ottawa, Canada: National Clearinghouse on Family Violence.

Miletski, H. (1995), *Mother-Son Incest: The Unthinkable Broken Taboo – An Overview of Findings*. Vermont, USA: The Safer Society Press.

Morrison, B. (2002). Bullying and Victimisation in Schools: A Restorative Justice Approach, *Trends and Issues in Crime and Criminal Justice*. February, No. 219.

National Clearinghouse on Child Abuse and Neglect Information (2004), *What is Child Abuse and Neglect?*. U.S. Department of Health & Human Services, Administration for Children & Families.

Panchal, T. & Shaikh, N. (1997), *Documentation of Police Cases of Sexually Abused Girls in Mumbai City Between 1994-95*. Mumbai: The Special Cell For Women and Children, Tata Institute of Social Sciences.

Reno, J., Holder Jr., E. C., Fisher, R. C., Robinson, L., Brennan, N., & Turman, K. M. (1999), *Breaking the Cycle of Violence: Recommendations to Improve the Criminal Justice Response to Child Victims and Witnesses*. Washington, D.C.: U.S. Department of Justice, Office of Justice Programs.

Ross, A. D. (1961), *The Hindu Family in Its Urban Setting*. Delhi: Oxford University Press.

Strang, H. (1999), *Restoring Victims: An International View*. Paper Presented at the Restoration for Victims of Crime Conference, Melbourne, Australia.

Struve, J. (1990), Dancing With the Patriarchy: The Politics of Sexual Abuse. In Hunter, M. (Ed.), *The Sexually Abused Male, Vol. 1*, USA: Lexington Books.

Valios, N. (2002), Women Abuse Too. *Community Care*. 14-20 March, 28-29

Victorian Government Department of Health and Community Services (1994). *Child Physical Abuse: Understanding and Responding*. Australia.

Virani, P. (2000), *Bitter Chocolate*. New Delhi: Penguin.

Widom, C. S. (1992), *The Cycle of Violence*. USA: National Institute of Justice.

M. INDRASELVI AND P. MADHAVA SOMA SUNDARAM

17

CHILD MALTREATMENT IN SCHOOLS: SELECTED RESULTS FROM A SURVEY OF RURAL SCHOOLS

INTRODUCTION

Child abuse, whether intra- or extra-familial, generally includes various forms of physical, sexual, and emotional abuse. Physical abuse includes acts such as punching, beating, kicking, biting, burning, shaking, or otherwise physically harming a child. Sexual abuse ranges from sexual touching to exhibitionism, sexual intercourse, and commercial exploitation. Emotional abuse includes acts or omissions that could cause serious behavioural, cognitive, emotional, or mental disorders. Operational definitions of these forms of abuse have been developed on the basis of three National Incidence Studies (NIS) conducted by the U.S. Department of Health and Human Services, and the Canadian Incidence Study of Child Abuse and Neglect (Sedlak & Broadhurst, 1996: Trocm & Wolfe, 2001).

Child abuse is an Intentional act that results in Physical or emotional harm to children. The term child abuse covers a wide range of behavior. From actual physical assault by parents or other adult care takers to neglect of a Child's basic needs. Child abuse is also some times called child maltreatment. Although the extent of child abuse is difficult to measure it is recognized as a major social problem, especially in industrialized nations. It occurs in all income, racial, religious, and ethnic groups and in urban and rural communities. It is however more common in some groups, especially those below the poverty line.

Cultures around the world have different standards in deciding what constitutes child abuse. In Sweden, for example the law prohibits any physical punishment of children including spanking, by contrast, in some countries of Asia, Africa, and the Caribbean, parents are expected to punish their children by hitting them.

TYPOLOGY OF CHILD ABUSE

There are several different types of child abuse and some children experience more than one form.

- Physical abuse includes deliberate act of violence that injures or even kill a child. Unexplained bruises, broken bones, or burn marks on a child may be signs of physical abuse.
- Sexual abuse occurs when adults use children for sexual gratification or expose them to sexual activities. Sexual abuse may begin with kissing or fondling and progress to more intrusive sexual acts, such as oral sex and vaginal penetration.
- Emotional abuse destroys childs self – esteem. Such abuse commonly includes repeated verbal abuse of a child in the form of shouting, threats and degrading or humiliating criticism other types emotional abuse are confinement, such as shutting a child in a dark closet, and social isolation, such as denying a child friends.
- The most common form of child abuse is neglect. Physical neglect involves a parent's failure to provide adequate food, clothing, shelter or medical care to a child. It may also include inadequate supervision and a consistent failure to protect a child from hazards or danger, emotional neglect occurs when a parent or care taker fails to meet basic needs for affection and comfort. Example of emotional neglect includes behaving in a cold, distant and unaffectionate way towards a child allowing a child to witness chronic or severe spouse abuse. Allowing a child to use alcohol or drugs and encouraging a child to engage in delinquent behaviour. Another form of neglect involves failing to meet a child's basic educational

needs either by failing to entroll a child in school or permitting a child to skip school frequently.

INSTITUTIONAL ABUSE

When child abuse was first brought to public and professional attention it was most commonly thought to occur within the family context, with parents as perpetrators (Kempe & Steele, 1962: Helfer & Kempe, 1974). In the mid 1970's David Gil (Gil, 1975) was the first to suggest that child abuse occurs at three levels:

- Intrafamilial
- Institutional and
- Societal.

A few years later Eliana Gil (Gil,1982) took this one step further, identifying three distinct forms of institutional child abuse

- The first is the overt physical, sexual, or emotional abuse committed by those individuals directly responsible for the child's care, most often childcare workers or foster parents.
- Program abuse and
- System abuse

Programme Abuse and System Abuse are unique to out-of-home settings, Program abuses occur when programs operate below acceptable standards or rely upon harsh or unacceptable methods to control behaviour and normally apply for the school environment. System abuse is not committed by a single individual or a single agency, but rather occurs when the entire childcare system is stretched beyond its limits. This type of maltreatment is often related to shortcomings of agencies responsible for the care and well being of children. Prolonged treatment, unnecessary removal from the home, misplacement and misdiagnosis due to inadequate assessment resources all may be viewed as forms of system abuse. Similar to other forms of abuse, the impact of system abuse may be devastating.

Traditional definitions of child abuse in institutions and organizations were also rooted in Goffman's (1961) model of the A total institution. This model defined a total institution as one in which almost every aspect of the child's life is controlled by the institution and by the same single authority, with common examples being institutions to care for people with physical or mental disabilities, children without family caregivers, or young offenders.

SCHOOL RELATED ABUSES

If one were to examine educational institutions in terms of potential risk for institutional abuse and subsequent psychological harm, a number of features stand out. Perhaps most striking is the non-voluntary nature of school and the large amount of time children spend in school. Between the ages of five and sixteen, children spend the majority of their time at school, which poses a risk for some forms of maltreatment in this setting. The fact that children may be at the same school with the same teacher(s) or other school personnel for many years creates the potential for ongoing abuse.

In addition, teachers are powerful figures in children's lives. Many children consider their teachers to be mentors and role models, particularly when the relationship extends outside of the classroom (e.g., coaching, tutoring). Teachers have a great deal of control over whether a child's classroom experiences are positive or negative. Teachers also have control over the child's marks. When a teacher abuses a child, the child may be reluctant to disclose for a number of reasons. Knowing that teachers are generally well respected, children may fear that they will not be believed. They also may fear that if they tell of the abuse they will lose their teacher's favor, their marks may suffer, or their teacher will make school life difficult for them.

When abuse does occur in an educational or vocational setting, the effects can be devastating. Children are left with feelings of shame, worthlessness, confusion, and guilt (Dolmage, 1995). Children may also experience Post-Traumatic Stress Disorder or similar symptoms, including avoidance of school and fear associated with educators; loss of trust in or fear of adults, especially educators; loss of interest in school; denial of or refusal to discuss the traumatic event; nightmares; and excessive crying (Hyman et al., 1988). As parents, survivors may be re-traumatized when they send their children to school, fearing that they, too, will be victimized.

As a consequence of these institutions' failure to act in cases of child abuse, the importance of an education and associated interest in learning and achievement may be compromised. Survivors are left feeling disillusioned with the system, either as a result of the abuse itself or how the abuse was handled (or mishandled), and as a result they avoid any reminders of school and school-related activities. These feelings may continue into adulthood and prevent victims and survivors from obtaining the same level of education or employment they might have otherwise obtained.

In many instances one also faces difficulties responding to allegations of abuse by a teacher, partly due to well-meaning safeguards that protect teachers from complaints lodged by students and parents. To by-pass such obstacles and minimize accountability, some district level administrators silently transferred teachers who were alleged to abuse students from one school to another school, resulting in further allegations. Nonetheless, in the developed countries, the professional and scientific literature on abuse by teachers is disproportionately focused on false allegations rather than the prevention and treatment of actual incidents of abuse (Anderson & Levine, 1999). In India, it must be mentioned here, that abuse in school has not received the kind of attentions that is required, from professional criminologists and sociologists, except for popular articles in magazines and newspapers.

PREVALENCE OF ABUSE

Child Abuse in India, as per the statutes, is covered in many sections of the IPC and other special Legislations. There is no separate classification for child abuse, as in many other developed countries. If one can take crimes against children as a sort of indicator on the prevalence of child abuse in the country, NCRB (2003) reveals that a total of 11,633 cases were reported in the country during 2003 as compared to 10,469 cases during 2002, reporting an increase of 11.1%. Among IPC crimes, Rape cases have increased by 16.5 percent (from 2532 cases in 2002 to 2949 cases in 2003) followed by Murder 13.0 per cent (1073 cases to 1212 cases), Exposure and Abandonment 12.1 per cent (644 to 722 cases) and Kidnapping & Abduction 10.7 per cent (2322 cases to 2571 cases). The following figure gives the details on the crime wise percent distribution for the year 2003.

Many researchers believe that statistics based on official reports do not accurately reflect the prevalence of child abuse. Definition of maltreatment varies from state to state and among agencies making such statistics unreliable. Professionals who interact with children-such as teachers, day-care workers, pediatricians, and police officers-may fail to recognize or report abuse. In addition, acts of abuse some times occur in the privacy of family's home and often go unreported.

Surveys of families, another way of estimating abuse, indicate that 2.3 percent of children in the United States or about 1.5 million children experience abusive violence each year. There are no such surveys conducted in India, and hence there are only guesstimates available.

Figure 1

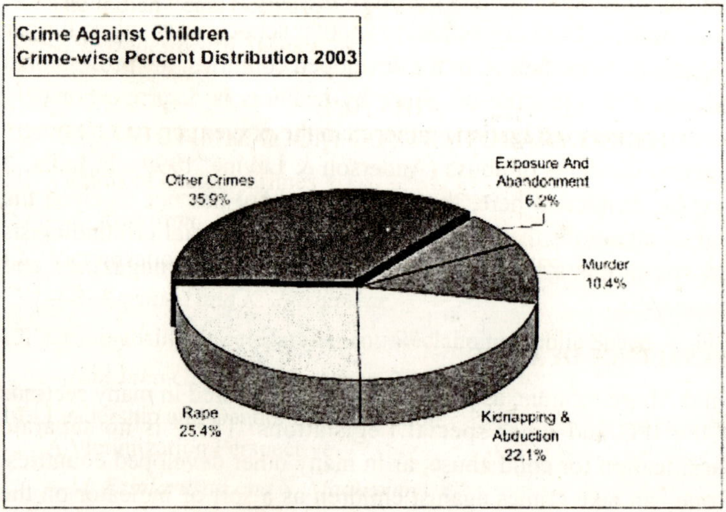

Crime Against Children
Crime-wise Percent Distribution 2003

Other Crimes 35.9%
Exposure And Abandonment 6.2%
Murder 10.4%
Kidnapping & Abduction 22.1%
Rape 25.4%

CAUSES

While, many people have difficulty in understanding why any person would hurt a child, the public often assumes that people who abuse their children suffer from mental disorders. But fewer than 10 percent of abuses have mental illness. Most abusers love their children but tend to have less patience and less mature personalities than other parents. These traits make it difficult to cope with the demands of their children and increase the likelihood of physical or emotional abuse.

CONSEQUENCES OF CHILD ABUSE

Over the past 25 years researchers and clinicians have described the varied and severe ways in which children's development and future mental health can be impaired by child abuse. Child abuse often results in cognitive and emotional distress or dysfunction. Children who have been abused may experience depression, anxiety, low self-esteem,

(Beitchman *et al.*, 1991; Berliner & Elliot, 1996; Green, 1993; Ammerman, 1986; Kolko, 1996) and somatic problems (Perring, 1992).

Theoretical explanations for understanding the immediate and enduring effects of child abuse on children's development take into account developmental processes and how they might interact with the particular pattern and trauma of maltreatment. Exposure to violence as a victim or witness poses a serious threat to American children. Widom (1992) reported a significant link between victimization in childhood and later involvement in violent crimes, revealing a cycle of violence. Those who had been abused or neglected as children were more likely to be arrested as juveniles and as adults for violent crimes. On average, abused and neglected children begin committing crimes at younger ages, they commit nearly twice as many offenses as non-abused children, and they are arrested more frequently. Widom also interviewed a large number of people 20 years after their childhood victimization. Findings from this follow-up study suggest that the long-term consequences of childhood victimization may also include mental health problems, educational difficulties, alcohol and drug abuse, and employment problems.

Trauma theory and developmental psychopathology each consider how exposure to traumatic events or the use of inappropriate childrearing methods can affect children's development diversely and progressively over time. Saunders and Kilpatrick found that approximately 2 million adolescents, ages 12–17, appear to have suffered from post-traumatic stress disorder (PTSD) — a long-term mental health condition characterized by depression, anxiety, flashbacks, nightmares, and other behavioral and physiological symptoms.

AIM OF THE STUDY

The major aim of the study was to understand the types of punishments awarded by schools in Tenkasi Taluk in Tirunelveli District of Tamil Nadu.

TOOL

A questionnaire that was specifically, constructed for the purpose of the study was used by the researchers. The tool elicited information on the personal details of the students like age, sex, school, and class of study, duration of study in the school etc., A separate scale was constructed to determine whether the students have been awarded any of the listed punishments, in the past one-year. The list of punishments that were included were, scolding, standing on the bench, raise the hands and made to stand, imposition, kneeling, made to stand in the sunlight, slapping, beating on the head, beating with scale, beating with a cane, beating on the knuckle, made to run around the ground, shaking the head, shaking by hair, pinching, boxing (pinching on the ear), made to clean the school/class, fine, use of threat, and use of fire. This scale had 20 items and the responses were, "Yes", "No" and a neutral response of "Don't Know".

Two scales were also constructed to measure the respondents' academic performance (7 items) and the problems that the respondents faced (9 Items) due to the punishments that they received at the school.

RELIABILITY AND VALIDITY

In order to establish the reliability of the tool, Cronbach Coefficient Alpha was calculated (Cronbach, 1949). The alpha values for the three scales are given in Table 1. To establish the validity of the tool, it may be mentioned here that a highly reliable tool, is always a valid measure. A scale that has a sound rational validity, coupled with a high index of validity, can be empirically proved to have high validity (Garrett, 1970). Hence, in order to establish the validity of the tool, Index of reliability was calculated.

Table 1
Reliability and Validity of Scales Used

Scale	*Number of Items*	*Cronbach Alpha*	*Index of Reliability*
Punishments Adopted in Schools	20	0.705	0.839
Academic Performance	7	0.679	0.824
Problems faced due to punishments received	9	0.699	0.836

THE STUDY AREA

The study was conducted among selected schools in Tirunelveli District, Tamil Nadu, India. The profile of the Tirunelveli district is given below.

Table 2
Tirunelveli District Profile

	Rural	*Urban*	*Total*
Population	14,15,742	13,08,246	27,23,988
Male	6,45,142	6,88,797	13,33,939
Female	7,26,945	6,63,104	13,90,049
Literates	8,91,282 (71.7%)	9,37,782 (80.79%)	18,29,064 (76.09%)
Male Literates	4,90,721	5,06,557	9,97,278
Female Literates	4,00,561	4,31,225	8,31,786
Illiterates	5,24,460 (28.30%)	3,70,464 (19.21%)	8,94,924 (23.91%)
Male Illiterates	1,98,076	1,38,585	3,36,661
Female Illiterates	3,26,384	2,31,879	5,58,263
Main Cultivators	1,09,016 (17.49%)	21,800 (4.38%)	1,30,816 (11.67%)
Agricultural labourers	1,98,037 (31.77%)	79,632 (16.01%)	2,77,669 (24.78%)
Household Ind. Workers	1,39,283 (22.34%)	1,08,638 (21.84%)	2,47,921 (22.12%)
Other Workers	1,77,038 (28.40%)	2,87,308 (57.76%)	4,64,346 (41.43%)
Total Households	3,67,607	2,94,337	6,61,944

SAMPLE

80 respondents were selected from government run and Privately managed schools in Tenkasi Taluk, in Tirunelveli district. The profile of the sample according to the type of schools is given in Table 3.

Table 3
Distribution of Sample by type of School

	Frequency	*Percent*
Government School	49	61.3
Private School	31	38.8
Total	80	100.0

The profile of the sample, by sex, is as follows

Table 4
Distribution of Sample by Sex

	Frequency	*Percent*
Male	38	47.5
Female	42	52.5
Total	80	100.0

Majority of the sample (52.5%) were female students and males formed 47.5% of the sample. The profile of the sample, by age, is as follows

Table 5
Distribution of Sample by Age

	Frequency	*Percent*
< 10 years	20	25.0
11 - 15 years	38	47.5
16 > years	22	27.5
Total	80	100

RESULTS AND DISCUSSION

The data collected was coded and analyzed using SPSS package. The major findings are discussed, below. Table 6 and Figure 2 show the punishments that were given to students.

Table 6
Punishments Awarded by Schools

	Yes		*No*	
Types of Punishments	*N*	*%*	*N*	*%*
Scolding	74	92.5	6	7.5
Standing on the bench	21	26.3	59	73.8
Raising the Hands & Standing	17	21.3	63	78.8
Imposition	63	78.8	17	21.3
Kneeling	66	82.5	14	17.5
Standing in the sunlight	55	68.8	25	31.3
Slapping	72	90.0	8	10.0
Beating on the head	31	38.8	49	61.3
Beating with scale	59	73.8	21	26.3
Beating with a cane	71	88.8	9	11.3
Beating on the knuckle	46	57.7	34	42.5
Run around the ground	34	42.5	46	57.5
Shaking by the head	21	26.3	59	73.8
Shaking by hair	21	26.3	59	73.8
Pinching	47	58.8	33	41.3
Boxing (pinching on the ear)	32	40.0	48	60.0
Made to clean the school/class	61	76.3	19	23.8
Fine	56	70.0	24	30.0
Use of threat	77	96.3	3	3.8
Use of fire	3	3.8	77	96.3

Use of threat is the most commonly used form of punishment (96.3%) by schools, followed by Scolding (92.5%). Beating with cane

(88.8%) and kneeling (82.5%) were also commonly used in schools. The other forms which are used and their percentages are given in figure 2.

Figure 2

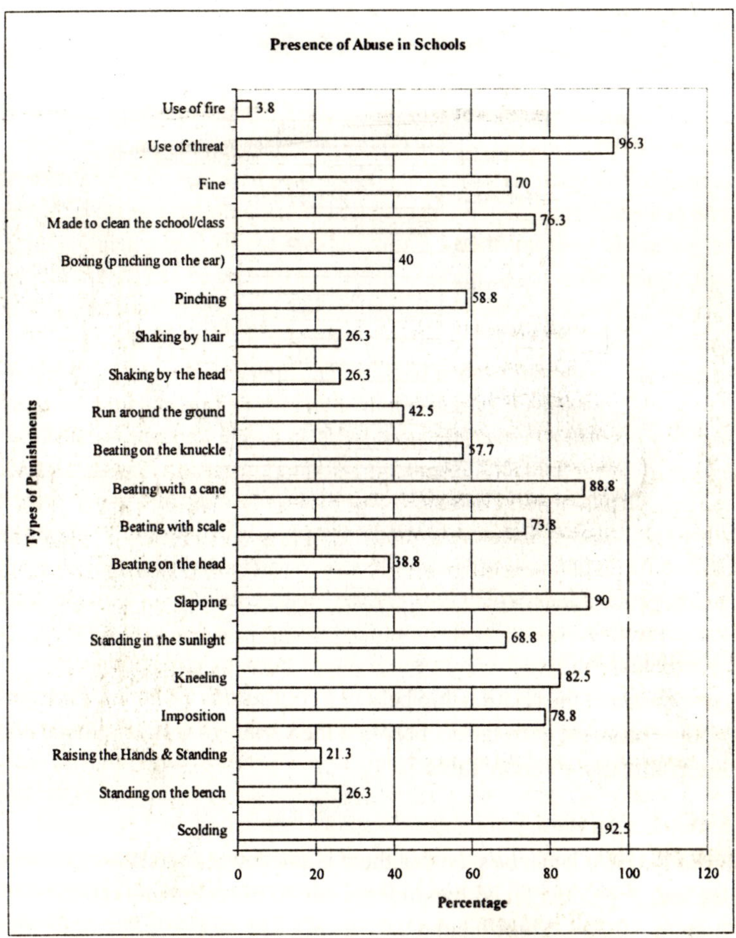

The study focused on the various problems faced by the students due to the various punishments given in the school. Fear /Anxiety is the major problem faced by students (91.3%), followed by stammering. It may be mentioned here that stammering as a consequence of punishments is a serious problem, which needs immediate attention of school administrators.

Figure 3
The other Problems Faced by Students

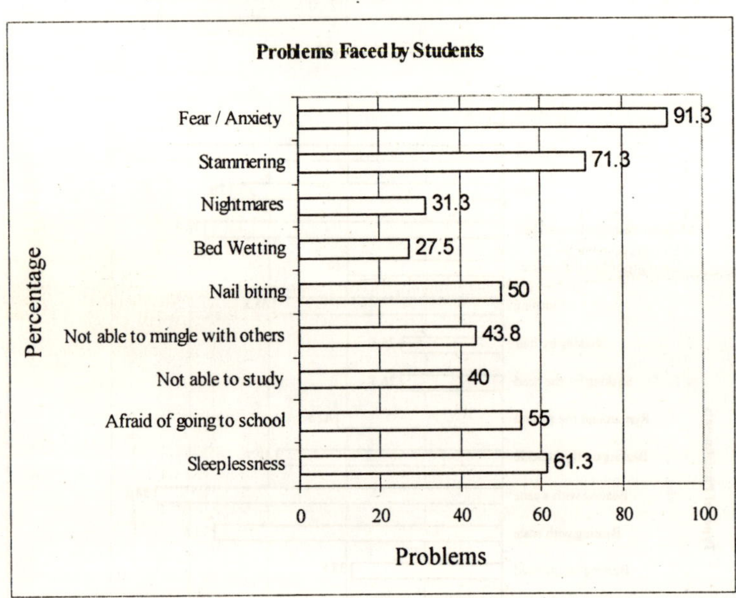

CORRELATION

To understand the relationship between continuous variables, Pearsons product moment correlation, between the variables was calculated and the results are given in Table 7.

AGE

From the table it can be seen that there is a negative correlation between age and Problems faced by students due to punishments received by them (r = 0.341: Significant a 0.01 level). The negative sigh indicates that as the age of the student increases the problems decrease and *vice versa.*

Age was, also, found to be positively correlated with, academic performance (r=0.351: Significant a 0.01 level). As the respondents age increased the academic performance also increased.

Figure 7

Correlation M*i*

		Age	Length of Study	Punishment Score	Academic Performance	Problems Faced
Age	Pearson Correlation	1	.164	-.007	.351**	-.341**
	Sig. (1-tailed)	.	.073	.475	.001	.001
	N	80	80	80	80	80
Length of Study	Pearson Correlation	.164	1	.249*	-.196*	.016
	Sig. (1-tailed)	.073	.	.013	.041	.445
	N	80	80	80	80	80
Punishment Score	Pearson Correlation	-.007	.249*	1	-.279**	.035
	Sig. (1-tailed)	.475	.013	.	.006	.377
	N	80	80	80	80	80
Academic Performance	Pearson Correlation	.351**	-.196*	-.279**	1	-.044
	Sig. (1-tailed)	.001	.041	.006	.	.351
	N	80	80	80	80	80
Problems Faced	Pearson Correlation	-.341**	.016	.035	-.044	1
	Sig. (1-tailed)	.001	.445	.377	.351	.
	N	80	80	80	80	80

* Correlation is significant at the 0.01 level (1-tailed)

** Correlation is significant at the 0.05 level (1-tailed)

LENGTH OF STUDY

From table 7, it can be seen that there is a positive correlation between length of study in the same school and punishment received, by the respondent (r=0.249: Significant a 0.05 level). As the length of study increased, the punishment score increased. This may be due to the fact that as the student studies for a longer time in the same school, the school authorities and the teachers try to take more liberty with the student and hence the relationship.

Further, there is a negative correlation between length of study and the academic performance (r = - 0.196: significant a 0.05 level). This result suggests that as the length increases the performance decreases. Looking this relationship in the light of the last finding, it can be understood that as the length increases, the punishment received also increases and probably due to this the academic performance decreases.

PUNISHMENT SCORE AND ACADEMIC PERFORMANCE

There is a negative correlation between punishment received by the students and their academic performance (r = - 0.279: significant a 0.01 level). This is understandable, as the punishment increases the student starts a disliking for the studies and his academic performance comes down.

INFORMING PARENTS ABOUT PUNISHMENTS

From Table 8 it can be seen that majority of the respondents (53%) do not tell their parents about the punishments received by them at the school and only some (33.8%) tell their parents. Since there is no communication in this regard with their parents, there is no adequate social support for the student and this explains the earlier finding of this study of why there is more fear and anxiety among the students, and the prevalence of stammering (Fig 3).

Table 8
Informing Parents about Punishments

	Frequency	*Percent*
Yes	27	33.8
No	53	66.3
Total	80	100.0

CONCLUSION

The study was undertaken to understand the types of punishments awarded by schools in Tenkasi Taluk, Tirunelveli District and the consequences of the punishments, on the students. The study found that

- Use of punishments was widely prevalent in the schools with use of threat, scolding and beating with cane leading the way.
- Though reported very less, the study found that even fire was used to punish the students.
- Punishments in the schools leave a permanent mark on the psyche of the students and fear/anxiety, stammering and sleeplessness, were the common consequences.
- Even though, teachers and the school, use punishments, for enhancing academic performance, this study found that punishment only has a negative impact on the academic performance.
- Students do not inform their parents about the punishments received by them and this still increases their Vulnerability.

REFERENCES

Ammerman, R. T., Cassisi, J. E., Hersen, M., Van Hasselt, V. B. (1986), Consequences of Physical Abuse and Neglect in Children. *Clinical Psychology Review, 6,* 291-319.

Anderson, E. M., & Levine, M. (1999), Concerns about Allegations of Child Sexual Abuse Against Teachers and the Teaching Environment. *Child Abuse & Neglect, 23,* 823-843.

Beitchman, J.H., Zucker, K.J., Hood, J.E., DaCosta, G.A., & Akman, D. (1991), A review of the short-term effects of child sexual abuse. *Child Abuse & Neglect, 15 (4),* 537-556.

Berliner, L., & Elliot, D. (1996), Sexual abuse of children. In J. Briere, L. Berliner, J. A Bulkley, C. Jenny, & T. Reid (Eds.), *The APSAC Handbook on Child Maltreatment* (pp. 51-71). Thousand Oaks, CA, USA: Sage Publications.

Cronbach, Lee, J. (1949), *Essentials of Psychological Testing.* Harper and Row. London.

Dolmage, W. R. (1995), Accusations of Teacher Sexual abuse of Students in Ontario Schools: Some Preliminary Findings. *Alberta Journal of Educational Research, Vol 41,* 127-144.

Garrett, H.E. (1970), *Statistics in Psychology and Education.* London, Longman.

Gil, D. (1975). Unravelling Child abuse. *American Journal of Orthopsychiatry, 45,* 346-356.

Gil, E. (1982), Institutional abuse of Children in out-of-home Care. *Child and Youth Care Review, 4(1-2),* 7.

Goffman, E. (1961), *Asylums: Essays on the Social Situation of Mental Patients and Other Inmates.* New York: Anchor/Doubleday.

Green, A. (1993), Child Sexual Abuse: Immediate and long-term effects and intervention. *Journal of the American Academy of Child and Adolescent Psychiatry, 32(5),* 890-902.

Helfer, R. E. & Kempe, C. H. (1974), *The battered child.* Chicago: The University of Chicago Press.

Hyman, I. A., Zelikoff, W., & Clarke, J. (1988), Psychological and Physical abuse in the Schools: A Paradigm for Understanding post-traumatic Stress Disorder in Children and Youth. *Journal of Traumatic Stress, 1,* 243-267.

Kempe, C. H., Silverman, F. N. & Steele, B. F. (1962), The Battered Child Syndrome. *Journal of the American Medical Association, 181,* 17-24.

Kilpatrick, D., and B. Saunders, *Prevalence and Consequences of Child Victimization,* Crime Victims Research and Treatment Center, Medical University of South Carolina, Research in Brief, National Institute of Justice, 1997.

Kolko, D. J. (1996), Child Physical Abuse. In J. Briere, L. Berliner, J. A Bulkley, C. Jenny, & T. Reid (Eds.), *The APSAC Handbook on Child Maltreatment* (pp. 21-50). Thousand Oaks, CA, USA: Sage Publications.

Perring, C. (1992), The Experience and Perspectives of Patients and Care Staff of the Transition from Hospital to Community Based Care. In S. Ramon (Ed.), *Psychiatric Hospital Closure: Myths and Realities.* London: Chapman Hall.

Sedlak, A. J., & Broadhurst, D. D. (1996), *Third National Incidence Study of Child Abuse and Neglect: Final Report.* Washington, DC: U.S. Department of Health and Human Services.

Trocm, N., & Wolfe, D. A. (2001), *Child Maltreatment in Canada: Selected Results from the Canadian Incidence Study of Reported Child Abuse and Neglect.* Ottawa: Minister of Public Works and Government Services

Widom, C. S., (1992), *"Cycle of Violence"* (Research in Brief), National Institute of Justice, U.S. Department of Justice.

A. MAHESH AND K. JAISHANKAR

18

VICTIMIZATION OF CHILD LABOURERS IN COTTON MILLS

INTRODUCTION

According to International Labour Organization's Bureau of Statistics (1998), there are 250-million child labourers in the age group 5-14 in the developing countries. Of them, 120 million children are working full time and are engaged in hazardous and exploitative occupations. New global estimates by the ILO reveals number of children who work, and of the numbers involved in each category of child labour for abolition, are presented in the Future without Child Labour Report in the year 2002. The estimates reveal several disturbing realities. Some 180 million children aged 5-17 (or 73 per cent of all child labourers) are now believed to be engaged in the worst forms of child labour, comprising hazardous work and the unconditional worst forms of child labour. This amounts to one child in every eight in the world. Of the some 171 million children engaged in hazardous work, nearly two-thirds are under 15 and therefore require immediate withdrawal from this work and rehabilitation from its effects.

While 67 million children in the 5-14 age group are engaged in non-hazardous child labour that they should not be undertaking by virtue of their age, many more children (111 million) are involved in work that actually jeopardizes their well being. Among older children aged 15-17 years (who are above the minimum age for employment), the estimates indicate that 59 million are involved in hazardous work.

This represents an alarming 42 per cent of all working children in this age group.

THE PROBLEM OF CHILD LABOUR IN INDIA

In India, according to 1991 census there were 11.29 million child workers. National sample survey figures for the year 1999-2000 indicated that there were 10.4 million child labourers. It is difficult to cite a current figure for the number of children engaged in child labour. This difficulty is attributed to the fact that the Indian Government "has been highlighted in its refusal to collect and analyze current and relevant data regarding the incidence of child labour. As on 1996, official figures continue to be based on 1981 census figures". The 1981 Indian census reports that there were 13.6 million child labourers in India. Indian government extrapolations of this 1981 data place the current number of child labourers at between seventeen and twenty million. This extrapolation seems highly unlikely as the official national sample survey of 1983 (of India) reports 17.4 million child labourers. While a study sponsored by the labour ministry concluded that the child labour force was 44 million. UNICEF cites figures ranging from seventy-five to ninety million child labourers under the age of fourteen. A universal difficulty in obtaining accurate data may be that individuals fail to report child labour participation during surveys for fear of persecution. Although figure for the number of child labourers varies they are all significantly high when considering that the Child Economic Activity rate for 1980-1991 was 13.5% for males and 10.3% for females. In comparison, other developing countries such as Sri Lanka and Malaysia (where data is available), have lower activity rates : 5.3% for males and 4.6% females in Sri Lanka, and 8.8% for males and 6.5% for females in Malaysia (SCLRCWS, 2005).

Historical census data shows on overall child work participation rate of 12.69% in 1961 and 7.13% in 1971. This data is misleading because the definitions of child labour are different in the two censuses (unpaid workers are not included in the 1971 census), thus a comparison cannot be completely valid. The data shows that in a span of 25% years, the proportion of children who are working has not changed significantly, but since comparisons with this data are not valid, this conclusion is questionable.

The 1981 census of India divided child labour into nine industrial divisions: 1) Cultivation, 2) Agricultural Labour, 3) Livestock, Forestry, Fishing, Plantation, 4) Mining and quarrying, 5) Manufacturing, processing, servicing and repairs, 6) Construction, 7) Trade and commerce, 8) Transport, storage and communication and 9) other services.

Child labour is a source of income for poor families. A study conducted by the ILO Bureau of statistics found that "children's work was considered essential to maintaining the economic level of households, either in the form of work for wages, of help in household enterprises or of household shares in order to free adult household members for economic activity else where. In some cases, the study found that a child's income accounted for between 34 and 37 percent of the total household income. This study concludes that a child labourer's income is important to the livelihood of a poor family. There is a questionable aspect of this study. It was conducted in the form as a survey and the responses were given in the parents of the child labourers. Parents would be biased into being compelled to support their decision to send their children to work, by saying that it is essential. They are probably right for most poor families in India; alternative sources of income are close to non-existent. There are no social welfare systems such as those in the worst nor is there easy access to loans, which will be discussed what is apparent is the fact that child labourers are being exploited, shown by the pay that they receive. For the same type of work, studies show that children are paid less than their adult counterparts (SCLRCWS, 2005).

A comparison of child wages to adult wages obtained by a study of child workers in the Delhi region of India. Although 39.5% of employers said that child workers earn wages equal to adults, if the percentage of employers admitting that wages are lower for children is added up, a figure of 35.9% is found. This figure is significant when taking the bias of employers into account. Employers would have been likely to descend their wages for child workers, by saying that children earn the same wages as adults. The fact that no employers stated children earned more than adults should also be noted. Other studies have also concluded that "children's earnings are consistently lower than those of adults, even where there two groups are engaged in the same tasks. The percentage of the population of India living in poverty is high. In 1990, 37% of the urban population and 39% of the rural population was living in poverty. Poverty has an obvious relationship which child labour and studies have" revealed a positive correlation - in some instances a strong one-between child labour and such factors as poverty (SCLRCWS, 2005).

CHILD LABOUR IN TAMIL NADU

According to a variety of sources, child labour is a serious problem in Tamil Nadu. In Tamil Nadu, according to 2001 census, there are lakhs child workers. 48.2% of them were male and 51.8% were female child workers. The survey conducted by Sarva Shiksha Abhiyan (SSA) in 2003 revealed that the number had dipped below one lakh and stood at 70,344 child labourers in Tamil Nadu. According to UNICEF (Vidyasagar, 1995), in 1991 there were 3.1 million children of school age (5-14 yrs) not attending school in Tamil Nadu. It is assumed that most of these children were working, either part or full time. Many children work in agriculture, but many also work in industrial occupations. The districts with the highest estimated numbers of child labourers were: Coimbatore (where Tirupur is located), North Arcot (where Ambur is located), Periyar (adjacent to Coimbatore) and Salem (David, 2002).

Elimination of child labour is official policy in Tamil Nadu. In November 1993, the Government of Tamil Nadu adopted a State Plan of Action for the Child in Tamil Nadu, which included targets for the elimination of child labour. These were: elimination of bonded child labour and child labour in the match and fireworks industries, elimination of all child labour (up to 14 years of age) in hazardous occupations and elimination of all child labour (up to 12 years of age) in all occupations by the year 2000.

Tamil Nadu policy is underpinned by that of the Government of India which has a constitutional mandate in favour of universal primary education. In 1986, the Government of India adopted the National Policy on Education (NPE) which made universal primary education the top priority (Government of Tamil Nadu, 1998).

The data and commentary presented in the Government of Tamil Nadu's 1997-98 Social Sector report, show that the Government of Tamil Nadu takes the view that the elimination of child labour requires the universal availability of primary and secondary school education of sufficient quality to enable all children to enrol in school and to retain them once enrolled. The Government is making a considerable investment to achieve that goal and the data show an improving trend, though a substantial number of children are still falling through the net (David, 2002).

CHILD LABOUR IN THE COTTON INDUSTRY

In looking at the cotton garments supply chain in Tamil Nadu we may need to look beyond the factory clusters of Tirupur and Chennai to the cotton growing and spinning industries, which are extensive in Tamil Nadu and adjacent states. Cotton is grown across the whole of western, central and southern India, with the exception of Kerala. The main producing states are Andhra Pradesh, Gujarat and Maharashtra. Tamil Nadu produced 475,000 bales in 1995-96, 2.9% of the India total (Sharma, 1999).

Child labour is reported to be common in cotton production. The following description refers to children working in *cotton production* in southern Andhra Pradesh (adjacent to Tamil Nadu): "Typically, 10-15 children are hired for 100-150 days per acre of cotton-seed production. Children as young as six works from 8:30 am to 6 or 7 pm and some boys even return to the field again from 9 pm to 12 am. The cotton seed production calendar has been standardised for the process of certification and marketing and has resulted in the regimentation of work schedules of children who are now continuously employed for 6-9 months in the year. In villages where labour is scarce, children are being 'tied' to contract farmers with advances of cash and grain to parents (typically Rs. 1000) and bonuses (a stainless steel tiffin carrier after two years, for example). Children's labour is extended well beyond the work day by paying them piece rates to de-lint the cottonseeds (Rs.10/ bag of 25kgs cotton) and catch pests (Rs.0.05/ worm). Physical force and holding back wages if a child's productivity is low are routine labour control practices. Many girls also now accompany their mothers for casual coolie work. They are paid daily wages but the mother must not only do her own work but also help her daughter keep pace. Consequently, more and more girls are being taken out of school (Ramamurthy, 2000)."

So far as the *Cotton Spinning* Industry is concerned, the major concentration is in Tamil Nadu, which (in 1992) had 440 spinning mills out of a national total of 846, employing 174,326 workers out of an India total of 1,055,020 (Kumar, 1997). The major concentration of Tamil Nadu mills was in Coimbatore (189 spinning mills). The cotton spinning industry association - the Southern India Mills' Association - is also based in Coimbatore. There are no published reports to hand of the incidence of child labour in cotton spinning, but Steve Grinter of the ITGLWF says that there is no child labour in the formal (large enterprise) export sector (David, 2002).

NEED AND SIGNIFICANCE OF THE PRESENT STUDY

The area of the present study is confined to the child labours working in the cotton mills of Sankarankovil Taluk, Tirunelveli District of Tamil Nadu, India. The existence of various factors is like cotton mills, match industries, plastic manufacturing companies, sugar factory give the employment to the local population of Sankarankovil. The Agriculture lands are also contribute the major role in the income generation to this rural locality; Beedi, Cotton, Chilly, Sugarcane are the major cultivation to the poverty is a predominant factor which affects the growth of the children in Sankarankovil. The extremely poor families cannot send their children to even if there are provisions of free and compulsory education. It appears that economic factor is a critical factor associated with child labour problem. Because of their poverty, parents cannot make any investment in their child's development; they are also reluctant even to support them. They want their children to fend for themselves as early as possible much better if they become a source of income to family. So they send their children to cotton mills for labour. The cotton mill contains the various units like colouring unit, dilation unit, stitching unit, cutting unit, wastages recycling unit in which the children not attained the 18 years of age are working in Sankarankovil. Due to ignorance and illiteracy, the parents do not understand the future career possibilities and the development of their children. This present study attempts to analyze the child labour in two cotton mills of Sankarankovil and try to identify the problems and give proper suggestions.

METHOD

The aim of the present study is to study the personal profile of the child labourers in cotton mills Sankarankovil, to find out the causes of child labour, and to examine various forms of victimization of child labourers. The data related to child labours were collected from the cotton mills Sankarankovil. The universe consisted of child labourers who were working in cotton mills Sankarankovil, Tirunelveli District. Purposive sampling method was adopted in for the present study. The samples of child labourers were selected from two cotton mills in Sankarankovil Taluk. The total sample size was 100. In the present study the researchers constructed an interview schedule and administered to the respondents. Primary data were collected in this present study. This includes their view on child labour for example, sexual abuse, physically abuse, verbal abuse, psychological abuse and caste based abuse. Percentage analysis was done using SPSS.

RESULTS AND DISCUSSION

Table 1 Socio Economic Characteristics and Table 2. Details Related to Industry

Socio-economic Characteristics	*N*	*%*	*Working Unit Type*	*N*	*%*
Age			Coloring Unit	39	39
9-11	14	14	Stitching Unit	20	20
12-15	73	73	Thread Separating Unit	26	26
16-18	13	13	Cutting Unit	15	15
Sex			*Wages (Rs.)*		
Male	49	49	300-600	22	22
Female	51	51	601-800	47	47
Religion			801-900	31	31
Hindu	75	75	*Frequency of Wages*		
Christian	25	25	Days	32	32
Caste			Week	59	59
SC	70	70	Month	9	9
BC	12	12	*Working hours*		
MBC	18	18	8.00	35	35
Education			8.30	65	65
Illiterate	10	10	*Rest Hours*		
Upto Middle School	80	80	½ hours	90	90
Upto High School	5	5	1 hours	10	10
Vocational	5	5	*Opinion about wages*		
			Satisfaction	14	14
			Dissatisfaction	86	86

Contd...

Socio-economic Characteristics	*N*	*%*	*Working Unit Type*	*N*	*%*
			Wages Equivalent to Work Done		
			Yes	19	19
			No	81	81
			Opinion about the Government Supervising Officer		
			Good Officer	58	58
			Bad	42	42
			Opinion on Inspection Period		
			Frequently	86	86
			Rarely	14	14
			Knowledge about the Government Officer		
			Yes	87	87
			No	13	13

The majority of the respondents 73% belong to age group of 12-15 years. Most of them were female and had studied up to middle school only. Table 1 shows the extent of prevalence of child labour, which proves that the economic conditions of the family is very poor and pathetic condition, where they have to live on the earnings of children.

Table 2 shows that most are employed in colouring units (39%) and paid weekly wages (59%). This table proves that eighty six percent of the respondents are dissatisfied with their wages and feel that they should be paid more for the work they are doing. 90% of the respondents were not given proper rest; this is the basic affecting factor in their working conditions resulting in poor performance and loss of health.

From Table 3 it is inferred that, 50% of the respondents say it is because of the poverty they are forced for child labour and up to 83% want to continue their education. 79% of the students want to play; it is basic of child to grow to have a positive development of their life. Table 4 shows that 78% of children are victimized by the government officials during inspection, shows the lack of awareness of officials in critical issues like child labour and poor performance of the officials who are supposed to protect them. 92% were victimized by the supervisors and most of them did not inform even to their parents (78%) nor police (82%). Even those who have complained to police (18%) failed to get proper response from them. 80% of the respondents were not compensated and 75% were allowed to work even after their victimization.

Table 3
Opinion – General and
Table 4. Opinion - Victimization

Opinion-General	*N*	*%*	*Opninion-Victimization*	*N*	*%*
Work same as Father's			*Victimized by Government Officials during Inspection*		
Yes	32	32	Yes	78	78
No	68	68	No	22	22
Reasons for Child Labour			*Victimized by the Supervisor*		
Poverty	50	50	Yes	92	92
Having no interest in the study	22	22	No	8	8
Forced by parents	21	21	*Types of Victimization*		
No earning member in family	7	7	Sexual Abuse	14	14
Interested in Continuing Education			Physically Victimization	21	21
Yes	83	83	Verbal Abuse	40	40
No	17	17	Caste based Abuse	25	25
Aspirations for the future			*Informed Parents about Victimization*		
Likes to continue work	49	49	Yes	22	22
Likes to get more training	12	12	No	78	78
Wants to switch over	20	20	*Complaint to the Police*		
Wants to go back to School	19	19	Yes	18	18
Ways of Spending Holidays			No	82	82
Playing	79	79	*Immediate Action Taken by Police (N=18)*		
Walking / Roaming	48	48	Yes	34	34
Taking Rest	33	33	No	66	66

Contd...

Opinion-General	*N*	*%*	*Opninion-Victimization*	*N*	*%*
Reading Books	12	12	*Opinion on Police Action (N=18)*		
Swimming	22	22	good	10	10
Watching TV.	60	60	Careless	42	42
			Denial of FIR	48	48
			Medical aid by Supervisor/ Company		
			Yes	21	21
			No	79	79
			Hospital where Medical Assistance was Received		
			Government Hospital	3	3
			Private Hospital	18	18
			Not Sufferings	79	79
			Compensation from the Management		
			Yes	20	20
			No	80	80
			Management permission to continue work after victimization		
			Yes	75	75
			No	15	15
			Based on physical strength	10	10

CONCLUSION

The results of this study have showed that the child labourers faced several problems in cotton mills and they are affected physically, mentally, emotionally. The child labourers get very less wages compared to their work load. So, they were not satisfied in their work because their basic needs are not fulfilled. The government should involve in this national problem and provide welfare measures for the child labourers working at cotton mills. Child labour may decline as incomes of our country rise, but there is nothing in theory or evidence that tells us such an outcome is inevitable. Perhaps more importantly, there are many policy tools available that can help alter family and firm decision making prior to a rise in income, such as a package of improved educational opportunities, increased inflow of child-displacing technologies from industrial countries, more efficient capital and labour markets, and educational attainment subsidies. Efforts to eliminate child labour must take all aspects of the problem into account and draw upon these and other mechanisms that have the potential for reducing child labour without inducing further hardship.

REFERENCES

Government of Tamil Nadu (1998), Chapter 12: Social Sector from Tamil Nadu – An Economic Appraisal 1997-98, Department of Evaluation and Applied Research, Chennai.

Kumar, P.S. Mohana, (1997), *Cotton Textile Industry*, Reliance Publishing House, New Delhi.

Ramamurthy, Priti, (2000), The Cotton Commodity Chain, Women, Work and Agency in India and Japan: The Case for Feminist Agro-Food Systems Research, *World Development* Vol. 28, No. 3, pp 551-578.

Sharma, Y.C., (1999), *Cotton Khadi in Indian Economy*, Navajivan Publishing House, Ahmedabad.

State Child Labour Rehabilitation cum Welfare Society (SCLRCWS) (2005), *Magnitude of Child labour* Retrieved on 18th May 2005 from http://www.childlabour.tn.gov.in/magnitude.htm.

Steele David, (2002), *Child Labour in Tamil Nadu: An Initial Survey.* Retrieved on 18th May 2005 from http://www.ethicaltrade.org/Z/lib/2002/05/chlab-lit/index.shtml.

Vidyasagar, R, (1995), *A Status Report on Child Labour in Tamil Nadu*, UNICEF, Madras.

S. M. MAHENDRA SIMHA KARNA AND S. RAMDOSS

19

CHILD VICTIMS OF TRAFFICKING: A TRANSNATIONAL PERSPECTIVE

INTRODUCTION

The trafficking of children for sexual purposes is an immense problem in most South Asian countries and India is the regional hub. Bangladesh and Nepal are the dominant source countries into India. Estimates vary, but a safe guess is that several thousand Bangladeshi girls and five to seven thousand Nepalese girls are trafficked out of the country and primarily to India each year. It is estimated that Nepalese children constitute 20% (40,000) of the estimated 200,000 Nepalese prostitutes in India. Girls as young as seven years are trafficked from economically depressed neighborhoods in Nepal and Bangladesh, to the major prostitution centers of Mumbai, Calcutta, and Delhi. In Mumbai, an estimated 90 percent of sex workers started when they were under 18 years of age; half are from Nepal. A similar profile is believed to exist in Calcutta, though Bangladesh surpasses Nepal as the primary source of children for Calcutta.

India is also a significant source and transit country. Many child prostitutes in the brothels of India's major cities come from rural villages and they are trafficked under the same guise as children from Bangladesh and Nepal. Indian female children are trafficked to the Middle East and Europe, often forced into sexual slavery. This is similar for the Bangladeshi and Nepalese children who pass through India en route to the Middle East and the West.

The reasons leading to the occurrence and rise in trafficking are common to all the South Asian countries. Poverty, lack of education, and the status of females and children from lower socio-economic backgrounds are all contributory factors. Lured by promises of good jobs or marriage, trafficking victims are frequently forced into debt bondage outside of the country. Traffickers living abroad often arrive in a village and convince a child's family to let her leave with them. For reasons of ignorance, abject poverty and a social perception of the girl child, parents willingly send their children. Upon arrival at the destination location, children are sold to "friends", "husbands"; and driven into prostitution. Criminal gangs conduct much of the trafficking and the porous international borders in South Asia facilitate their activities.

Recently, international tourism has emerged as a powerful factor-giving rise to victimization of vulnerable children in Commercial Sexual Exploitation (CSE). Worldwide travel has increased sevenfold since 1960. The tourism industry will soon be the biggest industry globally. Tourism is not the cause of child prostitution but it does provide easy access to vulnerable children. Mainly when the tourist is in a foreign land the anonymity obtained relieves him from several social and legal constraints which he otherwise faces in his own country. As a Japanese proverb goes, "the traveler knows no shame" or as a European one states, "the further I go from home the less moral I become". He thus ventures in sexual experiments and attempts to gratify all his socially unacceptable sexual desires and fantasies. Tourism reinforces racial prejudice in some ways and prompts some to exploit others whom they consider as inferior. Accompanying doctrines (again based on prejudices) help the tourists justify the exploitation by saying that sex with children is acceptable in the culture of the society they are visiting. While places like Goa, Kovalam, Mahabalipuram in Tamil Nadu and Puri in Orissa have earned wide ill reputation for being the paradise of the pedophiles the mainland tourism is not at all free from this scourge (Trafficking A Social-legal study 2001).

WHAT IS TRAFFICKING?

"The Illicit and clandestine movements of persons across national borders, largely form developing countries and some countries with economies in transition, with the end goal of forcing women and girl children into sexually or economically oppressive and exploitative situations for profit of recruiters, traffickers and crime syndicates, as well as other illegal activities related to trafficking, such as forced domestic labour, false marriages, clandestine employment and false adoption."(United Nations General Assembly, 1994).

Trafficking is defined as "the moving, selling or buying of women and children for prostitution within and outside a country for monetary or other considerations with or without the consent of the person subjected to trafficking: "Trafficking" means persons, agencies or institutions engaged in any form of trafficking: "Persons subjected to trafficking" means women and children victimized or forced into prostitution by the traffickers by deception, threat, coercion, kidnapping, sale, fraudulent marriage, child marriage, or any other unlawful means (SAARC, 2002).

THE EXTENT AND MAGNITUDE OF TRAFFICKING IN ASIA

Reliable estimates are few, and empirical data is limited on the number of women and children who are trafficked, from where and to what destinations. Existing studies in the Asia region provide only a partial picture of the extent and magnitude of the problem, often limited to the numbers involved in commercial sex work. The data on the numbers trafficked also varies widely, and a large number of cases go unreported.

Though there are a number of studies and reports on commercial sexual exploitation of women and children there are no reliable estimates of the extent and magnitude of trafficking and commercial sexual exploitation in Asia. There are major obstacles in trying to estimate the magnitude of the problem, among which are the social stigma and legal sanctions attached to it which inhibit easy identification, the stranglehold of gangs and brothels keepers enforced through violence which prevents identification of the women and child victims and the dispersed nature of the phenomenon, other than in certain localities of the metropolitan cities.

A survey sponsored by the Central Social Welfare Board (CSWB) in 1991 in six metropolitan cities of India indicated that the population of women and child victims of commercial sexual exploitation would be between 70,000 to 1, 00,000. It also reveled that about 30% of them are below 18 years of age. Nearly 40% of them were inducted when they were less than 18 years of age. The major contributory factor for the commercial sexual exploitation of women and children are poverty and unemployment of lack of appropriate rehabilitation. 70% of them are illiterates... 43%of them desire to be rescued. Most of those who want to leave have given the reasons of desire to save their children form commercial sexual exploitation and protection of the future of the children, fear of disease etc. the others continue to be exploited due to absence of alternative sources of income, social non-acceptability, family customs, poverty, ill heath and their despondence.

Commercial sexual exploitation is found in a concentrated manner in brothels arid red light areas. The more dispersed form may be found along major highways, in massage parlors, guesthouses, call girl rackets, cabaret shows, female escort services etc. The United Nations Fund for Women (UNIFEM) New Delhi Report " Trading in Human Misery" mentions "There are over 10 lakh children below the age of 16 years in various brothels in the South Asian region who are being abused for commercial sex. What is alarming is the fact that the age of entry into sexual slavery is fast decreasing. The Country Report on Pakistan suggests that there are approximately 20,000 children in prostitution near the Lahore station alone. The data for the rest of the country is not available. Male children form a substantial proportion among them".

India Today in 1990 quoted that there are over 5,00,000 girl victims of prostitution, below 18 year in India. The National Commission for Women states, "In Bombay alone 40,000 girls between the ages of 10-16 years are selling their bodies from their doorsteps". Statistics also suggests that about 61 per sent of the women in prostitution in India belong to the scheduled castes, other backward castes, and the scheduled tribes. The UNICEF report states there are about 5,000 prostitutes in Katmandu alone, of which 1000 are children. Maiti, an NGO from Nepal working on the problem of prostitution estimates that every year 5000 to 7000 girls from Nepal are trafficked into India for prostitution.

A Study conducted by Child Workers in Nepal (CWIN), 1987 indicated that about 2,00,000 Nepali girls and women were sold to Indian brothels of which 10 percent were between the age group of 14 to 18 years. South Asia Forum for Human Rights in its report of 1997 states about 50 per cent of the prostitutes in the brothels of India is a trafficked Nepali girl. China is no exception either as hundreds of thousand of girls mainly belonging to the minorities is trafficked into prostitution from china.

Asia Watch mentions that about 20,000 to 30,000 women and girls have been trafficked from Myanmar mainly into the brothels of Thailand. The Royal Thai Government estimates indicate that a majority of the approximately 9, 00,000 illegal migrants to Thailand are from Myanmar. Many of the Myanmar women and girls are first trafficked into Bangladesh as refugees and from there they are trafficked to the brothels in India. UNICEF quoted the 1996 report of NCWA that 20,000 to 40,000 girls under the age of 18 years were engaged in prostitution in Thailand. The CATW Philippines report of 1996 states that 10, 00,000 women of various nationalities have been trafficked into Thailand for the purpose of prostitution.

THE EXTENT AND MAGNITUDE OF TRAFFICKING IN OTHER COUNTRIES

"International Trafficking in women to the United states; A contemporary Manifestation of Slavery and Organized Crime, November 1999 writes Trafficking in persons, particularly women and children, is significant on nearly every continent. Gauging the level of trafficking with precision, however, is difficult since it is an underground industry. Estimates of the trafficking problem in the United States vary, given different definition of what constitutes trafficking and research based on limited case studies. At present no one U.S. or international agency is compiling accurate statistics. Nonetheless, government and non-governmental experts in the field estimate that out of the 7, 00,000 to two million women and children who are trafficked globally each year, 45,000 to 50,000 of these women and children are trafficked to the United States. Approximately, 30,000 women and children are trafficked annually from Southeast Asia, 10,000 from Latin America...." (Note: This number is only a preliminary estimate and represents cross border and international trafficking. It does not include internal trafficking within countries such as Thailand or India (Richards, 1999).

The UNIFEM (United Nations Fund for Women) states that every year 7 million women and girls are trafficked across the globe. Though the figures quoted for India vary, there is a common agreement among all observers that the problem has reached alarming and colossal proportions in India. Commercial Sexual Exploitation has come out of the traditional red light areas and spread almost everywhere. The traditional routes of trafficking of girls and young women, the evil social customs like Devadasi, Venkatsani, Basavi, Kolateeen, Bedia, are neither the only nor the main sources of induction of victims into the flesh trade. Girls and young women are being inducted from everywhere and being sold everywhere. Observers also agree on one more observation; the age at recruitment is fast going down.

The Philippines: Between 60, 000 to 1, 00,000 children are involved in the sex industry. Child prostitution flourished during the 1970s and1980s with US Navy presence.

Indonesia: Indonesia seems to be attracting ever increasing number of sex tourists. Boys are mainly involved in selling sex to the tourists, although teenage boys are among the transvestite group servicing local men in major cities.

China: Estimates range from 2, 00,000 to 5, 00,000 children. Girls from pastoral villages of the minority tribes in Yunan province in south western China are being tricked by phone offers of job and then being sold into prostitution in Thailand.

Vietnam: 20 per cent of Vietnam's growing commercial sex industry is comprised of children less than 18 years of age. The development of tourism is one of the main causes of increased child prostitution.

Thailand: Statistics vary greatly as to the numbers of children involved in the Thai sex industry. Figures range from 10,000 to 8, 00,000.

Sri Lanka: Estimates that around 10,000 children aged 6 – 14 are virtually enslaved in brothels and a further 5,000 aged between 10-18 years are working independently in tourist resorts.

Burma: Asia Watch estimated 10,000 Burmese girls and women are trafficked to Thai brothels every year.

South Africa: Women and young girls from Thailand, Taiwan, and Russia work in brothels in the suburbs of Johannesburg. Estimations of number of child prostitutes in the country range from several thousands to several hundred thousands.

Australia: Children are trafficked into Australia from several Asian countries.

USA, Canada: The supply of children to the sex trade is linked with homelessness and family breakdown. Teenage children, having been thrown out of home or having run away following physical mental and/or sexual abuse, neglect, parental drug or alcohol addiction sell sex for survival. In Canada, at Montreal alone there are several thousand juveniles involved in the sex trade.

Italy: Children aged 5 to 14 years have been found prostituted in Sicily.

CONVICTING THE VICTIMS

Going by the findings of a recent National Human Rights Commission (NHRC) - United Nations Development Fund for Women (UNIFEM) – Institute of Social Science (ISS) report, India seems to be rapidly emerging as a source, a transit point as well as a destination for trafficking in women and children. What is worse is that the traffickers go scot-free, while the victims those procured, taken in transit, re-sold and then subjected to long-term exploitation are arrested, charge sheeted, prosecuted and convicted. Further, those rescued by the official agencies are reported to be subjected to human rights violations during the rescue and post-rescue phase. The extent of their being trafficked is not insignificant; the failure to rehabilitate victims leaves them with no real alternative but to resubmit to a life of being abused. Majority of the trafficked victims, after their rescue, often face the revictimization in different phases (EPW, 2006).

THE PROFILE OF VICTIMS TRAFFICKED

The data collected in the course of a recent action research conducted in 11 States (of which 9 of them were large States) reflected that about a quarter of the trafficked persons were children below 16 years of age at the time of trafficking. About two-thirds of the adult victims were unmarried. Divorced/separated/deserted/widowed women also account for substantial numbers. A large proportion of the victims belong to the lower strata of society. Traffickers also have access to persons in middle and upper strata of society who are vulnerable for reasons other than poverty. Generally those who are trafficked are of the following categories:

- Marginalized women and children with poor economic resources and mostly engaged in the informal sector of employment;

- Those belonging to impoverished households in rural areas and urban slums;
- Unmarried, divorced, separated or widowed women;
- Illiterates or those with low education;
- Women and children of forlorn status because of disruption of home/families;
- Women and children with low awareness of their rights or their exploited situation;
- Orphans who have no caregivers are inducted into trafficking.
- Those who belong to communities that practice and legitimize commercial sex work because of cultural factors.

It is clear then, that women and girl children are especially most vulnerable. Cascading discrimination within and outside households, lack of education, nutrition, health, skills and employment, apart from domestic and societal violence make them easy prey for the greed of the traffickers. There is also the notion among the clientele of the traffickers that having sex with virgins is an insurance against HIV/ AIDS and STDs. This results in younger and younger girls being trafficked. On leaving the profession, the survivors of trafficking take up different vocations – petty business, domestic help in households, helpers in brothels etc. sometimes, they themselves become brothel owners or traffickers. They live miserable lives, devoid of dignity and self esteem.

TRAFFICKING - CAUSES AND CONSEQUENCES

The growing public debate, intensive discussions and reports over the years on the issue of trafficking in India have highlighted a multiplicity of causes for the problem. The magnitude of the problem is immense, with varying figures emerging from different sources. According to one study, the current estimates of the trafficked persons range between 2 to 3 million.

As reflected in International Convention, trafficking is a business. The simple market forces of demand and supply govern this phenomenon. On the demand side, the reasons for trafficking include increasing tourism and industrialization, rural-urban migration (particularly of males); expanding demand for commercial sex promoted by organized criminal networks, demand by employers for cheap labour and male dominated value systems.

There are many supply side reasons for trafficking. The first, of course, is poverty which is taken advantage of by traffickers for Commercial Sexual Exploitation (CSE). Erosion of traditional family systems and values has also created a social environment in which trafficking thrives. Gender disparities in access to skills and employment tend to feminize poverty driving women and girls and children into the network of traffickers. Economic disparities also create demand for trafficking from low income to high-income areas. Internal and international migration of women into the labour market has exposed women to the vulnerability of sexual exploitation. Opening up of international borders and relaxation of controls on account of globalization, facilitating international and cross border mobility, have also contributed to this vulnerability. Certain traditions have tended to institutionalize the offer of sex as a matter of religious practice, according social sanction to it. Drug smuggling and associated organized crime have also been potent forces which have strengthened trafficking.

The inter-relationship between migrating and trafficking deserves some elaborate mention. Within India over 200 million persons migrate annually, substantial numbers of them being women. People migrate for various reasons, the principal amongst which is lack of job opportunities in source areas and availability of the same in urban destination areas. The economic migrants, being people in need, become victims of trafficking. Women and children among migrants are deceived and coerced at the places of their origin, during movement and transit and at their destination. Undocumented migrants become especially vulnerable to trafficking. Large numbers of male migrants in particular areas also create demand for sex workers and these aids in trafficking. Ecological migrants that are person getting displaced because of environmental factors – like for example earthquake – lose their assets and means of livelihood, such person again are easy prey for the traffickers. Indeed, immigrant community networks themselves often emerge as prime movers of further migration. Side by side, trafficking networks also emerge, traffickers providing the link to migrant community networks. Original migrant also become traffickers. Feminization of poverty leads to feminization of migration and attendant trafficking. Recruitment of employment through intermediaries in India and abroad has also become a profitable industry, often for non-existing jobs. In this process women become more vulerable to trafficking.

Trafficking of girls takes place also under the grab of marriage and lure of employment. It has been found that districts with low sex ratio often become fertile ground for the operations of the traffickers because of the relatively lesser numbers of women and girl children. Here the girls are first brought in to be brides and later pushed into prostitution. There are media reports about trafficking of girls from Orissa and Assam to states with adverse sex ratios, such as Haryana and Punjab for "marriage" (DWCD, 2004).

Tourism is yet another factor, which deserves detailed mention. Tourists look upon the destinations as places for sex tourism as well. Abuse of male and female children by tourists has assumed serious proportions with the involvement of criminal pedophile networks. Sometimes, they abuse children in the name of running orphanages for them. Children are also sexually exploited for production of child pornographic materials, which are widely accessed through Internet technology. Those used for child pornography are often indigent persons and migrant workers. Bar girls from different places are extensively trafficked. Initially joining the bars as dancers and waitresses, over time, these girls get sucked into trafficking networks.

Psychological and moral consequences of commercial sexual exploitation of women and child victims are serious, life-long and even life threatening. About 60-80% of the victims suffer from more than one disease. Threat of unwanted pregnancy, maternity mortality, torture, physical injury, physical disabilities, mental traumas and disorders and sexually transmitted diseases including HIV/AIDS is ever present.

The life of a woman or child victim of commercial sexual exploitation is under constant fear of the police, of the pimps; of brothel keepers etc. the children of women victims are born and are brought up with the stigma of illegitimacy. Shunned by the majority, they are in danger of being caught up in the grip of various vices and criminal activities. They also develop a fatalistic attitude which makes rehabilitation difficult.

INTERNATIONAL INSTRUMENTS

A number of International Instruments are there to combat trafficking such as the United Nations Convention for the Suppression of the Traffic in persons and of the Exploitation of the prostitution of Others (1949); the United Nations Convention against Transnational Organized Crime (2000); the Convention on the Elimination of All Forms of Discrimination Against Women (CEDAW) (1979); the International Covenant on Civil and Political Rights (1966) and its First Optional Protocol; the Convention on the Rights of the Child (1989); the ILO Convention on the Worst Forms of Child Labor (1999); the Convention Related to the Status of Refugees (1951); the Supplementary Convention on the Abolition of Slavery, the Salve Trade, and Institutions and Practices Similar to Slavery (1956); the Optional Protocol to the Convention on the Rights of the Child on the sale of children child prostitution and child pornography (2000); the SAARC Convention on Preventing and Combating trafficking in Women and Children for Prostitution (2002). Despite these instruments, the problem of trafficking continues to rise in the world.

TRAFFICKING PREVENTION - THE ROLE OF INTERNATIONAL AGENCIES

There are a number of International agencies involved in the prevention and creating awareness about the problem faced by victims of trafficking. These agencies also fund to take up research studies on this issue. These agencies also conducted rehabilitation programs for the victims of trafficking. Some of the International agencies have been listed below.

USAID

USAID has responded to this problem by funding numerous anti-trafficking activities in recent years in conjunction with other donors. In 2000, USAID funded a large regional anti-trafficking effort for South Asia, managed by the United Nations Development Fund for Women (UNIFEM), focused on prevention and education in Bangladesh, India, Nepal, Pakistan and SriLanka. USAID-UNIFEM's funding for prevention strategy includes support for networking and alliance building among NGOs, community leaders, and the law enforcement community in an effort to generate political and community support for anti-trafficking initiatives.

UNITED NATIONS DEVELOPMENT FUND FOR WOMEN (UNIFEM)

The UNIFEM program is designing media strategies for disseminating information about the causes and consequences of trafficking and engages in grassroots campaigns to gain community support for the elimination of trafficking among vulnerable groups. It is creating an anti-trafficking resource center together with a new website and database system in order to facilitate information dissemination and public discussion. Some of the support for this South Asia regional program comes from USAID/Washington's Bureau for Asia and the Near East through a five-year regional effort designed to promote the economic, political and legal rights of women and children as a poverty fighting strategy.

FORD FOUNDATION

The Ford Foundation is a resource for innovative people and institutions worldwide. It's one source of support for these activities. It works, mainly by making grants or loans that build knowledge and strengthen organizations and networks. Since its financial resources are modest in comparison to societal needs, it focuses on a limited number of problem areas and program strategies within its broad goals.

INTERNATIONAL LABOR ORGANIZATION (ILO)

The International Labor Organization (ILO) in May 2001 released a report, "Stopping Forced Labor," that concluded that trafficking is contributing to a rapid increase in forced labor: "The person may enter into an agreement with the recruiting agent on an apparently voluntary basis but conditions at the destination point are likely to involve coercion, including physical restrictions on freedom of movement, abuse or violence, and fraud. Victims frequently find themselves trapped in debt bondage and other slavery like conditions."

UNITED NATIONS INTERNATIONAL CHILDREN'S FUND (UNICEF)

Presently working in 10 states but in limited way. Its objective is to strengthen the state and district level capacity to deal with the issue; study child labour, education and its linkages with trafficking; NGO networking and panchayat level work. In India and at both national and state levels UNICEF is working together to combat the trafficking and commercial sexual exploitation of children. UNICEF has been working together with the DWCD in preparing the Indian Plan of Action on Child Trafficking, and on its implementation.

UNITED NATIONS DEVELOPMENT PROGRAMME (UNDP)

UNDP is working on the issue of Trafficking and HIV-AIDS. The project is basically on re-integrating of the children back into the society.

UNITED NATIONS INTERNATIONAL DRUG CONTROL PROGRAM (UNDCP)

UNDCP has been dealing with drug trafficking, but now it has started working on issue of human trafficking and is doing regional work also. It is supporting a project of mobile task force at border-providing it with walkie-talkies and equipment necessary to deal with the issue.

PREVENTIVE MEASURES SUGGESTED:

The following measures are suggested to prevent, control and rehabilitate the child victims of trafficking.

1. The Central and State Governments of India should take up long term training-cum-income generation programmes under IRDP, Development of Women and Children in Rural Areas, CAPART Schemes, Khadi and Village Industries Commission Schemes, STEP, Socio-Economic Programme, NORAD, Rashtriya Mahila Kosh, Prime Minister Rozgar Yojana, Swarna Jayanti Shahri Rozgar Yohana, and other such existing schemes of the Government of India and State Government in identified areas on priority. Wherever necessary, assistance may be sanctioned under these schemes for benefiting families in which children are vulnerable to or at high risk of being trafficked and sexually exploited for commercial purposes.
2. Setting up of Family Counseling Centers and Short Stay Homes in high supply areas to provide counseling and guidance to single women, which is a high risk group, who are deserted, widowed, divorced, socially ostracized, to parents, to missing girls, illegally adopted girls, street children, child brides, bonded laborers etc., so that they get shelter and counseling.

3. Formation of Committees for the Protection of Rights of children at State, District Taluk and Village levels with membership of the public. These committees may be vested with the power of monitoring the registration and investigation of crimes against children, expediting the measures for the defense of the rights of children, providing assistance to children to defend themselves against criminal proceedings.
4. Formation of Watchdog committees, Community Surveillance Group, Neighborhood Policing for mobilizing all sections of society to counter crime against children. Students and youths in neighborhood and campuses to take responsibility for safety of girl students in the campus prevent violation of child rights within the campus and protect and defend victims of such violation.
5. Protective homes/shelter should be established for rehabilitation of victims of trafficking. Suitable provisions shall also be made for granting legal aid, counseling, job training and health care facilities for the victims.
6. Children are the most at risk of being trafficked when they are living or moving without parents or guardians. Projects that provide temporary shelters, non-formal education and skills training opportunities and build social networks for these children will reduce their risks of being trafficked.
7. Among the victims of trafficking, after their rescue the grown up children may be entrusted with the task of identifying, rescuing and rehabilitation of the children vulnerable to trafficking.
8. There must be a convergence of all departments like the law enforcement agencies, NGOs, Women and Child Welfare Department etc., to solve trafficking. If livelihood is the main problem, then there should be an alternative livelihood option provided to families, so that traffickers do not take undue advantage of their vulnerability.
9. The present legal framework to combat commercial sexual exploitation results in re- victimization of the victims of exploitation while the exploiters mostly go scot-free. Statistics reveal that the number of females arrested is roughly four times the number of males in the implementation of the ITPA

(Immoral Traffic Prevention Act). The present laws would therefore be reviewed to ensure that the victims of commercial sexual exploitation are not re-victimized and that all the exploiters, including clients, traffickers, parents/guardians and others who collude with them are made liable for punishment.

10. Training and awareness activities designed to increase awareness of the impact of trafficking as well as the rights and psychosocial needs of the victims and appropriate procedures and practices for respecting and protecting their rights, should be organized for law enforcement officials, including customs and immigration officials and border police, judges and prosecutors, medical personnel, social workers, journalists. Such programmes should include, inter alia, interviewing and confidence building techniques for communicating with child victims.
11. The media has to be sensitive when dealing with issues of child abuse and exploitation. Sensationalizing of issues is not being allowed and protecting the identity of victimised children are must dos for all branches of the media. Media watch groups to control the depiction of children and women as sex objects are also necessary. It must also have more child sensitive reporting and encourage family values.
12. Financial assistance should be provided to conduct studies to create a reliable and relevant data base on the high supply areas, routes, destinations, causes of commercial sexual exploitation, high risk groups, the exploiters, and the magnitude of the problem and rehabilitation of the victims of trafficking.

CONCLUSION

Among the victims of trafficking, a group, which faces several forms of victimization such as Physical, Verbal, Emotional and Sexual etc., are children. The exploitation of younger children aged between 7 to 12 years of age in sex tourism send an alarming signal to the global community for immediate action to prevent the trafficking menace. It is bounden duty not only of the government to prevent the trafficking in children but also of the community. Hence, the participation of community in prevention of trafficking in children assumes a greater significance. Unless the active participation of the community in the primary prevention of trafficking in children, there will be no end to the trafficking menace. With regard the rehabilitation of the trafficked children, the programs available are inadequate, considering the magnitude of the child trafficking in the world. Therefore, measures must be taken on priority basis to address the issue of rehabilitation needs of the trafficked children.

REFERENCES

A Reference Manual on Combating Trafficking in Tamil Nadu 2003, UNICEF.

A Report of the National Consultation Workshop on The Prevention of Trafficking of Women and Children at the Border source areas of Bihar, Sikkim, Uttaranchal, Uttar Pradesh and West Bengal 2001: Organised by Coalition for Rural Empowerment and Institute for Gender Justice.

A Report on Estimation of Child Prostitution in India – Human Rights Report, 1999.

A study conducted by USAID, India 1999.

Convicting the Victims, The Economic and Political Weekly: January 21, 2006.

End Child Prostitution in Asian Tourism (ECPAT) Bulletin, 1999.

Estimation of Nepali Girls in Indian Brothels – A Report *The Outlook* June, 1998.

Nayar, Reva (2002). *National Consultation Workshop on The Prevention of Trafficking of Women and Children at the border source areas of Bihar, Sikkim, Uttaranchal, Uttar Pradesh and West Bengal 2001*: Organised by Coalition for Rural Empowerment and Institute for Gender Justice.

Nepali Girls Trafficked into red light districts in Indian Cities, *The Outlook* March, 1998.

Population of Child Prostitution in India (1996) *India Today Magazine* March 1996.

Richards, Amy O' Neil (1999). International Trafficking in Women to the United States; A contemporary Manifestation of Slavery and Organized Crime. *ECPAT Bulletin* 1999.

SPARC (999).*Survey by Central Social Welfare Board* in November

UNICEF (1994).*Trafficking in Women and Children Asia Region* United Nations General Assembly

Department of Women and Child Development. (2004). *Trafficking of Women and Children in India: Challenges and Responses* Government of India, Ministry of Human Resource Development,

National Commission for Women. (2001). *Trafficking A Social-Legal Study*

S. Anantha Ambeth Selvi and P. Madhava Soma Sundaram

20

NO-LAW, LOW-ENFORCEMENT TRAP: A GLIMPSE OF VICTIMIZATION OF GIRLS THROUGH SOFT TRAFFICKING

INTRODUCTION

Trafficking in human beings is a serious violation of human rights and therefore a threat to the security of any country. Every year, international organizations, governments, and NGOs make numerous efforts to combat trafficking in human beings, and vast funding is poured into anti-trafficking activities. During recent years, the international legal framework has continued to develop. The last decade of the twentieth century saw an unprecedented level of international concern over the trafficking of human beings. Broad recognition of the links between trafficking and the exploitation of children in particular also emerged as the children's rights movement gained momentum during this period. Today, abhorrence of the slavery-like practices associated with child trafficking has put this criminal activity squarely on the international agenda as a distinct and egregious violation of children rights and comprising one of the worst forms of child labour.

People were first referred to as 'traffickers' as early as the mid-sixteenth century, although at that time the label implied neither wrongdoing nor internal or cross-border movements. Traffickers were simply traders, and the two terms were roughly synonymous. By the end of that century, however, 'trafficking' had become disassociated from trading and was used to refer to the sale of illicit or disreputable goods. It is in this form that it first appeared in the discourse of politics, law and social development, where it came to denote the smuggling of contraband – often drugs or weapons but not yet human beings – across borders for profit. Towards the end of the nineteenth century, when the term 'trafficking' finally came into common usage to also refer to the illicit trade in human beings and their displacement across borders or within a country, it represented an amalgamation of the various meanings attributed to the word at various times: movement, illicit trade, and people as merchandise.

DEFINITION

Trafficking is all acts involved in the recruitment, abduction, transport, harboring, transfer, sale or receipt of persons; within national or across international borders; through force, coercion, fraud or deception; to place persons in situations of slavery or slavery-like conditions, forced labor or services, such as forced prostitution or sexual services, domestic servitude, bonded sweatshop labor or other debt bondage. Analysts agree on the fact that there is no consensual definition of trafficking in human beings (Chew, 1999; Derks, 2000; Okolski, 2000; Oxman-Martinez, Martinez, Hanley, 2001; Salt and Hogarth, 2000; Toupin, 2002). Salt and Hogarth (2000) have identified 22 definitions of the concept of trafficking in their study. Moreover, authors use various terms such as alien smuggling, trafficking of aliens, illegal immigrant smuggling, human trafficking, trade of human beings, and commodification of human beings, thus adding to the confusion. However, Salt and Hogarth (2000) indicate that various government agencies now tend to make a very clear distinction between trafficking and smuggling, citing as examples the *United Nations Convention against Transnational Organized Crime,* also called the Palermo Convention (2000),

It should be noted that trafficking is also defined in the "International Protocol to Prevent, Suppress, and Punish Trafficking in Persons, especially Women and Children," which will be a supplement to the UN Convention Against Transnational Organized Crime. According to the Protocol,

> *"Trafficking in persons means the recruitment, transportation, transfer, harboring or receipt of persons: by the threat or use of kidnapping, force, fraud, deception or coercion, or by the giving or*

receiving of unlawful payments or benefits to achieve the consent of a person having control over another person, for the purpose of sexual exploitation or forced labor".

The first international treaty to address trafficking in human beings was the *International Agreement for the Suppression of White Slave Traffic* (1904). Today, the term has re-emerged on political and operational agendas around the world with an expanded meaning informed by current discourse on migration, changes in prostitution patterns, the feminist and gender debate, increased attention to human rights and, most recently, children's rights. In effect, 'trafficking' has proved a useful and simple label for a complex phenomenon, whose wide-ranging manifestations and root causes necessitate a multi-strategy response. It should be noted at the outset that the issue of the trade in human beings received attention first and foremost in relation to the trade in women (Bertone, 2000, Chuang, 1998, Derks, 2000), being associated with the phenomenon of the "white slave trade" that had been vigorously condemned by moral reformers and feminists in the late nineteenth century. Subsequent historical research revealed that there was little material basis for this crusade of purity (Corbin, 1990; Doezema, 2000; Rosen, 1982; Walkowitz, 1982), although Doezema (2000) refers to this question as the "myth of white slavery." This campaign in fact coincided with an increase in the number of migrant prostitutes in Europe during that period (Doezema, 2000).

Although a distinct issue, the trafficking of children is often discussed together with trafficking of women. This is not only because the same mechanisms and processes often apply to both, but also because much of the available data on trafficking of women is not clearly disaggregated by age. For example, many reports on the trafficking of women state that the majority of women coerced into prostitution are between 16 and 24 years of age. However, 16 and 17 year-old girls are children according to the *UN Convention on the Rights of the Child* (CRC) and the *ILO Worst Forms of Child Labour Convention (No. 182).* In order to set priorities for policy and programme interventions that combat trafficking of children, it is essential to understand the context and the magnitude of trafficking of those under the age of 18. At the same time, policy and interventions must make clear distinctions between the suppression of trafficking of adults and that of children. In the case of adults, the recognition of the right to make informed decisions and choices, even if this includes the choice to remain in exploitative situations, will continue to be an issue of debate and has to be considered in programme interventions. In the case of children, the international consensus is to withdraw them from exploitation without delay. Action to combat the trafficking of children can and should be an integral part of action to combat the trafficking of adults.

Determining whether or not a child or adult is being 'trafficked' requires a nuanced working definition of trafficking that distinguishes it from other types of activities. Trafficking as a distinct, discrete act does not really exist. It is, in fact, a combination or series of events that occur at places of origin, transit points and destinations, involving potentially both legal and illegal acts.

Various means can be used to entrap victims, including persuasion, deception, threats and coercion, and these can involve different actors, including recruiters, intermediaries, transporters, employers, brothel/inn operators, and even families and friends. The methods of entrapment, as well as the means of transport/movement and the nature of the exploitation, can also have significant regional and national variations. What transforms this chain of events into 'trafficking' is the exploitation of the child or adult who is being relocated, whether that exploitation occurs at the beginning, during or at the end of the trafficking process.

Traffickers have also taken advantage of the demand for cheap, unprotected labor, and the promotion of sex tourism in some countries (Miller & Alison, 1998). Exploitation, always illegal in international law and national laws, may occur at any point in the chain of events that, taken together, are recognized as trafficking. It may occur, for example, if the child is misled with false reports or promises, coerced, or otherwise forcibly recruited or handed over to transporters. It may also occur when the child is transported: a child might be told s/he is going to a nearby big city, only to be moved elsewhere, or a child or family might be charged an exorbitant fee in order to ensnare them in debt bondage. Trafficking may be said to have taken place when the child is recruited as a dancer but forced into prostitution, or by the withholding of wages or their payment to a third party. It may take the form of exploitative and/or abusive conditions to which the child is subjected, including physical and mental abuse or confinement, inadequate or non-existent health care, poor accommodation and hazardous work.

Aside from the lack of consensus on a definition, a number of authors have noted that there is no consistent theoretical framework that structures analysis and empirical research on this question (Okolski, 2000; Salt and Hogarth, 2000). Many authors introduce their comments by stating that globalization is the backdrop against which the trafficking in human beings has developed over the past 30 years (Beare, 1999; Bertone, 2000; De Dios, 1999; Kempadoo, 1998; Oxman-Martinez, Martinez, Hanley, 2001; Skrobanek and Sanghera, 1996; Toupin, 2002, Williams, 1999).

MAGNITUDE OF TRAFFICKING

Trafficking in persons, particularly women and children, is significant on nearly every continent. Gauging the level of trafficking with precision, however, is difficult since it is an underground industry. Estimates of the trafficking problem in many countries vary, given differing definitions of what constitutes trafficking and research based on limited case studies. At present, no international agency is compiling accurate statistics. Nonetheless, government and nongovernmental experts in the field estimate that out of the 700,000 to two million women and children who are trafficked, globally, each year, 45,000 to 50,000 of those women and children are trafficked to the United States. Approximately 30,000 women and children are being trafficked annually from Southeast Asia, 10,000 from Latin America, 4,000 from the Newly Independent States and Eastern Europe, and 1,000 from other regions (CIA, 1999).

The primary source countries for trafficking appear to be Thailand, Vietnam, China, Mexico, Russia, Ukraine, and the Czech Republic. Women have also been trafficked to the US from the Philippines, Korea, Malaysia, Latvia, Hungary, Poland, Brazil, and Honduras among other countries. Women have been trafficked to the US primarily for the sex industry (prostitution, stripping, peep and touch shows, and massage parlors that offer a variety of sexual services), sweatshop labor, domestic servitude, and agricultural work. Women have also been trafficked to provide maid services at hotels, peddle trinkets on subways and buses, and beg. The average age of the trafficking victim is roughly 20 years old. Some of the Asian women may have been initially trafficked overseas at a much younger age, but then worked in cities such as Bangkok before being trafficked again.

AIM OF THE STUDY

The major aim of the study was to provide a glimpse of the problems faced by the victims of soft trafficking.

TOOL

The researchers for conducting the study developed a questionnaire, specifically constructed, for the purpose. The tool elicited information on the personal details of the respondent like age, sex, type, place and length of work etc., and whether the respondent faced problems while they were working. The tool also enquired about who rescued them the respondent's present problems and the type of assistance that they require, at present.

THE STUDY AREA

To understand the demographics of the study area, table 1 gives the profile of Tirunelveli District, Tamil Nadu, India. The study was limited to the urban Tirunelveli.

Table 1
Tirunelveli District Profile

	Rural	*Urban*	*Total*
Population	14,15,742	13,08,246	27,23,988
Male	6,45,142	6,88,797	13,33,939
Female	7,26,945	6,63,104	13,90,049
Total Children (0 - 6)	1,72,659	1,47516	3,20,175
Male Children (0 - 6)	88,121	75,503	1,63,624
Female Children (0 - 6)	84,538	72,013	1,56,551
Main Cultivators	1,09,016 (17.49%)	21,800 (4.38%)	1,30,816 (11.67%)
Agricultural labourers	1,98,037 (31.77%)	79,632 (16.01%)	2,77,669 (24.78%)
Household Ind. Workers	1,39,283 (22.34%)	1,08,638 (21.84%)	2,47,921 (22.12%)
Other Workers	1,77,038 (28.40%)	2,87,308 (57.76%)	4,64,346 (41.43%)
Marginal Workers	1,06,402 (7.52%)	53,963 (4.12%)	1,60,365 (5.89%)

Contd....

	Rural	*Urban*	*Total*
Marginal Cultivators	5,749	951	6,700
	(5.40%)	(1.76%)	(4.18%)
Marg. Agri. labourers	59,311	19,075	78,386
	(55.74%)	(35.35%)	(48.88%)
Marginal Workers in Household	20,882	13,479	34,361
Industries	(19.63%)	(24.98%)	(21.43%)
Marg. Other Workers	20,460	20,458	40,918
	(19.23%)	(37.91%)	(25.52%)
Non-Workers	6,85,966	7,56,905	14,42,871
	(48.45%)	(57.86%)	(52.97%)

SAMPLE

During the problem formulation stage it was found, discussions with the *Moolachi* village level workers and public that certain villages in *Ambasamudaram taluk* were more vulnerable to trafficking and regularly girls from these villages are sent for six months to one year in industries else where. 35 girls of these villages were randomly selected for the study and the questionnaire was administered. The profile of the sample, by age, is as follows:

Table 2
Distribution of Sample by Age

Age	*Frequency*	*Percent*
13	2	5.7
14	9	25.7
15	10	28.6
16	12	34.3
17	2	5.7
Total	35	100.0

Majority of the sample selected for the study (34.3%) were in the age group of 16 years, 28.6% were 15 years and 25.7% of them were 14 years. Table 2 gives the details of the distribution by age.

RESULTS AND DISCUSSION

The data collected was coded and analyzed using SPSS package. The major findings are discussed, as under.

Table 3
Period of Working

Age	*Frequency*	*Percent*
< 1 Year	22	62.9
2-4 Years	13	37.1
Total	35	100.0

From Table 3 it can be seen that majority of the respondents were working less than one year, and the rest were working for a varying periods between 2-4 years.

Figure 1

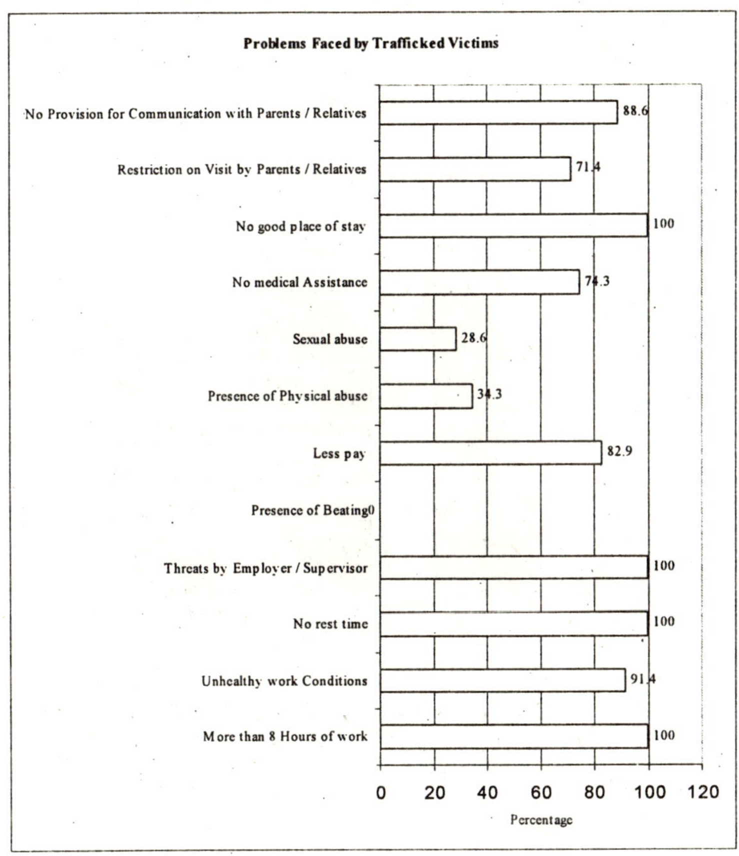

Figure 1 gives the details of the various factors faced by the trafficked victims. Threats by employers, lack of rest time, made to work for more than 8 hours of work, lack of good place to stay were problems faced by all the respondents (100%). Unhealthy working conditions were the next major problem faced by these victims (91.4%), followed by no communication facilities (88.6%). Even though presence of beating was no there (0%), sexual abuse was present in 28.6%. It may be mentioned here that, not many respondents would have agreed to this abuse, considering the stigma attached to it, and hence the figures may not represent the actualities.

Considering the other problems that the respondents face now due to trafficking, the study found that, 91.4% had emotional problems, 82.9% had health problems, and 65.7 % had financial problems. Figure 2 gives the details.

Figure 2

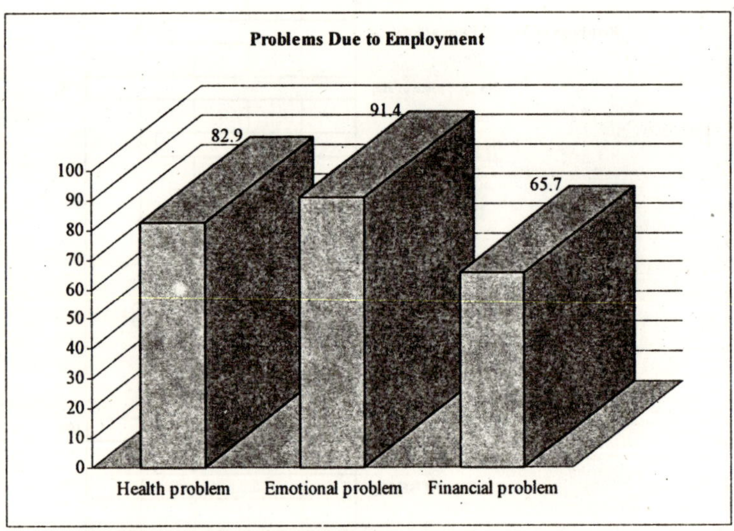

From Figure 3, it can be seen that, Majority of the respondents wanted assistance related to occupational avenues. Others required medical facilities, financial assistance, counselling services and educational services.

Figure 3

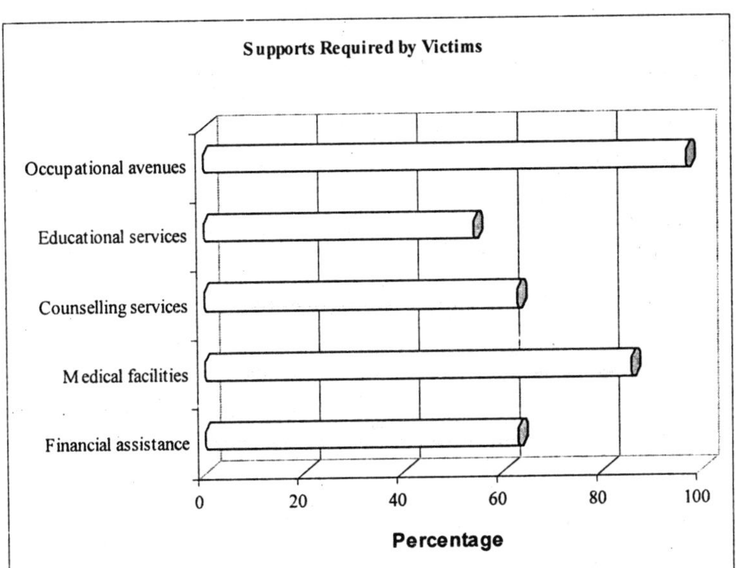

CONCLUSIONS

The study was conducted with an aim to study the rehabilitated victims of child trafficking, in a semi urban area. This study found that

- All the respondents faced problems like threats by employers, lack of rest time, made to work for more than 8 hours a day, lack of good place to stay were problems faced by all the respondents (100%).
- Unhealthy working conditions were the next major problem faced by these victims (91.4%), followed by no communication facilities (88.6%).
- The trafficked victims were in need of occupation, health assistance, financial assistance and counselling services

Considering the fact that there is a wide gap between the problems present and the services available, schemes may have to be developed in these vulnerable areas to combat trafficking in children.

REFERENCES

Beare, Margaret E. (1999), Illegal Immigration : Personal Tragedies, Social Problems, or National Security Threats? *Illegal Immigration and Commercial Sex. The New Slave Trade*. Phil Williams (ed.). London: Frank Cass Publishers, 11-41.

Bertone, Andrea Marie (2000), Sexual Trafficking in Women: International Political Economy and the Politics of Sex. *Gender Issues* 18, 1: 4-22.

Central Intelligence Agency Briefing (1999), Global Trafficking in Women and Children: Assessing the Magnitude, April.

Chew, Lin. (1999), Global Trafficking in Women: Some Issues and Strategies. *Women's Studies Quarterly* 1 and 2: 11-17.

Chuang, Janie (1998), Redirecting the Debate over Trafficking in Women: Definitions, Paradigms and Contexts. *Harvard Human Rights Journal* 11: 65-107.

Corbin, Alain (1990), *Women for Hire : Prostitution and Sexuality in France after 1850*. Cambridge, Mass.: Harvard University Press.

De Dios, Aurora Javate (1999), *Macro-Economic Policies and their Impact on Sexual Exploitation and Trafficking of Women and Girls: Issues, Responses and Challenges*, http://www.catw.-ap.org/Macro.htm.

Derks, Annuska (2000), *Combating Trafficking in South Asia, A Review of Policy and ProgrammeResponses*. Genève, Organisation Internationale pour les Migrations.

Derks, Annuska (2000), *Combating Trafficking in South Asia, A Review of Policy and Programme Responses*. Genève, Organisation Internationale pour les Migrations. http://www.iom.int.

Doezema, Jo. (2000), Loose Women or Lost Women. *Gender Issues* 18, 1:23-50.

Kempadoo, Kamala (ed.), (2000), *Global Sex Workers. Rights, Resistance, and Redefinition*. New York: Routledge.

Miller, Ali and Stewart, Alison (1998), Report from the Roundtable on The Meaning of Trafficking in Persons: A Human Rights Perspective, Women's Rights Law Reporter, Rutgers Law School, Fall/Winter. Vol. 20 Number 1.

Okolski, Marek (2000), Migrant Trafficking and Human Smuggling in Poland. *Migrant Trafficking and Human Smuggling in Europe : a Review of Evidence with Case Studies from Hungary, Poland and Ukraine,* Frank Laczko and David Thompson (eds.), Genève, Organisation internationale pourles migrations, 233-328. http://www.iom.int

Oxman-Martinez, Jacqueline, Andrea Martinez and Jill Hanley (2001), Human Trafficking : Canadian Government Policy and Practice, *Refuge, Canada's Periodical on Refugees* 19, 4: 19-23.

Rosen, Judith (1982), *The Lost Sisterhood: Prostitution in America, 1900-1918*. London: John Hopkins University Press.

Salt, John, Jennifer Hogarth (2000), Migrant Trafficking and Human Smuggling in Europe : A Review of the Evidence. *Migrant Trafficking and Human Smuggling in Europe: a Review of Evidence with Case Studies from Hungary, Poland and Ukraine.* Frank Laczko and David Thompson (eds.), Geneva: OIM,. 11-164. http://www.iom.int

Skrobanek, Siriporn and Jyoti Sanghera (1996), Sex Trade and Globalized Traffick in Women, *Atlantis* 21, 1: 95-99.

Toupin, Louise (2002), *La Question Du « Trafic Des Femmes ». Points de Repères dans la Documentation des Coalitions Féministes Internationales anti-trafic*. Montréal: Stella.

Walkowitz, Judith (1982), *Prostitution and Victorian Society: Women, Class, and the State*. Cambridge, Cambridge University Press.

Part - V

PERSPECTIVES ON WOMEN VICTIMIZATION

NANDINI RAI

21

SPATIO-TEMPORAL ANALYSIS OF VICTIMIZATION AGAINST WOMEN IN DELHI: AN EMERGING ZONE OF FEAR

INTRODUCTION

Crime and Violence is Omnipresent in all the living Society (Durkheim 1938), all sorts of spaces and places have experienced it at some point of time. Various disciplines have developed different perspective towards the study of crime and victimization. But geographers concerned in this area were specifically interested in the behaviour pattern of crime over the space. It also presumes that spatial structure of an area can be used to explain criminal behaviour in space. However, there are two aspects of the debate related to crime and its behaviour over the space; *one* is the area where offenders come from and *second* is the place where crime is committed. These two seldom intersect with each other; (Herbert 1972a;), as offenders chose to commit crime generally away from their vicinity.

Hence, in the above light it can be argued that place differs in terms of their levels of vulnerability of crime. Some areas seem to attract more criminals than other areas (Davidson 1989). The very different circumstances that surround incidences of victimization varies, this idea very well stemmed in a situational typology of crime. It became popular in 1980s and Davidson was the pioneer to this approach of study of crime. It is mainly based on the argument that certain spaces facilitate crime such as Rape and some places offers suitability to the offender. This framework offers the analysis along gender, different age groups of victim and certain spaces attracting more victimization.

The chapter maintains that for greater understanding of situation of crime against women in Delhi, one must have an idea about the existing gendered pattern of the various settings of crime. While attempting this chapter also looks upon the spread of Female victimization in India. The chapter is divided into four sections, *first* section deals with data and methodology, *second* is about looking at the situation of victimization in the country, third section contains the settings and profiles of women victimization at temporal and different spatial level and finally analysis of possible factors which may be contributing to victimization is presented in the fourth section.

DATA AND METHODOLOGY

According to the general perception, official crime records do not provide the accurate scenario (Guha, 2000) but they are certainly useful for broader analysis. However to determine the existing settings around gendered crime in Delhi, crime reported in the Newspaper has been used as the database. Though newspaper as a database also invites numerous criticisms. But because they provide good amount of information, so for micro level analysis it is used here as an optimal data source.

For churning out the broader picture of crime at the state level, information given in the National Crime Records Bureau published by the Ministry of Home Affairs has been availed. The period of analysis is a decade from 1992 to 2001. The details of the age group, place where victimization took place and victim's relation to the offender has been documented and tabulated from the newspaper. For the convenience of the analysis all the crimes reported against women has been brought under three categories. They are Violent crimes (attempt on life, dowry homicides etc.), Property crime (robbery, burglary and small thefts) and Sexual harassment (rape and other harassments) cases. Rates of crime at the region level analysis (obtained from different wards) have been calculated by dividing the number of incidences reported per ten thousand populations.

The analysis begins with a brief discussion on the situation of women victimization in various quarters of the country.

SCENARIO ACROSS THE COUNTRY

This section gives the broad detail of the interstate variation of the IPC (Indian Penal Code) crimes against women in India. It reveals that on average, bigger states of the like Rajasthan, Madhya Pradesh

Table 1
Rates of Victimization against Women in India , 1992-2001

Rates Calculated per lakh Total Population

S.N.	*States/UTs*	*92-93*	*94-95*	*96-97*	*98-99*	*00-01*
1	Andhra Pd	11	13	14	16	20
2	Arunachal Pd	08	08	08	12	14
3	Assam	06	09	13	13	15
4	Bihar	02	3.5	5.5	07	06
5	Goa	08	09	12	07	06
6	Gujarat	09	09	11	14	12
7	Haryana	9.5	10.5	12	16	16
8	Himachal Pradesh	12.5	13	13	12	13
9	Jammu & Kashmir	11.5	10	01	17	16
10	Karnataka	06	11	13	11	11
11	Kerala	04	06	09	15	16
12	Madhya Pradesh	17	20	21	21	23
13	Maharashtra	16	17	18	15.5	13
14	Manipur	07	04	04	03	04
15	Meghalaya	02	2.5	04	03	03
16	Mizoram	11	11	12	16	14
17	Nagaland	0.1	01	02	02	14
18	Orissa	06	08	11	13	14
19	Punjab	02	2.5	3.5	06	09
20	Rajasthan	16	18	21	24	23
21	Sikkim	6.5	10	10	06	04
22	Tamil Nadu	04	14	15	19	19
23	Tripura	9.5	08	10	09	11
24	Uttar Pradesh	09	09	7.5	10	11
25	West Bengal	06	08	09	09	08
26	A&N Island	14	09	08	08	11
27	Chandigarh	12	12	09	14	17
28	D&N Haveli	07	10	09	09	8.5
29	Daman & Diu	4.5	01	01	05	05
30	Delhi	36	16	19	19	17
31	Lakshadweep	00	00	00	00	01
32	Pondicherry	78	27	6.5	09	12
	India	08	12	12.5	14	14

Source: NCRB , 1992 to 2001

and Maharashtra are showing high reporting of the women victimization respectively. For the state of Rajasthan may be historical reasons can be attributed for poor gender well being and in Madhya Pradesh is a tribal dominated area which comprises of the most vulnerable group.

The smaller states such as Mizoram, Tripura and Arunachal Pradesh are also showing higher concentration, may be due to their various local determinants. Third important observation made from the data is that one of the highly protected areas Delhi is invariably maintaining its higher ranking. It is evident from the table that in the nineties Delhi has always maintained its position amongst the first five high crime prone region.

As per the analysis of NCRB and Newspaper database, different districts are reporting greater crime frequencies. Data from the newspaper suggests that district of South West and New Delhi are more unsafe zone for women. Northern and Western parts are reported safer. On the side, NCRB report says that areas around New Delhi and North districts share more fearsome space for women.

Table 2
District wise Situation of Crime as per NCRB and Newspaper

S.No.	*Districts*	*Rank as per Newspaper*	*Rank as per NCRB*
1	North West	9	7
2	North	5	2
3	North East	7	9
4	East	4	8
5	New Delhi	2	1
6	Central	3	4
7	West	8	6
8	South West	1	5
9	South	6	3

Source: National Crime Records Bureau 2001 Newspaper

TEMPORAL VARIATION IN WOMEN VICTIMIZATION

It has been observed that newspaper reports shares more violent crime than the other types. Decadal analysis of the data reveals that nearly half of the incidence are related to violence. Next to this comes the reportage of sexual harassment cases. In the year 1992-93 the share of violent crime to the total crime was 56%, which declined to the level of 45% in the moving year 2000-01. Reporting of the sexual harassment cases raised to the level of 31% in the end of 2000-01, and the highest growth (31%) was demonstrated in the year 1994-1995.

Age wise temporal analysis of the data, interprets that young and the middle aged women have the highest victim ratio as compared to the older population. It is quite contrary to the established belief, which says that fear of crime is higher among elderly and they are more vulnerable to victimization (Garofalo 1979, Akers:1987, Oh Hwan 2003). Total share of elderly victimization in the total victimization has consistently remained low (less than 10% of the total). Middle aged group categorically remains the most victimised and thus vulnerable age group.

Table 3
Temporal Profile of Victimization against Women in Delhi during 1992-2001

Figures in %

Profile of Victimization		*92—93*	*94-95*	*96-97*	*98-99*	*00-01*
Types of Victimization	Viol*	56	54	55	45	45
	Prop^	18	12	17	22	24
	SH+	26	34	28	33	31
Age wise	0-18	25	40	24	30	34
	18-45	61	42	54	51	50
	45-60	09	07	10	10	09
	60+	04	11	08	07	05
Place of Victimization	Residence	74	78	62	51	64
	Out-residence	13	08	11	16	15
	Workplace	05	06	03	07	05
	Public place	08	08	27	26	16
Time of Victimization	Post Midnight	07	06	02	09	07
	Day	41	36	34	36	40
	Night	50	52	61	48	41
Offender Relation & Nearness to Victim	Close Relatives	22	21	18	14	15
	Distant Relatives	08	08	04	07	06
	Acquaintances	39	46	43	40	42
	Strangers	31	25	35	37	36

Source: Newspaper
* Viol: Violent Crime
^ Prop: Property Crime
+ SH: Sexual Harassment

Women in Delhi are more at risk at the private places rather than the non private ones such as park, cinema etc. For all the decadal years, in-house crimes are reported greater in number in comparison to other location settings. For consistent one decade home-space has been reported as the place of frequent women victimization. This postulate goes quite contrary to the belief that home is the safest territory for women.. However , public place victimization is also on rise and now shares around 16% of the total which is 100% increase from the year 1992-93.

In majority of the cases offenders were known to the victims either as a relative or a common neighbour etc. It can be mentioned that the traditional perception of 'strangers only harm' shall be revised. Daytime frequency of victimization seemed less in the early nineties, but recently it is on mount. Though night time frequency of crime has remained greater.

VARIOUS SETTINGS OF VICTIMIZATION AGAINST WOMEN IN DELHI

Newspaper data provides us the details of places where offence has been perpetrated. It can be broadly divided into two as indoor or outdoor settings. For further understanding one more division can be obtained and that is private (including workplace) and public place. Of known locations, 64 % were inside residence and 31% at the outside residence and rest at the workplace locations. However the circumstances of the victimization varies with the different settings. Some salient categories have been discussed below.

Table 4
Place wise Settings of Victimization

Figures in %

N-1095	*Time of Victimization*	*Post Midnight*	*Day*	*Night*
Place of Victimiz-ation	Residence	6	38	56
	Out-Residence	7	31	62
	Workplace	6	51	43
	Public place	15	41	44
Time of Victimiz-ation	*Nearness of the offender to Victim*	*Relatives*	*Acquaintance*	*Stranger*
	Post Midnight	28	36	36
	Day	17	48	35
	Night	24	39	35

Source: The Newspaper

Inside or near the victim home are characterized by a greater evening or night time frequency which is 56% of the total cases. Victimization at workplace has greater daytime(51%) frequency, Incidents in public places as roads, parks, markets or places of entertainment has reported more night time frequency . Daytime incidences are mostly committed by day to day acquaintances.

The physical setting of attacks on women in Delhi reinforces some highlighting pattern. Attacks inside the residences are perpetrated the most by the acquaintances and near relatives as husbands and father of the victim etc. It has been demonstrated by the data that public place victimization has been perpetrated in the hands of the strangers (Table 4).

VULNERABILITY SETTINGS

There are number of personal variables which are related to the victim's exposure to risks of violence(Hough and Sheehy: 1986, Gottfredson: 1984). Gender and age of the victims are particularly relevant.

Table 5
Age wise Settings of Victimization in Delhi

Figures in %

Age wise V'mization	*Type of Victimization*			*Place of Victimization*			
	*Viol**	*Prop^*	*SH+*	*Resi-dence*	*Outside residence*	*Work place*	*Public Place*
0-18	27	15	59	56	21	6	17
18-45	60	20	20	65	12	5	18
45-60	60	28	12	74	4	4	18
60+	71	18	11	75	0	0	25

Source: Newspaper
*Viol: Violent Crime
^Prop: Property Crime
+SH: Sexual Harassment

When we look at the type wise victimization across different age groups in Delhi, there emerges certain highlighting features. Women of the middle age group along with the elderly population have been reported to experience more violent kind of incidences. Younger population (0-18 yrs) are reported to be victimized maximum (59%) for the sexual assaults. In house victimization is common for both mid aged and elder population. Elderly population is reporting violent assaults and property violence in the private place settings more.

While going through the general character of victimization against women in Delhi it is quite clear that particular settings are most attractive to the victimization. To understand this in the spatial terms the detailed discussion has been done at the ward level.

SPATIAL ANALYSIS OF THE VICTIMIZATION SETTINGS

Rates of crime has been used to understand the magnitude of the victimization from the long time. In the present chapter also for the descriptive analysis of the range of places settings profile of the victimization at the spatial scale, crime arte has been adopted for the

Table 6
Region wise Profile of Victimization against Women During 1992-2001

]Profile of Victimization in Various Zones (figures in percent)		*High Victimization Zone*			*Medium Victimization Zone*			*Low Victimization Zone*		
		*Viol**	*Prop^*	*SH+*	*Viol*	*Prop*	*SH*	*Viol*	*Prop*	*SH*
Age Group	0-18 Yrs	18	30	62	16	13	61	16	24	52
	18-45 Yrs	62	45	30	64	61	35	58	51	43
	45-60 Yrs	13	18	04	09	15	04	13	13	03
	60+	07	07	04	10	10	01	12	13	03
Place of V'miation	Residence	74	53	53	75	53	53	74	49	46
	Out-residence	11	13	23	11	13	23	13	00	30
	Workplace	02	06	07	02	06	07	02	16	10
	Public place	14	28	17	14	28	17	04	16	07
Time of V'mization	Post Midnight	06	08	05	04	05	08	08	02	09
	Day	38	53	37	33	49	34	39	51	26
	Night	54	34	49	58	46	49	49	42	54
Nearness of the Offender to Victim	Close Relative	54	00	04	39	02	08	35	00	12
	Acquaintance	22	22	68	35	33	73	28	36	62
	Strangers	24	78	18	26	65	19	37	64	26

Source: The Newspaper
* Viol: Violent Crime
^ Prop: Property Crime
+ SH: Sexual Harassment

spatial division. Census of India in 2001 has divided Delhi into one hundred and thirty four wards and nine NDMC charges. Rates of women crime has been calculated by dividing the number of incidence reported by the number of female population of the corresponding ward. The victimization rate calculated for the above wards and charges shows the mean victimization rate of women. According to the rates calculated 5% of the wards are reporting very high victimization rates, 8% of the wards are recording medium rate of victimization and rest of them are falling under the lowest reported area category. Above figures also reflects the tendency of spatial concentration crime. In the highest reporting area four persons per ten thousand population approximately and it is less than two women for the lowest reported areas.

It is evident from the data that sexual harassment (32%) incidences are reported maximum for the younger age group category. Further among the younger population, maximum concentration is found in the highest victimization zone (62%). Age group of 18-45 experiences violent incidences more frequently than other category.

The remarkable feature of the victimization in all wards are, that in all the places crime revolve around the home space. Women are made victims by their own near ones they are not spared at their own private places (Pain, 200). Even the place outside the residence but within the threshold of the residence have been demonstrating vulnerability for women. Property related offences against women is showing the tendency for daytime preference for all the areas. Whereas evening and nighttimes preference has been reported for the sexual harassment and violent offences.

Of all the cases reported in the newspaper, majority have been perpetrated by the near acquaintances. This is true for the all the victim zones of Delhi, however the numbers may vary. In all the regions, offenders were known to the victims of violent incidences, though in lower crime regions strangers also found to be the possible offenders. Property crime is the one, which is mostly taken up by the people other than the acquaintances.

SOME CORRELATES OF VICTIMIZATION

Various physiological and economic indicators have been used to establish the possible relationships with rates of victimization. Here in the chapter we have used some demographic and socio-economic variables to understand their relationship with the crime rate. The data has been drawn at the ward level from the Census of India at the ward level. Variables as sex ratio and population of female at the age group of 0-6 years (demographic indicators) and socio-economic indicators as, number of persons per household, percent literacy for total and female population, percent of illiterate population, scheduled caste population, number of main workers, non working population.

It is however, intriguing to note that literacy both for the total and for female population and main workers population for total and female exhibits positive (Table 7) association with the rate of women victimization in Delhi. The correlation has been run at the ward level data provided by census. However, though it shows absolutely significant relation with the variables the magnitude of effect is not high.

Table 7
Correlates of Victimization Rates with Select Indicators

S. N.	*Select Indicators*	*Victimization Rates*
1	Sex Ratio	-0.21
2	Number of Persons per household	-0.64
3	Percent of literate population to total	+0.277*
4	Percent of illiterate population to total	-0.024
5	Percent of female literate population to total female population	+0.267*
6	Percent of female illiterate population to total female illiterate population	-0.260*
7	Percent of Non-workers to total population	-0.249*
8	Percent of female Non-workers to total female Non-workers population	-0.263*
9	Percent of SC population to total SC population	-0.165
10	Percent of female SC population to total female SC population	-0.162
11	Percent of main workers to total main-workers population	+0.291*
12	Percent of female main-workers to total female main-workers population	+0.241*
13	Percent of 0-6 age group female population to female popn at this group	-0.239*

Source: Census of India,2001
*Significant at 0.01 level

CONCLUSION

The prevailing situation of victimization in different areas of Delhi certainly presents before us a fundamental question. It is as in the present age of rapid development where world has taken a form of global village. The issue of gender equality still remains unheard and uncared. As the rate of urbanisation is on rise and new million cities are emerging, the story of crime and victimization is getting worse. The fact to be noticed and the most cared for, is that women are not safe in the hands of their caretakers. Their private dominion home, a place of supreme comfort has also been challenged. So now the issue emerges to introspect the situation of family capital in urban area.

REFERENCES

Akers, R. L., (1987), 'Fear Of Crime And Victimization Among The Elderly In Different Types Of Communities', *Criminology* 25(3), 487-505.

Davidson, R. N., (1989), 'Micro Environments Of Violence', PP 59-85 in Evans, David J., and Herbert, David T., *The Geography of Crime*, Routledge pub., 59-85.

Durkheim, E. (1938), *The Rules of Sociological Method.* New York: Free Press.

Garofalo, M. R. (1979), 'Victimisation and Fear of Crime', *Journal of Research in Crime and Delinquency*, 16:80-97.

Gottfredson, M. R. (1984), 'Victims of Crime: The Dimensions of Risk', *Home Office Research Study Number 81,* London: HMSO.

Government of India (1992-2001), *Crime in India*, National Crime Records Bureau, Ministry of Home Affairs, New Delhi.

Guha, B., S. (2000), 'A Geography of Crime in India', Pp. 263-281 in Noble, A., G., Thakur, B., Mukherji, A., B., and Costa., F. J. (eds) *Geographic and Planning Research Themes For The New Millennium*, Vikas Publishing House Pvt Ltd., New Delhi.

Hough, M. and Sheehy, K. (1986), 'Incidence of Violence: Findings from British Crime Survey', *Research Bulletin,* 20: 22-26.

Morris, T. (1957), *The Criminal Area: A Study of Social Ecology*, London: Routledge.

Oh, Hwan, J. (2003), 'Assessing the Social Bonds of Elderly Neighbours: The Role of Length of Residence, Crime Victimization, and Perceived Disorder', *Sociological Enquiry*, 73 (4): 493-510.

Pain, R. (2000), 'Place, Social Relations and the Fear of Crime: A Review', *Progress in Human Geography,* 24 (2): 365-387.

STANLEY B. YELDELL

22

BATTERED WOMEN'S SYNDROME: CIVIL REMEDIES FOR THE VICTIMS IN UNITED STATES

INTRODUCTION

Divorce or separation provides escape from tortuous abuse, but it cannot be equated with a civil right to redress compensation for personal injuries. Equally arcane and unworthy is the notion that a wronged spouse or partner, who has been injured at the hands of her or his mate, can and should resort to an arsenal of private sanctions (Giovine v. Giovine, 1995).

Civil tort actions arising out of domestic violence, (Jewitt V. Jewitt, 1993) can offer redress for abused victims. Although, there is an emerging trend among victims to file civil tort actions, the practice has not become widespread (Atkins, 1999). Victims most often seek legal recourse through the judicial system by obtaining a protective order or by assisting the state to criminally prosecute the abuser. (Atkins, 1999).

PURPOSE

This chapter will examine significance of tort law for victims of domestic violence. In addition, it will explore the existing barriers to recovery in a civil tort action initiated on behalf of domestic violence victims. The focal point of the chapter will be an analytical examination of the concept of a new civil tort called the *"Battered Women's Syndrome"* (BWS). This analysis will be utilized as an example the

New Jersey judicial decision that created this specialized remedy for battered spouses to demonstrate the potential for the reform of tort law.

SIGNIFICANCE OF CIVIL TORT LAW FOR DOMESTIC VIOLENCE VICTIMS

The pursuant of a monetary judgment is very important for victims who endured financial abuse during an abusive relationship (Buel 1999). The batterers will seek to control their victims by halting access to the couple's finance and to make budgeting decisions (Buel 1999). The results of numerous studies revealed that 51 percent of battered women had no access to a credit card account, 34 percent had no access to a checking account, and 21 percent could not obtain cash in any form. When a victim has no means to support herself and her children, she may return to him because she is in financial despair (Buel, 1999).

According to Professor Barbara Hart, "The most likely prediction of whether a battered woman will permanently separate from her abuser is whether she has the economic resources to survive without him." (Hart, 1990). Many battered women who divorce their abusers must sacrifice their financial security as a result (Hart, 1990). The ability to recover a judgment in a tort action is very important to victims who lose financial stability as a consequence of leaving their abusers.

RATIONALE

A judgment against the abuser may be futile; the abuser may not be dischargeable in bankruptcy and there is no time limit for collection and not all judgments may ripen into collectable judgments (Austern, 1997). One may argue that the pursuance of a civil tort action against an abuser maybe futile, especially if the abuser is not financially able to fulfill a monetary judgment. This argument assumes that domestic violence occurs only in lower socioeconomic households; it disregards the fact that a substantial number of middle and upper class women, many of whom are professionals. Domestic violence is a secret usually silent affair (Johnson, 1995).

A US Justice Department's 1994 National Crime Victimization Survey found less then a ten percent difference in the rate of a domestic violence between households earning less then $10,000 a year and those earning more then $50,000 a year (Johnson, 1995). Finally, domestic violence is a plague that endangers female victims from all socioeconomic status, and the prospect of obtaining civil tort remedies should not be dimmed simply because the victims found in low-income groups may not directly benefit from this remedy.

BENEFITS

Some victims believe their chance of recovery is not possible; since their abusers do not have the financial resources to satisfy a judgment. However, the initiation of a civil tort suit against the wrongdoer provides numerous benefits. Some of the benefits are listed below:

1. The pursuance of a civil tort can provide a sense of justice and vindication for a victim who has never had an advocate in the past to defend and protect her from an abuser. (Buel, 1999)
2. Tort law is supposed to punish wrongdoers and deter future misconduct.
3. The civil tort against the abusers articulates a message to the community that domestic abuse will not be tolerated.
4. Abusers will be accountable for their wrongful conduct and victims will feel free in revealing the pain they have endured (Horman and Thatcher, 1996).
5. The number of tort actions filed against the abusers will increase public awareness and education regarding domestic violence (Buel, 1999).

IMPEDIMENTS

Historical Development

It was not until the mid-nineteenth century, when the Married Women's Property Acts (MWPA) was passed. Women were given property rights and the rights to sue (N.H. Rev.Stat.Ann, 1983). The English Common Law held that the husband and wife represented a union as a single entity. Women posed no separate rights for themselves (Fort, 1993). As a result of the MWPA's women could now defend, their property rights (Fort, 1993). Not withstanding the MWPA laws, courts continued to prohibit tort actions between spouses by accepting the inter-spousal immunity doctrine (Fort, 1993). The rationale for the inter-spousal immunity was to promote harmony in the marriage; to prevent fraudulent civil suits from being filed (Fort, 1993).

The early 1970's saw numerous jurisdictions began to repeal the inter-spousal immunity doctrine (Fort, 1993). However, Georgia and Louisiana continued to adhere to the doctrine, but Florida, Delaware, and Hawaii abolished the inter-spousal immunity doctrine (Tonsing, 1993).

Statute of Limitations

The statute of limitations for most torts of assault and battery is only a few years. The torts of assault and battery are usually for two years from the date of its inception or occurrence. Most courts perceive the abuse as discrete and separate acts, with the result that each incidence of assault or battery runs its own statute of limitations (Fort, 1993). If a victim endured abuse for five years before she filed a tort action against her abuser, she was only able to recover damages for the last two years.

The incidences of abuse are treated as isolated acts of violence (Ducate, 1998). The courts are beginning to treat torts arising from domestic violence as continuing torts. A continuing tort is one who has been abused over a period of time in which it involves wrongful conduct that is repeated until desisted. Each day will create a separate cause of action (Fort, 1993). The statute of limitations for a continuing tort is tolled until the injurious conduct ceases.

Joinder and Res Judicata

There are important procedural issues that must be addressed when developing strategies for commencing a tort action, especially when the victim is married to her abuser. If the victim is considering a divorce, she must decide whether the tort action should be joined with the divorce proceeding or filed as a separate action. This division will depend on the law of the Jurisdiction where the victim initiates the suit.

There are paramount issues regarding joinder and especially the need to ensure that a subsequent tort lawsuit is not barred by the doctrine of res judicata (Fort, 1993). A few states like Texas and Tennessee encourage joinder of all action in the interest of judicial economy (Twyman V. Twyman, 1993).

However, New Jersey is the only state that requires joinder of all these actions (Lewbowitz, 1996). In New Jersey, if a victim fails to institute suit against her abuser at the time of the divorce then res judicata prohibits her from pursuing that action in a later proceeding. The doctrine of res judicata will prejudices victims who are initially more interested in legally separating themselves from their abusers and who fail to bring a tort suit against their husband at the time of the divorce, possibly out of fear or ignorance of the law or other concerns (Lewbowitz, 1996). The rationale for prohibiting joinder is that tort claims are legal in nature and should be kept separate from divorce actions, which are equitable in nature (Tonsing, 1993).

CREATION OF THE BATTERED WOMEN SYNDROME TORT

The creation of the battered women's syndrome as a civil tort for domestic violence victims was decided in the New Jersey case Giovine V. Giovine. (Giovine V. Giovine, 1995).

GIOVINE V GIOVINE

Creation of the Battered Women's Syndrome

It was the first case in the United States to recognize that separate acts of assault and battery in the area of domestic violence consisted of a continuous tort that tolls the statute of limitation until the tortuous conduct desists. (Regent U.L.Rev, 1997). The formation of their new cause of action articulates domestic violence in order to impede the abuser's force for the tortuous conduct.

Facts and procedural History of Giovine

Christina and Peter Giovine married on May 1, 1971. They had three children in 1975, 1979 and 1983. On December 31, 1978, the Giovine separated and in 1980, Peter filed for a divorce. Christina answered and counter claimed for divorce, alleging extreme cruelty and habitual drunkenness as alternative grounds for divorce. The counter claimed also cited two specific acts of assault and battery, and occurring in March of 1972 and the other on December 28, 1978. It further alleged that Christina suffered emotional distress as a result of those acts a continuous and unbroken wrong commencing on or about March 1972 and continuing until December 28, 1978" (Giovine v. Giovine, 1995) pending the existing case,. The Giovine reconciled and resumed living together in July of 1982 and both parties requested that their attorneys discontinue the action. The case was dismissed on October of 1982.

The couples separated a second time in September of 1993 and in July of 1994; Mrs. Giovine again filed a complaint for divorce and domestic abuse. Mr. Giovine answered and counter claimed and moved to strike particular causes of action alleged in Mrs. Giovine's eleven count complaint as being subject to the statue of limitations. The trial judge granted the defendant's motion, striking any alleged tortuous claims that occurred before June 30, 1992. The New Jersey Supreme Court-Appellate Division granted Mrs. Giovine's motion for appeal. The appellate Court decision determined that the statute of limitations is tolled for a wife diagnosed with the battered woman's syndrome.

The court also held that a domestic violence victim can sue her abusive spouse for physical and emotional injuries sustained by continuous acts of battering during the course of marriage as long as expert testimony established that the wife was incapable of improving or altering her situation unilaterally, (Giovine V. Giovine, 1995). The appellate court stated: Battered Women's Syndrome is more correctly the medical condition resulting from continued acts of physical or psychological misconduct. Because the resulting psychological state composed, of varied but identifiable characteristics is the product of at least two separate and discrete physical or psychological acts occurring at different times to overcome the statute of limitations, it is imperative that the tortuous conduct giving rise to the medical condition is considered a continuous tort (Giovine V. Giovine, 1995).

The Giovine's court relied on the decision (Cusseaux V. Picket, 1994) in which a New Jersey trial court held that the BWS was a cognizable cause of action.

The court set the elements of a BWS cause of action:

1. Involvement in a marital like intimate relationship; and (2) physical or psychological abuse perpetrated by the dominant partner to the relationship over an extended period of time; and (3) the afore stated and abuse has caused recurring physical or psychological injury over the course of the relationship; and (4) a past and present inability to take any action to improve or alter the situation unilaterally (Giovine V. Giovine, 1995).

DIAGNOSIS OF THE VICTIM

The court required the victim to satisfy a diagnosis in which they relied upon the research of Dr. Leonore Walter (Vt. L.Rev, 1982).

According to Dr. Walter, the Battered Women's Syndrome is characterized by a woman's learned helplessness as she endures a cycle of abuse that consists of three phases:

1. First phase consist of tension building and involves minor assaults (Walker, 1979) the woman's attempts to control the phase by appeasing the batters and by taking responsibility for the abuser's behavior (Moore, 1992).
2. Second phase, the violence has increased and the abuser is out of control and she is in danger.
3. Third phase or the final phase comprises the honeymoon period. The abuser feels remorseful and asks the victim to forgive him. The cycle repeats itself repeatedly and she feels a sense of helplessness (Walker, 1979).

The court made it clear that the medical condition of the battered woman's syndrome occurred only after the woman is battered at least twice (Giovine V. Giovine, 1995).

ANALYSIS OF THE GIOVINE CASE

The Giovine case represents a major hallmark within the judicial system; since it creates a new cause of action for victims. The holding in the Giovine case appears to limit the victim's recovery for the abuser tortuous conduct. The court concluded that only a wife diagnosed with the BWS could sue her batterer and receive damages for physical and emotional injuries.

By requiring expert testimony to document the battered woman's syndrome, the court will hinder low-income victims from filing a tort lawsuit because of the lack of financial resources to do so (Atkins, 1999).

In order to recover based upon the holding of Giovine, a victim would have to submit evidence of complete helplessness and mental incapacitation and be medically diagnosed of suffering from battered women's syndrome.

The court filed to address some of the dangers that victims face when they attempt to assert or employ their legal pursuits. It is not unusual for a victim of domestic violence to file civil or criminal charges against her battered and then drop them before any legal action can be taken against the batterer. Some of the charges maybe dropped because of religious, economic, or social reasons; a victim may fear the batterer will retaliate against her, friends, or family members.

JUDICIAL INTERPRETATIONS OF THE BATTERED WOMEN'S SYNDROME CIVIL TORT REMEDY

The New Jersey Giovine judicial decision is a landmark or a case of first impression for the battered woman. The impact of the decision was to provide the domestic violent victim the legal vehicle to initiate a civil tort.

However, numerous states have adhered to the Giovine decision. The subsequent state judicial decisions rendered various interpretations regarding the establishment of a civil tort for victims of domestic violence.

IDAHO

The state of Idaho judiciary utilized the intentional infliction of emotional distress for victims of domestic violence. In Curtis v Firth, 850 p.2d. 749, 753-54 (Idaho, 1993): The court held that the tort of intentional infliction of emotional distress was a continuing tort in the context of domestic violence.

ILLINOIS

The supreme court of Illinois followed the New Jersey Giovine decision. In Feltmeier v. Feltmeier 207 ILL.2d263.; 798 N.E.2d.75; (2003): The supreme court of Illinois affirmed the lower court' rulings, stating that Mrs. Feltmeier did suffer from intentional infliction of emotional distress because Mr. Feltmeier's conduct was outrageous and had a high probability to cause emotional distress was severe. The supreme court of Illinois cited the Giovine case, stating that when the defendant has power over that person; and in the cases of a battered spouse, the injured party will remain in the abusive relationship because the abuser has exercised dominance over the victim for an extended duration. Also, the Illinois Supreme court that the issues of domestic violence should not be exempt from civil litigation.

LOUISIANA

The Louisiana court of Appeals interpreted the marital tort a continuous tort in the context of domestic violence. Moreover, the Laughlin v. Beard, 515 so.2d 480, 482-83, (La Ct. App. 1987): held that a continuous tort only applies when continuing conduct results in continuing damages.

NEW MEXICO

The New Mexico court of appeals sets a qualifying threshold for the marital tort for victims of domestic violence. In Hakkia v Hakkia, 812.p2d 135-26: (NM, Ct App. 1991): required a higher threshold of outrageousness in the marital context when one spouse sues the other for intentional infliction of emotional distress.

OREGON

The state of Oregon rejected the continuous tort theory as it applies to domestic violence matters. In Davis v. Bustick, 580p.2d.544,547-48,Cor. 1978): refuse to apply the continuous tort theory in the context of domestic violence.

TEXAS

The Texas judicial decisions articulated limited recovery of the intentional and negligent infliction of emotional distress. However, the court of appeals examined the cycle of violence concepts according to the continuing tort doctrine.

1. Twyman V. Twyman, 855 S.W.2d 619, 627, (Texas, 1993); limiting recovery of intentional infliction of emotional distress only upon proof that the defendant acted intentionally or with reckless disregard for the probability of inflicting severe emotional distress on the plaintiff.
2. Boyles V. Kerr, 855.S.W. 2d. 593, 594, (Tex. 1993), Refusing to adopt the tort of negligent infliction of emotional distress after a girlfriend sued her former boyfriend for video tapping them, having sexual intercourse, and showing the videotape to others.
3. Toles V. Toles 45.S.W. 8dd.252 (2001), The Appellate court of Texas held that Mr. Tole's action continued a cycle of violence according to the continuing tort doctrine, which gives the totality of all of the incident, considered together.

CONCLUSION

Some point out that domestic violence victims are injured twice: once by their batterer and then again by a sometimes hostile judicial system.

(Fort, 1993) This may not be the result of insensitivity. Some appellate courts appear to not recognize the importance of their decisions as they relate to domestic violence and continue to impede the victims in recovering judgments against their batterers by maintaining the historical aspects of the interpersonal immunity doctrine. Also the courts refused to toll the statute of limitations for traditional torts and required or encouraged joinder of all claims against the battered by prohibiting or barring any further claims through the doctrine of res judicata .

It has been argued that the present system of tort remedies is sufficient to provide legal redress for abused victims. However, the present law does not take into consideration regarding the complexities of and abusive relationship and the frequent roadblocks a victim will encounter if she attempts to depart from her batterer or assert her rights.

Moreover, New Jersey has made significant progress by creating the battered women's syndrome cause of action, but there are a few problems in the new tort. Nevertheless, the judiciary of other jurisdictions should follow New Jersey's lead and consider moving in the direction of creating said tort.

A proposed tort of partner abuse can potentially provide victims complete recovery for the abuse endured in a battering relationship. Although, this chapter only provides abuse tort that might appear to resemble elements of the Battered Women's Syndrome. Courts are more than equipped to articulate the guidelines of the law and dismiss frivolous claims and transform partner abuse into a cognizable course of action.

The judiciary maybe hesitant to foster this change in their jurisdictions, but Present treatment of tort law should create exceptions for domestic violence victims. Tort law needs to be tailored in a way to remind everyone that no one deserves to be treated with disrespect or abuse.

REFERENCES

Adams, David., (1989), *Identifying the Assaultive Husband in Court: You Be the Judge*, Boston B.J., July-Aug 23.

Atkins, Daniel G., (1991), *Striving For Justice with the Violence Against Women Act and Civil Tort Actions*, 14 Women's L.J. 69, 71.

Buel, Sarah M., (1999), Family Violence, *Texas Prosecutor*, Mar-April.

Cole, Constance Ward., (1984), Intentional Infliction of Emotional Distress Among Family Members, 61 *Den U.L. Rev*. 553.

Ducate, Richard., (1998), The Things I Wish Family Court Judges Know About Domestic Violence, *Family Law Commentator*.

Gosselin, Denise K., (2003), *Heavy Hands*, 2nd Ed. Prentice Hall.

Hart, Barbara. (1990), Assessing Whether Batterers Will Kill, in Confronting Domestic Violence: Effective Police Response 1, 2, CPA Coalition Against Domestic Violence ed., (1990) *Separation Violence- Police Response*.

Horman, Dave and Rebecca Thatcher., (1998), Najera Must Pay $8 Million in Divorce *Colo Law*, Oct.

Jerry, Edwin J. and Kristin K. Proctor., (1993), Infliction of Emotional Distress in the Middle Ground., 27 *Tex Trial Law*. F.5

Johnson, Hillary., (1955), The Truth About White Collar Domestic Violence, *Working Women*, Mar.

Lebowitz, Jill., (1996), Pursuit of Tort Claims For Domestic Violence in New Jersey, 17 *Women's Rights L*. Rep. 259.

Meadows, Robert J., (2004). *Understanding Violence and Victimization*, Prentice Hall 3rd.

McDevitt, Jack and Judith M. Sgarzi, (2003), *Victimology*, Prentice Hall.

Schafran, Lynn H., (1995), There's No Accounting For Judges, 58 *Albany L. Rev*. 1063.

Sutchell, James C., (1993), Tradition, Distortion and Creation: Three Approaches to "Battered Women's Syndrome in Tort," 8 *Regent U.L. Rev*. 83.

Tate, Julie Bliskey., (1995), "I Was Raped and Sued." *Ladies Home Journal*.

Tonsing, Heather., (2001), Battered Women Syndrome as a Tort Cause of Action, 12 *J.L. and Health*, 407.

Walker, Lenore., (1979), *The Battered Woman*, Harper and Row.

Rashmi Mishra and Sujata Biswal

23

VICTIMS OF DOMESTIC VIOLENCE: A STUDY FROM HUMAN RIGHTS PERSPECTIVE

INTRODUCTION

All human beings are born free and equal in dignity and rights. The prevalent gender based violence, sexual harassment and exploitation against women are offensive to human dignity and human rights. The need for protection of rights of women gained global recognition during the international decade of women (1975-85) and has steadily gained momentum since then. This recognition became International Law in 1979 when the UN General Assembly adopted the Convention on the Elimination of All Forms of Discrimination Against Women (CEDAW). During the year 1993, India joined other countries of the world and ratified CEDAW and committed itself to work for elimination of all types of discriminations, which place women at disadvantage.

The United Nations Declarations of the Elimination of Violence against Women, adopted by the General Assembly in 1993, defines violence against women as 'any act of gender-based violence that results in, or likely to result in physical, sexual or mental harm of suffering to women, including threats of such act, coercion, or arbitrary deprivation of liberty, whether occurring in public or in private life'. The Declaration states that violence against women encompasses but is not limited to the following:

(a) Physical, sexual and psychological violence occurring in the family, including battering, sexual abuse of female children in the household, dowry-related violence, marital rape, female genital mutilation and other traditional practices harmful to women, non-spousal violence and violence related to exploitation;

(b) Physical, sexual and psychological violence occurring within the general community, including rape, sexual abuse, sexual harassment and intimidation at work, in educational institutions and elsewhere, trafficking in women and forced prostitution;

(c) Physical, sexual and psychological violence perpetrated or condoned by the State, wherever it occurs.

Violence against women can take several forms including domestic violence, intimate partner violence, sexual assault and abuse, rape, incest, and elder abuse. Violence includes both actual and threatened violent acts of physical, psychological, or sexual in nature directed against women. Domestic violence is any form of physical, sexual or emotional abuse, which takes place within the context of a close relationship. In most cases, the relationship is between partners and also the victims and more likely to female partners. When woman is being physically or sexually associated by someone she lives with, or is being threatened by them that is domestic violence. It is the controlling behaviour which includes all kinds of physical, sexual and emotional abuse within all kinds of intimate relationships. Domestic violence against women is increasingly being recognized as a violation of their human rights and a serious deterrent to development as evident in the Vienna accord of 1993 and the Beijing platform of 1995.

DOMESTIC VIOLENCE: A HUMAN RIGHTS PROBLEM

It is realized that men beat up women because of their own insecurity. They perceive themselves as inferior in some way to women and so to prove their security by hitting them. Domestic violence is perhaps the most understated of all crimes. Domestic violence as a global problem was brought out in through a UN report published on November 30, 1989. For the first time ever, violence against women within the home became an officially acknowledged part of UN agenda. Jane Connors, law lecturer at London's school of Oriental and African studies who authored the UN report said "It is a popular misconception that the home is a place of safety, violence against women in the street does occur, but the more like place for it to happen is in the home. The person most likely to perpetrate the assaults is the husband".

Domestic violence against women both violates and impairs or nullifies the enjoyments by women of their human rights and fundamental freedoms. The long standing failure to protect and promote those rights of freedoms in the case of domestic violence against women is a matter of concern to all states and should be addressed effectively. Recognizing that domestic violence against women is a manifestation of historically unequal power relations between men and women, which have led to domination over and discrimination against women by men and to the prevention of the full advancement of women, and that violence against women is one of the crucial social mechanisms by which women are forced into a subordinate position compared to men.

Women can experience physical or mental abuse throughout their life cycle, in infancy, childhood and adolescence, during adulthood or older age while violence has severe health consequences for the affected. It is a social problem that warrants an immediate co-ordinate response from different sectors.

DOMESTIC VIOLENCE AGAINST MAIDSERVANTS

Women workers are employed in the organized as well as the unorganized sectors of the economy. A high proportion of workingwomen in India are employed in the unorganized sector. They are the most vulnerable section of the Indian economy. They substantially belong to economically weaker sections of the society in highly hazardous and arduous occupations as agricultural labourers, construction workers, maidservants and informal labouers without any advantage of social security and other privileges. They work and live under subdued conditions with family and children, devoid of proper living and working conditions, equal wages, but receiving humiliating treatment.

Maidservants have become an integral part of middle and upper class society. These servants are often, an exploited class and are forced to under take this manual work, as they are not fit for other occupations. Their wages are comparatively low, service condition far from being ideal and they are at the mercy of their employers. Their social status is low and little or no prospect of advancement.

The affluent sections of people in the society have a plethora of need, but they do not have sufficient manpower to satisfy these needs. They employ maidservants to maximize the comforts and to maintain dignity and prestige and also as a status symbol. Employed women, who have settled in the organised sectors and other fields, are required to fulfill the role expectations as a housewife along with the duties as employees outside. In this situation the employed housewife requires some help in household chores to lessen her burden because her work role invariably encroaches on her time and energy, approximately allocated to the housewife's role. One of the ways of lessening her burden in the house is to employ maidservants. These factors have contributed to the galloping demand for housemaids.

Though women were working as maidservants from time immemorial, in the past they were a few working in the houses of the rich and rulers. The twentieth century has witnessed a rapid development of the middle class, accompanied with the education and employment of women. The women domestic servants are mostly engaged in household activities like scrubbing utensils, washing clothes, sweeping the house, mopping the floor, assisting the employer in the kitchen and going to the market.

The maidservants work under trying conditions. Their standard of living, their problems, aspirations, their relationships with their family members are some of the areas those are to be probed for their upliftment. Most of them are uneducated, poor family background and the life is often not very happy. Their husbands are sometimes unemployed or if employed spend their earnings on themselves. Many of these under privileged women do not have access to control over economic resources, which increases their vulnerability to violence. The crime scenario of the state of Orissa is distressing in respect of violence against women. Domestic violence against women has been rising alarmingly since 1991. In Orissa, violence against women viz. Dowry homicide, dowry suicide, dowry torture, bride burning and non-dowry torture are exhibiting an increasing trend in 1999 and 2000 (Mishra, 2001).

In India, research in the area of domestic violence has been restricted to violence against women, dowry related violence and wife battering (Devasahayam, Able and Jothimurthy, 1989; Devasia and Devasia, 1984; Devi Prasad, 1990; Devi Prasad and Vijayalakshmi, 1998; Lata, 1989; Mahajan, 1989 Samuel, 1998). A recent multi site household survey on domestic violence in India found that approximately 50 per cent of women had experienced at least one form of physical or psychological violence at least once in their lives (The Hindu, 2002).

When there are numerous studies on women working in different kinds of occupation. Very few research studies are available on domestic maids in the country. As they are less, they have not been widely published. No scientific and in-depth study on maidservants has so far been undertaken particularly in the context of domestic violence against women.

In the light of these considerations that the present study focuses on domestic violence against women in unorganized sector, particularly on maidservants with the following objectives:

(i) To identify different types of domestic violence against maidservants.
(ii) To find out different causes responsible for domestic violence against maidservants.
(iii) To suggest ways and means for preventing/ reducing domestic violence against women and maidservants in particular.

METHODOLOGY

The empirical study has been designed to study domestic violence against maidservants, which has reflected the seriousness of the problem in the society. Owing to the fact that domestic service is an unorganized activity, the servants are not geographically bound to any particular area in terms of their employment or residence. In the present study the sample is confined to 50 maidservants (married) employed in different residences from the capital city of Bhubaneswar, Orissa, India by following purposive sampling method.

Statistics on domestic violence tend to be understated often because victims do not incidents or are reluctant to mention them to survey interviewers. In the present study, rapport has been established with the respondents from the very beginning. They were assured that the information provided by them will be kept confidential. Accurate and comparable data on violence against women have been recorded to strengthen advocacy effort, policy matters to understand the problem and to guide the design of preventive interventions.

A questionnaire pertaining to socio-economic background information has been administered among the respondents. It also consists of four broad areas of domestic violence viz. physical (including sexual violence), verbal violence, social and emotional violence and causes responsible for their occurrence. Each of the areas consisted of items contributing to those aspects of violence like physical violence includes 14 items, verbal violence with 2 items, social violence having 6 items and emotional violence containing 4 items.

The severity of violence was measured using the following key:

(a) Any means not adopted is considered as never or no violence.
(b) Any of the means adopted once or twice in a month constituted mild degree of violence.
(c) Any of the means adopted once or twice in two weeks constituted moderate degree of violence
(d) Any of the means adopted every day constituted a severe degree of violence.

After the collection of field data, processing has been done to put these data into some definite forms. Data have been processed and analyzed by using appropriate statistical tools and techniques.

RESULTS AND DISCUSSION

Domestic violence against women has become so very normal in home everywhere in the world that those who suffer violence accept it as the way of life. It was only in 1983 that legislation was passed by the Indian Parliament, which took cognizance of the 'cruelty' that led to un-natural deaths of large numbers of women. Section 498A provided opportunities to women of publicly stating that they were treated with cruelty within four walls of their homes. This catapulted a very private sphere into public arena.

Domestic violence can take a number of forms such as physical assault, sexual abuse and rape, threats and intimidation, which are criminal offences. In addition, it also includes destructive criticism, pressure tactics, and disrespect, breaking trust, isolation and harassment. There are four broad areas of domestic violence namely, physical violence (including sexual violence), verbal violence, social violence and emotional violence. Physical violence component refers to violence by the use of means such as beating, kicking, pushing and so on. Sexual violence refers to the use of means such as forced sex or the deprivation of sex or any act sexual in nature performed without consent or understanding. Verbal violence component refers to means such as the use of abusive language or threats that the family uses. Social violencc component refers to the demeaning or disrespectful acts shown to family members in social situations. Emotional violence component of violence refers to the intentional deprivation of love, affection, sympathy or care by family members.

Table 1
Types of Domestic Violence towards the Respondents

Sl. No.	*Types of Violence*	*Present F(%)*	*Not Present F(%)*	*Mild F(%)*	*Moderate F(%)*	*Severe F (%)*
1	*2*	*3*	*4*	*5*	*6*	*7*
Physical Violence						
1.	Pushing	29 (58.00)	21 (42.00)	0	3 (10.34)	26 (89.66)
2.	Slapping	13 (26.00)	37 (74.00)	0	4 (30.77)	9 (69.23)
3.	Punching	27 (54.00)	23 (46.00)	13 (48.15)	12 (44.44)	2 (7.41)
4.	Biting	23 (46.00)	27 (54.00)	12 (52.17)	8 (34.78)	3 (13.05)
5.	Pinching	16 (32.00)	34 (68.00)	8 (50.00)	5 (31.25)	3 (18.75)
6.	Throwing objects	28 (56.00)	22 (44.00)	4 (14.29)	14 (50.00)	10 (35.71)
7.	Kicking	23 (46.00)	22 (44.00)	3 (13.05)	8 (34.78)	12 (52.17)
8.	Hit with hard objects	13 (26.00)	37 (74.00)	2 (15.38)	4 (30.77)	7 (53.85)
9.	Choking	14 (28.00)	36 (72.00)	14 (100.00)	0 (2.00)	0 (2.00)
10.	Bleeding Injury	14 (28.00)	36 (72.00)	14 (100.00)	0	0
11.	Forced Sex	26 (52.00)	24 (48.00)	12 (46.15)	6 (23.08)	8 (30.77)
12.	Deprive of food	16 (32.00)	34 (68.00)	11 (68.75)	5 (31.25)	0

Contd....

Sl. No.	*Types of Violence*	*Present F(%)*	*Not Present F(%)*	*Mild F(%)*	*Moderate F(%)*	*Severe F (%)*
1	*2*	*3*	*4*	*5*	*6*	*7*
13.	Punish with Cigarette butts	10 (20.00)	40 (80.00)	10 (100.00)	0	0
14.	Pulling the hair	11 (22.00)	39 (78.00)	2 (18.18)	9 (81.82)	0
	Verbal Violence					
1.	Use of abusive and filthy language	26 (52.00)	24 (48.00)	8 (30.77)	10 (38.46)	8 (30.77)
2.	Verbal threats	16 (32.00)	34 (68.00)	5 (31.25)	7 (43.75)	4 (25.00)
	Social Violence					
1.	In public places	12 (24.00)	38 (76.00)	0	9 (75.00)	3 (25.00)
2.	In the Presence of Family Members	28 (56.00)	22 (44.00)	6 (21.43)	12 (42.86)	10 (35.71)
3.	In the Presence of Relatives	13 (26.00)	37 (74.00)	8 (61.54)	2 (15.38)	3 (23.08)
4.	In the Presence of Neighbours	10 (20.00)	40 (80.00)	0	6 (60.00)	4 (40.00)
5.	In the Presence of Friends	12 (24.00)	38 (76.00)	7 (58.33)	3 (25.00)	2 (16.67)
	Emotional Violence					
1.	Deprivation of love and affection	16 (32.00)	34 (68.00)	8 (50.00)	8 (50.00)	0
2.	Deprived of Appreciation	12 (24.00)	38 (76.00)	6 (50.00)	6 (50.00)	0
3.	Deprived of Care and Sympathy	13 (26.00)	37 (74.00)	0	9 (69.23)	4 (30.77)
4.	Deprived of sex	12 (24.00)	38 (76.00)	5 (41.67)	3 (25.00)	4 (33.33)

Note: Figures in the Parentheses Indicate Percentages.

Table 1 analyses different types of domestic violence against maidservants mainly by their husbands and in-laws.

PHYSICAL VIOLENCE

With regard to different types of violence, it was found that most of the respondents suffered from physical-violence compared to verbal, social and emotional violence. While analyzing physical violence, Table-I revealed that out of 14 dimensions of physical violence, pushing, throwing objects, punching and forced sex types of violence were more prominent compared to others. In this context of prominent types of violence, more than 50 per cent respondents reported mild to severe forms of violence.

By analyzing the severity of violence it was found that 89.66 per cent respondents suffered from severe form of pushing type of violence. It has highlighted the fact that most of the respondents suffered this type of violence every day. While 46 per cent reported violence in the form of biting and kicking, only 32 per cent respondents suffered from violence in the form of pinching and deprivation of food. 28 per cent reported physical violence in the forms of choking, bleeding injury and 26 per cent reported mild to severe form of violence to that of hit with hard objects and slapping. It was noteworthy to mention that most of the respondents suffered from the types of violence viz slapping, hit with hard objects and kicking every day.

VERBAL VIOLENCE

52 per cent of the respondents reported verbal violence in the form of use of abusive and filthy language from mild to severe forms. By analyzing the severity of violence it was also found that around 31 per cent suffered from severe form of that type of violence. Thirty two per cent respondents reported verbal violence in the form of verbal threats. Table-I revealed that most of the respondents suffered from the violence in the form of use of abusive and filthy language compared to verbal threats every day. While 16 per cent of the respondents reported verbal violence in the form of verbal threats, most of the respondents suffered from the former type of verbal violence compared to the later everyday.

SOCIAL VIOLENCE

In respect of social violence majority of the respondents (56 per cent) reported mild to severe forms in the category of "in the presence of family members". While 26 per cent reported in the presence of relatives, most of them reported it in the mild form. With regard to social violence in the form of violence in public places, in the presence of friends, 20 per cent respondents reported the occurrence of social violence in the presence of neighbours. By analysing the severity of social violence it was also found that majority of the respondents suffered it in the presence of neighbours and family members every day.

EMOTIONAL VIOLENCE

Deprivation of love and affection form of violence was reported by 32 per cent respondents from mild to moderate forms. While 26 per cent respondents reported that they were deprived of care and sympathy, most of them (69 per cent) suffered from moderate form of violence. It further highlighted the fact that 24 per cent reported emotional violence in the form of deprived of appreciation and deprivation of sex.

CAUSES OF DOMESTIC VIOLENCE

Violence against women within the family does not constitute an occasional, rare incident, but is a regular, systematic and structural manifestation of social control. The present study has been a systematic exploration of the problem. The primary purpose of the work was to explore the nature of domestic violence and the causes responsible for that violence.

Table 2
Causes of Domestic Violence Against the Respondents

Sl. No.	*Causes of violence*	*Frequency*	*Percentage*
1.	Dowry demands because of greed attitude of in-laws	17	34.00
2.	Dowry demands because of financial problem	23	46.00
3.	Alcohol, gambling and bad habits of causes demands of dowry	43	86.00
4.	Extra marital affairs and bio-gamy	15	30.00
5.	Adverse attitude of in-laws	17	34.00
6.	Continuous birth of female child	9	18.00
7.	Childlessness	3	6.00
8.	Husband mentally and physically handicap	14	28.00

It was evident from Table 2 that out of different causes of violence against respondents, 86 per cent reported that alcohol; gambling and bad habits of husbands were major causes of dowry demands. While 46 per cent of the respondents reported that dowry demands were causes because of financial problem, 34 per cent of the respondents reported the fact that dowry demands were because of greed and adverse attitude of in laws. While 30 per cent respondents reported that extra-marital affairs and bigamy caused violence, 28 per cent respondents viewed that it is because of their husbands were mentally and physically handicap. Eighteen per cent respondents reported that, continuous birth of female children, caused violence and only 6 per cent had reported childlessness was the main cause of violence against women.

It was revealed from the study that social condition, patriarchal structure of our society, dowry demands, drunkenness, immorality, cruelty, addition to drugs, sickness were the primary causes responsible for domestic violence against women. As most of the husbands were unemployed, sitting at home without a job, they imagine the wife insulting them looking down upon them because they were dependent upon her, they imagine her enjoying with other men at place of work. Unemployed men were found biting their wife on trivial domestic issues.

When the husbands demand money from the maidservants, conflict occurs and they become irritable. In such an emotional situation they beat their wives even if they give their earnings.

Many violence acts were also committed under the influence of alcohol or drugs. The use of alcohols in course of time caused a great and irresistible craving for it. The evil effects of alcohol result in heavy damage of the mind and the body and results in susceptibility to crimes. Excessive drinking results in starvation for the family members, assaults and quarrels between husband and wife, between father and child, desertion, beating cruelty etc.

The results obtained from the study illustrated that among the different types of domestic violence, certain types of violence appeared to be more frequently experienced that the others. It was found that the frequency of physical violence was much higher compared to other areas of violence viz. social violence, verbal violence and emotional violence. In most of the cases (86 per cent), the perpetrators of violence were alcoholic and gambler husbands.

Families represented in the study hail from the lower strata of society as evinced by low income averages, type of occupation held and educational background. Such families were also found with high degree of physical violence. It is compatible with the observation made by Bhatti, (1989). However, other categories of violence (social, verbal and emotional violence) in the form of mild to severe were also prevalent among the maidservants. It was revealed from the present study that in a large number of cases (90 per cent) suffered from severe form of pushing type of physical violence.

Two persons who contribute most to dowry torture, non-dowry torture are the victim's of husband and the mother-in-law. Thus brides living in households headed by dominant and authoritarian mothers-in-law and uncompromising and un-adjusting husbands have noticeably higher victimization rates. The wide range of abuse experienced by victims mainly came from their husbands and mother-in-laws.

All the components under different types of domestic violence are both exclusive as well as inclusive. The study illustrated that, in the presence of physical violence, the remaining forms of violence viz. social, verbal and emotional were also present and absent.

It was found that women in the age group of 25-35 years, who were often constrained by the presence of very young children, did not seem to come forward to report readily.

Most of the maidservants (95 per cent) do not even know that cruelty is a crime and there are laws that can protect them. Majority of the respondents were illiterate (80 per cent). A very few who were aware of such laws were not prepared to set them in motion to seek relief. They were convinced that their alcoholic husbands have nothing to give them; they were more of a liability, yet they wanted their association for social security and status.

CONCLUSION

Violence within the home constitutes, more often than not, a private affair because of the high value attached to family as an indisputably sacrosanct social institution. Clergy and secular counselors are often trained to see the goal of saving the marriage at all costs, rather than the goal of stopping the violence. They tend to motivate the woman to compromise even at the risk of her own interests in order to prevent family disruption and to protect the children. Since violence against women is a critical factor in the development paradigm of women, their communities and society at larger, it is important to create greater awareness on domestic violence among the public and relevant professionals. Awareness programmes should also be organised by the Human Rights Protection Cells, State Women Commission supported by social agencies as well as by non-government organizations.

The role of the police is crucial in case of domestic violence, particularly in investigation process, which includes the first information report. But police often do not support to women. They try to dissuade women from filling charges, do not intervene in domestic quarrels and do not consider wife beating a crime. The familiar fact of inordinate delays in disposing of cases is a deterrent to the victims. There should be special courts to handle these cases. This will help in the quick disposal of cases and reinstate the people's faith in judiciary.

The flexibility of judiciary as well as police system should be rectified through proper amendment, enactment and policy formation, so that the tortured and harassed women would get proper justice along with the punishment to the culprits. Women's organizations play a major constructive role in generating awareness and providing assistance to the victims. They should also be given locus standi to plead on behalf of the victim. They should be permitted to meet the victim in the rescue home so that they can offer the necessary help, guidance and reassurance.

Thus, the measures suggested for reducing violence against women are: (1) Legal literacy of women or creating awareness of rights through media, published literature and voluntary agencies (2) Judicial activism, *i.e.* given liberal and creative interpretation of law than literal or technical interpretation. (3) Constant monitoring of justice and to examine the impact of legislation. (4) Monitoring rescue homes. (5) Strengthening free legal aid societies. (6) Effective functioning of family courts and family counseling services.

Above all there is a need to reform the images of women that have been created over centuries by history, mythology and social customs. Women must be considered as individuals who are equal to men in their own rights. Parents should not impose crippling restrictions on their daughters, which prevent them from thinking and acting independently. The legislators must treat women as participants and not merely as recipients. Women also have to be assertive and develop a self-identity so that they can lead a life of security and dignity.

REFERENCES

Bhatti, R.S. (1989), Socio-Cultural Dynamics of Wife Battering. In: S.Sood (Ed.), *Violence Against Women*, Jaipur: Arihant Publishers, pp 45-56.

Devashayam, M. Abel, R and Jothimurthy, S. (1989), Violence Against Women: An Opinion Survey Among Village Women in K.V. Kuppam Block. In: Unit for Family Studies (ed) *Research on families with problems in India* (volume 2), Bombay: Tata Institute of Social Sciences PP 526-529.

Devasia, V.V. and Devasia, L. (1984), Victim Offender Relationship in Female Homicide by Male: A study conducted in Maharashtra. *The Indian Journal of Social Work*, 45 (3) PP 317-323.

Devi Prasad, B. (1990), Dowry Related Violence Towards Women: A Sociological Perspective. In: S. Sood (Ed) *Violence Against Women*, Jaipur: Arihant Publishers, 293-310.

Devi Prasad, B. Vijayalakshmi, B. (1998), Dowry related Violence towards women: Some Issues. *The Indian Journal of Social Work*, 49 (3) 271-280.

Lata P.M. (1989), Violence within the Family: Experience of a Feminist Support Group. In: S. Sood (Ed), *Violence, Against Women*, Jaipur: Arihant Publications, 223-236.

Mahajan, A. (1989), Instigators of Wife Battering. In: S. Sood (Ed.) *Violence Against Women.* Jaipur: Arihant Publisher, 119-127.

Mishra, R. (2001), *Violation of Human Rights: A study on Violence Against Women in Orissa.* Paper presented in the seminar on Human Rights and Women's Empowerment' Organised by Utkal University, Bhubaneswar, Orissa.

Samuel. A.S. (1998), *A study of factors related to be or not to be an Abusive Conjugal System*, Unpublished M. Phil Dissertation, Bangalore: NIMHANS.

The Hindu (2002), *Legislation: Intimate enemy*, Sunday, 4th August, P4.

World Health Organisation (1997), *Violence Against Women in Families.* Geneva: WHO.

KUSA KUMAR SHAHA

24

ALLEGED DOWRY DEATH: A MEDICO LEGAL EVALUATION

INTRODUCTION

Alleged Dowry Deaths are frequent occurrence in India. The investigation of such a case is very difficult mainly because of complex situation such as the false counter allegations from complaints and accused parties. Such cases need thorough investigation for launching the prosecution. Therefore it is imperative to study the prevalence of Dowry Death. In order to check and prevent such occurrences Sec 304B, 498A IPC have been introduced and 174 & 176 Cr PC have been modified but still the occurrences are increasing day by day. In the present study an attempt is made to analyze the data statistically collected on such cases, highlighting the various aspects in order to let the legal system and medico – legalist take necessary action in preventing this social evil and discriminated the true case from false fabricated ones.

MATERIALS AND METHODS

Between Jan. 1998 and Dec. 2002, 152 cases of Alleged Dowry Death were autopsied, amounting to about 32.7% of all the female autopsied cases received in the mortuary of the M.K.C.G. Medical College & Hospital Berhampur (Orissa) during the same period. Detailed analysis of the cases was based on the medical records and evaluation of autopsied reports and was as per the criteria laid down in Sec 304 B IPC, Sec 498(A) IPC and Sec 113A & B of IEA.

Sec 304 B IPC: Where the death of a women is caused by burns or body injury or occurs otherwise than under normal circumstances within seven years of her marriage and it is also shown that before her death she was subjected to cruelty or harassment by her husband or any relatives of husband for securing any properties or valuable security from her or her relatives, such deaths shall be called 'dowry death'. Who ever commits dowry deaths shall be punished with imprisonment for a term which shall not be less than 7 years but which may extend to imprisonment for life.

Sec 498(A) IPC: Who ever being the husband or relatives of husband of a woman subjects such woman to cruelty shall be punished with imprisonment for a term which may extend to three years and will be liable to fine.

113(A) IEA Presumption as to abatement of suicide by a married woman.

113(B) IEA Presumption as to 'Dowry Death' if that death caused within 7 years of marriage.

OBSERVATION

During the period of five years 2441 postmortem examinations were conducted out of which 465 were females. Among the females 152 cases had first hand allegation of Alleged Dowry Death who were all-Hindu and were isolated for the study Table 2. All the 152 cases so selected were subdivided according to their cause and manner of death on the basis of first hand history and police report. 12 cases were alleged to be accidental in nature. In conducting the postmortem examination and subsequent follow up & investigation the postmortem findings were consistent with the history given by the police in 11 cases. But in one case (accidental Burn) the burn was found to be postmortem in nature and the cause of death was detected as manual strangulation. This was subsequently confirmed by further police investigation.

95 cases having alleged suicidal history were investigated. In 93 cases, the postmortem findings were consistent with the history and inquest report but 2 cases of hanging were found to be postmortem origin and death was due to manual strangulation which was subsequently confirmed by further police investigation and follow up.

On reviewing the postmortem findings of all 152 cases of Alleged Dowry Death and subsequent follow up, 11 cases were established as accidental death and 4 cases were due to some disease process. These 15 cases (11+4) were dropped from further studies when it was confirmed that the death were by no means related to dowry. Remaining 137 cases were isolated as study material.

DISCUSSION

On analysis the Table 1, it was derived that the male to female ratio of unnatural deaths was found to be 4.2:1. It is because in the locality less attention has been given to education & economically independence of females. Most of the women are engaged in house hold works. Large proportions of unnatural deaths among the females were due to Alleged Dowry Death comprising 137. It indicates that dowry related deaths has not spared this locality and is almost at par with the incidence observed in other areas of the country. Careful postmortem examination and sincere investigation have its own reward in ascertaining the truth. There is a chance that the so-called eyewitness can speak false hood, but the dead will never speak lie.

Table 1
Incidence of Alleged Dowry Death

Year	*Total No*	*Male*	*Female*	*ADD*	*%(ADD)*
1998	466	383	83	27	32.5
1999	476	385	91	33	36.3
2000	503	402	101	31	30.7
2001	495	403	92	32	34.8
2002	501	403	98	29	29.6
Total	2441	1976	465	152	32.7

ADD - Alleged Dowry Death

Out of 137 cases of alleged dowry deaths 93 cases were suicidal and 44 cases were homicidal Table 2. Hanging (59.1%) was the commonest method of suicide and burn (72.7%) was the commonest cause of homicide (Table 3A). The maximum number of dowry deaths occurred between age 18 – 22years (62%) followed by 23 – 26years (33.6%) and gradually decreasing as age advances (Table 3B). Commonest method of death was hanging (50.6%) in the age group of 18 – 22 years where as burning (58.7%) in 23 – 26years (Table 4A). 113

cases (82.5%) were from rural areas while 24 cases (17.5%) were from urban areas. Both suicide (83.9%) and homicide (79.5%) occurs more in rural areas as compared to urban area (Table 3C). Hanging (42.5%) is the commonest method of death in rural areas where as Burn (58.3%) appears to be the major method in urban areas (Table 4B).

Table 2
Nature of Deaths in Alleged Dowry Death Victims

	Methods Adopted	*Suicide*	*Homicide*	*Accidental*	*Natural Disease*	*Total*
First hand history And Police Report	Hanging	57	00	00	00	57
	Burn	20	32	07	00	59
	Poison	18	05	00	00	23
	Strangulation	00	04	00	00	04
	Drowning	00	00	04	00	04
	Fall from Height	00	00	04	00	01
	Acute Appendicitis	00	00	01	02	02
	Acute Pneumonitis	00	00	00	02	02
	Total	95	41	12	04	152
After Post-Mortem Examination	Hanging	55	00	00	00	55
	Burn	20	32	06	00	58
	Poison	18	05	00	00	23
	Strangulation	00	07	00	00	07
	Drowning	00	00	04	00	04
	Fall from height	00	00	01	00	01
	Acute appendicitis	00	00	00	02	02
	Acute Pneumonitis	00	00	00	02	02
	Total	93	44	11	04	152

Most of the dowry deaths in this study occurred in joint family i.e. 126 cases (91.8%) in comparison to the nuclear family *i.e.* in 11 cases (8.2%) (Table 3D). It is apparent that hanging (38.9%) was the most common method of death followed by burn (37.3%). Where as strangulation was observed only in joint family (Table 4D). Dowry torture inflicted by the in laws was more unbearable in comparison to the tortures inflicted by the husband alone. 116 cases (84.7%) belong to low socio economic status where as 21 cases (15.3%) belong to middle socio economic status, both suicide and homicide occurs more frequently in LSES (Table 3E). The social consistency reveals that female of this area mostly staying indoors as housewife, were commonly victim of both suicidal and homicidal assault. They adopt hanging and burn as a common practice due to easy availability of materials and combustible substances in the house. Majority of the victims of LSES adopt hanging (45.7%) as a common method of death followed by burn (35.3%). Where as burn (52.4%) followed by poison (38%) was adopted as a method in MSES (Table 4D).

Table 3
Manner of Death

A	*Intentional*	*Suicide (93)*	*%*	*Homicide (44)*	*%*	*Total (137)*	*%*
	Hanging	55	59.1	00		55	40.1
	Burn	20		32	72.7	52	37.9
	Poison	18		05		23	16.8
	Strangulation	00		07		07	5.2
B	*Age wise*						
	<18	00	00		00		
	18-22	65	69.9	20	45.4	85	62
	23-26	23	24.7	23	52.3	46	33.6
	27-30	05		01		06	
	>30	00		00		00	
C	*Area*						
	Rural	78	83.9	35	79.5	113	82.5
	Urban	15	16.1	09	20.5	24	17.5
D	*Family*						
	Joint	82	88.2	44	100	126	91.8
	Nuclear	11		00		11	8.2
E	*S.E.Status*						
	LSES	79	84.9	37	84	116	84.7
	MSES	14		07		21	15.3
	HSES	00		00			
F	*Education*						
	Illiterate	47	50.5	30	68.2	77	56.2
	Under	30	32.2	03		33	24
	Graduate	07		09		16	
	Matric	09		02		11	
	Graduate						
G	*Place*						
	In-Laws	85	91.4	44	100	129	94.2
	Parental	08		00		08	5.8

Contd.

A	*Intentional*	*Suicide (93)*	*%*	*Homicide (44)*	*%*	*Total (137)*	*%*
H	*Duration of Marriage*						
	<1 year	23	24.7	22	50	45	32.8
	1-2 year	31	33.3	05		36	26.3
	2-3 year	15		00		15	26.3
	3-4 year	11		05		16	
	4-5 year	08		05		13	
	5-6 year	05		02		07	
	6-7 year	00		05		05	
I	*Time of day*						
	Morning	43	46.2	15	34.1	58	42.3
	Mid-day	03		13	29.5	16	
	Evening	35	37.6	06		41	29.9
	Night	12		00		22	

Most of the cases (56.2%) occur among illiterate and uneducated class and number decreases with higher education. Due to lack of education and unawareness of the law regarding the women's right and privileges they have no other option left before them except succumbing to dowry torture and death. Homicide (68.2%) is found more common than suicide (50.8%) in illiterate group (Table 3F). 129 cases (94.2%) occurred in laws/husband house and 8 cases (5.8%) occurred in potential house of victim. No case of homicide had occurred in parental house (Table 3G). Both suicide and homicide cases occurred in in-laws / husband house and rarely some suicide cases were found in parental house. Number of cases of hanging in in-laws/husband house was 53 (41%) and burn was 52 (40.3%) but not a single case of burn and strangulation was found in parental house (Table 4F).

Table 4
Methods Adopted

(A) Age	*Hanging (55)*	*%*	*Burning (52)*	*%*	*Poison (23)*	*%*	*Strangu-lation (07)*	*%*	*Total*
<18	00		00		00		00		00
18-22	43	50.6	22		15		05		85
23-26	10		27	58.7	07		02		46
27-30	02		03		01		00		06

Contd.

(A) Age	*Hanging (55)*	%	*Burning (52)*	%	*Poison (23)*	%	*Strangulation (07)*	%	*Total*
(B) Area									
Rural	48	42.5	38	33.6	20		07		113
Urban	07		14	58.3	03		00		024
(C) Family									
Joint	49	38.9	47	37.3	23		07	5.5	126
Nuclear	06		05		00		00		011
(D) S.E.Status									
LSES	53	45.7	41	35.3	15		07		116
MSES	12		11	52.4	08	38	00		021
HSES	00		00		00		00		000
(E) Education									
Illiterate	28	36.4	28	36.4	14		07		77
Under matric	20	60.6	08	24.2	05		00		33
Matric	02		11		03		00		16
Graduate	05		05		01		00		11
(F) Place									
In-Laws	53	41	52	40.3	17		07		129
Parental	02		00		06	75	00		008
(G) Duration of Marriage									
<1 year	14	31.1	21	46.7	05		05		45
1-2 year	17	47.2	12	33.3	05		02		36
2-3 year	05		02		08		00		15
3-4 year	07		06		03		00		16
4-5 year	07		06		00		00		13
5-6 year	05		02		00		00		07
6-7 year	00		03		02		00		05
(H) Time of Day									
Morning	31	53.4	18	31	03		06		58
Mid-Day	00		15	93.7	01		00		16
Evening	17	41.5	10		14	34.1	00		41
Night	07		09		05		01		22

Maximum incidence of death occurred during the first 2 years of marriage out of which (32.8%) had occurred with in 1st year of marriage and (26.3%) between 1–2years of marriage. Tendency to commit suicide (33.3%) was at peak between 1–2 years of marriage (Table 3H) and the method was mostly hanging (47.2%) followed by burn

(33.3%) (Table 4G). On the contrary homicide occurs during the 1st year of marriage and the method of death was mostly burn (46.7%) followed by Hanging (31.1%) (Table 4G). The possibility of such occurrence even after 6 – 7 years of marriage cannot be ruled out. The peak time period for suicide death was (46.2%) between 6am – 12 noon followed by (37.6%) between 6pm – 12 night where the cause of death was hanging. For homicide the peak time period was 6am – 12 noon (34.1%) followed by 12 noon to 6pm (29.5%) where the cause of death was burn (Table 3 I & 4 H).

CONCLUSION

The routine activity and rational approaches should direct attention to a variety of measures, such as creating neighborhood watch programs, informant hot lines to report suspected violence against brides and easier access to shelters for battered wives. In the longer term, a public health approach to the problem of dowry death should consider possibilities for restricting access to the lethal agents such as insecticides. Finally bride, families need to be educated about sign of abuse, the dangers of using marriage brokers and the risk of sending their daughters away to distant families whom they barely know. Reinforcement of cultural value of non-violence, educating women about their rights and strengthening family ties would help in this cause. Also strengthening the government's efforts to prohibit the practice of dowry payments will further improve the existing evil. Unfortunately but realistically, we must concede that – Alleged Dowry Death has always been and always be with us. The most energetic efforts of law enforcement authorities will never eliminate dowry related death. However, let us at least try to decrease its toll.

Sohini Basu

25

SEXUAL HARASSMENT IN INDIA: A THEORETICAL FRAMEWORK

INTRODUCTION

Violence against women is universal, cutting across regions, religions, ethnicities, economic positions and educational standards. Sexual violence is one of the three most important aspects of abuse of women, the other two being physical and psychological, though they often crisscross each other. But research on sexual abuse in the West where gender studies have begun much earlier than in the East, is still to go a long way, while it is in its infancy in the Third World countries.

Sexual violence implies some kind of direct sexual assault like rape, forcible molestation, excessive sexual demand from unwilling partner and the like. But sexual harassment is objectively less direct and severe and implies more indirect suggestions and approaches in behaviour involving oral, physical and psychological gestures like teasing and taunting remarks, embarrassing jokes and vulgar humour, lewd gestures and unwelcome flirting, display of pornographic materials and sexual exposures, unwanted invitations and sexual favours, and touching like patting, stroking, fondling, hugging, only sometimes upping to sexual assault including attempted or actual rape. We are concerned here with sexual harassment at workplace.

Here we should remember the culture-specific factors. *è.g.* in developed industrial countries large numbers of women have been joining the workforce for many decades, resulting in emergent patterns of sexual harassment at places of work and researches thereon, while in a country like India, women have started joining offices and factories in good numbers rather recently and the phenomenon and study of sexual harassment are comparatively new. Again, maids helping in household chores, whole time as well as part-time, are very common in urban and semi-urban areas of our country and they sometimes become victims of sexual harassment by the adult male members of the households. This is rarely seen in developed countries in recent times because such maids are very small in numbers and work for a very limited time in households, though sexual exploitation was quite rampant in the days when slaves worked in households or in the colonial days in our country when the rich *Sahibs* maintained a good workforce in their households.

In Western countries research on sexual harassment at the workplace was restricted to just prevalence of this type of violence even 20 years ago, though absolutely reliable database is yet to be authenticated. Commenting on the lack of information about sexual harassment, MacKinnon laments, 'Even social scientists didn't study it, and they studied everything that moves' (1987: 106). Again, as Welsh (1999) points out, depending on the samples used, 16% to 90% of US working women were found to experience sexual harassment in their lifetime (E.g. Brooks and Perot, 1991; Gutek, 1985; Terpstra and Baker, 1989; US MSBP, 1981). In Canada, surveys using random samples of the general population find that lifetime sexual harassment rates for women vary from 23% (Welsh and Nierobisz, 1997) to 51% (Gruber, 1997). These variations highlight the major problems confronting the empirical study of sexual harassment that is related to survey measurement issues. Naturally, the problem is much greater in our country where techniques of analysis have not advanced very much for societal reasons and for developing nature of the country. During the last decades, however, there have been a good number of more sophisticated and theoretical studies in the developed countries on the nature, measures, causes and consequences of sexual harassment at workplaces (Welsh, 1999). However, one important point not adequately touched by Western scholars is the culture or country specificity of the problem. The author's endeavour, here, is to try to develop a theoretical framework of such a study in a country like India.

NATURE AND LEGALITY OF SEXUAL HARASSMENT

Though some readymade definitions may be forwarded in answering the basic question" what is sexual violence at workplace?" ; the apparent differences between the objective findings and subjective perceptions of the abused have to be resolved or either of them has to be accepted as the basis of the study. Whether or not the alleged sexual conduct or behaviour constitutes sexual harassment must be determined, according to US and Canadian courts and tribunals, by an objective test (Aggarwal, 1992). For an objective test, they have used the standard of a 'reasonable person' rather than the perception of a harassed or a harasser. Moreover, the behaviour in question should be examined and tested against the norm of 'socially acceptable conduct' in the community. Here the difficulty in finding out the prevalence of sexual harassment objectively at workplace is much more in a developing country like India than in a developed country and, more importantly, the perception and proneness to report of a more shy and tradition bound and less outspoken abused in India may differ from that of one, say, in the USA or Canada where, permissiveness in sex-related activities seem to be wider than in our country.

On the other hand, since harassment, according to many, is basically a matter of feeling, one may agree with Aggarwal that 'sexual behaviour that a person finds personally offensive may be considered sexual harassment' (1992:7). However, Aggarwal (1992) himself admits that because of the complexity of human behaviour it is difficult to pinpoint what exact behaviour any particular individual will perceive as harassment. To one person an arm around the shoulder may be perceived as a gesture of affection, while to another person the same gesture may be offensive or harassing.

But here we must not only take into account the personal differences but also cultural differences. Though it is often difficult to draw the line between what is 'acceptable' and what 'unacceptable' behaviour in the workplace is, we must try to standardize the normal area of acceptability in the light of broad socio-cultural background of a country as far as possible. Again, an offended person may not report or express her feeling of harassment, which is of special consideration in our country. That is why good qualitative studies are necessary to corroborate some objective findings by properly interviewing supposed victims to bring into light their offended feelings. This has recently started in industrialised countries. E.g. the Sexual Experience Questionnaire (SEQ) was used by Fitzgerald et al. (1988) to assess the experience of sexual harassment of women in the workplace. The items in the SEQ are again grouped into three types of sexual harassment: Gender Harassment (GH), Unwanted Sexual Attention (USA) and Sexual Coercion (SC). But this is yet to start properly in our country.

Raymond (2003) rightly points out that in India, studies find that sexual harassment is still endemic, often hidden and present in all organisations, but it is still not viewed as a grave problem though it touches lives of nearly 40% to 60% of working women. Again, in India it has been only 7 years since sexual harassment was first recognized by the judiciary as human rights violation and gender-based systemic discrimination that affect women and their livelihood. According to the Supreme Court of India, sexual harassment is any unwelcome sexual behaviour such as physical contact, a demand or request for sexual favours, sexually coloured remarks, showing pornography and any other physical, verbal or non-verbal conduct of a sexual nature.

The Supreme Court of India has also given mandatory guidelines for prevention of sexual harassment enjoining employers by holding them responsible for providing congenial environment for women. But 'the issue still remains under carpets'. Very important for India's socio-cultural context is the fact that the said guidelines apply to both organised and unorganised work sectors and to all women working part-time, on contract basis or in voluntary capacity because in our country, unlike in developed countries, women working in the organised sector constitute only 17% of the total female workforce (Nath and Rustagi, 2003)[1].

In this connection one must refer to the draft bill of 2004 on sexual harassment of women at workplace, an improved version of the draft bill of 2003, which is yet to be passed as an Act. Article 2(o) of The Sexual Harassment Of Women At The Workplace (Prevention And Redressal) Bill 2004 defines sexual harassment as 'any unwelcome sexually determined conduct whether physical, verbal or non-verbal, including but not limited to, sexual advances, demands or requests for sexual favours, molestation, sexually nuanced gestures, comments, remarks or jokes either verbal, textual, graphic or electronic' (2004:4)[2]. This definition is more comprehensive than that given by the Supreme Court, apart from being enumerative rather than exhaustive.

More important is Article 2(p), which lists 15 enumerative and not exhaustive items under workplace including not only factory/mine, agricultural farm, construction site, shop, office, banking/financial institution, hotel/restaurant, hospital/nursing home, court/police station etc. but also house/dwelling place, street, any form of transportation and any public place. The latter four are important in India's socio-cultural context because sexual harassment is widely seen in our country in households, crowded buses or trains, fairs or socio-religious assemblages and on roads.

Sexual harassment is viewed often behaviourally-psychologically, legally as well as economically. Canada Labour Code 1985 defines sexual harassment as: *Any conduct, comment, gesture or contact of a sexual nature that is either likely to cause offence or humiliation to any employee, or that might, on reasonable grounds, be perceived by that employee as placing a condition of a sexual nature on employment or on any opportunity for training and promotion*[3].

This definition, given from the point of view of labour law, takes into consideration the psychological aspect of undesirable behaviour on the part of the abuser as well as the feeling of humiliation on the part of the abused, and the employment-related economic aspect. Such a definition based on identifiable descriptions divides sexually related behaviour in two categories – sexual annoyance and sexual coercion (Waks and Starr, 1982). The former implies sexually related conduct that is hostile, intimidating or offensive to the employee, which, though not directly linked to any benefit or harm, often creates a bothersome work environment. The latter, on the other hand, is sexual harassment directly resulting in some tangible job gain or loss.

The US Equal Employment Opportunity Commission (EEOC) laid down the guidelines on sexual harassment in 1980. The guidelines define sexual harassment as 'unwelcome sexual advances, requests for sexual favours, and other verbal or physical conduct of a sexual nature' and set out the following three criteria for determining whether an action constitutes unlawful sexual behaviour: *'when submission to the conduct is either an explicit or implicit term or condition of employment; when submission to or rejection of such conduct by an individual is used as the basis for employment decisions affecting such individual; or when such conduct has the purpose or effect of unreasonably interfering with an individual's work performance or creating an intimidating, hostile or offensive working environment'.*

Aggarwal (1992) rightly points out that Human Rights Tribunals in USA and Canada, in initial cases, held that it had become almost essential to establish that resistance by the victims to sexual overtures led to specific adverse job-related consequences, such as dismissal, suspension or shift change, i.e. *quid pro quo*. Thereafter the tribunals also recognized that sexual harassment is also linked to hostile and offensive work environment. Thus 'quid pro quo' and 'hostile and offensive working environment' came to denote two types or implications of sexual harassment. In the context of legal position taken by the Indian judiciary also Raymond (2003) observes that sexual harassment at workplace is generally classified into two distinct types. 'Quid pro quo' means sexual favours or advances in exchange for work benefits and it occurs when consent to sexual behaviour is made a condition for employment or refusal to comply with such a request is met with retaliatory action such as dismissal, demotion and difficult work conditions. 'Hostile work environment' is a pervasive form of sexual harassment involving work conditions or behaviour that make the working atmosphere 'hostile' for the woman to be in.

However, two points are to be noted in this connection. First, 'quid pro quo' and 'conditions of work' like humiliating and offensive work environment are not entirely exclusive to each other. Actually, hostile and offensive work environment is created or becomes aggravated when the harasser punishes the victim who resists sexual advances with job-related reprisals (McPherson vs. Mary's Donuts, 1982)[4]. Secondly, and definitely more important for social scientists, Prof. Cumming (McPherson's case, 1982) recognized the relationship of 'cause and effect' between 'sexual harassment' and 'job-related consequences'. In fact, for the social scientists unlike for many legalists, 'sexual harassment' is a cause and 'hostile and offensive work environment' and 'job-related consequences', either one or both of which may follow, are the results.

THE THEORETICAL EXPLANATIONS

The causes of sexual harassment are diverse and therefore it is unlikely that a single model or approach could adequately address the complex nature of the problem. Actually, most sexual harassment studies offer descriptive models that primarily describe covariates than offering explanation as to why sexual harassment occurs (Tangri and Hayes, 1997). Still, as Welsh (1999) points out, grounded in feminist, social psychological frameworks, several models exist that break explanations of sexual harassment into the primary correlates of sex harassment like target characteristics, occupational or organisational characteristics and offender characteristics and theoretical explanations of sexual harassment like power dominance and sex-roles spillover models.

Five such models are briefly described below as explanations of sexual harassment.

(a) Natural/Biological Model, as discussed by Tangri, Burt and Johnson (1982), and later followed to some extent by writers like Studd and Guttiker (1991), views sexual harassment as the natural outcome of men's stronger sex drive and men's role as the sexual aggressors. Sexual harassment, according to this model, is neither sexist nor discriminatory but is a manifestation of biological relations between men and women.

(b) Organisational Model focuses on the role of organisations by way of offering following diverse set of explanations for sexual harassment. Underlying many of these explanations are the ways power differences in organisations promote sexual harassment and perpetual inequality (Rospenda, Richman and Nawyn, 1998).

   (i) Some organisational models emphasise how inequities in structural or formal power in organisations lead to sexual harassment – *e.g.* managers may use their position to harass subordinates (Benson and Thomson, 1982; MacKinnon, 1979). Sometimes harassers may be co-workers (Gutek, 1985) and also subordinates (Grauerholz, 1996; McKinney, 1994; Rospenda *et al.*, 1998); a fact which highlights that conceptualization of organisational power must be broadened to include informal sources of power such as personality, expertise and access to critical information (Cleveland and Kerst, 1993).

(ii) Some approaches discuss the issue of sexual harassment in terms of numerical dominance of males over females in certain workplaces (contact hypothesis). The contact hypothesis (Gutek *et al.*, 1990; Gruber, 1998) views sexual harassment as a function of the contact between men and women in the workplace.

(iii) The sex-role spillover theory (Gutek and Morasch, 1982; Gutek, 1985) attributes sexual harassment to the carryover into the workplace of gender-based expectations which are irrelevant to, and inappropriate for, work. This happens most often when the gender ratio is heavily skewed toward either men or women because such situations render 'femaleness' more salient and visible (Kanter, 1977; Stockdale, 1996).

(iv) Many researchers are turning to organisational culture to explain why sexual harassment occurs in some organisations and not in others (*e.g.* Kauppinen-Toropainen and Gruber, 1993, Hulin *et al.*, 1996; Pryor *et al.*, 1993).

(v) Looking at the organisation of work, alienating work conditions may be partly responsible for women's experiences of sexual harassment in male-type jobs. Some researchers see men's harassment and sexual horseplay in the workplace as an attempt to overcome boring work (*e.g.* Hearn and Parkin, 1987; Hearn, 1985).

(c) A variety of approaches focus on Individual Level characteristics of harassment targets or victims to explain sexual harassment. Individual characteristics make some women more vulnerable than others. E.g. single women and young women may experience higher levels of sexual harassment than other women (Gruber and Bjorn, 1982; US Merit Systems Protection Board, 1981). Similarly, young age not only captures the impact of youth as such but is also a sign of low seniority or poor job status (Gruber, 1998).

(d) The Socio-Cultural Model holds that sexual harassment in the workplace is a manifestation of general male dominance in society (Farley, 1978; MacKinnon, 1979). According to this model, harassment is a mechanism for maintaining occupational and economic male dominance over women, and men and women are socialized in ways that maintain this structure of dominance and subordination. Males are supposed to be aggressive and assertive, where as women are socialized to be passive and sexually attractive, and even to feel responsible for their own victimization (Tangri *et al.*, 1982).

(e) Again, researchers like Vaux (1993) suggest that sexual harassment is a form of 'moral exclusion' in which males feel entitled to their superior position and justify their behaviour disregarding any harmful consequences towards less powerful opposite sex.

Following Finkelhor's (1984) four-preconditioned model of child sexual abuse, O'Hare and O'Donohue (1998) develop the Four-Factor Model 'on the assumption that the variables related to sexual harassment can be grouped into four factors which must be met for harassment to occur:

1. Motivation (*e.g.*, sexual attraction and/or power needs);

2. Overcoming Internal Inhibitions against harassment (*e.g.*, viewing sexual harassment as illegal or immoral, victim empathy, outcome expectancies); 3. Overcoming External Inhibitions against harassment (*e.g.*, explicit grievance procedures and consequences to harassers); and 4. Overcoming Victim Resistance (*e.g.*, her ability to recognize and stop premonitory behaviour to harassment)' (O'Hare and O'Donohue, 1998: 565). In a way this model combines the relevant factors mentioned before. Factors 1 and 2 relate to individual variables of the harasser, factor 3 focuses on organisational and socio-cultural situational factors that are relevant in sexual harassment incidents and factor 4 addresses individual factors related to the potential victim of sexual harassment.

No doubt the above explanations try to delve deep into the issues involved in sexual harassment. But none of them seem to focus all the dimensions that may contribute to sexual harassment particularly in a country like India. Indian culture does not give much value to biological urges since it is supposed to believe in curbing unsocial show of instincts. At the same time, however, it permits greater latitude to the male than female members of society. The organisational factors like hierarchical power structure, organisational culture, organisational work pattern and the like relate mainly to organised sector and more particularly to big organisations. Hence, they cannot explain sexual harassment in large unorganised sector and in small organisations of India. Again, some of the above explanations often overlap. *e.g.*, individual-level correlates like age and marital status are taken into account in socio-cultural model by some researchers (*e.g.* Kauppinen-Toropainen and Gruber, 1993; Padavid and Orcutt, 1997). Moreover, cultural legacy or tradition, which is so very important in our country in developing personalities of both the harassed and the harassers, has not been given due weightage. Similarly, the above models do not pay due attention to the factor of education or literacy, which is significant in a country having millions of illiterates. Above all, the biggest gap in the above explanations is that the entire dimension of the economic factor has not been taken into account almost in disregard of developing nations. Quid pro quo is not that ostensible in a country like India. On the other hand, feminisations of poverty and subsistence level of living compel the women in many cases not to resist sexual harassment. Actually, sexual harassment appears to be a phenomenon determined by variables at multiple levels including individual, organisational, socio-cultural, economic and also developmental in case of developing countries. Thus, a multi-dimensional model is required to be developed to adequately address its etiology in a country like India.

THE AFTERMATH

'Research indicates that the consequences of sexual harassment to both the organisation and to the individual are substantial' (O'Hare and O'Donohue, 1998:562). Organisations have to pay a price in two ways. Directly they are faced with the costs of lawsuits, damages and compensations, whenever applicable. Organisations are faced also with the indirect or hidden costs of job turnover, reduced productivity, absenteeism and medical insurance claims. According to one US study (US Merit Systems Protection Board, 1981), sexual harassment of its employees cost the Federal Government an estimated US$189 million during the two-year from May 1978 to May 1980. These costs comprise of hidden costs of job turnover, emotional and physical stress, absenteeism, decline in individual productivity and decline in workgroup productivity. Moreover, the existence of sexual harassment in the workplace adversely affects employee morale thereby reducing productivity and increasing absenteeism. Another price not taken into account by the concerned researchers is the loss of goodwill, a factor which in a country like India with minimum pervasiveness in the sexual field is of importance.

At the personal level, the adverse effects are psychological, physical and economic. From the psychological point of view, Welsh remarks, 'Research on the consequences of harassment is limited' (Welsh, 1999: 183). As Gutek and Koss (1993) point out, most studies tend to list possible outcomes, with little regard to the prevalence or the complex processes underlying them. Recent researches by psychologists, however, attempt to respond to such criticisms. Sexual harassment is linked to anxiety, depression, sleep disturbances, nausea, stress and headache (Crull, 1982; Fitzgerald, 1993; Gutek and Koss, 1993). The sexually harassed also experience a greater lifetime risk of post-traumatic stress disorder (PTSD) and major depression than women who have never been sexually harassed (Dansky and Kilpatrick, 1997). The effects of bullying on the individual as developed by Scott and Stradling (2001) may also be applied to sexual harassment thereby showing its vulnerability to PTSD and indicating that harassment is as distressing to the victim as being exposed to a physical attack or injury. Apart from this last noted comparison, the concerned researches hardly take into account physical injury or disability of sexually harassed. There are also workplace-related negative psychological effects like lowered morale (US Merit Systems Protection Board, 1981 and 1987), decreased job satisfaction (Gruber, 1992), decreased perception of equal opportunity (Newell et al., 1995) and damaged inter-personal work relationship (Culbertson et al., 1992). As Tehrani (2001) points out in connection with the effects of bullying, we may say even the threat of being harassed can be the cause of stress and ill-health. Some of these disadvantages may also affect the harassers, though this point has not been duly emphasised in the noted researches.

Researchers (*e.g.* Gutek and Dunwoody, 1988) draw our attention to job-related consequences of sexual harassment. They include loss owing to being absent from work, disruptions in career and the like. Though these have adverse economic effects, these studies do not term them as 'economic'. But in a country like India these are associated with some other economic losses and hence we prefer to categorise these losses together as economic rather than simply job-related.

Important items in this respect are costs of medical treatment of both physical and psychological disorders, cost of litigation etc. The economic loss for many poor working women of our country is often disastrous. Again, from our perspective, we should also investigate into the consequences of sexual harassment in the developmental process. Harassment inhibits the victims to take part in development related activities, and more broadly to join the working force, which are so essential in our country where still many women are confined within their homes. There is also a sociological dimension in a country like ours. Here women, when raising complaints of sexual harassment, are in an extremely hostile environment with the risk of backlash, humiliation, psycho-physical injury and loss of confidentiality. In fact, the fear and reality of being stigmatized as targets of harassment and the consequent erosion of self-esteem is an evil effect sociologically as well as developmentally.

With the above in mind, and of course taking into account the researchers in the West, our researchers should develop a workable map of consequences of sexual harassment. The map should include, among other things, effects of sexual harassment on the loss of self-confidence, capability and efficiency of the harassed and the impact upon society as a whole.

DYNAMICS OF REMEDIAL MEANS

Since sexual harassment has become widespread and its consequences extremely damaging, there is a compulsion in all writing on the issue to suggest remedial measures. In USA and Canada, due, if not overdue from our point of view, emphasis has been given on legal measures. 'Preventing harassment and enforcing appropriate workplace behaviour appear to be the best, if not the only 'cure' for employer liability' (Aggarwal, 1992: 316). Consideration, therefore, has to be given to the development of programmes that meet the preventive standards outlined by the courts, Human Rights Tribunals and Human Rights Commissions in those countries. The US Supreme Court in Vinson's case (1986)[5] and the Supreme Court of Canada in Janzen's case (1989)[6] opine that the employer has an affirmative duty to investigate complaints of sexual harassment and to deal appropriately with the offenders. It is also the duty of the employers to investigate promptly and thoroughly. In fact, in those countries the employer is always legally liable for any supervisory actions that affect the victims' employment states such as hiring, firing, promotion or pay during such investigations. Remedial and preventive actions go hand in hand – one cannot be effective without the other in legally combating sexual harassment in the workplace.

The legal guideline often indicates the measures that employers should take to prevent sexual harassment. Foremost, employers should have a clear, precise and comprehensive written policy on sexual harassment, not only to avoid legal liability in a court action but also to restore human dignity in the workplace (Aggarwal, 1992). In a comprehensive sexual harassment policy, the employer should make a commitment to make and keep the work environment free from sexual harassment and convey that commitment to all of its employees from top to bottom. The policy must also include penalties for the harasser, remedies for the victim and provision for appeals. The policy should also state the intent and purposes of the employer concisely and clearly. If prevention is the most effective tool an employer can use for the elimination of sexual harassment, preventive action, which is provided for in many laws and judgments, should include communication, education and training. Unless there is enough emphasis on sensitisation, awareness and prevention at the workplace, legal provisions for complaint and investigation mechanisms, penalty and redress are hardly likely to be successful. Gruber and Smith (1995) found that women responded more actively to unwanted sexual attention when the workplace implemented several measures like formulation of a policy, providing proper complaint mechanism, preaching, communication, education and training for dealing with the harassment problems.

In India, the draft bill referred to before, though more comprehensive than the Supreme Court guidelines and include a variety of formal and informal workplaces within its scope, it contains, as Tejani (2004) points out, ambiguities and omissions and fails properly to institute rules relating to occupations where there is no clearly identifiable employer, and even workplace at times – a common feature of unorganised sector of employment in India. However, the present draft bill incorporates a two-tiered grievance mechanism – an Internal Complaints Committee (ICC) and another district level body called the Local Complaints Committee (LCC).

Informal sector workers can go directly to the LCC, which will be chosen from a group of experts including the NGO representative whose role naturally will be crucial as the only 'external member'. According to Tejani (2004), however, there should have been an arrangement at the block level and for covering informal workers comprehensively by providing different grievance mechanisms and procedures for each 'workplace'.

Researchers pay no less attention to organisational culture and functioning to fight sexual harassment. Organizations can proactively create an environment in which the organisation and the individual employees can show respect to one another. Though written mainly in relation to bullying, Walker (2001) looks at how an organisation's culture, standards and values impact on an employee's perception of what is acceptable behaviour. In her work in health trust, Walker discusses how her organisation introduced a dignity at work policy that created a framework for addressing (bullying and) harassment issues. Tehrani (2001) looks at building a culture of respect through the use of a total quality approach. The advantages of using total quality as a way of changing organisational culture is built upon the well-tried and tested processes and systems that have been used with success within many organisations. It recognizes that there is a need to include all the stakeholders in the process – owners, managers and supervisors, other categories of employees and even outsiders who interact with the organisation, and NGOs and government officials whenever applicable. This universal participation increases the likelihood of success. Rains (2001) provides a very practical account of how the Royal Mail introduced a peer 'listener' scheme that resulted in a number of benefits. Aggarwal (1992) in this respect emphasizes on communication, education and training on organisation's policy and healthy working environment.

Furthermore, developing a good organisational climate and fighting a discriminatory practice like sexual harassment is not only the responsibility of the employers but also of the employees. Here our attention is naturally drawn to the important role the unions can play in reducing the occurrence and impact of harassment. Aggarwal raises a very pertinent question: 'If unions have made the elimination of discrimination in the workplace a high priority, should they not be 'active' in seeking elimination of sexual harassment from the workplace?' (1992: 354). He further suggests that collective bargaining as a continuing institutional relationship between the employer entity and a labour organisation should include a clause on sexual harassment – a measure adopted by a few unions in the West. This is significant in our country where unions are gradually shifting from militant to constructive line for the sake of development.

However, what seems to be missing in the above discussions and what is extremely important in a country like India is that violence against women in general and sexual harassment in particular must be tackled by the entire society. There should be a continuous campaign and propaganda programme against all sorts of discrimination and inequity, especially involving women. The world is still largely patriarchal and hence sexual harassment at the workplace will go on for quite sometimes. But in Indian cultural tradition, patriarchy with all its associated characteristics of male superiority is more rooted and requires legal, administrative NGO-level intervention, particularly relating to women's organisations, and others concerned, to weed it out. In fact, in a country like India, the problem of sexual harassment is to be combated not in isolation but together with different issues of sexual discrimination and this requires social networking. Moreover, all concerned are to realize that sexual harassment is not only an issue of social justice; it is very costly in terms of obstacles to developmental processes.

CONCLUSION

This review seems to touch the surface of many issues with which researchers are currently struggling. In need of further study is the mechanism of complaint or identification of sexual harassment and its relationship to legal, institutional and societal environment. The author attempts to identify the need for a practical, conceptual and methodological framework by which harassment is to be viewed in the workplace particularly in our country. Instead of organisations and researchers spending most of their time in defining and describing which behaviours can be categorized as harassment, the emphasis should be shifted towards defining how organisational and communal cultures and participation can ensure the rights and dignity of the workforce. Obviously this change will require a conscious shift from the current emphasis on the negative aspects of sexual harassment to one in which the rewards for positive interpersonal relationships are beneficial to all stakeholders including the society.

Again, studies of the outcomes of sexual harassment cases focus on victim, perpetrator and harassment characteristics without utilising theoretical insights from the sociology of law, organisation and inter-human relationships in general. As a result, researchers often fail to examine the impact of sexual harassment within the wider societal context. In fact, sexual harassment is more generally a function of workplace dynamics in the context of cultural and attitudinal background of the entire society.

Finally, since sexual harassment, like any other form of discrimination, is a concern not only of the abused but also of the society as a whole, the problem has to be addressed by all and should be included in the mainstream of the problem of interpersonal relationship. No doubt, the evil results of sexual harassment are to be made known to all concerned by proper information, education and communication (IEC). That it is unwanted from the point of view of social ethics should be highlighted. But moral propaganda is not enough. In a developing country like India the cost of sexual harassment in terms of developmental activities should be properly focused and it is to be concretely shown that development processes will be immensely benefited if all kinds of gender discrimination including harassment are mitigated.

REFERENCES

Aggarwal, A.P. (1992), *Sexual Harassment in the Workplace*, Toronto and Vancouver, Buttersworth.

Benson D.J., Thomson G.E. (1982), Sexual harassment on a university campus: The confluence of authority relations, sexual interest and gender stratification. *Soc. Probl.* 29: 236 –251.

Brooks, L., and Perot, A.R.(1991), Reporting sexual harassment: Exploring a predictive model. *Psychology of Women Quarterly*. 15(1): 31-47.

Cleveland J.N., and Kerst M.E. (1993), Sexual harassment and perceptions of power: an underarticulated relationship, *Journal of Vocational Behaviour.* 42: 49- 67.

Coles, F.S. (1986), Forced to quit: Sexual harassment complaints and agency response. *Sex Roles*. 14: 81-95.

Crull, P. (1982), Stress effects of sexual harassment on the job: Implications for counselling. *American Journal of Orthopsychiatry*. 52: 539-44.

Culbertson, A.L., Rosenfeld, P., Booth-kewley, S., Magnusson, P. (1992), *Assessment of sexual harassment in the navy: Results of the 1989 Navy-wide survey*, San Diego, CA, Navy Personnel Res. Dev. Ctr.

Dansky, B.S., Kilpatrick, D.G. (1997), Effects of sexual harassment. In O'Donohue, W. (ed.), *Sexual harassment: Theory, research and treatment*, New York, Allyn & Bacon, pp. 152 - 174.

Farley, L. (1978), *Sexual Shakedown: The Sexual Harassment of Women On the Job*, New York, McGraw-Hill.

Finkelhor, D. (1984), *Child Sexual Abuse: New Theory and Research,* Free Press, New York.

Fitzgerald L.F. (1993), Sexual harassment: Violence against Women in the Workplace. *American. Psychology.* 48:1070-1076.

Fitzgerald, L.F., Shullman, S.(1993), Sexual harassment: A research agenda for the 1990s. *Journal of Vocational Behaviour*. 42: 5- 27.

Fitzgerald, L.F., Shullman, S., Bailey, N., Richards, M., Swecker, J., Gold, Y., Ormerod, A.J., and Weitzman, L. (1988), The Incidence and Dimensions of Sexual Harassment in Academia and the Workplace. *J. Voc. Behav.* 32: 152- 175.

Fitzgerald, L. F., Swan, S., Magley, V. (1997), But was it really sexual harassment? Legal behavioural and psychological definitions of the workplace victimization of women. In O'Donohue,W.(ed.), *Sexual harassment: Theory, research and treatment*, New York, Allyn & Bacon, pp. 5- 28.

Grauerholz E. (1996), Sexual harassment in the academy: the case of women professors. In Stockdale, M.S. (ed.), *Sexual Harassment in the Workplace: Perspectives, Frontiers and Response Strategies*, Vol. 5, Women and Work Series. Thousand Oaks, CA, Sage, pp. 29-50.

Gruber, J.E. (1992), A typology of personal and environmental sexual harassment: Research and policy implications from the 1990s. *Sex Roles*. 22: 447- 464.

Gruber, J.E. (1997), *An epidemiology of sexual harassment: Evidence from North America and Europe*. In O' Donohue, W. (ed.), *Sexual Harassment: Theory, Research and Treatment*, New York, Allyn & Bacon, pp. 84-98.

Gruber J.E. (1998), The Impact of Male Work Environments and Organizational Policies on Women's Experiences of Sexual Harassment. *Gender & Soc.* 12(3): 301-320.

Gruber, J.E., Bjorn, L. (1982), Blue-collar Blues: the Sexual Harassment of Women Autoworkers. *Work Occupation.* 9(Aug.): 271-298.

Gruber, J.E., Smith, M. (1995), Women's Responses to Sexual Harassment: A Multivariate Analysis. *Basic and Applied Social Psychology*. 17: 543-562.

Gutek B.A. (1985), *Sex and the Workplace,* San Francisco, Jossey-Bass.

Gutek B.A., Cohen, A.G., Konrad, A.M. (1990), Predicting Social-sexual behavior at work: a contact hypothesis. *Acad. Mgmt. J.* 33: 560-577.

Gutek, B.A., Dunwoody, V. (1988), Understanding sex and the workplace. In Stromberg, A. H., Larwood, L., Gutek, B. A. (eds.), *Women and Work: An Annual Review,* Vol. 2, Sage, Newbury Park, CA.

Gutek, B.A., Koss, M.P. (1993), Changed women and changed consequences of and coping with Sexual Harassment. *Journal of. Vocational Behaviour.* 42: 28-48.

Gutek B.A., Morasch, B. (1982), Sex-ratios, sex-role Spillover, and Sexual Harassment of Women at work. *J. Soc. Issues,* 38: 55-74.

Hearn, J. (1985), Men's Sexuality at work. In Metcalf, A., Humphries, M. (eds.), *The Sexuality of Men*, London, Pluto, pp. 110-128.

Hearn, J., Parkin, W. (1987). *'Sex' at 'Work': The Power and Paradox of Organisation Sexuality*, Brighton, Wheatsheaf.

Hulin, C., Fitzgerald, L.F., Drasgow, F. (1996), Organizational influences on sexual harassment. In Stockdale, M.S. (ed.), *Sexual Harassment in the Workplace: Perspectives, Frontiers and Response Strategies*, Vol. 5, Women and Work Series, Thousand Oaks, CA, Sage, pp. 127-151.

Kanter, R.M. (1977), *Men and Women of the Corporation*, New York, Basic Books.

Kauppinen-Toropainen, K.,Gruber, J.E. (1993), Antecedents and outcomes of woman- unfriendly experiences. *Psychology of Women Quarterly.* 17:421-456.

McKinney, K. (1994), Sexual harassment and college faculty members. *Deviant Behav.* 15(2): 171- 191.

MacKinnon, C. (1979), *Sexual Harassment of Working Women*, New Haven, Yale Univ. Press.

MacKinon, C. (1987), *Feminism Unmodified: Discourses on life and law*, Cambridge, MA, Harvard Univ. Press.

Nath, S.K., Rustagi, P. (2003), Using Statistics for Gender-Responsive Policy Analysis and Advocacy, Paper from India group presented at the UNESCAP/UNIFEM Workshop, Bangkok.

Newell, C.E., Rosenfeld, P., Culbertson, A.L. (1995), Sexual harassment experiences and equal opportunity perceptions of Navy women. *Sex Roles*. 32 (3-4): 159-168.

O'Hare, E.A., O'Donohue, W. (1998), Sexual harassment: Identifying risk factors. *Archives of Sexual Behaviour*. 27, 6: 561-580.

O'Donohue, W. (1997), *Sexual harassment: Theory, research and treatment*, New York, Allyn & Bacon.

Padavid, I., Orcutt, J.D. (1997), Perceptions of Sexual Harassment in the Florida legal System: a Comparison of Dominance and Spillover Explanations. *Gender Soc*. 11(5): 682-698.

Pryor J., Lavite, C., Stoller, L. (1993), A Social Psychological Analysis of Sexual Harassment: The Person/Situation Interaction, *Journal of Vocational Behavior.* 42:68-83.

Rains, S. (2001), Don't suffer in silence: Building an effective response to bullying at work. In Tehrani, N. (ed.), *Building a culture of respect: Managing bullying at work*, London, Taylor & Francis.

Raymond, N. (2003), Sexual Harassment at work. [www.indiatogether.org/combatlaw /vol2issue3/harass.htm].

Rospenda, K.M., Richman, J.A., and Nawyn, S.J. (1998), Doing Power: the Confluence of Gender, Race, and Class in Contrapower sexual Harassment. *Gender & Society*. 12(1): 40-60.

Studd, M., Gattiker, U. (1991), The Evolutionary Psychology of Sexual Harassment in Organizations. *Ethiol. Soc.Biol*. 12: 249-90.

Scott, M., Stradling, S. (2001), Trauma, Duress and Stress. In Tehrani, N. (ed.), *Building a Culture of Respect: Managing Bullying at Work*, London, Taylor & Francis.

Scheidner, K.T., and Swan, S. (1994), Job-related, Psychological, and Health-related outcomes of Sexual Harassment, Paper presented at the Ninth Annual Conference of the Society of Industrial and Organizational Psychology, Nashville, TN.

Stockdale, M.S. (1996), What we know and what we need to learn about sexual harassment. In Stockdale, M.S. (ed.), *Sexual Harassment in the Workplace: Perspectives, Frontiers and Response Strategies*, Vol. 5, Women and Work Series, Thousand Oaks, CA, Sage, pp. 3-25.

Tangri, S.S., Burt, M.R., and Johnson, L.B. (1982), Sexual Harassment at Work: Three Explanatory Models. *J. Soc. Issues*. 38: 33-54.

Tangri, S.S., Hayes, S.M. (1997), Theories of Sexual Harassment. In O'Donohue, W. (ed.), *Sexual Harassment,* Boston, Allyn and Bacon, pp. 112-129.

Tehrani, N. (2001), A total quality approach to building a culture of respect. In Tehrani, N. (ed.), *Building a culture of respect: Managing bullying at work*, London, Taylor & Francis.

Tehrani, N. (2001), Preface. In Tehrani, N. (ed.), *Building a Culture of Respect: Managing Bullying at work*, London, Taylor & Francis.

Tejani, S. (2004), Sexual Harassment at the Workplace: Emerging Problems and Debates. *Economic and Political Weekly*. XXXIX, 41: 4419- 4494.

Terpstra, D.E., Baker, D.D. (1989), Outcomes of Sexual Harassment Charges. *Acad. Mgmt. J*. 31:185-194.

United States Merit Systems Protection Board (1981, 1987), *Sexual Harassment in the Federal Workplace: Is It a Problem?* U.S. Government Printing Office, Washington, DC.

Vaux, A. (1993), Paradigmatic Assumptions in Sexual Harassment Research: Being guided without being misled. Special issue: Sexual Harassment in the Workplace. *Journal of Vocational Behavior.* 42: 116-135.

Waks, J.W., Starr, M.G. (1982), The Sexual Shakedown in Perspective: Sexual Harassment in its Social and Legal Contexts, *Employee Relations L.J.* 7, 567-572.

Walker, V. (2001), A Proactive Approach. In Tehrani, N. (ed.), *Building a Culture of Respect: Managing bullying at work*, London, Taylor & Francis.

Welsh, S. (1999), Gender and Sexual Harassment, *Annual Review of Sociology..* 25, 169-190.

Welsh, S., Nierobisz, J. (1997), How Prevalent is Sexual Harassment? A Research note on Measuring Sexual Harassment in Canada. *Canadian Journal of.Sociology.* 22(4): 505-522.

NOTES

1. National Sample Survey Organization (NSSO) in its sample survey on 'Employment and Unemployment' estimated that during 1999-2000 female workforce stood 124 millions, about 31% of total workforce of which more than 88% belongs to rural workers.
2. See http://wcd.nic.in/draftbillonsexualharassmentonwomen.htm
3. As cited in Aggarwal (1992)
4. McPherson vs. 'Mary's Donuts', (Ont. 1982), 3 C.H.R.R D/961 (Cumming)
5. Meritor savings bank v. Vinson (1986), 106 S. Ct. 2399, 40 E.P.D.
6. Janzen v. Platy Enterprises (Man. 1985), 6 C.H.R.R.D/2735 (Henteleff).

Part - VI

VICTIMS ASSISTANCE: AN ATTEMPT AT CONVERGENCE OF EXISTING SERVICES

STANLEY B. YELDELL

26

VICTIM ASSITANCE CENTERS AT HIGHER EDUCATIONAL INSTITUIONS: A BLUE PRINT FOR THE FUTURE

INTRODUCTION

The Victimology course is a very interesting and diverse vehicle for providing students with the opportunity to study and research the numerous problems that crime victims encounter. My interest in this field evolved from teaching the Victimology Course over duration of twenty-five years or more within the Law/Justice Studies Department at Rowan University. The course sparked our interest to conduct research within the sixteen counties of New Jersey on the various needs of the "Victim Assistance Agencies" or organizations. The research was conducted by surveys, which provide us with definitive data to formulate and implement a College or University Victim Assistance Center. It will be envisioned that the center will serve as a core of knowledge and training for the numerous Victim Assistance Agencies and Organizations. Also, the Center would invite the Victim and Victim Assistance Organizations to actively participate within this unique learning process rather than the consumption by passive osmosis.

It is believed that the Criminal Justice System has been said to be a set of scales, with the accused on one side and the victim on the other side. Many victims and their advocates argue that there should be a balance of rights between the involved diverse parties. The mission of the Center would be to provide a core of knowledge for Victim

Assistance Organizations through training and technical support for advocates. This will increase and expand the resources for victim service providers and allied professionals. The research disclosed that there was a definitive need to organize and categorize the victim assistance agencies and organizations according to the services rendered by each. Also, the numerous victim assistance programs were unaware of the other organizations and especially, the complementary and supplementary services offered to crime victims.

The research enabled us to identify and categorize the victim assistance organizations as follows:

VICTIM ASSISTANCE ORGANIZATIONS

1. Victim/Witness Advocacy Programs
2. Shelter and Safe House Centers
3. Solace and Dove Centers
4. Family and Counseling Service Centers
5. Coalition Against Rape and Abuse Centers
6. Sex Crime Units and Rape Specialist
7. Battered Women's Shelters
8. Family Violence Programs
9. Domestic Abuse and Rape Crisis Centers
10. Sexual Trauma Resource Centers
11. Anger Management Programs
12. Networking Groups
13. Court Preparation and Escorting Services
14. Victim Support Groups
15. Victims of Crime Compensation Board
16. Children Justice Center
17. Family Violence and Prevention Services

It was determined that the college or university was considered to be geographically positioned as the focal point of the surrounding jurisdictions of the victim assistance organizations, in which the Center would be easily accessible to the community and related agencies.

VICTIM AWARENESS

The university would serve as a research center for victim awareness or victim assistance centers throughout the state. Moreover, the university would continue to formulate and develop relevant literature for enhancing the organizations capabilities.

CREATION OF POETIC HOMICIDE CENTER

The survivors of Homicide Victims would be able to express their bereavement by writing poetic expressions about their family members or friends as another avenue of therapeutic and spiritual healing. An online program would be designed to post the poems.

CATEGORIZE VICTIM ASSISTANCE ORGANIZATIONS

The victim Assistance Organizations would be categorized by the following:

1. IRS 501(c) (3) status
2. Jurisdiction –county
3. Capabilities
4. Services rendered
5. Group Affiliations
6. Duration of the Organization

The categories will be subject to change based upon its mandated duties and responsibilities.

CLASSIFYING OF POETIC HOMICIDE VICTIM SURVIVORS PRESENTATIONS

The Poetic Homicide victim survivors presentations will be classified by its:

1. Title of Presentation
2. Presentations on CD or DVD
3. Written Expressions

SCHEDULING POETIC PRESENTATIONS

It will be the responsibility of the poetic center to schedule dates and the duration for receiving expressions. The designed website would list the requirements for using expressions posted online.

VICTIM ASSISTANCE CENTER'S OBJECTIVES

The Victim Assistance Center's Objectives are listed below:

1. To conduct extensive research on the various victim assistance organizations, services and their capabilities.
2. To foster meaningful partnerships with the victim assistance organizations by developing staff.
3. To increase victim assistance internships with the university or college.

4. To formulate a "Poetic Homicide Center" within the university or college.
5. To formulate a statewide victim assistance directory.
6. To formulate a state and federal legislative research unit.

HOW THE OBJECTIVES MAY BE ACHIEVED

The Victim Assistance Center's objectives may be achieved in the following ways:

1. To Conduct Extensive Research of the Victim's Assistance Organization's Financial Strengths.
2. To Classify the Victim Assistance Organizations Based on Services Rendered and Capabilities.
3. To Execute an Internship Agreements with the Victim Assistance Organizations.
4. To Develop and Implement a Poetic Homicide Victim Survivor Center with an online Internet site.
5. Design a Victim Homicide Survivor Questionnaire to Ascertain Individual and Community needs.

FORMULATION OF POETIC HOMICIDE CENTER

The poetic center will provide the survivor victims the opportunity to express themselves in writing. A substantial number of individuals find writing to be very therapeutic; many victims have difficulty in expressing their feelings verbally.

Victim Homicide Poetic CD'S or DVD'S

The CD or DVD can be tendered to relatives, friends and members of the victimization community; it can be duplicated and played for a great duration.

Online Internet Communications

The online internet web site will serve as an excellent vehicle for the victim-survivor of the homicide to register their poetic thoughts by using a very reliable resource. An innovative communication vehicle can be established by emailing or postal mail per request.

Scheduled live chats could be provided so individuals could exchange ideas and share their thoughts at the same time. The site would be monitored frequently as to alleviate inappropriate chats.

FORMULATION OF A VICTIM ASSISTANCE RESEARCH CENTER

Victim – Clock

The victim assistance research center will be required to establish the victim clock. The victim clock articulates a time line or crime computation of violent crime and property offenses. It is measured in seconds and minutes; for example, a victim of violent crime is victimized every 19 seconds. The victim clock can be obtained from the National Crime Victimization Survey (NCVS) The Bureau of Justice Statistics records the victims statements and their victimization encounters.

Victimization Data

The victimization concept is a dynamic process that emerges through a series of stages. The stages commence with the appropriate factors and go through the precipitation conditions that result into harmful consequences. This victimization data will be obtained from the Victim Assistance Centers, Witness Protection Centers, County Prosecutors Office and other related victim services.

Intake of Data

The intake unit of the research center must obtain intake victim data from the following resources:

1. County Prosecutor's Office
2. Municipal Courts Clerk Office
3. Superior Courts Criminal Case Managers
4. Juvenile Intake Officers
5. Trial Courts Administrators
6. Family Court Administrations

The intake unit will be required to contact or obtain the recorded criminal complaints and disposition of each; the intake unit will have to classify the crimes according to the seriousness to the minor offenses.

Dissemination of Data

The data will disseminate to the Victim Assistance Organizations located within the twenty-one counties; the Victim Assistance Organizations will be able to access the Data from the internet research bank.

Utilization of Data

The data will be utilized by the research units of the centers to:

1. Identify new areas of victim awareness
2. Formulate legislative concerns
3. Aid in the formulation of seminars
4. Assist victim organizations for the purpose of servicing its members
5. To provide financial and technical support for the development of protocols to victim assistance programs.

FORMULATION AND DEVELOPMENT OF A VICTIM ASSISTANCE DIRECTORY

Classification of Victim Assistance Organizations

The victim assistance center will be based upon the type of service. The directory will classify the organization as follows:

1. Victim Witness Organizations
2. Stalking Victims
3. Homicide Services – Post Mention Clean up Services
4. Elderly Abuse Centers
5. Domestic Violence Units
6. Sexual Assault Centers
7. Victim Financial Resource Organizations and
8. Suicide Centers etc.

Description of Services

The victim organization will be listed in alphabetical order and according to a complete description of the services rendered. The services would be earmarked:

1. Emergency-immediate
2. Long Term Service
3. Short Term Service
4. Referrals Information and
5. Financial Assistance etc.

Jurisdictional Limitations

The victim organizations will limit their assistance or services to the geographical boundaries. However, the directory may be utilized to ascertain the services that the victims will receive within their geographical locations.

HISTORICAL INFORMATION

Each organization will be required to submit a historical statement which explains its origin and changes since its original inception. This historical information will be utilized to assist the organization in the development of potential strengths and identify areas of weaknesses.

LEGISLATIVE UNIT

Role of the Unit

The primary role of the legislative unit is to provide legislation that has an impact on crime victims and victim assistance organizations.

Origin of Innovative Legislation

The legislative unit will be responsible for the formulation and development of innovative legislation that can be used to enhance victims rights such as: the production of a modified victim's rights card. This card may be used by the victim assistance organizations when advising victims and the card may be distributed to victim assistance organizations.

Liaison to Federal and State Legislatures

The legislative unit will be required to contact the state and federal legislatures. The unit must make recommendations of victim's needs and the enhancement of their rights. It is believed that the liasion can provide "think tank information regarding the field of Victimology".

HORIZONTAL LEGISLATION

The unit will be required to formulate and develop legislation for the horizontal crime victims. This will encourage horizontal victims to assist their immediate family members.

Vertical Legislation

The legislative unit will research the various areas that impact vertical victims. These victims are usually placed in position to provide the following help:

1. Financial
2. Housing
3. Food
4. Legal Resources

The vertical assistance will be to members of the immediate and extended family.

NETWORKING

Linkage to Organizations

The central theme of the victim assistance center is to link the various victim organizations to each other. The importance of the linkage is to enhance the services that can be offered to the victims.

Support Mechanism

The victim assistance centers will provide a support mechanism for the victim organizations. The centers will be able to assess the organizations in the formulation of policies and procedures as it relates to emergency and non-emergencies rendered.

Supplemental Assistance

The victim assistance center will be able to provide supplemental assistance in maintaining the organizations, services. The center would provide supplemental assistance by:

1. Initiating Funding Activities
2. Disbursement of Funds to need Organizations
3. Conducting Educational Seminars
4. Examination of the Organizational Business Plan

Exchange of Services

The organization will be able to exchange vital services that are being delivered to the victims. The exchange of services is an excellent vehicle to enhance the duration of organizational existence. This process will lessen the drain of service.

Curtailment of Duplication

The essential ingredient of the center is to eliminate the duplication of services being rendered by competing organizations. It is believed that an amicable resolution be submitted to the organizations so that they may become more focused.

Consortiums

The consortium should be planned and developed based upon a quarterly schedule. The Consortiums will consist of the formulation and implementation of productive seminars.

First Quarter

The consortium for the first quarter should be devoted to the instruction of the prevailing issues that needs to be addressed.

Second Quarter

This quarter will be dedicated to the forum of providing linkage capabilities for the organizations. The quarterly session would be used to produce a written document or articulating the linkage benefits to each.

Third Quarter

This quarter is dedicated in identifying the trends as it affects the victim. The trends maybe coming from:

1. Judicial Decisions
2. State Legislation
3. Federal Legislation
4. International Conferences

The trends will keep the center and the organizations with-up to date literature that can be utilized for the enhancing victims services.

Fourth Quarter

The success of any vital center or organization is to design and develop an awards ceremony for the numerous participants in the field of Victimology. The ceremony would identify the recipients as:

1. Volunteer of the year
2. Aided victims in life threatening situations
3. Enhanced the understanding of the victim dilemma and
4. Fighting for victim's rights etc.

SUMMARY

Linkage of Services

The establishment of the regional victim assistance center at a university or college will provide an invaluable resource for victim organizations. Moreover, the center will supply an important ingredient in the linkage of critical services for victims.

Think Tank for Organizations

The center will provide victim wisdom for the victim organizations; it will serve as a think tank for the organization. Moreover, the centers will farther the tapping of victim awareness benefits and especially as it enhance victim rights.

Sustaining Victim Awareness

The central role will be promoting the principles of victim awareness and its impact on the victims and society.

The center may sustain victim awareness by:

1. Mass Media Campaigns
2. Production of Victim Literature
3. Producing TV Programs that Educate the Youth
4. Victimology Courses should be Incorporated into the Curriculums of Elementary, Secondary, and Higher Education.

Judicial Approval

The judiciary has been concerned about the constant problems of the financial difficulties that victims incur. There is a demonstrated need to seek judicial approval in assisting crime victims with their financial problems. There is a need to seek judicial approval for innovative financial resources such as the use of a spousal abuse credit card.

Poetic Homicide Compilation

"Poetic Homicide Writings" would be categorized into groups according to the types of victims and the survivors. The Poetic Homicide unit will extend beyond the local university or college. Moreover, an International book of Poetic Homicide compilations can easily be produced or coupled with copyright certification. Finally, the poetic center can be the shining star in the background and will enhance victims self esteem throughout the world.

NATTI RONEL

27

GRACE THERAPY FOR RECOVERING VICTIMS: A RESTORATIVE 12-STEP BASED THERAPY

Therapy for Victims of Crime may wear various forms, as in other fields of intervention. Amongst, a growing approach is the spiritual one, which focuses on individuals' spiritual beliefs and way of life. More often than not, this approach underlines restoration as both a goal and a path for recovery. In this chapter, I will present *Grace Therapy* - an innovative spiritual and restorative therapy for victims of crime, partially based on the well-known 12-step program (see appendix 1).

The 12-step program, originally created in 1935 by suffering alcoholics on the basis of their personal experience in recovery (Kurtz, 1988), is adapted to other fields of intervention, usually as self-help program. It may also be adaptive as a professional model which I call *Grace Therapy* (Ronel, 2000). This model is widely disseminated in the addiction field (*e.g.* Miller, 1998; White, 1998); nevertheless it also emerges in other areas. For example, *Grace Therapy* was adapted as a professional restorative intervention for male batterers (Ronel & Claridge, 1999; Ronel & Tim, 2003). In these adaptations, the program's emphasis is on human imperfection and powerlessness as a starting point of self-struggle, and on gradually rising spirituality (Kurtz & Ketcham, 1992).

Although spirituality is central to humanity (Kalo, 1981), is as older as human civilization and is presented in most known cultures, it was mostly removed from mainstream social sciences until recently (Slife, Hope & Nebeker, 1999). However, this tendency has been changed and during the last decade there is a growing body of spiritual based social science literature (*e.g.* Aponte, 1998; Giacalone & Jurkiewicz, 2003; Miller, 2005; Miller & Delaney, 2005). Accordingly, Wolman (2001) emphasizes the role of spirituality in everyday activities and relationship. Kass and Lenox (2005) claim that when individuals practice life as an agent for spiritual growth, they achieve their full choice of human potential. Consequently, the re-discovery of a spiritual based intervention (*e.g.*, Richards & Bergin, 1997) is but a natural step.

Brende (1993, 1995) asserts that survivors of victimization have unresolved moral and spiritual needs which may be paralleled to those of recovering addicts. Amongst are guilt-ridden memories, unhealed emotional wounds, alienation and the need for spiritual surrender (Brende & McDonald, 1989). Based on these, Brende created a spiritual 12 themes model of therapy that corresponds to the original 12-step program. On the same line I will describe here *Grace Therapy* as parallel but different model for intervention with victims.

GRACE THERAPY VIEW ON VICTIMIZATION

Although harm inflicted upon individuals is the origin of victimization, not all that causes harm causes victimization. Harm is an external event forced upon individuals, but victimization is a personal experience, an experience of the self. This experience is subjectively related to the way one perceived the harmful event (Andzenge, 2005; Hulsmann, 2006). Following the harmful event and its subjective perception by the self, a process of victimization may arise. It is a process of the formation of the victimized self. This process, although subjective, may work hidden from the individual's sense of awareness. Hence, individuals may deny the victimization although the victimization process may shape their selves. In the following, "victimization" will relate to the subjective experience, whether conscious or hidden from the self.

Harm and its following victimization process are always forced upon individuals. Therefore, any victimization contains an experience of powerlessness. Individuals are powerless over their victimization, and this powerlessness characterizes the victimization process. We may define two stages during the construction of the powerlessness experience: (a) primary powerlessness over the wounding event(s); (b) secondary powerlessness over the influence of victimization on life afterwards. This distinction plays a major role during intervention. For example, David, 28 years old married man was group raped as an adolescent during a period of three months. Since, in his everlasting, almost-alive fantasies, he re-attempts to control the rape-situations, but in vain. While his powerlessness over the rape was primary, his attempts to solve it in his fantasies were a major constituent of his secondary victimization. In this case, the distinction was a starting point for recovery. Accordingly, the secondary powerlessness stands in the center of intervention.

Analogous to the addiction process (Ronel, 2000), we may illustrate.three levels of the secondary powerlessness: (a) behavioral; (b) mental; (c) spiritual. The first level relates to the visible realm – the behaviors that correspond to the victimization process. Powerless individuals may feel as though they are locked in circular processes: after they are driven to initiate a typical behavior, they are unable to stop it, despite the known negative results. It is a behavioral spin - behavior may lead into more of itself, regardless of the initial intention. For example, Talia, a woman who was emotionally, severely abused by her husband, was trapped in ineffective attempts to avoid any conflict with him by pleasing him. The harder she tried to please him, more conflicts she met, but felt unable to stop. Frequently she told her husband lies in order to gain domestic peace, but still her attempts were in vain. As a result she felt unauthentic, unethical and the burden of guilt. Usually, recovery begins in this level by an attempt to abstain from the typical behavior, parallel to the alcoholic's abstinence from alcohol. Accordingly, Talia began her recovery journey with an abstinence from telling her husband lies, thus risking the wished peace. Gradually she resumed her self-dignity.

Underneath the visible realm lies the mental one. Here we find the mental (emotional and cognitive) processes that correspond to the victimization experience, such as guilt, shame, fear, self-image, sense of dissociation, an attitude of avoidance and more. These processes lead one into the behavior of powerlessness. For example, Talia experienced strong anxiety concerning her husband negation of her. This anxiety drove her to the ineffective pleasing behaviors.

Intervention in this level, as we will see later, support the wished abstinence already discussed.

A major characteristic of *Grace Therapy* is the inclusion of the spiritual level in the description of powerlessness. The spiritual level is considered as the phenomenological root of the powerlessness. In this level we find a process of self-centeredness, a process by which the person's major concerns are directed toward oneself. Although it is typical to most humans, during the victimization process one's attention is turned toward oneself more intensively and extensively, to the degree of masking other experiences. Talia, for example, was mostly occupied by her fears as well as fantasies of loving relationship with her husband, to the point of masking her ability to live creatively in the world. David, who was also mentioned above, perceived the whole world through "the lens" of his own victimization. Everything was seen as relating to his own pain and continuing suffering, thus limiting his ability to see the world as it is and to fully participate in it. A growing self-centeredness disrupts one's faith, will and ability to love. Since it is considered as the root of the powerlessness, *Grace Therapy* directs recovery in this level.

RECOVERY BY *GRACE THERAPY*

Based on its pragmatic, self-help source, *Grace Therapy* provides recovering victims with pragmatic suggestions in an attempt to meet to the everyday manifestations of their powerlessness; defining a behavior over which one feels powerless and abstaining from it is a typical pragmatic suggestion. For example, Nili, a young, unmarried woman who was victimized in dating violence and date rape, noticed that she is over-concerned about being rejected by others. Hence she was driven to please people in order to avoid any risk of rejection. Unfortunately it enables others to take advantage over her weakness and even to abuse her. Therefore, her abstinence was from pleasing behaviors – not to be confused, of course, with her good-hearted, free-choice behaviors. She defined typical pleasing patterns and attempted to abstain from these known reactions, even though she still felt tension.

The leading principle in this and other suggestions is expressed by the well-known Serenity Prayer: "God grant us the serenity to accept the things we cannot change, courage to change the things we can, and wisdom to know the difference" (Alcoholics Anonymous, 1957,

p. 196). Through different stages of recovery, individuals gradually learn to distinguish between what it is impossible for them to change (*e.g.* their painful past) and what it is within their ability (*e.g.* their reaction towards their past). Experience proved, time and again for most of us are that the less people can change – the more they would love to, but the more people can change, the less they would dare to. Talia, for example, worked hard but in vain to change her husband behavior and attitude towards her. On the other hand, she feared changing her own behavior and attitude. Moving from the first to the second became a possibility after a process of acceptance, considered a key one during *Grace Therapy* recovery.

The Serenity Prayer connects serenity to acceptance. Accepting the fact that her husband was a violent man who emotionally abused her, Talia was unexpectedly calmed. It gave a sound explanation to her suffering and directed possible actions. Another example is Dalia, a woman who was sexually abused by her father since early childhood and up to late adolescence. Her recovery passed through the recognition that her father raped her. Accepting her powerlessness over his behavior relieved her sense of guilt. As we can see, acceptance has the potential to paradoxically show recovering victims the way out of their powerlessness and to resume their strength. Nili, for example, accepted her pleasing tendency, and gradually reduced it.

Acceptance is an active voice, which opposes the marked submissiveness that many victims present. It helps the recovering victims to face reality with gradual emotional relief and sense of self-strength. While the submissiveness of victims may be experienced as meaningless, deterministic burden with sense of separation and loneliness, the active acceptance opens a path towards meaningful experience of free choice and sense of connectedness and wholeness. Approaching it is gradual, through self-struggle.

Grace Therapy constitutes a faith-based, non-religious but spiritual model of self-struggle and transformation. All the above examples represent courageous struggles for self-transformation with certain degree of success. A major aim in recovery is to support the struggling victims in the direction of gaining meaningful spiritual life that are related to a Higher Power, as one understands this power. Unfortunately a broader description of this aim extends my limits here. A related aim is to challenge the cognitive distortions caused by the victimization, and to go beyond emotional obstructions such as resentment, anxiety and fear. Since resentment and fear are crucial elements of the victimization process, they will be further discussed.

It is natural that harms inflicted upon individuals cause anger towards the harming person. However, when the event is over, in most cases the anger is still alive and may even grow stronger. This current rage over past event(s) is resentment. Although natural, resentment actually connects the suffering victims to the harming offender. By resentment, the victim emotionally relates to the offender. Thus, although the victimizing event is over, the resentment keeps it alive in the victim's mind. Resentment ties the victim to the event and to the aggressor. It is an unpleasant experience that has no effect on the aggressor but harms only the resentful individual. But is it necessary?

By learning its character, recovering victims can understand resentment as a natural emotional reaction. But as a known AA saying assert, "Feelings are not facts". Therefore, resentment is a changeable emotion that can be eliminated. *Grace Therapy* offers recovering victims with a way out of resentment that may even lead, gradually, to forgiveness and restoration of relationship, when possible. For example, Mira, a young woman, daughter of two addicted parents who grew-up with her grandparents, was sexually abused by her uncle and emotionally abused by her grandfather. Not typically, her stronger resentment was towards her grandfather but not towards her uncle, whom she perceived to be also a victim of the same grandfather. Initially she refused to face this resentment, but during her recovery it became a crucial step. She then took a process of overcoming the resentment (unfortunately its description is beyond the scope here). After several weeks, the resentment subsided. She was able to create new relationship with her grandfather, with a marked relief.

Similar to resentment, fear and anxiety are expected natural outcomes of victimization. During the abuse, offenders usually treat their victims as objects, which may lead to alienation of the victimized self. Usually no other person prevented the abuse; hence the victimized self experiences sense of loneliness. One's powerlessness, loneliness and alienation challenge the individual's sense of control. Fear and anxiety may arise when people doubt their ability to control coming situations or events of life. In a way, fear is an alarming emotion based on experienced harm. But unfortunately, fear has more than positive attention for known risks. It may expand and be generalized up to limiting the victim's life. Fear and anxiety may rule one's life and lead into the described submissiveness. Therefore emerges the need to liberate the victimized self from their oppressing power. How can they be removed?

Again, the pragmatism of the Serenity Prayer paves the way for self-liberation. Usually, conscious and intent efforts are incapable of removing the fear or the anxiety. Fear and anxiety are leading experiences of the victimized self and one is incapable of transforming them. A recovering victim is powerless over one's fear or anxiety. Therefore, an acceptance is needed – to accept the powerlessness over fear or anxiety and the possible lack of control. Fear or anxiety constitutes the subjective reality, whether one accepts it, fights it or avoids everything while waiting for the fearful emotion to be over. But acceptance opens a new option, that is, to struggle actively in life *with* these emotions and *without* the wished sense of control. Instead of helpless fight against the fear or the anxiety, and as an alternative to the passive submissiveness to their destructive paralization, a recovering victim learns how to be active while ignoring ones fearful emotions. During this process one acknowledges the limitation of self and its ability to control, accept this limitation and the subsequent fear or anxiety, but consciously acts as though there is no fear or anxiety. Again paradoxically, acceptance of one's limitation brings almost an immediate relief. In addition, when one accepts the limitation of the human self, a spiritual transformation becomes a possibility and faith may be awakened (Kurtz & Ketcham, 1992). Usually, the awakening of faith eliminates the "being alone" feeling and therefore supports the recovering victim in the struggle to react in spite of the fearful emotions. Gradually, these emotions are diminished until they almost dissipate.

CONCLUSION

Victimization, as was claimed here, is a process of the self, originating in harmful events. During recovery, the victimized self needs to go through a transformation. *Grace Therapy* offers such a transformation, based on one's self-struggle. Being a spiritual way, *Grace Therapy* directs the transformed self into the realm of theistic faith. A major component of the transformation process is the setting of the Spirit as a goal. When this process occurs, a recovering victim can gain a new perspective on life and on one's wished achievements. Simultaneously, one usually experiences new hope. A main source for this hope is the subjective experience of support that one receives during the process. Experience of support lies within the spiritual experience, and it may renew the ability to love and to receive love. Finally, the relationship with the world is restored; one no more feels alone.

REFERENCES

Alcoholics Anonymous (1976), *"Alcoholics Anonymous"*, NY: AA World Service Office.

Alcoholics Anonymous (1957), *"Alcoholics Anonymous Comes of Age"*, NY: AA World Service Office.

Andzenge, R. (2005), *"Cultural and Geopolitical Contexts of Victimization in the Developing Countries"*, Paper presented at the XXI, Post Graduate Course on Victimology, Victim Assistance, and Criminal Justice. Dubrovnik, Croatia: Inter University Center.

Aponte, H. J. (1998), Love, the Spiritual Wellspring of Forgiveness, An Example of Spirituality in Therapy. *Journal of Family Therapy, 20*, 37-58.

Brende, J. O. (1993), A 12-step Recovery Program for Victims of Traumatic Events. In J.P. Wilson and B. Raphael (eds.), *International Handbook of Traumatic Stress Syndromes* (pp.867-877). New York: Plenum Press.

Brende, J. O. (1995), Twelve Themes and Spiritual Steps. In G. S. Everly, Jr. and J. M. Lating, *Psycotraumatology* (pp. 211-229). New York: Plenum Press.

Brende, J. O., and McDonald, E. (1989), Post-traumatic Spiritual Alienation and Recovery in Vietnam Combat Veterans. *Spirituality Today, 41* (3), 319-340.

Giacalone, R. A., and Jurkiewicz, C. L. (2003), Right from Wrong: The Influence of Spirituality on Perceptions of unethical Business Activities. *Journal of Business Ethics, 46*, 85–97.

Hulsmann, L. (2006), *The Problematic Relationship between Victims and Criminal justice: How to Prevent Secondary Victimization.* Paper Presented at the XXII. Post Graduate Course on Victimology, Victim Assistance, and Criminal Justice. Dubrovnik, Croatia: Inter University Center.

Kalo, S. (1981), *The Undaunted.* Jaffa: DAT (Hebrew Edition).

Kass, J. D., and Lenox, S. (2005), Emerging Models of Spiritual Development: A foundation for Mature, Moral, and Health-promoting behavior. In W. R. Miller and H. D. Delaney (eds.), *Judeo-Christian Perspectives on Psychology* (pp. 185-204). Washington, DC: APA.

Kurtz, E. (1988), *AA the story*. San Francisco: Harper & Row.

Kurtz, E., & Ketcham, K. (1992), *The Spirituality of Imperfection*. New York: Bantam Books.

Miller, W. R. (1998). Researching the Spiritual Dimensions of Alcohol and other drug Problems. *Addiction, 93*(7), 979-990.

Miller, W. R. (2005). What is Human Nature? Reflections from Judeo-Christian perspectives. In W. R. Miller and H.D. Delaney (eds.), *Judeo-Christian Perspectives on Psychology* (pp. 11-29). Washington, DC: APA.

Miller, W.R., and Delaney, H. D. (2005), Psychology as the Science of Human Nature: Reflections and Research Directions. In W.R. Miller and H.D. Delaney (eds.), *Judeo-Christian Perspectives on Psychology* (pp. 291-308). Washington, DC: APA.

Richards, P. S., and Bergin, A. E. (1997), *A spiritual strategy for counseling and psychotherapy*. Washington, DC: APA.

Ronel, N. (2000), From self-help to Professional Care: An expansion and an application of the 12-Step Program. *Journal of Applied Behavioral Science, 36,* (1), 108-122.

Ronel, N., and Claridge, H. (1999), Grace Therapy: A new approach to the Treatment of Male Batterers. *Contemporary Justice Review, 2* (3), 283-308.

Ronel, N., & Tim, R. (2003), Grace Therapy: Meeting the Challenge of Group Therapy for male Batterers. *Clinical Social Work Journal, 31* (1), 63-80.

Slife, B.D., Hope, C., and Nebeker, R.S. (1999). Examining the relationship between religious spirituality and psychological science. *Journal of Humanistic Psychology, 39* (2), 51-85.

White, W. L. (1998), *Slaying the Dragon: The History of Addiction Treatment and Recovery in America*. Bloomington, IL: Chestnut Health Systems/ Lighthouse Institute.

Wolman, R. N. (2001), *Thinking with your soul*. Tel Aviv, Matar (Hebrew Edition).

APPENDIX 1

THE 12-STEP PROGRAM

1. We Admitted we were Powerless over alcohol - that our lives had become Unmanageable.
2. Came to believe that a power greater than ourselves could restore us to sanity.
3. Made a decision to turn our will and our lives over to the care of God as we understood Him.
4. Made a searching and fearless moral inventory of ourselves.
5. Admitted to God, to ourselves, and to another human being the exact nature of our wrongs.

6. We're entirely ready to have God remove all these defects of character.
7. Humbly asked Him to remove our shortcomings.
8. Made a list of all persons we had harmed, and became willing to make amends to them all.
9. Made direct amends to such people wherever possible, except when to do so would injure them or others.
10. Continued to take personal inventory and when we were wrong promptly admitted it.
11. Sought through prayer and meditation to improve our conscious contact with God, as we understood Him, praying only for knowledge of His will for us and the power to carry that out.
12. Having had a spiritual awakening as the result of these steps, we tried to carry this message to alcoholics, and to practice these principles in all our affairs.

(from Alcoholics Anonymous, 1976, pp. 59-60).

D. Rufus and S. Ramdoss

28

TAMIL NADU STATE VICTIM ASSISTANCE FUND: A STUDY OF THE BENEFICIARIES

INTRODUCTION

The sufferings of the victims of crime need to be healed as far as possible. A civilized society (State) is identified not only with how its prisoners are treated but also with how the victims of crime are treated by it. In this context, it is the bounden duty of the State to provide the meaningful assistance to the victims of crime, wherever necessary, to the extent possible. Assistance may be of different kind's viz. the legal, medical and financial depending upon the nature and gravity of victimization caused. Victim assistance and its related synonyms (support, advocacy, aid, help, services), generally means the application of direct personal action designed to reduce the suffering and increase the recovery of crime victims. In the broadest sense this encompasses such activities as: victim restitution, victim rights, victim compensation, case status information, support groups, victim/offender mediation and reconciliation, hot – lines, crisis intervention, victim counseling and therapy, emergency medical services, social services, companionship, protection from secondary victimization (Dussich, 1976; Webster, 1989).

Victims of crime need to be treated with respect for their dignity. The victims need support and assistance from the State to redress their grievance. It appears that the victims of crime now avail some kind of assistance either from the State or from the NGOs or from both. More specifically, the victims of violent crimes in Tamil Nadu get financial assistance from the State of Tamil Nadu under the Scheme 'Victim Assistance Fund'. Though, this fund was meant only for victims of violent crimes, this initiative of the State of Tamil Nadu, India deserves a greater appreciation. Despite the small quantum of financial assistance, this effort of the State recognizes the sufferings of the victims to some extent and attempts to provide them some financial assistance.

The more common victims served are victims of violent crimes, burglary victims, and special categories (especially in the United States). Since victim needs are greatest immediately following their victimization, programs which are responsive to early assistance are the most appreciated by victims while those which deal with victim well after the victimization offer only limited services for those with long term problems (Dussich, 1999).

The idea that the state should provide financial reimbursement to victims of violent crime for their losses was propounded initially by English penal reformer Margery Fry in the early 1960s. Spurred by the impulse to grant a new kind of welfare to people in need, New Zealand's was the first legislature, in 1963 to adopt a victim compensation program, with Great Britain passing a similar law shortly thereafter. In 1965, California became the first state in North America to establish a compensation program in 1965, soon followed by New York. The idea spread methodically in the United States, with 32 states administering compensation programs by 1979. Most evolved from a welfare to a justice orientation, in which victims were seen as deserving compensation whether they were in need or not. Compensation programs also sought to promote involvement by victims in the criminal justice system because they required victims to report to the police and, in many cases, to cooperate with the prosecution. In the early years, administrators of victim compensation programs were not always passionate advocates of victims' broader concerns, but from the start, their programs were of both practical and symbolic value – they represent the first public recognition of society's responsibility to victims and have been the cornerstone of all the victim service schemes that have followed (Young, 1998).

In the years leading up to 1985, the World Society of Victimology invested significant resources to develop a body of knowledge which create a declaration on behalf of crime victims and victims of the abuse of power. It was in Milan, Italy where the formal Declaration of Basic Principles of Justice for Victims of Crime and Abuse of Power was first created and subsequently accepted by the delegates. Later that year, on 29 November, the United Nations' world wide strategy to effect change in the member countries so that victims might be "treated with compassion and respect for their dignity and that they are entitled to prompt redress for the harm that they have suffered through access to the criminal justice system, reparation, and services that will assist their recovery" (United Nations, 1999).

Three countries that developed the earliest and most comprehensive programs are the United States of America, England and the Netherlands. England and the United States began providing services about the same time, 1973 and 1974. In England the first independent support scheme was begun in Bristol and concerned mostly with burglary victims (Mawby and Walklate, 1994). The first programs in the United States were funded by the federal Law Enforcement Assistance Administration (LEAA) and were a mix of police based and prosecutor based programs (Balus, 1975; Callahan, 1975; Roberts, 1991).

In the Netherlands the first support services were developed as experimental projects in 1975 in the towns of Hoorn and the province of South Limburg. These two programs had strong links to probation and mediation (Van Dijk, 1989). Other countries also became involved in providing victim assistance in the late 1970s and early 1980s, primarily influenced by the USA, England and the Netherlands. These included Canada (McClenahan, 1987), South Australia (Paterson, 1991), New Zealand (Taylor, 1994), Wales, Scotland, Spain (Vidosa, 1989), France (the National Institute for Assistance for Victims - INAVEM in Paris) (Piffaut, 1989), Mexico (Fundacion Para Atencion A Victimas Del Delito – IAP in Mexico City), Argentina, Belgium, Croatia, Israel (Young, 1994), Germany, (Mawby and Walklate, 1994).

One of the unique differences in the European programs, generally, has been the focus on legal advice and financial assistance. This is to be compared with North America, which is more concerned with crisis counseling from professional therapists and criminal justice system advice (Young and Stein, 1983), and in Britain the focus is on sympathetic support and general advice (Mawby and Walklate, 1994).

Assistance programs can lead victims to a new place and thereby reduce the risk of future violence. Working with the victim immediately following the crime is particularly important. At the point of crisis, people may be more inclined to make changes in their behaviour, their lives, and their surroundings, and this makes them more receptive to assistance programs (Anderson, Chenery and Pease, 1995). In addition, prompt reaction can provide more effective prevention because the risk of revictimization is greatest immediately after the incident (Anderson et al, 1995).

THE TAMIL NADU STATE VICTIM ASSISTANCE FUND – AN OVERVIEW

The Crime Victims must be provided with services/assistance immediately after the victimization. The kind of service or assistance may vary according to the nature of harm suffered. The legal provisions with regard to the restitution to the victims of crime in India are found in the Code of Criminal Procedure, 1973 under Sections 357, 358 and 359 and under Section 5 of the Probation of Offenders Act, 1958. But, in the Code the term compensation is used which actually refers 'restitution'. India does not have an exclusive law to deal with victims of crime or for that matter to provide victim assistance like other countries, the Victims of Crime Act, 1984 (United States of America); the Justice for Victims of Crime Act, 1986 (Canada); The Victims of Offences Act, 1987 (New Zealand) and the Criminal Justice Act, 1988(United Kingdom). In this context, the State of Tamil Nadu established a fund called "Victim Assistance Fund" assumes a greater significance in terms of rendering financial assistance to the specific categories of victims of violent crimes. Tamil Nadu is the first ever State to establish such a victim assistance program in the whole of India.

The Government of Tamil Nadu sanctioned an amount of Rs.One Crore towards the creation of the fund called 'Victim Assistance Fund' during 1995 – 96. This amount is placed at the disposal of the Director General of Police who will sub – allocate the amount to the Commissioners of Police of Madras (now Chennai), Madurai and Coimbatore and the Superintendents of Police in other districts with reference to requirements. The Victim Assistance Fund is for the grant of financial assistance to the legal heir of the victims of murder and the victims of grievous injury and rape. Preference will be given to women and children. In the case of murder, the assistance will be provided, if the breadwinner is killed. The cash relief will be sanctioned to victims or legal heir (in the case of murder) on the following scale.

Type of victimization	*Scale of Assistance*	*Beneficiary*
Murder	Rs.10, 000	Legal heir (dependent)
Grievous injury	Rs.5, 000	The victim
Rape	Rs.5, 000	The victim

Source: Abstract, Home (Police – XII) Department, Govt. of Tamil Nadu, 1995.

THE PRESENT STUDY

The present study was carried out with the following objectives:

1. To understand the problems faced by the beneficiaries in availing the "Victim Assistance Fund" given by the Government of Tamil Nadu.
2. To study the utilization patterns of the assistance received by the beneficiaries.
3. To understand the opinion of the beneficiaries on the Victim Assistance Fund.

METHODOLOGY

The methodology of the present study includes the Universe of the study, Sample and Sampling method, and Research Tool, Data collection and Analysis of the data.

UNIVERSE OF THE STUDY

The Universe of the present study consisted of the beneficiaries of the Tirunelveli district of Tamil Nadu who availed the State Victim Assistance Fund from the Government of Tamil Nadu during the period 1997-2003.

SAMPLE AND SAMPLING METHOD

A total of 30 Beneficiaries of the Tirunelveli district (a southern district which is more prone to violent crimes) of Tamil Nadu who availed the State Victim Assistance Fund from the Government of Tamil Nadu were chosen from the Beneficiaries' population. Purposive sampling technique was employed to choose the respondents from the universe.

RESEARCH TOOL

A semi – structured Interview Schedule developed by the researchers was used to collect the primary data from the respondents (beneficiaries) chosen for the study. The Tool comprised of 16 items covering the personal profile of the respondents, the problems, if any while availing the assistance fund, the utilization patterns of the fund and the opinion of the respondents over the Victim Assistance Fund.

DATA COLLECTION

The present study used both the primary data and the secondary data pertaining to the objectives of the study. The primary data was collected from the respondents chosen from the universe of the study. A semi – structured Interview Schedule constructed for the purpose was used to collect the primary data. The secondary data i.e. the addresses of the beneficiaries and the case details etc were collected from the office of the Commissioner of Police, Tirunelveli City of Tamil Nadu.

DATA ANALYSIS

The present study used the univariate analysis viz. the frequency analysis to analyse the primary data and the interpretations were made based on the results.

RESULTS AND DISCUSSION

The results of the present study presented in the table followed by the discussion.

Table 1 shows the personal characteristics of the respondents (beneficiaries) such as age, educational qualifications, caste and religion. With regard to the age of the respondents, a majority of the respondents were in the age group of 26 – 40 years. The educational qualification of the beneficiaries range from primary school level to graduation. A sizeable per cent of the respondents were illiterates. With regard to the caste of the respondents, it was found that a significant per cent of the respondents belonged to Backward Caste (37%) and Other Caste (27%) followed by Scheduled Caste (23%) and Most Backward Caste (13%). With regard to the religion of the respondents it was found that a majority of the respondents were Hindus (70%) followed by Christians (20%) and Muslims (10%).

Table 1
The Profile of the Respondents

Age	*Frequency (N=30)*	*Percentage*
18 – 25 years	5	17%
26 – 40 years	20	67%
41 – 60 years	3	10%
61 and above	2	6%
Education		
Illiterate	5	17%
Primary	5	17%
Middle School	10	33%
High School	8	27%
Higher Secondary	1	3%
Graduation	1	3%
Caste		
SC	7	23%
MBC	4	13%
BC	11	37%
OC	8	27%
Religion		
Hindu	21	70%
Christian	6	20%
Muslim	3	10%

Table 2
Types of Victimization for which the Assistance was availed

Types of Victimization	*Frequency (N=30)*	*Percentage*
Murder	17	57%
Rape	2	6%
Grievous Hurt	11	37%

Table 2 reveals the types of victimization for which the Assistance Fund was availed by the beneficiaries. The Victim Assistance Fund is given to the victims of murder, rape and grievous hurt based on their economic conditions and their character. Of the total respondents who availed the Victim Assistance Fund from the Government of Tamil Nadu, victims of murder formed a major portion (57%) followed by victims of grievous injury (37%) and rape victims (6%).

Table 3
Time taken to receive the Victim Assistance Fund

Time Taken	*Frequency*	*Percentage*
Within 6 months	12	40%
6 – 12 months	17	57%
12 – 18 months	1	3%

Table 3 reveals the time taken to avail the Victim Assistance Fund by the respondents. For a majority of the respondents it took 6 –12 months to avail the victim assistance fund (57%) whereas 40% of the respondents availed the fund within 6 months. For a meagre per cent of the respondent it took 12 – 18 months to avail the victim assistance fund. Providing immediate assistance to the crime victims is very essential. Anderson, Chenery, and Pease, (1995) observed that working with the victim immediately following the crime is particularly important. At the point of crisis, people may be more inclined to make changes in their behaviors, their lives, and their surroundings, and this makes them more receptive to assistance programs. In addition, Anderson et al (1995) argued that prompt reaction can provide more effective prevention because the risk of revictimization is greatest immediately after the incident.

Table 4
The Current status of the case

Current Status	*Frequency*	*Percentage*
Disposed	23	77%
Trial is on	6	20%
No idea	1	3%

Table 4 reveals the current status of the case of the respondents. A majority of the cases were disposed (77%). 20% of the cases were on trial stage. It is significant to note here that 3% of the respondent was not informed about the status of the case. It was a case of murder. Of the cases disposed, majority of the cases were ended up in acquittals (74%). Only 22% of the cases saw the conviction of the offenders. In one case, mediation was employed to settle the issue. It is a welcome measure considering the number of cases pending in the courts in India. Mediation is good for both the victim and the victimizer and also to the society at large.

Table 5
Whether Bribe was given to avail the Fund

Bribed	*Frequency*	*Percentage*
Yes	3	10%
No	27	90%

Table 5 shows whether bribe was given to avail the victim assistance fund. A vast majority of the respondents did not bribe either the police or any other government official they contacted to avail the fund (90%). 10% of the respondents bribed the government officials to get the legal heir certificates. These respondents were the dependants of the deceased persons. To avail the victim assistance fund in a murder case, one has to produce the legal heir certificate, which is mandatory. It is the bitter fact that the practice of coercive and collusive type of corruption continues to exist in our society. What is shocking here is that the victims who lost their loved ones too not spared from paying bribe to get the certificates. On the contrary, the police were very cooperative and compassionate to the respondents in availing the victim assistance fund. They also provided the transportation facility to the respondents to receive the fund. The respondents also said that they came to know about the availability of the victim assistance fund only through police.

Table 6
The Utilization Patterns of the Fund by the respondents

Utilization Patterns	*Frequency*	*Percentage*
Consumption purpose	9	30%
Children's education	4	13%
Savings	8	27%
Medical expenses	10	33%
Repayment of debt	5	17%
House repair	2	7%
To generate income	1	3%
Case expenses	1	3%

Table 6 reveals the utilization patterns of the victim assistance fund by the respondents. A significant per cent of the respondents used the fund for the medical treatment (33%). 30 per cent of the respondents used the assistance for the consumption of food. 27% of the respondents deposited the fund in the savings account for future use. 17% of the respondents utilized it for the repayment of the loan they incurred to perform the last rites to the deceased member of the family. This is the economic condition of the some of the families where the breadwinner is murdered.

Table 7
Opinion of the Respondents on the Victim Assistance Fund

Opinion	*Frequency*	*Percentage*
The Quantum of the Fund should be increased	25	83%
Employment should be provided	5	17%

Table 7 shows the opinion of the respondents on the victim assistance fund. All the respondents appreciated and welcomed the victim assistance program of the government of Tamil Nadu. While appreciating the State government, majority of them (83%) also opined that the quantum of the victim assistance fund should be increased. 17% of the respondents said that the State government should provide employment rather than the victim assistance fund. This is interesting point to be considered by the State at least in some deserving cases where the breadwinner of the family is murdered. Considering today's cost of living the quantum of the victim assistance given to the crime victims is not satisfactory. Furthermore, the victim assistance fund is only a short-term assistance, which cannot provide a permanent solution to empower the crime victims.

RECOMMENDATIONS

The study recommends the following measures to the different agencies that come into contact with crime victims.

1. The present quantum of amount in the victim assistance is not sufficient. The State may consider enhancing the quantum of fund from the present Rs.10, 000 to Rs.50, 000 to the victims of murder; Rs.5, 000 to 25,000 to the victims of rape and Rs.5, 000 to Rs.25, 000 to the victims of grievous hurt.
2. The State should provide the assistance fund immediately, *i.e.* within one month from the date of crime victimization.
3. The State may consider providing special privileges to the victims of violent crimes in getting the employment in public

sector or private sector depends upon their educational qualification. The state should also assist them to start a small-scale business by getting them some loans.

4. Mere monetary assistance from the state is not enough. Victims should be offered psychological counseling especially to the victims of rape, in order to prevent Post Traumatic Stress Disorder (PTSD).
5. The police may consider extend their helping hand to assist the victims in getting the legal heir certificate, death/injury certificate and income certificate wherever possible. Otherwise, there will be a chance for the secondary victimization.
6. The Non – Government Organizations may assist the crime victims to get the State Victim Assistance Fund or may create a financial assistance scheme specifically for the victims of violent crimes. They may also consider providing counseling to the victims of crime in general and the rape victims in particular.

CONCLUSION

Based on the findings it is concluded that majority of the respondents did not face any problem in availing the victim assistance fund. Only meagre per cent of the respondents faced problem i.e. they had to bribe the officials concerned to get the legal heir certificate. It is a morale boosting fact for the police that none of the police officers received bribe from the respondents. Rather, the police were cooperative and supportive and they also provided transportation facility to the victims to receive the assistance. Majority of the respondents received the fund within a period of 6-12 months. Such period is not an immediate assistance and none of them received any other assistance from other sources like, Non – Government Organizations, voluntary organization etc. The truism that has emerged within the victim assistance arena is that "good victim assistance is good crime prevention." Victims who are not treated have a greater likelihood of taking their anger and frustrations out on other persons, often repeating the same violence committed on them, and thus continuing an unending cycle of violence (Dussich, 1999). The respondents utilized the assistance fund for various purposes, inter alia; medical treatment was cited by more number of the respondents. Hence, the State may consider providing medical aid also in addition to the victim assistance fund. Considering the cost of living today in the 21st century, the quantum of the assistance fund is not reasonable; therefore it has to be enhanced. However, 'The State Victim Assistance Fund' was found to be useful for the victims of violent crimes as something is always better than nothing.

REFERENCES

Anderson, D. Chenery, S. and Pease, K: (1995), *Biting Back: Tackling Repeat Burglary and Car Crime* (Crime Detection and Prevention Series Paper No.58), London: Home Office.

Balus, Mary E. (1975), *Integrated Services for Victims of Crime: A County Based Approach*. Washington D.C: The National Association of Countries.

Callahan, Leo F. (1975), The Victim Advocate: Programmed Police Response for Crime Victims. The Police Chief. (April).

Dussich, John P. J. (1976), Victim Service Models and Their Efficacy. In: Emilio C. Viano, *Victims and Society*, Washington D. C : Visage Press.

Dussich, John P. J. (1999), *Implementation of the United Nations' Declaration of Basic Principles of Justice for Victims of Crime and Abuse of Power*. Lecture Delivered at the University of Madras on 11 February, 1999.

Dussich, John P. J. (1999), *Victim Assistance Program Possibilities*. Lecture delivered at the University of Madras on 12 February, 1999.

Mawby, R. I. and Walklate, S. (1994), *Critical Victimology: International Perspectives*. London: Sage Publications.

McClenahan, C. A. (1987), *Victim/Witness Services: Vancouver, British Columbia, Canada*, Paper Presented to the American Criminological Association Annual Conference.

Montreal, as cited in Mawby and Walklate, (1994) infero.

Paterson, Andrew (1991), Victim Services in South Australia, In Kirchhoff, G.F., Kosovski, E. and Schneider, H., J. (Eds.,). *International Debates of Victimology*, Monchenglabach: WSV Publishing.

Piffaut, G. (1989), *Concrete Achievements Toward the Implementation of the Fundamental Principles of Justice for Victims*. In Heuni.

Roberts, Albert R. (1991), Delivery of Services to Crime Victims: A National Survey, *American Journal of Orthopsychiatry*, 61 (1). January.

Taylor, J. J. (1994), *Support to Community by Victim Support Groups*, Paper presented to the 8th International Symposium on Victimology, Adelaide, Australia, August.

United Nations (1999), *Handbook on Justice for Victims: On the use and application of the United Nations Declaration of the basic principles of Justice for Victims of Crime and Abuse of power*. Office for Drug Control and Crime prevention, Center for International Crime prevention. Retrieved on August 15, 2005 at www.ojp.usdoj.gov/ovc

Van Dijk, Jan J. M. (1989), *The Challenge of Quality Control: Victim Support in the Netherlands*. Unpublished paper cited in Mawby, R. I. and Walklate, S. (1994) Supra.

Webster, L. (1989), *Sexual Assault and Child Sexual Abuse: A National Directory of Victim Services and Prevention Programs*, Washington D. C: U.S. Government Printing Press.

Young, Marlene A. and Stein, John H. (1993), *The Victim Service System: A Guide to Action*, Washington, D. C. : NOVA.

Young, Marlene A. (1994), *Victim Services: Towards a New Millennium in Victim Assistance*, Paper presented to the 8th International Symposium on Victimology, Adelaide, Australia, August.

Young, Marlene A. (1998), *Victim Rights and Services – A Modern Saga*. National Organization for Victim Assistance Retrieved on 28th April 2006.

Anna Ryding

29

TRANSFORMING THE SORROW TO ANGER, THE VICTIM TO SURVIVOR: A CASE STUDY OF ORGANIZED VICTIM SUPPORT WORK IN SWEDEN

The Norwegian Criminologist Niels Christie constructed a typology of an "Ideal Victim", which has become a minor classic. The ideal victim is a person or a category of individuals who – when hit by a crime – most readily get complete and legitimate status as a victim. An ideal victim answers to the following description:

- The victim is weak.
- The victim is involved in a respectable project.
- The victim is to be found on a place he or she can't be blamed for.
- The perpetrator is big and evil.
- The perpetrator is unknown and has no personal relationship with the victim.

While I'm inspired by Christie's ideal victim type (1985), my aim is, however, to develop his analysis, by showing that the definition of victim status is an ongoing, complex project, and not a "one shot deal". In the Swedish voluntary victim organization, which I have been studying from the year 1999, the support workers try to make the persons, hit by a crime, *and start* seeing themselves as victims. However, the work ideology becomes more complicated as they also try to make the people *stop* seeing themselves as such. The victim is expected to be strong *and* weak, active *and* passive, sad *and* angry, and all these emotional states have definite time limits. The "victims" are supposed to become "survivors", "reorient", go back to their normal life, as soon as possible.

EMOTION WORK AND IDEOLOGY

The organization *"Brottsofferjouren"* apply a certain ideology of emotion in their support work, which I will describe and analyze in this chapter, from a critical victimological point of view. The ideology is connected to a popular psychological folk theory of crises. A crime victim is expected to feel strong guilt, shame and fear due to the experience of crime. The victims are recommended to accept the emotions as "a normal reaction to an abnormal experience". However, the victims are also recommended to "go back to normal"; and within this image of "normality" there seems to be limited space for extreme emotions. The persons who are named "crime victims" get guidance in their "emotion work" by the volunteer workers (see Hochschild 1984).

The American sociologist Arlie Hochschild is a pioneer in the Emotional sociology field of research, a field that has increased and reached recognition within the last decade. She established the term "emotion work", which stands for the, often unnoticed, work we do when we construct or adapt emotions, in accordance with institutionalized ideals in society. The victims are encouraged to perceive themselves through an identification with certain emotional ideals. However, the theory of crises seems to have a double-edged function. Not only the victim (or persons aspiring to victim status) is encouraged to identify with the emotional images, taken from the theory of crises, but likewise the support person gets guidance from the theoretical images in their emotion work. They define people (clients) as victims (or not victims), through comparison with the theory. The crime victim identity is viewed in light of a psychological "theory of crisis", by the members within the organization. The 'crisis' is described as a linear process, which goes from the phases of "shock" and "reaction" to the phases of "processing" and "reorientation".[3] Accordingly, an important part of the support work is to encourage the individual to pass from the passive "reaction" to the more active "processing" and "reorientation". This process could as well be rephrased as going from the role of "victim" to "survivor".

I will describe and analyze a support talk between a crime victim and a support person. The victim is a woman who was attacked by an unknown man in the park in broad daylight. She does not only live up to the moral image, linked to the concept of an ideal victim, but also embraces the identity as a victim "in crisis". This notwithstanding, her narrative is not automatically accepted, but is edited, revised and altered by the support person guiding the support talk, which I will describe and analyze. But first I will give a short description of the method and perspective used.

METHOD AND PERSPECTIVE

The analysis is based on a case study. The case study also forms a part of my PhD thesis. I have a qualitative approach and have conducted seventeen interviews with support workers of different kinds: for example voluntary support persons, crime victim assistants, crime victim coordinators and board members at national as well as local levels. The material also consists of field observations of different kinds. I have been observing activities and meetings taking place at two local victim organizations. The activities that I have observed are member meetings and support person meetings, a "drop-in-activity"[1], a support person education, support talks between a support person and a crime victim, and supervision meetings of support persons by a psychologist.

Critical vs Positivistic & Activist Victimology

I use a critical Victimological Perspective, which differs from the two main perspectives in the Victimology field of research: the positivistic and activistic approach (or radical, see Fattah 1991, Wallace, 1998 and Walklate,1989). The positivistic approach differentiates between the role of an academic and an activist and between facts and values. Classical victimologists like Mendelsohn and Von Hentig created typologies intended to show typical victim traits or situations (see Grothe-Nielsen & Snare 1998). Within this tradition they seem to take the meaning of the concept of victim for granted; the term is treated as if it was only descriptive. The lack of neutrality or objectivity of the term (see Boutellier 2000), is something that the activist (or "radical") Victimology approach has recognized and emphasized. This approach may be seen as a critic towards the positivistic Victimology. It questions the role of the state and the law, in relation to the definition and treatment of crime victims. Certain groups are discriminated within society, for example by being blamed for their victimization while hit by crime, according to this view. The approach is closely linked to the fight for women and human rights. The critical Victimological perspective, which my perspective is mostly influenced by, is similarly to the activist approach, critical towards positivism. I use a Symbolic Interactionist approach. My intent is to study an interaction and definition process, in relation to a specific field: the voluntary crime victim organization, *"Brottsofferjouren"*, in Sweden. Similar to sociological studies of deviance it is the social processes, whereby images of (ideal) victims are constructed which is the main focus. Through an Interactionist approach it is crucial to see how actors organize, value and make sense of events and behavior in relation to a taken for granted, normative interpretative structure, as well as time order. I ask questions like: How is a crime victim (client) defined within the organization? How can a person be expected to *become* a victim and *stop being* a victim at the same time? What kind of emotion work and ideology is used and prescribed?

THE SUPPORT PERSON AS COACH

The victim role is a temporary status. After having adopting it the victim advocates are expected to take the role as an agent, (or "survivor"). The process of crises may be described as a predicted path from victim to survivor. Strauss (1997) uses the metaphor of a running path to highlight the common sense notion of 'development':

... the end of the path represent the final goal; and the closer to it the runner the more 'advanced' he is. The observer, who stands outside the race, possesses tools for measuring crudely or precisely the amount of progress. The metaphor assumes fixed goals against which the aspirants' movements can be chartered. The movement can be conceived as a series of stages or as steps along a continuum. Too slow progress or too quick, as well as failure to reach the final norm usually leads to 'trouble'.

And he defines a coaching relationship as follows:

A coaching relationship exists if someone is trying to move someone else along a series of steps, when those steps are not entirely institutionalized or invariant, and when the learner is not entirely clear about their sequences (although the coach is) (1997:112).

In line with these images, the support persons in *"Brottsofferjouren"* may be seen as coaches, guiding the persons who have been hit by crime through the different stages of the victimization process. Through the use of the theory of crisis (described above), the support persons come to think of the development of the victim identity as a rather clear-cut and linear process. The experience of crime (or victimization) is the beginning, and the recovering of the victim (which sometimes may include the prosecuting of the offender) is the end. As Strauss (ibid) writes, the movement of the person taking part the "development" is typically expected to be in accordance with a certain time order. This seems also to be the case within the context and interpretative structure of "Brottsofferjouren". There are more or less implicit norms of how quickly the victims should move from one stage to the other. An important part of the coaching task, performed by the support persons, is to point out the next step at the right moment. This includes, however, also encouraging the persons to take the step, foresee what will happen when they have taken it, as well as taking them back into the path if they drop out. If we move back to the Support talk again, this could easily be analyzed as a kind of coaching, by the support person, of the status passage of the Maria.

THE SUPPORT NARRATIVE – EDITED & REVISED

Maria is organizing her narrative as a contrast between the *before* and the *after* experience of crime. The "before" is constructed as the everyday life process of "trying to get along"- In spite of an previous experience of being burned out, she had recovered, she tells. It's a narrating style which Riessman Kohler (1990) calls a "habitual narrative". In contrast, the "after" is as linked to the sudden outburst of many negative and strong emotions, an order that is turned into chaos.

Maria: I was working at a health centre but a week ago I returned to my old work place, unfortunate, it was that I… had had trouble from being burned out. But I managed in a rather good way, and now I'll return to my ordinary job and work half time. Before the accident happened, that is (unclear voice)

The support person: Was that before-

Maria: Before, before (mm). and then this happened and I felt awfully bad, awful, felt completely powerless, insecure, instable, afraid in a way…

Although it's Maria who introduces the timeframe by saying "before the accident happened", the support person is no passive receiver, but a co-narrator. She helps her creating and organizing of the narrative by asking the question "was that before?". Alma is a support person and as such she is not supposed to question the experience of the victim, or her version of what has happened to her, according to the "emotion rules" within the organization (Hochschild 1984). Therefore the reaction from the support person, showed below, is somewhat surprising. Instead of contrasting the normal time before the crime with the abnormal after, like Maria does, she answers through emphasizing the normality of the current situation. She even defines it as healthy:

The Support Person : Yes, it is... totally, such a reaction is healthy to have, you *should* react like that, but it's difficult and heavy.

The last phrase shows an understanding for Maria's version (it's difficult and heavy). Maria chooses answering to the last confirmation of her difficulties, instead of the description of her as "healthy". She doesn't just use the extreme form of expression but continues to include a more extreme content of the narrative. The situation grew worse, she tells, because of bodily experiences, problems with sleeping, unclear mind and so on:

Maria: *Very* hard, very hard! Mostly, I was worried that I had, before the accident because of burn out, *raised blood pressure* so now the situation was growing worse, my fear was enormous, plus that I couldn't sleep at night, it was a... myself, I described, like a Babylon salad in my head...

Support person: And there was nobody who could help you when it was urgent? I guess not–

This time, the support person seems to accept Maria's version, at least she doesn't argue against it. She also makes a connection to a taken for granted view within the Organization, which is the victim's right to support, and the belief that such support in the society is absent (which is the voluntary Organization's *raison d'étre*): The support person is a co-narrator of the story and her words "when it was urgent" may be seen as an effort to organize the story in accordance with a culturally defined chronological time structure (see Riesman Kohler

1990). However, it may also be a proposition that Maria's situation is not urgent anymore, but has (or should have) reached another phase in the process.

Awful Vs Healthy

Maria's story seems to be an act of balance. As Clark (1992:43) writes, to get sympathy from others, a person must follow certain rules of a "sympathy etiquette", which guides the giving and taking of sympathy in social life. The foremost rule is not to manipulate other's sympathy by pretending to need it, for example giving exaggerating or false claims. Serious trouble is not part of the everyday life, but examples of extraordinary events. Maria has to narrate her experience in a way that mobilizes understanding and sympathy at the same time as it appears trustworthy and not exaggerated. She uses several rhetorical tools in her act of balancing. Firstly extreme case formulation and intensifying (Pomerantz 1986, Tannen 1987). She doesn't only say that she felt bad, but awfully bad, and not that she had only been powerless but completely powerless. Secondly she uses listing, drops many words after each other that describe similar emotions (afraid, insecure, instable). A detailed description may have as purpose to make the listener to involved in the speaker's emotions (named *pathos* in classical rhetoric, Johannesson 1996) and the right to sympathy (which is named *ethos*).

From Clark's (ibid) perspective one can assume that also the support person's simultaneous correction and confirmation of Maria's version is part of a balancing act. She calls her reaction as healthy and right (you should react like that) but says that it's difficult and heavy. To question the victims' emotions is taboo within the victim's movement and it is called a secondary victimization. When Maria's negative definition of her emotions is redefined into a more optimistic version, it may be interpreted as a proscribed provocation or even an oppression. Why is the support person using a term like healthy for the experience of the victim advocate? A possible explanation is that the victim identity may be seen as unattractive, as it has connotations as weakness, and loss of control, which is (partly) negatively valued in an individualistic culture (Ryding 2001, Wood and Rennie 1994). It risks creating hopelessness and passivity, which is in conflict with the aim of the support person and support organization. Like Burke

(1969:18) has described it, it demands convincing vocabulary of change and a new appealing image to identify with, for a person to start looking at him- or herself as a person in progress.

The term "healthy" may, from that perspective, be seen as an effort to exchange Maria's unhealthy emotions for images that relate to a context of fitness and vitality. These images may in turn be associated to order and purity, that contrast with a threatening chaos and dirt, according to Mary Douglas classical study of purity and danger (1966). In this way, the victim not only be encouraged to take a more positive future orientation but also avoid being judged as deviant. The support person's description may be another a way of saying: "everybody in your situation react this way", a formulation that has as a function to show that everybody in a certain category are irresponsible for a condition (Pomerantz ibid). In this way normality and innocence, are emphasized, as Potter point at, the question of normality is closely connected to the question of regularity (see also Zerubavel 1981).

Transforming fear to Courage, Sorrow to Anger

In the description above, it's through the reformulation of the experience as a crime victim that a change is expected to happen. In the following example the support person not only tries to make Maria changing perspective of her emotions, but tries to change the emotion itself. It is an example of what Hochschild calls "deep acting": a change of the emotional experience and not only of the expression. It is showed how the categorization not only is directed backwards (establish innocence) but also prescribes future actions and emotions. It's not enough to appear morally impeccable in the occasion of the crime, like the typology of Christie seems to suggest. The person's perceived action after the crime is influencing the assignment of victim status as well. Paradoxically, the categorization prescribes opposite emotions. To be a victim means to be a victim of uncontrollable emotions, due to the experience of crime, but only to begin with. The next step of the process of crises and victimization is to retake control and transform the passive emotions to active. Fear may be transformed to courage, sorrow and despair to anger.

The victim process is expected to go from the role of victim to the role of survivor, from naming to claiming (Felstiner et al, 1981). Part of this process is the active effort to "go back to normal", and not "let the offender rule life". The interaction is continued by the support person referring to a psychologist (who is a leader within the organization) and she's citing him, suggestion that Maria should try to overcome her fear by "going out". Her initiative to bring in the voice of an authority seems effective at first, as Maria seems impressed, stating that she will "take notes and remember". However, after she has got the advice, she says that she already has tried that, but still experiences fear. Her speech now becomes fragmentized:

Support Person: Yes, I have talked a little bit with-, we have a psychologist who's name is ——— and he has been giving me some instructions.

The Maria: Yes I'll take notes and remember.

Support person: That it's, he thinks that it's very good for you to go out, if you tried to overcome this fear through taking walks. And if you could walk alone, I could walk after you, or may be you have a friend who could go with you.

Maria: I have walked a few times with my partner, we've done that.

Support Person: Oh yes, how did you feel?

Maria: Four days after, and I was insecure, after all- myself- I don't dare, go far from- and look... and then you become (unclear voice) I prefer not to bring bags.

After having confirmed the fear of Maria is legitimate, the support person, by pointing to time, implicitly is giving a cue that the Maria shouldn't feel afraid anymore. In other words she seems to put further pressure on her to move towards "survivor status". Maria does not seem to agree, however, about the fear having disappeared, but she seems a bit more optimistic, as she describes it as decreasing over time:

Support Person: ...Yes I understand very well, but now it has been about five weeks then.

Maria: I think sixteenth of April, it's soon two months.

Support Oerson: It's soon two months, yes, how do you think you're doing now? Do you think the fear has gone back a little?

Maria: I think it's decreasing eventually.

The support person then once again is leading her further towards the "right path", through hinting that the passive feeling is expected to lose power. Maria doesn't agree, however, but continues to tell the other about her feelings of weakness. Like before the support person then is naming the troubling emotions as "natural", but is advising her to transform the emotions into anger. When Maria is confirming that she *has* felt and expressed rage, the support person is satisfied:

Support Person: Yes, well Maria, and then there is that a natural reaction is to be in despair, afraid (unclear voice) but that one tries to get piss- you know?

Maria Oh yes, yes.

Support Person: Do you understand?

Maria: Yes I *was*, indeed, yes I was.

Support Person: Pissed off, that is?

Maria: Yes, angry, *angry,* and it worried me, aggression, and I have been setting about my husband unfortunately.

Support Person: Yes, (laughs a little) that, he would have to put up with, really, he just has to because–

The support person does not show sympathy for the worries of Maria, that her anger has been expressed towards an innocent party: her husband. Another aspect of the last quotation I'd like to emphasize is the avoidance of the word "pissed off", as if it was taboo. She seems conscious of the fact that the expression she recommends isn't completely culturally accepted, especially for women. To investigate these aspects a little bit further, I'd like to discuss the emotion anger from a phenomenological perspective. The victim is expressing worries about the same anger that the support person was portraying as ideal. It almost seems like they are talking about different kinds of anger. Their different views of the emotion can be analyzed through Jack Katz's (1999) insightful studies of the experience – and expressions – of anger in everyday life.

The state of anger is described as a form of victimization; a bodily experience of being compelled by forces beyond ones control ("taken by emotion"). Katz describes it as a feeling of "moral impotence", which is referring to the passivization of the angry person. It is portrayed as the painful experience of losing control over one's identity project. However, it is only the first step of the experience of anger that is seen as victimizing (Katz 1999:49). The next step is constituted by the angry person's efforts to overcome the anger. In this way the "wet", degrading humiliation can turn into a "hot", sensual feeling, with an "oppositional" force, Katz writes (Katz, 1999). The importance of opposition might be relevant in relation to the context of the crime victim organization.

The function of anger is not only to reveal a tension of the person, but also to create a new meaning of the situation, as well as of the person's self; a new moral meaning, through which the angry person is able to return as a moral agent with a recovered face. Maria, seems to be displaying a tension between two selves or two realities, by using a contrast narrative. She appears to be in a state of transition, or being located between two perspectives. She has experienced something traumatic, and therefore being unable to see herself as the same person as before. However, she does seem ready to take the step towards a new "strong" sense of self yet, which is creating a tenstion within the support talk.

COMPETING FRAMES - BUREAUCRACY VS AUTHENTICITY

It is not only a psychological discourse, influencing the work and emotion ideology of the organization, but a discourse of law and morality as well. To act within a survivor role, to go through the crises, is to master the bureaucratic process; see to that one gets the economic compensation and legal rights. This aspect is showed below when the support person gives Maria advice of how to get her rights as a victim. She gives information about the right to economic compensation for harm due to the crime, as well as free counseling from a psychiatrist. It is significant that the Maria changes from talking in first person to the impersonal "you". The Support person is addressing her as a representative of the group of "crime victims" and she responds as such. But they have different focus in their talk. Maria's emotions get a different meaning from their diverging perspectives. While the support person has an action oriented approach, and represents a social policy or bureaucratic view of her emotions, Maria is more interested in the impact of the emotions for her personally:

Support Person: These brochures you may have already? You have the right to get damages for violation for example, and then it's best to ask…

Maria (interrupts) Mhm and you *do* feel violated.

Support Person: So… Oh yes, you do- And then you'd better get-

Maria (interrupts) I never knew to what extent you could feel-

Maria answers with atrocity stories (Dingwall 1977), about her fruitless efforts to see a doctor and psychiatrist, in spite of her serious problems with heart beating, and high blood pressure and so on. The support person could have stressed how people don't understand, she could have created an initiated pact with the victim against "others". She could moreover have acted expert, saying "this is an example of secondary victimization, see much of that..." However, none of these things happen. The support person continues taking the perspective of bureaucracy and doesn't engage in the atrocity stories. She starts talking about Maria's capacity to go back to work, which appears as sharp contrast to Maria's detailed trouble talk and her fight for a legitimate sick role:

Maria: I tried to call psychiatrist, /—/ there are no, it is very very rare /—/ I turned two times to the care center, then doctors don't have time.

Support Person: No time?

The Maria: No… so I said some harsh words, and told that "I'm not from here, I feel incredibly bad" and I can't understand that they are saying no, so a doctor finally received me, but very stressed, she was, the woman, had no time.

Support Person: Yes, but you could start to work then.

Maria: Yes, that's that, I don't want to /—/ I think my understanding of the whole thing is that people don't understand… Because it was completely, I couldn't direct my thoughts, possibilities, fear made me think "I'll never be good enough". When I started to work, *I didn't manage!*

Support Person: But you *did* start to work?

Maria: Yes, anyway, I did, I thought, maybe it's good, sometimes it's good, you get in to this kind of… work /—/ I'd like to see (em em) others and come in-

Support Person: I think that's good for you as well, the best for you, if you can do that.

Maria continues to hold on to her account of other people's incapability to understand her situation. In the last sequence she is focused upon her boss who thinks she should go back to her job, while she doesn't feel ready. Instead of Maria's party, the support person is creating an alliance with this "other people", incapable of understanding her and pushing her to start work.

The descriptions by support organization of the situation of victims are often based upon the absence of insight into the problems of crime victims, which includes responsible persons like doctors and subordinates. In other words Maria's effort to get a recognition of this kind, wasn't far fetched although she doesn't get it from the support person. Why doesn't she get the recognition? Why does the support person act like she does? My interpretation is linked to the understanding of the victim identity as an ongoing, socially controlled process. If Maria wants to continue to be seen as a victim she must, paradoxically, stop acting like one. Like Strauss writes, status passages are expected to follow a certain time structure. In analogy with Parson's theory of the sick role, the individual has to show signs that he or she is trying to recover, in order to be free from conventional requirements and expectations. It seems like Maria, as an example of a person trying to get victim status, must show that she is able to leave the experience behind and reorient to the "normal", to get enduring sympathy and support. The support person's job as a coach is to show the next step at a certain moment. Although she risks intimidating the other if she put too much pressure, which is what seems to happen in the support talk in the following sequence. The support conversation is continuing by a "back sliding" (Strauss 1997). Maria returns to a previous phase within the victimization (or crises) process. She starts to blame herself again, which makes the support person encouraging her to get back on "the track":

Maria: ... I was ashamed, I thought there's something extremely wrong...Maybe it is something else which is the problem.

Support Person: You... you have no guilt in this you know...

Maria: I felt-

Support Person: It *felt* that way. *Why?!*

Maria: I thought that I shouldn't walk through the par, usually I would surely avoid ... And it was my fault, and "how could you be so stupid?" Moreover I've always thought that in my life, I never used to catch any mystical types... sight of me...I thought a couple of times that I always managed, nobody ever molested, not (unclear voice) jump into my life, ugh!

The support person tries to lead her back to the right path, both by the form and the content of her speech. She resists the personal guilt (Saying "you have no guilt"). Maria defends her view ("I felt") whereas the support person interrupts and correct her, saying, "*it* felt that way". The formulation is depersonalized, *I* is exchanged to *it.* The support person is moreover repeating the phrase "felt" in a way that the meaning changes., which may show the ambivalence of the rhetoric of emotionality. When Maria says *I felt* it is a defense for her version of reality; the feeling appears, from her point of view, as an expression of authenticity and truth. The support person is in turn emphasizing the impersonal and irrational character of emotions. As an alternative to "pathos", using an emotional argument, she uses "logos", a rationale argument. It's a fact that she's not guilty because she's a crime victim. However it's clear that the discourse around the crime victim issue is not only consistent of "logos" but also of "pathos" and "ethos". The emotional and moral understanding are linked in a way that is not always made explicit.

FINAL WORDS – THE AMBIVALENCE OF "VICTIMIZATION"

To end this chapter I'd like to point to a dimension of the concept of victim (or victimization). There is an emotional and a moral (or political) meaning attached to the term, and they are connected in an rather ambiguous way, which is not always made explicit. Within the context of the crime victim organization *"Brottsofferjouren",* that is the focus of my study, the notion of crime victim is linked to an extraordinary emotional state ("in crisis") and to a certain moral position (innocence, and of the right to compensation). In spite of these rather passive connotations, the concept is also linked to expectations of future action. Persons hit by crime are assumed to need help to direct the blame. This means to persuade people to start seeing themselves as victims. The model gets more complicated however, as another part of the persuasion is to make the persons stop seeing themselves as victims. This means that the "clients" are encouraged to turn the "weak" feelings (sorrow, fear, and humiliation) into "strong" ones (anger, righteousness) within a certain time limit.

The redefinition of the experience may also be seen as a change of time perspective; the experience which, from the perspective of Maria, is an involuntary disruption becomes, from the support person's point of view, a turning point and a new beginning.

It is the crime victim's representation of reality that is honored by the victim organization. On a structural level, the victims get the privilege to interpret their situation. This notwithstanding, in this concrete interaction Maria's subjective story seems restrained and defined from the social and organizational context. As Foucault (1972) puts it, "power is a feature of both the structure of the situation, and interactants' move within them" The narrative of the victim has to be edited and revised by the support person to fit the general and expected course of events: the process of support work, of victimization and crises. In this way a tension between the intended result of a collective identity as a crime victim, and Maria's personality require to be seen as a unique person, with a unique experience, also seems to be produced. Using Mead's (1972) vocabulary, one could say that the support person succeeds to take the role of "the generalized other", but fails to take the role of "the significant other".

REFERENCES

Boutellier, H. (2000), Crime and Morality: The Significance of Criminal Justice in Post-Modern Culture, Dordrecht: Kluwer Academic.

Burke, Kenneth, (1969), *A Rhetoric of Motives*, Berkley, California: University of California Press.

Christie, N. (1986), 'The Ideal Victim', in E. Fattah (ed.) *From Crime Policy to Victim Policy*, pp.1-17. London: MacMillan.

Clark, H. H. (1992), *Arenas of language use.* Chicago: University of Chicago Press.

Cullberg, J. (1992), *Kris och utveckling ('Crisis and Development').* Stockholm: Natur och Kultur.

Dingwall, R. (1977), Atrocity Stories and Professional Relationships. *Sociology of Work and Occupations*, 4: 371-396.

Fattah, E. (1991), From Crime Policy to Victim Policy, the need for a Fundamental Policy Change. *International Annals of Criminology*, vol. 29, nos. 1-2, pp. 43-60.

Felstiner, W. L. F., Abel, R. L., & Sarat, A. (1981), The Emergence and Transformation of Disputes: Naming, Blaming, and Claiming, *Law & Society Review*, 15, 631-654.

Foucault, M. (1972), *The Archeology of Knowledge*, (A. M. Sheridan-Smith trans), London: Tavistock.

Johannesson, Erik (1996), En Agitator söker sina roller. Ingår i: Agitatorerna. : Johannesson, Kurt (ed.) Stockholm : Carlsson, S. 248-315.

Katz, Jack. (1999), *How Emotions Work*, Chicago: University of Chicago Press.

Mary Douglas (1966), *Purity and Danger: An Analysis of the Concepts of Pollution and Taboo,* Harmondsworth: Penguin Books.

Mead, Margaret. (1972), *Blackberry Winter: My Earlier Years*, New York: William Morrow & Company, Inc.,

Nielsen, Beth Grothe & Snare, Annika (1998), Viktimologi, Om forbrydelsens ofre: teori og praksis (Victimology. On the victims of crime: theory and practice), Århus: Århus Universitetsforlag.

Pomerantz, A. (1986), Extreme case Formulations: A way of Legitimizing Claims. *Human Studies* 9, 219-229.

Riessman, C. K. (1990), Strategic uses of Narrative in the Presentation of Self and Illness, *Social Science & Medicine,* 30(11), 1195-1200.

Ryding Anna (2001), "*Det ställdes så mycket krav krav krav... men jag ville ju ha brottsoffer" – Om brottsofferstöd som gåvoutbyte och definitionsprocess.*" Paper presenterat på kriminologisk konferens, Lund 2001.

Ryding Anna (2005), *Välviljans variationer. Moraliska gränsdragningar inom brottsofferjourer*. 2005, Dept. of Sociology, Lund University, Sweden

Strauss, Valerie, (February 16, 1997), Meaning of UDC Cuts Depends on Viewpoint. *The Washington Post.*

Tannen, Deborah (1987), Repetition in Conversation: Toward a poetics of talk. *Language* 63, 574 605.

Walklate, S. (1989), *Victimology: The Victim and the Criminal Justice Process* Unwin Hyman.

Wallace, H. (1998), *Victimology: Legal, Psychological and Social Perspectives*, Boston, Allyn and Bacon.

Wästerfors, David (2004), *Berättelser om mutor. Det korruptas betydelse bland svenska affärsmän i Öst- och Centraleuropa*, 2004, Brutus Östlings Bokförlag Symposion, Box 148, 241 22 Eslöv

Wood, Linda A. and Heather Rennie (1994), Formulating Rape: The Discursive Construction of Victims and Villains. *Discourse & Society*, Vol. 5, No. 1, 125-148.

Zerubavel, Eviatar (1981), *Hidden Rhythms: Schedules and Calendars in Social Life,* Chicago: University of Chicago Press.

NOTES

3. The crisis theory by Cullberg (1992) is established in Sweden (and has equivalents in other countries). It is used by many different professions, and areas, in their efforts to make sense of experiences of sickness or disability (see Ryding 2005, Wästerfors 2004). An example of the establishement of the theory is that it is mentioned under "crisis" in the Swedish National Encyclopedia (1993).
1. When crime victims had possibility to see and be supported by support persons in a specific place one evening every week.

M. G. Huddar

30

FARMERS' SUICIDES AND COMPENSATION: AN EXAMINATION OF VICTIM ASSISTANCE IN KARNATAKA

India is an agricultural country where 72.2 percent of the population lives in villages and 65 percent of the total agrarian population is engaged in agriculture. The contribution of this sector to GDP is 24 percent. Agriculture is an important and dominant sector of India's economy as it is the main source of food for the growing population. Even today agriculture and agro-related activities constitute the backbone of India's economy. India achieved self sufficiency in food production within few decades of her political emancipation. It can be attributed to remarkable success of Green Revolution and series of land reform measures taken by the government. The production of food grains reached 212 million tones in 2001-02. Now, per capita availability of food grains is 539 grams per day and it was just 395 grams in 1950s (Ruddas Datt and Sundaram, 1987).

Karnataka is one of the eight largest states of the country. It has nearly five and half crores of population of which 76 percent of people live in villages. About 65 percent of them are engaged in agriculture. Contribution of agriculture to the total income of the state is 49 per cent. About 78.3 percent of the agricultural land is rain fed. 125 lakh hectares of land is used for agricultural purpose. The major food crops of this state are rice, ragi, jowar, maize, millets, wheat and pulse and major cash crops are ground nut, sugarcane, cotton, tobacco, coconut, coffee etc (Gutal, 2004).

Agriculture in India is largely dependent on natural rainfall. Out of the total 142 million hectares of net sown area, 92.6 million hectares area is dependent on natural rainfall. About 49.4 million hectares is yet to be irrigated. The major crops grown under dry land area are rice, jowar, pulses, oil seeds, cotton etc. The farmers of this area are completely dependent on timely rainfall *i.e.*, on bounties of nature. But, the rainfall in India is not only irregular but also unpredictable. Failure of monsoon naturally results in the failure of crops. That is why Indian Agriculture is called as 'gamble of monsoons' (Tyagi, 1984). Since 2001, monsoon failed successively for a period of three years in some states of India including Karnataka. Consequently, there was a drought. Failure monsoons and failure of crops has adversely affected the farming community of this state. The small and marginal cultivators under these circumstances fail to repay the loan that they have borrowed from institutional and non-institutional sources of finance. The cultivators of Karnataka like farmers of other states do not save anything for future. Whatever they earn is just sufficient to meet their basic requirements of life. Failure of rain, failure of crops, lack of remunerative prices for the agricultural products due to dalals and commission agents, exorbitant interest charged by money lenders etc. have created some sort of helplessness and frustration in farming community. This situation made the farmers to face endless miseries, helplessness and frustration. Consequently, some farmers who have failed to face this kind of stress and anxiety preferred to kill themselves. Emile Durkheim, the famous French sociologist and an authority over the study of suicide calls such acts of self destruction as *'anomie'*.

The high rate of suicides among farmers of Telangana region of Andhra Pradesh caught the attention of politicians, policy makers and also the academicians of the country by the end of 1990 (Revathi, 1998). The pesticides used by farmers failed to control the pests due to adulteration which resulted in the loss of crops. In some parts, the farming community was supplied with inferior quality of seeds. The disgusted farmers committed suicide. The suicidal current gradually spread to other states. One of the reports says that in India more than 3000 farmers committed suicides in a short span of three years (2003-2004). In Karnataka suicide rate is highest. The statistics given by the Directorate of Agriculture, Government of Karnataka on suicide states that of 846 reported cases of suicides in 2003-04, 809 suicides were of the farmers. According to one estimation on an average four farmers commit suicide every week (Deccan Herald, 2004).

The Government of Karnataka initially paid the compensation of rupees one lakh to the families of the victim. The suicides by farming community went on increasing without any check. Later, it was felt by government machinery that the payment of compensation could be one of the reasons for these acts of self destruction. Further, it was also felt that some people in agrarian India started to equate suicides due to personal reasons with the suicides due to failure of crops so as to get compensation from the state.

Drought, scanty rains and failure of monsoons, failure of crops, is not a new phenomenon for the farming community of northern part of Karnataka. In past they were facing such a critical situation with lot of courage and self confidence. But, now farmers lack these qualities. The things have changed now. In past, farmers were investing minimum amount on agricultural inputs as they were using traditional seeds, manures and primitive implements. Only to meet some unproductive expenditure they were dependent on non-institutional sources of finance comprising sahukars, mahajans and other money lenders. The institutional sources of finance were either absent or were beyond their reach. Consequently the burden of debt on them was minimum. Above all they were facing crisis of life either with well knit or strongly integrated joint families or with religious ethics provided by their religion (Assadi, 1998).

With the Invention of state-of-art agricultural implements, HYV seeds, effective pesticides and chemical fertilizers and with the ever increasing demand for a agricultural products farmers showed lot of interest in incorporating new methods of cultivation. They started cultivating cash crops, like sugarcane, ground nut, tobacco which can fetch them more income. They are investing too much on HYV seeds, chemical fertilizers and pesticides and also on agriculture implements like harvesters, tractors etc. This is how labour intensive farming transformed itself into capital intensive farming. The procedure of getting loans has been simplified. Consequently, the present farming community is at the risk of falling in debt trap than ever before.

Those who have studied the farmer's distress and anguish identified the following causes for the distress.

- Failure of Crops – Failure of crops due to the failure of rainfall, drought, destruction of crops due to pests and use of low quality seeds.
- Increasing prices - Increasing prices of seeds, fertilizers and pesticides, in toto increasing prices of all agricultural inputs.
- Financial stress – This is due to price crash of agricultural prices and debt burden.
- Scarcity of water – due to failure of rainfall, failure of bore wells, sharp decrease in ground water tab
- Improper supply of electricity by KPTCL and consequently inability of the farmers to supply water to the fields.
- Inadequate services by the agricultural departments to provide proper counseling on farm technologies.
- Failure of the governmental institutions to meet out the needs and aspirations of the farming community.

Discussing the causes for farmer's suicides, Dr. R. Dwarakanath, Former Chairman, and Karnataka Agriculture Commission opines that average farmer had become more vulnerable today with disappearance of barter system and traditional practices. Emphasizing the importance of joint family, Deshpande (2002) asserts that in joint family each member was secure. The joint families in olden days were extending moral support to its members at the time of all crises. The majority of victims who committed suicides were surprisingly came from nuclear families. Even Durkheim in his monumental contribution, 'La Suicide' speaks of the co-relationship that exists between family size and incidence of suicides. According to him there exists an 'inverse relationship between family size and tendency towards suicides'. Durkheim (1952) writes: "A person is almost certainly well insured morally when isolated and left to himself than when constantly under beneficent discipline of family surroundings". Deshpande (2002) also feels that failure of social institutions to instill and establish confidence among those who are on the verge of breakdown is one of the main factors responsible for the suicide among farmers.

In response to the alarming hike in 'farmers' suicides the Government of Karnataka appointed a Joint Legislative Committee (2002) to study the farmers' problems with reference to suicides in detail and submit a report on it to the government. Accordingly, the committee studied sixty reported cases of suicidal deaths of farmers and submitted a report to the government. It came with several recommendations. There was pressure on the government both inside and outside the assembly for the payment of compensation to the affected families of the victims. Contrary to this pressure, the Joint Legislative Committee clearly stated in its recommendations that the confidence building measures should be taken instead of paying compensation to the farmer's families (Hariyabbe Prem Kumar, 2003; Mohan Yagati, 2003).

The Government of Karnataka commissioned an 'Expert Committee' in August 2002, under the Chairmanship of Dr. G. K. Veeresh, Former Vice-Chancellor of the University of Agricultural Sciences, Bangalore to study the 55th and 56th recommendations of Joint Legislative Committee. It was asked by the government to find out the causes for farmers, suicides and suggest remedial and preventive measures. The 'Expert Committee, involved academicians drawn from various disciplines namely Economics, Sociology, Psychiatry and Agricultural sciences. The task before the Committee was to examine thoroughly the 55th and 56th recommendations made by Joint Legislative Council. Those recommendations were related with the payment of compensation and confidence building measures to be taken by the government in the interest of the farming community.

The 'Expert Committee' studied 130 cases of suicides throughout the state and submitted a detailed report to the government in April 2003. It made certain recommendations.. The expert committee fully agreed with the 55th and 56th recommendations of the Joint Legislative Committee that the confidence building measures should be taken instead of paying compensation to the families of the victims. Some notable recommendations of the committee are:

- A separate 'Farmers Welfare Department' should be established in the state and it should function under the direct supervision of the Chief Minister.
- Farmers Welfare Fund (FWF) should be created and measures should be taken for its proper utilization.
- The farmers who have crossed 60 years of age should be considered as 'senior farmers' and special concessions should be extended to them.
- Health insurance plans should be designed at the state level for the benefit of farming community.

- 'Farmers Communication centres' should be strengthened and farmers should be encouraged to engage themselves in income generating activities which are complimentary to agriculture like poultry, dairy, mushroom cultivation, sericulture etc. They should be given basic infrastructure along with subsidized financial support.
- Measures should be taken for the regular supply of electricity for agricultural purposes.
- The irrigation facilities should be extended to non-irrigated areas.
- Necessary amendments may be brought to the existing Land Reforms Act.
- Measures should be taken to educate the farmers along with general public regarding the harmful effects of alcohol. To create awareness among the farmer's special measures should be taken at village panchayat level. The village panchayat should be empowered to grant/cancel the license to arrack shop.

Analysing the causes for farmer's suicides the Committee found that consumption of alcohol, ill health and family problems have also contributed to the farmers' suicides. Committee pointed out that failure of crops was one of the causative factors but not the chief cause.

The Government of Karnataka accepted the recommendations of the Committee. But in the mean time there was mounting pressure on the government to pay the compensation to the families of the victims. The Government appointed a 'Cabinet Sub-Committee' to implement the recommendations of the expert committee.

As an immediate measure the government announced the special package of Rs. 856 crores to the farmer's community and the following measures were taken.

- The farmers were exempted from the payment of interest on crop loans. Further they were exempted from the payment of water tax and land revenue.
- Arrangements were made to supply the seeds at the subsidised rates to the small and marginal farmers.
- The small scale and the marginal farmers were encouraged to grow horticultural crops. To reach this objective the loan facility was extended.

- Support price was given for certain agricultural products.
- The farmers were exempted from the penalty for the non-payment of electricity bill used for the purpose of irrigation.

The Cabinet Sub-committee further framed the guidelines for the payment of compensation to the families of the farmers who have committed suicide.

- The farmer who has committed suicide should have possessed the cultivated land in his name.
- He should have taken the crop loan from any institutional financial agencies and should have possessed the documents to the effect.
- Mere FIR by police is not a sufficient ground to get the compensation. The Assistant Commissioner of particular district / taluka has to ascertain the facts of suicide by visiting the victim's family and submit the report to the government. On the basis of this report the issue of paying compensation will be settled.

In order to mitigate the problem of rural indebtedness the Government of Karnataka has banned the private money lending business since 2002.

Following Table gives the detailed account of total suicides of farmers of Karnataka and the compensation given to the victims, family by the government.

Year	*No. of Suicides*	*No. of Families to whom Compensation is given*	*Total Compensation amount (in rupees.)*
2001-02	81	23	2,30,000
2002-03	52	07	62,000
2003-04	708	195	1,95,00000

If we look at the compensation given to the victim's families in different years we will come to know that during 2001–02, 23 families of the victims have received an average compensation of Rs. 10,000. However, during 2002-03 only 7 families *i.e.*, 12.28 per cent of the total victim's families became successful in getting compensation from the state. The average compensation received by those seven families was just 8857.14 Rupees. However, during 2003-04 about 27.54 percent were successful in receiving the compensation.

The Government of Karnataka gave direction to the district authorities to pay compensation to the victim's families if the death of victim is due to the loss of crop and he was unable to pay the debt of authorized financial institutions. As per the guidelines compensation is given in seventeen cases in the current financial year (Samyukta Karnataka, 2004).

The Present Coalition Government of Karnataka has taken certain measures to provide relief to farmers in distress. They include extending irrigation facilities to the un-irrigated areas, restructuring of farm credit, a temporary moratorium on all debt repayment, enhanced access to seeds and providing the loan facilities to the farmers at the rate of 6 percent per annum etc.

In spite of the various confidence building measures initiated by the state government the suicides by the farming community continued unchecked. To check this trend the following measures are suggested.

- The cooperative farming should be encouraged so as to derive benefits of large scale cultivation, and government should take initiative to consolidate small uneconomic holding.
- The existing co-operative societies should be strengthened. The efforts should be made to establish multi-purpose co-operative societies in all villages catering to the diverse needs of agriculturists.
- The farmers should be motivated to grow the crops which suit with the agro-climatic conditions and they should be encouraged to engage in organic farming .
- The farmers should be enlightened about the methods of using pesticides, manure fertilizers, suitable crop pattern through the proper media.
- The farmers counseling centres should be established at the village panchayat level.

REFERENCES

Assadi, Muzaffar (1998), Farmers' Suicides: Signs of Distress in Rural Economy, *Economic and Political Weekly*, April 4, 1998.

Deccan Herald (English daily)– *Spectrum* Vol. No. 16. Oct. 12, 2004.

Deshpande, R. S (2002), Suicides by Farmers in Karnataka: Agrarian Distress and Possible Alleviatory Steps, *Economic and Political Weekly*, June 29, 2002.

Durkheim, E. (1952), *Suicide- A Study in Sociology*, translated by John, A Spoulding and George Simpsons, London: *Routledge and Kegan Paul.*

Gutal, Shalmili (2004), Focus on Global South Web Site (online at www. focusweb.org).

Hariyabbe Prem Kumar (2003), *Maddunte Ee Maranakke?* Published in Sudha (Kannada Weekly), Vol No. 60, 37th Issue, Sept. 11 2003.

Mohan Yagati (2003), *Raitar Jeevakke Bele Illave?* Published in Karmaveer (Kannada Weekly), Vol.60, 50th Issue, Oct. 5 2003.

Revathi, E. (1998), Farmers Suicide: Missing Issues, *Economic and Political Weekly*, May 16 1998.

Ruddar Datt and Sundaram K. P. M. (1987), *Indian Economy,* New Delhi, S Chand and Company (Pvt.) Ltd.

Samyukta Karnataka (Kannada Daily)– Vol. No. 71 Dated Oct. 11-2003, and Vol. No. 72 Dated Aug, 5 -2004.

Tyagi B. P. (1984), *Agricultural Economic and Rural Development*. Meerut (UP): Jai Prakash Nath and Co.

INDEX

I

J